Models of Bounded Rationality
Volume 3

Models of Bounded Rationality

Volume 1
Economic Analysis and Public Policy

Volume 2
Behavioral Economics and Business Organization

Volume 3
Empirically Grounded Economic Reason

Models of Bounded Rationality

Volume 3

Empirically Grounded Economic Reason

Herbert A. Simon

The MIT Press
Cambridge, Massachusetts
London, England

This book was set in Times Roman on the Monotype "Prism Plus" PostScript Imagesetter by Asco Trade Typesetting Ltd., Hong Kong, and was printed and bound in the United States of America.

Library of Congress Cataloging-in-Publication Data

Simon, Herbert Alexander, 1916–
Models of bounded rationality.
Includes bibliographies and index.
Contents: v. 1. Economic analysis and public policy—v. 2. Behavioral economics and business organization—v. 3. Empirically grounded economic reason.
1. Economics—Addresses, essays, lectures. 2. Social choice—Addresses, essays, lectures. 3. Decision-making—Addresses, essays, lectures. 4. Economics—Psychological aspects—Addresses, essays, lectures. 5. Industrial organization—Addresses, essays, lectures. I. Title.
HB171.S5633 330 81-18620
ISBN 0-262-19205-5 (v. 1) AACR2
ISBN 0-262-19206-3 (v. 2)
ISBN 0-262-19372-8 (v. 3)

To the memory of George Leland Bach and to Richard M. Cyert

Economists, administrators, and warm friends who, as Deans of Carnegie Mellon University's Graduate School of Industrial Administration, created an exciting environment in which behavioral economics flourished.

Contents

	Introduction	ix
	Acknowledgments	xv
I	**THE STRUCTURE OF COMPLEX SYSTEMS**	1
I.A	**Causal Ordering**	
I.1	Causality in Economic Models	9
I.2	Causal Ordering, Comparative Statics, and Near Decomposability *(with Y. Iwasaki)*	13
I.3	Causality and Model Abstraction *(with Y. Iwasaki)*	43
I.B	**Simulating Large Systems**	
I.4	Simulation of Large-scale Systems by Aggregation	105
I.5	Prediction and Prescription in Systems Modeling	115
II	**THE ADVANCE OF INFORMATION TECHNOLOGY**	129
II.1	The Rural–Urban Population Balance Again	137
II.2	The Impact of Electronic Communications on Organizations	145
II.3	The Steam Engine and the Computer: What Makes Technology Revolutionary	163
II.4	Managing in an Information-Rich World	173
II.5	On the Alienation of Workers and Management	183
III	**MOTIVATION AND THE THEORY OF THE FIRM**	197
III.1	A Mechanism for Social Selection and Successful Altruism	205
III.2	Organizations and Markets	217
III.3	Altruism and Economics: A Summary Statement	241
III.4	Altruism and Economics: Social Implications	257
IV	**BEHAVIORAL ECONOMICS AND BOUNDED RATIONALITY**	267
IV.A	**Behavioral Economics**	
IV.1	Preface to *Handbook of Behavioral Economics*	275
IV.2	Behavioral Economics	277
IV.3	Bounded Rationality	291
IV.4	Satisficing	295

IV.B Empirical Methods in Economics
IV.5 Behavioral Research: Theory and Public Policy 299
IV.6 Methodological Foundations of Economics 319
IV.7 Preface to *La Théorie Moderne de l'Enterprise: L'Approche Institutionnelle* 337

IV.C Initial and Boundary Conditions in Economic Theory
IV.8 On the Behavioral and Rational Foundations of Economic Dynamics 343
IV.9 Rationality in Psychology and Economics 367

IV.D The State of Economic Science
IV.10 The Failure of Armchair Economics 387
IV.11 Why Economists Disagree 401
IV.12 The State of Economic Science 421

IV.E Economic Reasoning in Words and Pictures
IV.13 Effect of Mode of Data Presentation on Reasoning about Economic Markets *(with H. J. M. Tabachneck)* 433

Index 445

Introduction

About a decade and a half ago, I assembled and reprinted in two volumes the principal papers in economics that I had published up to that time. Since then, excellent health and a lifetime addiction to scientific work have permitted me to continue my research activity with only a gradual and modest shortening of my work day, and the resulting new assemblage of economics papers now fills a third volume. I offer the same reasons for reprinting them that I gave for publishing the first two volumes: the papers may be of some historical interest; ideas and their motivation may sometimes be seen more clearly in the early stages of their emergence than after they have received extensive polishing; and the republication gives me an opportunity to comment on the papers in this general introduction and in the introductions to the four sections into which the book is divided.

When I undertook this new project, I expected to arrange the papers in the same eight categories that I used in Volumes 1 and 2; but that didn't work out because the nature of my preoccupations had changed substantially from the earlier period. Several of the topics prominent in my work of the 1940s and 1950s are hardly represented at all in the present volume: specifically, the application of economics to governmental administration and policy, and rational choice under uncertainty and technological change (except for change associated with the new information technology).

Those topics are now largely replaced by others that have occupied my attention in the 1980s and 1990s. The first of these is the formal representation of causal ordering (closely connected with the identification problem) in dynamic systems. A second topic, not new but requiring a new look almost year by year, concerns the implications for our society of the new information systems that are being generated as products of the rapid development of computers and electronic communication networks. A third topic is the nature of employee and managerial motivation in the business firm, and specifically the implications for economics of the propensity of human beings to identify with the goals of organizations. A fourth topic, almost a "metatopic," is the state of economics itself, and its slowly but progressively changing attitudes toward formal theory vis à vis empirical research. So the section headings here, reflecting these new foci of my interests, are somewhat different from those in Volumes 1 and 2. Yet, if one wishes to seek for continuities, they are not wholly absent. The reader interested in linking the volumes can use the following guide:

This Volume (Vol. 3)	**Volumes 1 and 2**
Part:	*Related Sections*:
I.B. Simulating Large Systems	IV. Structure of Economic Systems
II. The Advance of Information Technology	VI. The Economics of Information Processing
III. Motivation and the Theory of the Firm	V. The Business Firm as an Organization
IV. Behavioral Economics and Bounded Rationality	VII. Economics and Psychology, and
	VIII. Substantive and Procedural Rationality
I. The Structure of Complex Systems	2. Causes and Possible Worlds, in my *Models of Discovery* (1977), essays on philosophy of science.

But I can claim continuities of an even more fundamental kind. Wherever I have been working in my peripatetic career—in public administration, business administration, economics, cognitive psychology, artificial intelligence and computer science, even philosophy—my central preoccupation has been with the nature of the thought processes that people use in making decisions. This topic can be (and needs to be) followed into every domain of human activity, and what we discover about it in any particular domain almost always casts light on thinking and decision making in other domains. So I am not wandering too far from the concerns of *Homo œconomicus* when I study the forms taken by bounded rationality in such human activities as chessplaying, making medical diagnoses, composing music, coaching shot-put, discovering scientific laws, making investment decisions in business firms, or even managing universities.

I have not brought back the products of research in these esoteric lands to this volume, but just their implications for economics. I hope that at least some of my readers will be encouraged by the hints given here to pursue their studies into foreign disciplines like cognitive psychology, where they will find strong empirical foundations for behavioral decision theory and bounded rationality as well as valuable suggestions on experimental and observational methodologies. All of these can be helpful for verifying the applicability to economics of the behavioral decision theory that has emerged from this research in other domains.

Other Work in Economics

As from the previous two volumes of *Models of Bounded Rationality*, I have omitted from the present volume researches that have been published as books: in particular, *Reason in Human Affairs* (1983); *Economics, Bounded Rationality and the Cognitive Revolution* (with Massimo Egidi, Robin Marris, and Riccardo Viale, 1992); and my 1993 Mattioli Lectures on economics, given at Bocconi University in Milano, which will appear in 1997. I have included, however, a half dozen or so short papers published in handbooks and encyclopedias, and a pair of prefaces to books, because they summarize in succinct form my present views on a number of topics, and thereby provide a common framework for the other papers.

Related Research in Cognitive Science

A theme that echoes through this volume (as it does through the last half of Volume 2) is that main-line economics has neglected its empirical chores. It has gathered too little factual evidence on how the economy and the firms and individuals in it actually operate, and has spent too much time spinning gossamer webs of mathematical theory that are attached to the world only by hypothetical "facts" having little or no basis in observation. I would like to mention, before a reviewer of the book does so, that you will also find little systematic empirical research in the papers reprinted here. Apparently I am guilty of the very crime of which I accuse main-stream economics.

In extenuation, I would point out that during the period covered by these papers a very large part of my research was empirical, in particular, research on human problem solving and decision making—but not research specifically applied to the phenomena of economics. Many of the results of my psychological work during this period can be found in the second volume of my collected psychological papers, *Models of Thought, Volume 2* (1989), in a contribution to methods for gathering data,

Protocol Analysis (with Anders Ericsson, 1984, 1993), and in a theoretical and empirical study of problem solving in science, *Scientific Discovery* (with Pat Langley, Gary Bradshaw, and Jan Zytkow, 1987).

In addition Howard Richman, Fernand Gobet, Jim Staszewski, and I (1995) have carried out numerous experiments and computer simulations dealing with the processes of perception, learning, and memory, using and extending the EPAM theory, a computer program. And Yulin Qin (1990), Hermina Tabachneck, Anthony Leonardo (1995), and I have been comparing and contrasting human reasoning that uses propositional representations with reasoning that uses pictorial—or graphic—representations (one product of this work, dealing with supply-demand diagrams, is reprinted as the final chapter in this volume).

As I observed above, much of this work, and the work of many others along similar lines is quite relevant to both the substance and methodology of research on economic decision making, for it provides a wealth of evidence in support of the boundedness of human rationality and, more important, a great deal of information about the processes human beings, in fact, use to make decisions, solve problems and learn. The extrapolation from this information to a deeper understanding of how economic actors, in particular, make decisions, solve problems, and learn is not a particularly long or arduous step.

Economists who are skeptical about the need to introduce bounded rationality into economics often complain about the vagueness of the bounded rationality thesis. It is, indeed, vague until it is filled in with concrete empirical knowledge about how human decisions are actually made; but the skeptics are wrong in thinking that no such "filling" is now available. The work just noted provides a substantial amount of it, as does the research of those who have followed the behavioral theory into direct field study of decision making within firms, and those who are now gathering and interpreting substantial laboratory evidence about experimental markets. These sources can provide empirically sound auxiliary assumptions and boundary conditions for our theories to replace those that are now largely supplied by armchair speculation.

Economists like Thomas Sargent, who have paid the phrase "bounded rationality" the compliment of borrowing it in titles of books or papers (see his *Bounded Rationality in Macroeconomics*, 1993), miss the point of it when they continue to base their models on *a priori* hypotheses about behavior instead of grounding them in fact established by direct observation.

References

Ericsson, K. A. and Simon, H. A. (1993). *Protocol analysis.* Cambridge, MA: MIT Press.

Langley, P., Simon, H. A., Bradshaw, G. L., and Zytkow, J. M. (1987). *Scientific discovery: Computational explorations of the creative processes.* Cambridge, MA: MIT Press.

Qin, Y. and Simon, H. A. (1990). Imagery and problem solving. *12th Annual Conference of the Cognitive Science Society.* Hillsdale, NJ: Lawrence Erlbaum Associates, 646–653.

Richman, H., Staszewski, J., and Simon, H. A. (1995). Simulations of expert memory using EPAM IV. *Psychological Review, 102,* 305–330.

Sargent, T. J. (1993). *Bounded rationality in macroeconomics.* Oxford: Oxford University Press.

Simon, H. A. (1977). *Models of discovery.* Boston, MA: D. Reidel.

———. (1982). *Models of bounded rationality.* Cambridge, MA: MIT Press, Volumes 1 and 2.

———. (1983). *Reason in human affairs.* Stanford, CA: Stanford University Press.

———. (1989). *Models of thought, Volume 2.* New Haven, CT: Yale University Press.

———. with Egidi, M., Marris, R., and Viale, R. (1992). *Economics, bounded rationality and the cognitive revolution.* (Edited by Egidi, M. and Marris, R.), Aldershot, England: Edward Elgar.

———. (1997) *Economic decision making.* (1993 Mattioli Lectures, Bocconi University, Milano). (In press.)

Tabachneck, H. J. M., Leonardo, A. M., and Simon, H. A. *CaMeRa: A Computational model of multiple representations.* Complex Information Processing Working Paper #530, Department of Psychology, Carnegie Mellon University, 23 February 1995, to be published in *Cognitive Science*, 1997.

Acknowledgments

The community of science is the most rewarding of all fellowships, for it combines friendship and partnership with the vigorous exercise of the mind. In bringing together this third volume of my economics papers, I must (and am delighted to) acknowledge again the many friends who have inhabited the halls of science with me. In addition to these old friends, two new colleagues join, in this volume, the list of co-authors of my papers on bounded rationality. I am grateful to them for permitting me to reprint here papers I have written with them.

With Yumi Iwasaki I revisited the problem, to which I had devoted much energy in the 1950s, of formalizing the description of the causal relation. In her dissertation work, on which our joint papers here are based, she was able to revise and extend the previous definition of causal ordering to handle both systems of differential equations and combined systems of differential and algebraic equations, so that we can now deal with causality in static, dynamic, and mixed systems.

My work with Hermina Tabachneck, while she was a doctoral student and a postdoc in the Psychology Department at Carnegie Mellon, explored a much newer (for me) question: how people use visual displays—diagrams, graphs, charts—and the corresponding mental images as tools for reasoning. This is not a topic peculiar to economics, but economics is an excellent area of application for studying the problems it raises. We need only recall Marshall's discussion, in the introduction to his *Principles*, of the relative advantages of words (his text), diagrams (his footnotes), and equations (his appendix) for thinking through economic issues. In light of the role that diagrammatic and algebraic reasoning has played and plays in economics, I thought it appropriate to include in this volume a joint paper with Dr. Tabachneck on that topic.

In Cambridge, the editorial staff of the MIT Press have been, as always, extremely cooperative and helpful in carrying out the labors involved in bringing my book to press, and in this case, especially Terry Vaughn, Ann Sochi, and Deborah Cantor-Adams. I am indebted, also, to several anonymous reviewers who suggested improvements in the new introductory material. On the Pittsburgh end of the operation, I owe special gratitude to my secretary and assistant, Janet Hilf, who has had the tasks of assembling suitable copies of the papers incorporated in this volume, securing necessary permissions, and generally managing my affairs so that I could find time to carry out the writing and editing part of the enterprise that was left to me. Their help, in Cambridge, Pittsburgh, and the e-mail lines between, made it possible to bring the project to fruition, and I thank them all.

Sources

The author and the MIT Press wish to thank the publishers of the following essays for permission to reprint them here.

Part I The Structure of Complex Systems

I.A Causal Ordering

I.1 Causality in economic models. In J. Eatwell, M. Milgate, and P. Newman (Eds.), *The New Palgrave: A Dictionary of Economics*. London: Macmillan, 1987, Vol. 1, 382–383. © 1987 Macmillan Press Ltd.

I.2 Causal ordering, comparative statics, and near decomposability (Y. Iwasaki and H. A. Simon). *Journal of Econometrics*, 39, 1988, 149–173. © 1988 Elsevier Science B.V., Amsterdam, The Netherlands.

I.3 Causality and model abstraction (Y. Iwasaki & H. A. Simon). *Artificial Intelligence*, 67, 1994, 143–194. © 1994 Elsevier Science B.V., Amsterdam, The Netherlands.

I.B. Simulating Large Systems

I.4 Simulation of large-scale systems by aggregation. In R. F. Geyer and J. van der Zouwen (Eds.), *Sociocybernetics* (Vol. 2). Leiden: Martinus Nijhoff Social Sciences Division, 1978. © 1978 Kluwer Academic Publishers.

I.5 Prediction and prescription in systems modeling. *Operations Research*, 38, 1990, 7–14. © 1990 by Operations Research Society of America.

Part II The Advance of Information Technology

II.1 The rural–urban population balance again. *Regional Science and Urban Economics*, 12, 1982, 599–606. © 1982 Elsevier Science B.V., Amsterdam, The Netherlands.

II.2 The impact of electronic communications on organizations. In R. Wolff (Ed.), *Organizing industrial development*. Berlin: Walter de Gruyter, 1986. © 1986 Walter de Gruyter and Company.

II.3 The steam engine and the computer: What makes technology revolutionary. *EDUCOM Bulletin*, 22(1), Spring 1987, 2–5. © 1987 Inter-University Communications Council, Inc.

II.4 Managing in an information-rich world. In Y. K. Shetty and V. M. Buehler (Eds.), *Competing through productivity and quality*. Cambridge, MA: Productivity Press, 1988, 45–54. © 1988 Utah State University.

II.5 On the alienation of workers and management. Hamilton, Ontario: McMaster University, 1981. © 1981 McMaster University.

Part III Motivation and the Theory of the Firm

III.1 A mechanism for social selection and successful altruism. *Science*, 250, 1990, 1665–1668. © 1990 American Association for the Advancement of Science.

III.2 Organizations and markets. *Journal of Economic Perspectives*, 5, 1991, 25–44. © 1991 the American Economic Association.

III.3 Altruism and economics. *Eastern Economic Journal*, 18(1), 73–83, 1992. © 1992 the Eastern Economic Association.

III.4 Altruism and economics. The American Economic Review, *Papers and Proceedings of the 105th Annual Meeting of the American Economic Association*, 83(2), 1993, 156–161. © 1993 the American Economic Association.

Part IV Behavioral Economics and Bounded Rationality

IV.A Behavioral Economics

IV.1 Preface to B. Gilad and S. Kaish (Eds.), *Handbook of behavioral economics*. Greenwich, CT: JAI Press Inc., 1986. © 1986 JAI Press, Inc.

IV.2 Behavioural economics. In J. Eatwell, M. Milgate, and P. Newman (Eds.), *The New Palgrave: A Dictionary of Economics*. London: Macmillan, 1987, Vol. 1, 221–225. © 1987 Macmillan Press Ltd.

IV.3 Bounded rationality. In J. Eatwell, M. Milgate, and P. Newman (Eds.), *The New Palgrave: A Dictionary of Economics*. London: Macmillan, 1987, Vol. 1, 266–268. © 1987 Macmillan Press Ltd.

IV.4 Satisficing. In J. Eatwell, M. Milgate, and P. Newman (Eds.), *The New Palgrave: A Dictionary of Economics*. London: Macmillan, 1987, Vol. 4, 243–245. © 1987 Macmillan Press Ltd.

IV.B Empirical Methods in Economics

IV.5 Behavioral research: Theory and public policy. In *The 1979 Founders Symposium, The Institute for Social Research: Honoring George Katona*. Survey Research Center, The University of Michigan, 1980, 11–36. © 1980 the Institute for Social Research.

IV.6 Methodological foundations of economics. In J. L. Auspitz, W. W. Gasparski, M. K. Mlicki and K. Szaniawski (Eds.), *Praxiologies and the philosophy of economics*. New Brunswick, NJ: Transaction Publishers, 1992. © 1992 Transaction Publishers. All rights reserved.

IV.7 Preface to H. Gabrie and J. L. Jacquier (Eds.), *La Théorie Moderne de l'Enterprise: L'Approche Institutionnelle*. Paris: Economica, 1994. © 1994 Economica.

IV.C Initial and Boundary Conditions in Economic Theory

IV.8 On the behavioral and rational foundations of economic dynamics. *Journal of Economic Behavior and Organization*, 5(1), 1984, 35–55. © 1984 Elsevier Science B.V., Amsterdam, The Netherlands.

IV.9 Rationality in psychology and economics. *The Journal of Business*, 59, 1986, S209–S224. © 1986 The University of Chicago. All rights reserved.

IV.D The State of Economic Science

IV.10 The failure of armchair economics (report of an interview). *Challenge*, 29(5), November/December 1986, 18–25. © 1986 Challenge.

IV.11 Why economists disagree. *Journal of Business Administration*, 18(1&2), 1988/89, 1–19. © 1988/89 The University of British Columbia.

IV.12 The state of economic science. In W. Sichel (Ed.), *The state of economic science: Views of six Nobel laureates*. Kalamazoo, MI: W. E.

Upjohn Institute for Employment Research, 1989. © 1989 the Upjohn Institute for Employment Research.

IV.E Economic Reasoning in Words and Pictures

IV.13 Effect of mode of data presentation on reasoning about economic markets (H. Tabachneck and H. A. Simon). *American Association for Artificial Intelligence Spring Symposium Series: Working Notes*, 1992, 59–64. Copyright held by authors.

Models of Bounded Rationality
Volume 3

I THE STRUCTURE OF COMPLEX SYSTEMS

The five papers of this part deal with two distinct, but related, topics: causal ordering (cause-effect relations) and the simulation of large-scale systems. Although my interest in both topics arose originally out of questions in economics, it is evident that neither topic is specific to that field. In fact, in recent years, my research on causal ordering has been largely set in the context of artificial intelligence systems for doing qualitative reasoning in physics, and my two essays in this volume on system simulation were addressed to the use of large simulation models in studying world energy needs and environmental constraints.

Causal Ordering

I initially undertook to understand the formal nature of causal ordering in the 1950s, during my association with the Cowles Commission for Research in Economics, located at that time at the University of Chicago. The Cowles research on the estimation of systems of structural equations provided a natural setting within which to explore questions of causality, for the whole point of structural estimation is to be able to predict the effects of manipulating exogenous policy instruments after (known) alterations have occurred in the mechanisms of the system under study. To achieve this requires understanding what is cause and what is effect. There is little I can add to the cogent statements by Jascha Marschak and Tjalling Koopmans of the rationale for the Cowles approach to estimating simultaneous equations, published in Cowles Commission Monographs 10, *Statistical Inference in Dynamic Economic Models* (1950) and 14, *Studies in Econometric Method* (1953).

The formal theory of causal ordering at which I arrived turned out to be closely related to Sewall Wright's earlier concept of path analysis, and both formulations were soon exported to political science and sociology, where they have had a substantial impact over the years on empirical work using regression analysis. The basic ideas are summarized in Chapter I.1.

These ideas have had less impact on econometrics and statistical practice in economics, which have sometimes been reluctant to recognize that the data that enter into regressions are, in principle, insufficient by themselves to allow unique identification of all (even of most) of the system parameters. Securing complete identification requires additional prior specification of the equation system. Econometricians have been too willing to use formal statistical criteria (e.g., the notion of "Granger causality"), often recommended by their convenience in application, to choose structures independently of their empirical meaning or veridicality, and have been relatively indifferent to the body of prior knowledge about the phenomena that often exists and that should constrain the set of plausible structures. In a classic paper, Koopmans and Reiersøl (1950, p. 169–170), made the point very well, many years ago:

> One might regard problems of identifiability as a necessary part of the specification problem. We would consider such a classification acceptable provided the temptation to specify models in such a way as to produce identifiability of relevant characteristics is resisted. Scientific honesty demands that the specification of a model be based on prior knowledge of the phenomenon studied and possibly on criteria of simplicity, but not the desire for identifiability of characteristics in which the researcher happens to be interested.

The issue here is at one with the broader issue (dealt with, formally and in principle, by the Bayesians, but not well incorporated in contemporary statistical practice) that the data from a single experiment or a single set of observations cannot be interpreted meaningfully except in the context of what is already known about the phenomena from previous experiments and previous observations. To paraphrase John Donne: "No experiment is an island entire of itself." Fortunately, causal ordering and the estimation of structural relations has attracted new interest in the past five or ten years, and produced some powerful new conceptual and computational ideas for achieving such estimation. I refer especially to the work of Peter Spirtes, Clark Glymour and Richard Scheines (1993) at Carnegie Mellon and Judea Pearl and his colleagues at UCLA.

My own recent work on causality, represented by Chapters I.2 and I.3, has taken quite a different direction. When Yumi Iwasaki, as part of her dissertation work in Computer Science at CMU, undertook to use the causal ordering ideas as a tool for describing qualitatively the behavior of many-variable physical systems, difficulties arose in handling dynamic systems, especially when the behavior was constrained by one or more conservation laws, or when some of the system's variables were derivatives or integrals of other variables. Overcoming these difficulties required extending the formal theory of causal ordering to dynamic systems and to mixed systems with static and dynamic components. A first version of our results, published in the *Journal of Econometrics*, is printed here as Chapter I.2. We gradually arrived at a fuller and more rigorous treatment of mixed systems, which appears here as Chapter I.3. Since it was published in an artificial intelligence journal, this expansion of the theory of causal ordering is not yet widely known among econometricians.

Our final treatment of causality in mixed static-dynamic systems turned out to be closely related to a topic on which I worked with Albert Ando in the late 1950s: the dynamic behavior of nearly-decomposable systems (Simon and Ando, 1961). Each of the parts of a nearly-decomposable system has strong internal links among its sub-parts, but the several top-level parts are bound together with each other only by comparatively weak linkages. In our paper, reprinted as Chapter IV.2 of Volume 1 of *Models of Bounded Rationality*, we showed that nearly-decomposable systems possess very special properties that lend themselves to separating short-term from long-term behavior. Near-decomposability allows the long-term behavior to be studied on an aggregative basis without concern for internal details of the parts; and allows the short-term behavior of each part to be studied independently of the behavior of the other parts.

Near-decomposability provides a rationale for partial equilibrium analysis in economics (or in any dynamic systems that have the near-decomposability property). It has many uses in the study of large, complex systems, and has been exploited, for example, in the analysis of computer operating systems (Courtois, 1977). Section 5 of Chapter I.3 joins the two ideas of causal ordering and near-decomposability, showing how the presence of near-decomposability permits the links within single system components to be represented statically in the causal analysis, while the between-component links are represented dynamically.

The methods that I and my colleagues have proposed for dealing with causal relations and with the near-decomposability of large systems, although initially conceived in response to problems in econometrics, have received much more attention in engineering and computer science (and in biology, for that matter) than they have in economics. I hope that their presence in this volume will help bring them again to the attention of economists, and show how they can be applied to a wider range of systems than were encompassed by the earlier formulations.

Simulating Large Systems

The papers in Part I.B stem not from my academic research but from my involvement for about 25 years in public policy questions (for example, air quality, world energy needs, global warming and environmental quality generally) through service on the President's Science Advisory Committee, the Committee on Science, Engineering and Public Policy of the National Academy of Sciences, and on several other committees of the Academy or the National Research Council. Here "hard" science and the behavioral sciences are inextricably intertwined, and the "softness" of all of the sciences, including the "hardest," becomes eminently clear as soon as we emerge from the laboratory and engage the complexity of the real world. We must then ask what data and methods are available to us for applying reason to understanding and dealing with this complexity.

The rapid growth of computer speed and memory capacity has stimulated an equally rapid growth in our appetite for understanding the behavior of very large and complex systems by modeling them. Perhaps meteorologists were the first to learn that it is easy for this appetite to outgrow the capacities of even the largest and most modern computers and to make demands that cannot be met for precise data on initial and boundary conditions. By now, the lesson has been taught to many others, as well. We have been further sobered in our modeling ambitions by the rather new awareness that some of the systems of interest may, in their mathematical structures, be chaotic and hence more or less intractable from a classical computational standpoint. Chapters I.4 and I.5 do not address the topic of chaos, but, setting that problem aside, ask how best (in the interest of addressing policy questions) to model systems containing very large numbers of variables when initial and boundary values and the shapes of the functions connecting the variables are known only to rough approximations.

Four central themes run through these chapters. First, to keep the computational load within acceptable limits, we must ask just what variables we need to estimate and at what levels of accuracy or approximation. Second, there may be enormous savings in computation, especially if a system is nearly decomposable, if the questions we wish to answer only call for estimating a small number of aggregate quantities. Or, we can structure the computations so that after estimating the steady-state behavior of component systems, we use aggregates for the steady state to estimate the dynamic behavior of the complete system.

Third, in addressing typical world-modeling problems (human energy needs and environmental constraints, the population problem, global warming, and so on), we do not need to extrapolate year-by-year predictions into a distant future, but are better advised to compute steady-state scenarios for alternative futures at various target dates. After all, our object is not to predict the future, but to guide our society into it, aiming at desirable goal states. Modeling of goal states can help us in designing acceptable futures. Again, the savings in computation when detailed prediction is avoided will usually be enormous, allowing the models to be enriched in size, complexity, and realism. Fourth, we can again help make our task computationally feasible if we aim at satisficing and give up the illusion that we can optimize. Here, as elsewhere, the best is often the enemy of the good.

As can be seen from this brief introduction, all five chapters of Part I investigate how bounded rationality (still severely bounded, in spite of all the help we can get from present and prospective computers) can cope with the problems of shaping a desirable future in the face of the world's immense complexity.

References

Courtois, P. J. (1977). *Decomposability: Queueing and computer system applications.* New York, NY: Academic Press.

Hood, W. C. and Koopmans, T. C. (Eds.) (1953). *Studies in econometric method.* Cowles Commission Monograph No. 14. Chicago, IL: Cowles Commission for Research in Economics.

Koopmans, T. C. (Ed.) (1950). *Statistical inference in dynamic economic models.* Cowles Commission Monograph No. 10. Chicago, IL: Cowles Commission for Research in Economics.

Koopmans, T. C. and Reiersøl, O. (1950). The identification of structural characteristics. *The Annals of Mathematical Statistics* 21, 165–181.

Simon, H. A. (1953). Causal ordering and identifiability, in W. C. Hood and T. C. Koopmans (Eds.), *Studies in econometric methods.* New York, NY: Wiley. pp. 49–74.

Simon, H. A. and Ando, A. (1961). Aggregation of variables in dynamic systems. *Econometrica* 29, 111–138.

Spirtes, P., Glymour, C., and Scheines, R. (1993). *Causation, prediction and search.* New York, NY: Springer-Verlag.

I.1 Causality in Economic Models

Causal notions arise when we seek to understand the workings of a complex system by analysing it into component subsystems and mechanisms. Thus, if we wish to understand the quantities of strawberries that are produced and consumed and the prices at which they are exchanged, we may consider a number of mechanisms that affect quantity and price. What mechanisms we will include depends on how widely we draw the boundaries of the system to be examined.

For example, we may include (1) a weather mechanism that determines the amount of rainfall; (2) a productivity mechanism that determines the yield of strawberries per acre; (3) a supply mechanism that determines the acreage sowed in strawberries; and (4) a demand mechanism that determines the quantity of strawberries purchased. In this formulation, each mechanism, which might be represented by an equation, determines the value of a particular variable as a function of some other variables (not specified in the account above). The variable whose value is so determined (dependent variable) may be called the *effect* of the working of that particular mechanism, while the values of other variables entering into the mechanism (independent variables) are the *causes* of that effect.

In the example before us, we might write:

$$R = r; F = f; T = t \qquad (1)$$

$$Y = f_1(R, F, T) \qquad (2)$$

$$A = f_2(p) \qquad (3)$$

$$Q = YA \qquad (D)$$

$$p = f_3(Q) \qquad (4)$$

Here R is rainfall, and r a positive constant; Y is the yield per acre, F the amount of fertilization with f a constant, and T the amount of tillage with t a constant; A is the acreage sowed, and p the market price; and Q is the total yield. Equation (D) represents a definition, not a separate mechanism. In equation (4), p is taken as the dependent variable, since Q is assumed already to be determined by (2) and (3) (cobweb assumption).

Causal Ordering

The system of equations defines a *causal ordering* among the variables. The value of R is determined exogenously, as are the values of F and T.

That is to say, they are determined in some larger system of which the mechanisms described in the equations are only a subset. The value of Y follows from those of R, F, and T. The values of A, Q, and p are determined simultaneously. Thus, the equations determine a partial ordering:

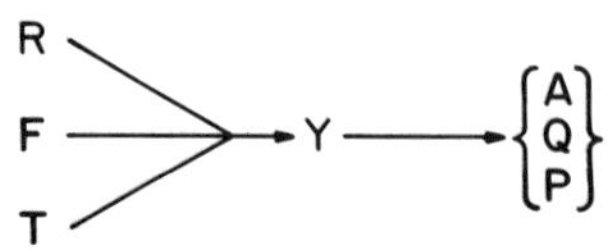

Figure 1.1

Notice that the asymmetry that underlies this ordering cannot be interpreted as the asymmetry of logical implication, for from '*A* implies *B*' we can infer that 'not-*B* implies not-*A*', while from, 'Heavy rainfall causes the yield to be large' we cannot conclude that '*A* small yield causes a scanty rainfall.' The most accurate mode of expression is: 'The amount of rainfall determines (causes) the amount of yield'—large or small in both cases. The asymmetry reflects a distinction between exogeneity and endogeneity of variables, based, in turn, upon controllability (in the case of variables that can be manipulated directly), or time precedence. Thus R is exogeneous to mechanism (2) on the assumption that the weather is unaffected by changes in the yield of strawberries. (That this is an empirical assumption is clear from the fact that widespread cultivation *can* cause changes in climate.)

If we wish to remove the ambiguity from the causal relations among A, Q, and p, we may assume (as in the classical cobweb theory) a time lag, replacing p in equation (3) by the exogenous and predetermined variable, p_{-1}. Then the causal ordering becomes:

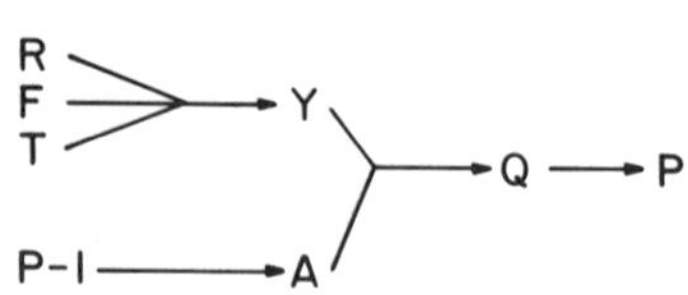

Figure 1.2

Now it is clear why we took p as the dependent variable in equation (4). Introducing the time lag requires making an empirical assumption—specificially an assumption about how farmers form expectations about future prices. In a rational expectations model, for example, this lag would not be admissible.

Formalization

To formalize these ideas, consider a system of n simultaneous linear equations in n variables (*linear structure*). We assume that each equation represents a mechanism. In some linear structures, certain subsets of equations can be solved independently of the remaining equations (*self-contained subsets*). Consider the *minimal self-contained subsets* of a system (those that do not themselves contain smaller self-contained subsets). With each such subset, associate the variables that can be evaluated from the subset alone (endogenous variables), and call them *variables of order zero*. Next, substitute the values of these variables in the remaining equations of the system, and repeat the whole process, obtaining the variables of order one, two, and so on, and the corresponding minimal self-contained subsets of equations. If a variable of some order occurs with non-zero coefficient in an equation belonging to a subsystem of higher order, then that variable is one of the causes of the values of the endogeneous variables of the latter set.

Thus, in our original example, equation (1) is the minimal self-contained subset of zero order, and R is its variable; (2) is the minimal subset of first order, and Y its variable; while (3), (D), and (4) constitute the minimal self-contained subset of second order, and A, Q, and p are their variables. The exogenous variables, F and T, can be regarded as parameters of the system, or equations parallel to (1) can be added for them, so that each belongs to a separate minimal self-contained subset of order zero.

Identifiability of Causal Ordering

The causal ordering among variables in a linear self-contained structure depends on which variables appear with non-zero coefficients in which equations. Consider a set of observations of the variables satisfying the equations of such a structure. Clearly these observations will also satisfy a new structure made up of equations that are arbitrary linear combinations of equations drawn from the original set. But different combinations of variables will generally appear in the equations of the new structure than appeared in the equations of the original structure. Taking these linear combinations 'blends' the separate mechanisms represented by the original equations. Hence, the causal ordering is not preserved under such a transformation, although the same empirical observations are compatible with both sets of equations.

From this consideration it follows that causal ordering cannot be inferred from simultaneous observations, no matter how numerous, of the variables of a structure. Additional assumptions must be made to identify a unique structure from the observations. The *identification problem* of econometrics is the problem of finding a sufficient number of prior assumptions to determine a unique set of equations, each corresponding to a mechanism, and such that the *set* of equations fits the observations. The equations thus determined are usually called *structural equations*, while algebraically equivalent equations derived from them by linear combination are called *reduced form* equations.

The assumptions needed to identify structural equations may be derived from prior knowledge about mechanisms (e.g., our knowledge that the weather affects crops, but crops do not usually affect the weather). Where experimentation is possible, holding particular variables constant while varying others, experimental findings are a powerful source of empirically valid identifying assumptions. Sometimes, there is prior knowledge, also, that particular mechanisms are independent of each other (that farmers make their decisions independently of consumers, and vice versa). Whatever their source, the identifying assumptions are genuine empirical assertions, and cannot be made arbitrarily or for reasons of statistical convenience if the correct causal inferences are to be drawn. So-called 'spurious' correlation is best interpreted as a relation between variables that does not have causal force because it was estimated from equations that did not correspond to independent mechanisms.

Bibliography

Goldberger, A. S. and Duncan, O. D. (1973). *Structural Equation Models in the Social Sciences.* New York: Academic Press.

Hood, W. C. and Koopmans, T. C. (1953). *Studies in Econometric Method.* New York: Wiley.

Simon, H. A. (1977). Causes and possible worlds. Section 2, in H. A. Simon, *Models of Discovery*, Dordrecht: D. Reidel.

I.2 Causal Ordering, Comparative Statics, and Near Decomposability

(with Yumi Iwasaki)

1 Introduction

It is the purpose of this chapter to review an old account of causality [Simon (1953)] in order to see how it can be revised and extended in the light of more recent thinking about causality in dynamic systems and about systems that are nearly decomposable [Ando, Fisher and Simon (1963)]. Its novelties lie largely in showing to what extent the causal analysis of a system is invariant as we pass from a description of the system's dynamics to a description of its equilibrium or steady state, and as we pass from a coarse-grained to a fine-grained description of the system, or vice versa, by disaggregation or aggregation.

The 1953 account of causal ordering provided a formal treatment of the syntax of causality, applicable to systems of simultaneous equations, together with a less formal model-theoretic treatment of its semantics. In a later paper, Simon and Rescher (1966) elaborated the semantic aspects and discussed their relation to the counterfactual conditional. The present paper, while self-contained, rests on these two previous accounts.

Since our own recent concerns with the concept of causality have involved applications to physical rather than economic systems, we have little to offer by way of illustrations from economics. That is regrettable in the context of this volume, but unavoidable. But whatever the source of the examples we use, the conceptual issues are completely general—as applicable to social or biological as to physical systems.

2 Causality

Causality arises when a mechanism links phenomena. If the mechanism is a lever, the phenomena are the movements of the bodies resting on its arms. The lever links the movement of the body on one arm to the movement of the body on the other arm. As we shall see, there is more to the causal relation than simply the linkage, for the linkage is symmetric while the causal relation is asymmetric.

As another example, if the phenomena are the weather during a growing season, the acreage of wheat planted by farmers, and the size of the wheat crop, then the link among these phenomena is the mechanism that determines the production of wheat. In a mathematical model of this situation, the three phenomena will be represented by three variables and the mechanism by an equation (in this case the production function) relating the variables that the mechanism links. The production function defines a symmetric linkage among the phenomena, for any one of the variables can be written as the dependent one, and the other two as independent. Additional assumptions must be supplied to convert this linkage into a causal ordering.

Formal treatments of the foundations of the sciences for a long time avoided notions of causation and spoke only of functional relations among variables. Nevertheless, in informal descriptions of real-world phenomena, statements of the form "A causes B" are exceedingly common. Saying "electric current flowing through a resistor causes it to heat up" appeals more strongly to our intuitions than saying "heating up of a resistor causes electric current to flow." Our main purpose here is not to *validate* these intuitions, but to provide an operational definition of causality in a system that matches our intuitive notions of causality, and to study its relevance to the behavior of the system.

In the example just given, the intuitively correct causal account is that which takes the weather and the acreage of wheat planted as the (mutually independent) causal variables, and the size of the wheat crop as their joint effect. We can introduce the necessary asymmetry as follows: We define two new mechanisms, one that determines the weather, independently of the acreage of wheat or the wheat crop; and one that determines the acreage planted, independently of the weather or the wheat crop. Each of these two new mechanisms can be thought of as linking a phenomenon to other unmentioned phenomena that are outside the system under consideration. Phenomena so linked are exogenous variables of the system being analyzed.

Given a set of phenomena and a set of linkages among them, we can describe the system by a matrix of 0's and 1's, as follows: We assign a column to each phenomenon and a row to each mechanism. If phenomenon i is linked by mechanism j, then we place a 1 in the intersection of the ith column with the jth row of the matrix. In all other cells of the matrix we place 0's.

We now need three definitions:

DEFINITION 1 A *structure* is a matrix of 0's and 1's with n columns and m rows, such that in any subset of k rows of the structure, 1's appear in at least k distinct columns.

DEFINITION 2 A structure is called *self-contained* or *complete* if $n = m$, that is, if it has exactly as many columns as rows.

DEFINITION 3 A *minimal self-contained subset* is a subset of rows of a self-contained (i.e., complete) structure such that the subset is self-contained but does not itself include a self-contained proper subset.

With these definitions, we define causal ordering [Simon (1952)] among phenomena described by a self-contained structure as follows. Given a self-contained structure S, let S_0 contain all minimal complete subsets of S; then S_0 is called the set of minimal complete subsets of zero order. Since S_0 is self-contained, the values of all the variables in S_0 are, in general, determined by the mechanisms in S_0. By eliminating these values for all the occurrences of these variables in the rows of the set $(S - S_0)$, one obtains a new self-contained structure, which is called the derived structure of first order. Let S_1 be the set of minimal complete subsets of this derived structure. It is called the set of complete subsets of 1st order. Repeat the above procedure until the derived structure of the highest order contains no proper subset that is self-contained. Let V_1 be the set of columns (corresponding to variables) containing 1 in the ith row of the matrix for $i = 1, \ldots, n$. Then for each V_i for $i = 1, \ldots, n$, we will say that the element (or elements) belonging to the minimal complete subset of the highest order among all its elements is *directly causally dependent* on the elements belonging to minimal complete subsets of lower orders.

The above procedure provides an operational definition of a causal dependency structure in a system that models a piece of the real world. It must be emphasized that the structure only pertains to the *model* being analyzed, and only denotes causal relations in the real world to the extent that this model is veridical. The question of how the "real" causal relations in a physical device can be discovered and verified will be addressed when we come to the topics of possible worlds and empirical evidence for structure.

Let us apply our definition of causal ordering to the structure representing the wheat production function and the functions that determine weather and acreage planted. The matrix of this structure, shown below, is self-contained:

Wheat	*Weather*	*Acreage*
1	1	1
0	1	0
0	0	1

It should be observed that the second row, taken by itself, is also a self-contained structure, as is the third row. These are obviously minimal self-contained structures, since each consists of a single mechanism with a single phenomenon. We will assign causal priority in the entire system to these phenomena. If they appear in other mechanisms as well, we will regard them as the causal phenomena in those mechanisms, and the phenomena linked to them as their effects. Thus, the second and third phenomena also appear in the first mechanism; hence, the weather and the acreage planted are causes of the size of the wheat crop, which is the effect.

The weather and acreage in this case are not causally dependent on any other phenomena in the structure. Whenever, as in these cases, there is a mechanism that contains only a single phenomenon (a row of the matrix with only one 1), the variable corresponding to the phenomenon in whose column the 1 appears is an *exogenous variable*. The values of exogenous variables are determined by mechanisms that lie outside the system under consideration.

The causal ordering relations thus derived are shown in figure 1. In the figure, the direct causal dependency relations are indicated by arrows connecting phenomena. "Phenomenon 1 → phenomenon 2" means that phenomenon 2 is directly causally dependent on phenomenon 1.

Cause-and-effect relations can be chained. Phenomena that are effects in one mechanism may be causes in another. A slightly more complex example will illustrate how this chaining works. In the matrix M shown

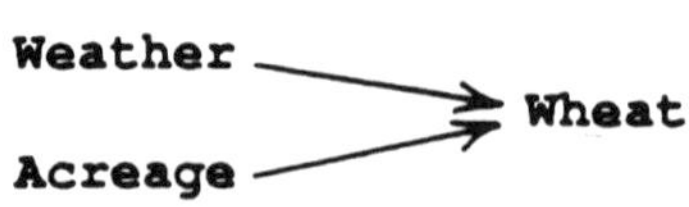

Figure 1
Causal ordering in the agriculture system

below, each of the first three mechanisms, with their linked phenomena, V_1, V_2, and V_3, respectively, are minimal self-contained subsets. Therefore, V_1, V_2, and V_3 correspond to exogenous variables. We will designate by A_{fg} the gth minimal self-contained subset of order f.

	V_1	V_2	V_3	V_4	V_5	V_6	V_7
M_1	1	0	0	0	0	0	0
M_2	0	1	0	0	0	0	0
M_3	0	0	1	0	0	0	0
M_4	1	1	1	1	1	0	0
M_5	1	0	1	1	1	0	0
M_6	0	0	0	1	0	1	0
M_7	0	0	0	0	1	0	1

Minimal Complete Subsets of Zero Order

Subset	*Mechanisms*	*Phenomena*
A_{01}	(M_1)	(V_1)
A_{02}	(M_2)	(V_2)
A_{03}	(M_3)	(V_3)

Removing the first three rows and columns from the matrix, we obtain the derived structure of first order, shown below:

Derived Structure of First Order

	V_4	V_5	V_6	V_7
M_4	1	1	0	0
M_5	1	1	0	0
M_6	1	0	1	0
M_7	0	1	0	1

Minimal Complete Subset of First Order

Subset	*Mechanisms*	*Phenomena*
A_{11}	(M_4, M_5)	(V_4, V_5)

In the derived structure of first order, the pair of mechanisms, M_4 and M_5, and the corresponding pair of phenomena, V_4 and V_5, constitute a minimal self-contained subset of the residual matrix. But V_1, V_2, and V_3 are all linked to the set $M_4 - M_5$ of the original matrix. Hence, V_1, V_2, and V_3 are causes of V_4 and V_5. Repeating this process, we obtain the derived structure of the second order, which cannot be reduced further:

Derived Structure of Second Order

	V_6	V_7
M_6	1	0
M_7	0	1

Minimal Complete Subsets of Second Order

Subset	*Mechanisms*	*Phenomena*
A_{21}	(M_6)	(V_6)
A_{22}	(M_7)	(V_7)

We see that V_4 is linked to V_6 by M_6; hence V_4 is a direct cause of V_6. Similarly V_5 is linked to V_7 by M_7; hence V_5 is a direct cause of V_7. And finally, V_1, V_2, and V_3 are indirect causes (via V_4 and V_5) of V_6 and V_7. Since V_4 and V_5 are linked by the pair of mechanisms, M_4 and M_5, these two phenomena cannot be ordered causally—there is mutual causation, or feedback, between them. The network of the causal relations in matrix M, is shown in figure 2.

The causal relation is *not* truth functional. That is to say: A causes B does not imply that not-B causes not-A. That rain causes the wheat crop to be large does not imply that a small wheat crop causes it not to rain. On the contrary, lack of rain causes the wheat crop to be small. The asymmetric causal relation is a functional relation between variables, not a relation of logical implication between the values of those variables. In the example, the causal relation is perhaps best stated: the quantity of rain determines (causes) the size of the wheat crop. The asymmetry of the linkage arises from procedures for determining which variables (phe-

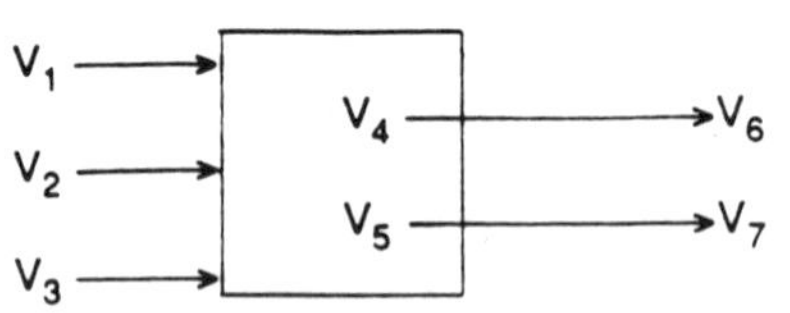

Figure 2
Causal ordering in matrix M

nomena) linked by a mechanism or set of mechanisms are the dependent variables and which are the independent variables.

3 Extended Causality

The standard definition of causal ordering that we have just reviewed is too limited to capture all the ways in which we use the term "causality" to characterize the relations among variables of a system of static simultaneous equations. In particular, we generally regard the individual equations of such a system as describing causal mechanisms, and the individual terms of an equation as stating a causal relation between the independent variables in that term and the dependent variable of the equation.

But to treat the dependent variable in an equation as *causally* dependent, we must already have introduced a causal asymmetry, and not simply a computational asymmetry, between the dependent and the independent variables. How can we avoid circularity in making such a distinction? We do it by regarding the system of static equations as representing the equilibrium of a systems of dynamic equations.

Suppose that we begin with a system of linear first-order differential equations in canonical form

$$dy_i/dt = f(y_1, y_2, \ldots, y_n), \qquad i = 1, \ldots, n.$$

We can regard y_i as the dependent variable of the *i*th equation, since the value of $y_i(t + dt)$ is determined by the values of all of the y's at time t. Hence, we can draw direct causal arrows to y_i from all of the variables that appear in that equation with non-zero coefficients. The total set of arrows for the whole group of equations defines the causal ordering of the system.

Now consider the equilibrium obtained by setting all the derivatives equal to zero. We may retain the connection of each equation with the derivative that previously appeared in it, and regard this variable as the causally dependent variable of the equation. In this way we can preserve the causal ordering of the dynamic system in speaking of the relations among variables in the static equilibrium system. The labeling of the equations with their dependent variables identifies the equations and prevents us from replacing individual equations with linear combinations of them.

In a later section, we will examine in greater detail the derivation of causal orderings for static systems from the orderings of dynamic systems, where the former correspond to the equilibria of the latter. Before we do this, we must say something about the semantic meaning of causal relations.

4 Possible Worlds

Our matrix scheme gives us a formal calculus of causal relations, but the important question, from a semantic standpoint, is what kind of justification needs to be, and can be, provided for our assumptions about phenomena, mechanisms, and linkages.

Let us consider the single mechanism that links the wheat crop with the weather and with the acreage of wheat planted, and let us again assume that the last two of these phenomena are the independent variables, while the first is the dependent variable. This is equivalent to assuming that there is a two-dimensional space of possible worlds, one dimension representing a range of possible values for the weather, the other representing a range of possible values for wheat acreage. Corresponding to each point in this space there is a determinate size of the wheat crop. The functional relation between a point in the space and a crop size represents the mechanism linking the weather, the wheat acreage, and the wheat crop.

What we are calling "possible worlds" here are, of course, "small worlds." In the large, there is only one possible world—the one we actually live in and experience. But by suppressing time subscripts and eliminating all phenomena save a few that are of interest to us, we obtain a space of a small number of dimensions where *all* points, at least within some range, may represent events in the actual world. We may actually experience, or observe, a wide range of weather phenomena, and a wide range of acreages planted in different years.

Our justification for ignoring other phenomena in representing the small world is that they appear not to affect the functional relation that we observe among the subset of variables we have selected. (Or if other phenomena affect it, we may be able to treat these effects as small "random" perturbations of the basic relation.) If we are mistaken, and ignore variables that, in fact, have large effects upon the dependent variables, this error will be revealed to us in the failure of the function to fit the data well.

5 Sources of Asymmetry

But our observations of phenomena and functional relations among them do not give us grounds for treating such relations as asymmetric and thereby dividing our phenomena into causes and effects. The asymmetry must be introduced by making assumptions about which phenomena can be considered to be exogenous, and such assumptions must be justified on some other basis. Two ideas have been prominent in the discussion of this question: manipulability of phenomena and precedence in time.

Manipulability When a phenomenon can be manipulated by the experimenter or observer, that phenomenon can be regarded as exogenous to the rest of the system, and the system will therefore contain a mechanism that is linked to that phenomenon alone. Thus, the acreage of wheat planted by farmers can be regarded as determined by the decisions of farmers, hence as exogenous, hence as representable by an equation in which acreage planted is the only variable.

Time precedence It is often assumed that precedence in time is a necessary, though not sufficient, condition for causality. Thus, we may take the temporal relation between the weather during the growing season and the size of the final crop as a reason for regarding the weather as exogenous to the production of wheat. However, our basis for postulating a causal relation in this case goes beyond time precedence. We also have prior belief that there are mechanisms that cause wheat to grow, and that the presence of moisture in appropriate quantities is essential for the operation of these mechanisms. Then our causal attribution at the macroscopic level of the three equations we wrote above rests upon assumptions that there exists a valid theory explaining the relation at a more microscopic level. The microscopic theory may be validated, in turn, by experimental evidence, relying on manipulability for causal attribution. In this case no infinite regress is involved in the attribution, and the time precedence is inessential. On the other hand, the microscopic theory may take the form of differential equations, in which case the time precedence, and hence the causality, becomes explicit.

Prepotency There are other bases for causal attribution besides manipulability and time precedence. One such base is the principle of prepotency. When we see large or powerful phenomena interacting with small or weak phenomena, we usually treat the large or powerful phenomena as the causes, and the small or weak phenomena as the effects. Thus, we would ordinarily say that the Sun causes the Earth to revolve, rather than that the Earth causes the Sun to rise and set. One may wonder whether the acceptance of this Copernican viewpoint would have been easier had the Sun been visually larger than the Earth.

Similarly, the principle of prepotency might justify our regarding the weather as a cause of the wheat crop, rather than the wheat crop a cause of the weather. The energies involved in producing the weather are so great compared with the energies consumed in the growth of the wheat that it is hard to conceive of the causal relation as reversed. Of course, if we take a longer time span into consideration, agricultural practices might, in fact, produce changes in the weather. Indeed, it is generally believed that such agriculture-produced alterations of the weather have taken place over the past several millenia. We will return to the causal treatment of feedback mechanisms in a later section of this paper.

There is another reason why prepotency may be a fallible criterion of causality. Certain subsystems of natural or man-made systems may serve as control structures for the larger system. Thus, the nervous system controls the movements of the body of an organism, and a system of electronic switches may control the operation of a power system. It is a characteristic of subsystems specialized for control that they employ very small amounts of energy to control very large amounts of energy; they are often referred to as energy amplifiers. Nevertheless, in the causal hierarchy, the control system stands above the system it controls. Before we apply the principle of prepotency, therefore, to determine a causal hierarchy, we must first look for the presence of control structures that violate the principle.

6 Possible Worlds and Identifiability

The existence of small worlds is essential to the identifiability of structural equations. A classical illustration of this is the case of economic market equilibrium, where price and quantity remain fixed at some constant value as long as no disturbing external phenomena cause the supply curve or the demand curve to shift. Since all observations are identical, and fall at the intersection of those curves, the slope of neither curve can be estimated.

On the other hand, if the small world we are studying belongs to a larger world in which parameters that affect the positions of supply and demand curves may take on different values at different times, then there is at least a possibility that the slopes of the curves can be measured. Of course this is only a necessary, not a sufficient, condition.

Let us suppose that we can enlarge our small world to a middle-size world by including the measurements of some additional variables. Let us suppose further that we have knowledge that these new variables are exogenous to the original system: that their values are determined independently of the mechanisms that determine the values of the small-world variables. Then, provided that the new variables influence the values of the variables in the original small world, they can become a powerful source of identification of the mechanisms of the latter.

For example, if we enlarge the small world of the market in equilibrium to include the weather, and treat the weather as an exogenous variable, then, in the middle-size world, changes in the weather will displace the supply curve and we may be able to identify the demand curve.

For identifiability, it is not always necessary that the exogenous variables be fully observable. It may be enough that we know something of their correlations, or lack of correlation, with each other and with the variables of the small world.

As we shall see in a moment, the introduction of exogenous variables produces asymmetries among the variables linked by the mechanisms of the small world that enable us to make causal statements about the relations of these variables. The links themselves may be perfectly symmetrical. (In the case of two forces linked by a lever, either force may be regarded as the cause that produces the other via the linkage.)

7 Empirical Evidence for Structure

There is a close relation between causal ordering and the identifiability of a linear structure. Determining the causal ordering in a system depends on describing it in terms of a set of mechanisms, each of which creates a linkage among a subset of the systems's variables. The decision to postulate the presence of a mechanism in a system of variables may rest on either theoretical or empirical grounds, or both. For example, if we wish to write the structural equations for a bridge truss, we will postulate a linkage between nodes in the truss that are visibly connected, and we will assume that no mechanism links nodes that are not so connected. Of course, if a very large magnet were located at one of the nodes, we might be wrong; but in any event, the presence of a force, hence a mechanism, linking any two nodes is to be determined empirically, in the light of whatever theories we have about the phenomena and whatever observables are implied by those theories.

The linkages need not depend on the presence of visible physical connections. In writing structural equations for a system of social relations among people, we might take the occurrence of communication between two people as a necessary condition for a direct linkage between them. (If our theories included ESP as a basis for linkage, we might not require even oral or written communication as a condition!) And, as indicated by the example of a magnet, the linkages need not be directly observable without special instruments.

Combining two or more mechanisms that are part of the description of the system may, and usually will, change the causal ordering of variables and equations, because it can change the pattern of zeros and non-zeros in the matrix of the system. Replacing equations in a linear structure by linear combinations of two or more equations does not alter the *solution* of the system—in fact, it is precisely by making such combinations that solution algorithms proceed. In the econometric literature, we call the transformed equations *reduced forms* to distinguish them from the original *structural equations*.

Here lies the connection between causal ordering and identifiability. Structural equations are equations that describe direct causal linkages, and the assumptions we make to secure identification of an equation system are precisely assumptions as to what those linkages are—what phenomena are connected directly to what other phenomena by mechanisms.

A linear system is completely identified if no linear combination of two or more equations can be substituted for one of the original equations without violating the prior constraints that define the structure of the system. And we have just seen that these prior constraints are the causal assumptions we make in defining the direct linkages among variables, that is to say, the mechanisms.

If we strip from a system of equations those equations, and the corresponding mechanisms, that determine the values of the exogenous variables, what remains is a subsystem that is not self-contained, but which describes the internal linkages of the system. In this subsystem, the causal ordering of the variables is not unequivocally determined, since the system could be completed in a number of different ways by selecting different variables to be the exogenous ones, and adding an equation to determine the value of each of these.

In our weather–acreage–crop example, we could remove the equation that defines the acreage planted as an exogenous variable, and replace it by an equation defining the size of the wheat crop as the exogenous variable. Intuitively, this doesn't make sense as a causal picture of the situation, demonstrating that our causal intuitions are semantic and prior to our designation of the equations. Of course, if we redefined the variables so that "weather" became "predicted weather" and "wheat crop" became "desired wheat crop," then the new system would make good sense, and the first equation relating the three variables would be interpreted not as agronomic but as describing farmers' decision processes (i.e., their model of the production function).

8 Effects of Changes in Structure: Comparative Statics

The causal ordering of variables in a structure can be used to simplify the analysis of the effects of altering one or more mechanisms while the remainder remain unchanged. All subsets of variables can be regarded as exogenous relative to the other subsets of the same or higher order. For example, in the example of fig. 2, if M_6 is altered, only the value of V_6 will be changed, since all other variables are exogenous relative to A_{21}. On the other hand, if M_5, in A_{11}, is altered, then the values of V_4, V_5, V_6, and V_7 will be changed, while V_1, V_2, and V_3 will remain unchanged. Moreover, if M_5 is altered and we are interested only in the effects on the variables in A_{11}, we can restrict our analysis to the equations M_4 and M_5 of that set, taking no account of the other subsets, except insofar as the (unchanged) values of V_1, V_2, and V_3 enter into the solutions of the equations of A_{11}.

Because of the indescribable complexity of the world we live in, we necessarily restrict our analyses of events to small or middle-size worlds, abstracted from their larger environments and characterized by very small numbers of equations. We see that the notion of causal ordering provides us with a rigorous justification of this essential practice. If the small worlds we choose for study correspond to complete subsets of the mechanisms of the larger world of which they are parts, then simplifying our analysis in this way does not at all invalidate our conclusions. This justification for partial equilibrium analysis was proposed some forty years ago by Richard M. Goodwin (1947).

We may be concerned, however, that our characterization of a small world will almost never be exact, and in particular, that there may be feedback from the small world to the larger environment in which it is embedded. Earlier, we remarked that even the weather might be affected, at least in the long run, by agricultural practices, and that we would therefore not be wholly justified in treating rainfall as an exogenous variable. The objection is valid, but not necessarily fatal to the practice of using small worlds for our analyses. If we can assume continuity in the functions of our system, so that the values of all variables will vary continuously with the values of the others and with the values of the system parameters, then small world analysis will be valid approximately and in the limit [Fisher (1961) reprinted in Ando, Fisher and Simon (1963)].

For example, in our wheat production model, we might replace the 0's in the mechanism determining the weather by ε's, allowing for a feedback from agricultural practices to the weather. As long as the ε's are small, weather will still behave approximately as an exogenous variable, and the feedback can be ignored. A change in the first mechanism, the wheat production function, can be analysed in first approximation without taking account of a change in the weather that it might cause.

Feedback will have two kinds of effects upon the behavior of a system. First, it will perturb slightly the equilibrium values of variables that are upstream in the causal hierarchy from a disturbance. Second, it will perturb slightly the characteristic roots of the system, and thereby change slightly the speed and manner of the system's return to equilibrium after it has been disturbed. We turn now to a consideration of this and other questions of dynamics.

9 Causality in Dynamic Systems

A linear oscillator provides us with an example of a simple dynamic system. Consider a spring of length L that requires a force of strength kx to stretch or compress it (as x is positive or negative, respectively) to length

$x + L$. By Newton's Second and Third Laws, the spring will exert a restoring force of the same magnitude and opposite sign: $-kx$. Hence, if stretched and released, its motion will be given by

$$dv/dt = -kx, \tag{1}$$

where

$$dx/dt = v. \tag{2}$$

The first equation represents a mechanism, linking the position of the spring to its acceleration, which changes its velocity. The second equation is definitional, for velocity is simply the time rate of change of position. But the equation can also be thought of as a mechanism that describes change in position as a function of velocity. We call the second mechanism M_x.

If we approximate this system by one with a discrete time interval, we obtain equations like

$$v_{t+1} = v_t - kx_t, \tag{3}$$

$$x_{t+1} = x_t + v_t, \tag{4}$$

where the causal relations are more obvious. By suppressing the time subscripts (see the earlier discussion of possible worlds), the above system of difference equations can be represented by the following matrix. The rows represent mechanisms and the columns variables (i.e., phenomena). There is 1 in position (i,j) if and only if the jth phenomenon is linked by the ith mechanism,

	v	x
M_v	1	k
M_x	1	1

In a causal interpretation, this is simply a two-variable minimal complete set, a feedback loop, in which the velocity causes changes in position and the position causes changes in velocity.

The linear operator could have been represented, using the second derivative, dx^2/dt^2, as a single differential equation of second order in the variable x:

$$d^2x/dt^2 = -kx. \tag{5}$$

However, by introducing $v = dx/dt$ explicitly, we described the system with a pair of first-order differential equations. More generally, by defining new variables in terms of derivatives [as in eq. (2)], any system of differential equations can be represented as a first-order system in the larger set of variables. If the sum of the orders of the differential equations in the original system was n, then the new system will have n first-order equations.

Moreover, if the equations are all linear in the first derivatives of the variables, then we can write the system in a canonical form by taking linear combinations of the equations so that the first derivative of a different variable is the left-hand side of each and no derivatives appear on the right-hand sides:

$$dx_t/dt = f_i(x_1, \ldots, x_n), \qquad i = 1, \ldots, n. \tag{6}$$

We will call such a system a self-contained dynamic structure.

DEFINITION 4 A *self-contained dynamic structure* is a set of n first-order differential equations in canonical form, such that in any subset of k equations of the structure at least k different variables appear on the right-hand sides.

Given a self-contained dynamic structure in canonical form as defined above, for each differential equation in the structure, we will say that the variable whose derivative appears on the left-hand side is *directly causally dependent* on the variables that appear on the right-hand side. If the derivative of a variable is a function of the variable itself only, then the variable is exogenous since it is not directly causally dependent on any other variables in the structure.

We give an example of a self-contained dynamic structure that is slightly more complicated than the previous example. It is a model of the ecosystem of a lake presented in Puccia (1985).

Let L be a dynamic structure in the following four variables:

N = amount of nitrate,

P = amount of phosphate,

G = quantity of green algae,

B = quantity of blue-green algae,

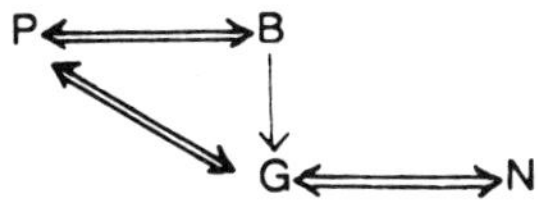

Figure 3
Causal ordering in structure L

Green algae consume nitrate and phosphate. Blue-green algae consume phosphate and inhibit the growth of the green algae. The generation of chemicals in biochemical systems is self-damping since each output derives from some precursor. The situation may be described by the following differential equations, where the c's are positive constants:

$$dN/dt = -c_1G - c_2N,$$

$$dP/dt = -c_3G - c_4B - c_5P,$$

$$dB/dt = c_6P,$$

$$dG/dt = -c_7B + c_8N + c_9P.$$

Each of the equations in the structure L is interpreted as the mechanism determining the rate of change in the amount of the corresponding substance or organism. The causal relations among variables in the structure are shown in figure 3.

If we set all of the derivatives on the left-hand sides of the equations in a self-contained dynamic structure equal to zero, at the same time adding to the right-hand side of each equation the dependent variable (if it does not already appear there), we will have the matrix for a static structure that corresponds to the equilibrium of the dynamic system. We have already shown how a change in mechanism leaves unaltered the values of variables that are prior to that mechanism in the causal hierarchy, and how this constancy holds approximately even when some of the 0's in the matrix are replaced by ε's. We can use this matrix to analyze the behavior of the system when, having been in a state of equilibrium, it is disturbed by a change in the coefficients in one or more of the mechanisms and moves to a new equilibrium.

We can also use the matrix to analyse the behavior of the dynamic system itself provided that the differential equations are linear. Let us return to the case of the block-triangular matrix, and for simplicity, begin with the special case where all the minimal complete subsets (of all orders) consist of a single mechanism each, so that the system is triangular. Consider now the characteristic roots of the system of differential equations. Since the first equation has a single variable and hence can be integrated independently of the others, there will be a unique characteristic root associated with that equation and this root will determine completely the behavior of the first variable.

We can now use the solution of the first equation in the integration of the second, which will give us two characteristic roots, the one associated with the first equation and another that we can associate with the second equation. Continuing in this way, we can associate a unique characteristic root with each equation and hence with the variable whose derivative appears on the left-hand side of that equation. Consequently, the speed of return of any variable to equilibrium will depend only on the size of the characteristic root of the equation belonging to that variable and the sizes of the characteristic roots associated with all equations that precede it in the causal hierarchy.

In the more general case of a block-triangular matrix, the characteristic roots will be associated, not with individual equations but with the minimal complete subsets, since the equations of each such subset must be solved simultaneously. Again, the dynamics of a particular variable will depend only on the characteristic roots associated with the subset to which it belongs, together with the characteristic roots of subsets that precede it in the causal hierarchy.

Since the characteristic roots of a system of differential equations are continuous in the coefficients of the equations, these results can be extended, in first approximation, to the case where some of the 0's in the matrix have been replaced by small ε's and where the matrix is therefore not exactly triangular. In this case, the dynamic behavior of a variable may be slightly affected by the dynamics of mechanisms lower in the causal hierarchy, but will be determined primarily by the dynamics of the variables in its minimal complete subset and above.

In may be useful to illustrate some of these characteristics of the dynamic behavior of causally structured systems with the simple example of a two-variable triangular system, where a, b, c, m, and n are positive constants:

$$dx/dt = -ax + m,$$

$$dy/dt = bx - cy + n.$$

Let x_0 and y_0 be the initial values of x and y, respectively, and x^* and y^* their final values in equilibrium. The characteristic roots of the equations will be $\lambda = -a, -c$.

It is easy to show that we will have

$$x = x_0 e^{-at} + x^*,$$
$$y = (b/(c-a))(x^* - x_0)e^{-at} + [(y_0 - y^*) - (b/(c-a))(x^* - x_0)]e^{-ct} + y^*.$$

Moreover,

$$x^* = m/a,$$

while

$$y^* = (n + bx)/c = (n + (bm)/a)/c.$$

In both its dynamic and equilibrium behavior, x depends only upon the coefficients of the first equation, while y depends upon the coefficients of both equations, as was inferred earlier from the causal ordering.

If a weak feedback is added to the system by making

$$dx/dt = -ax + \varepsilon y + m,$$

where ε is small in comparison with the other parameters, then λ will take on slightly modified values, $-a'$ and $-c'$, which will differ from $-a$ and $-c$ by terms of the order of $\varepsilon b/a$ and $\varepsilon b/c$, respectively. The equilibrium value of x will now be

$$x^* = mc/(ac - b\varepsilon) + \varepsilon n/(ac - b\varepsilon),$$

and y will have a similarly slightly perturbed equilibrium value.

10 Short-term and Long-term Dynamics

Consider a system composed of subsystems in which the principal strong forces link variables belonging to the same subsystems, while only weaker forces connect variables belonging to different subsystems. Under these circumstances, when the equations of the system are arranged in near block-diagonal form, the blocks will correspond to subsystems. Moreover, the non-zero elements outside the blocks will be small compared with the within-block elements. Let P be the matrix of such a dynamic system. P looks like

$$P = \begin{bmatrix} P_1 & & & \\ & P_2 & & \\ & & \ddots & \\ & & & P_N \end{bmatrix},$$

where the P_i's, for $i = 1, \ldots, N$, are square submatrices of P, and the elements of P outside the submatrices are either very small or zero. If P^* is the diagonal matrix of the same dimensions as P and with the same submatrices P_1 to P_N, P can be expressed as

$$P = P^* + \varepsilon C,$$

where ε is a very small real number and C is an arbitrary matrix of the same dimensions as P. A matrix that can be put in this form is called a *nearly completely decomposable* matrix.

For a dynamic system to be stable, all of its characteristic roots must be negative. We will assume in the discussion to follow that this condition is always satisfied. If all the roots are arranged in ascending order of the absolute values of their real parts, then the contribution of the roots toward the end of the list to the dynamic behavior of the system will be damped rapidly, and will be of importance only to the short-term behavior of the system. For the middle term and the long term, we can ignore these roots and treat the system as having a smaller number of degrees of freedom, corresponding to the number of roots we retain.

Applying this fact to a nearly decomposable dynamic system, it has been shown [Ando, Fisher and Simon (1963)] that the short-term dynamics of the system are associated only with the relative movements of the variables within each block, while the long-term dynamics are associated with the between-block linkages (i.e., the linkages defining the causal ordering). More specifically, the behavior over time of a nearly decomposable system can be described in the following four stages:

1. Short-run dynamics—Variables in each subsystem are moving toward their relative equilibria independently of other subsystems.

2. Short-run equilibrium—The most significant root (i.e., the one with smallest absolute value of the real part) of each subsystem dominates the behavior of that subsystem.

3. Long-run dynamics—The variables in each subsystem move together toward overall equilibrium while maintaining relative equilibrium in each subsystem.

4. Long-run equilibrium—Finally, the most significant root of the entire system dominates.

Thus, if we are interested in the short-term dynamics of the system, we can examine the behavior of each block, each subsystem, in isolation from the behaviors of the others; while if we are interested only in the long-term dynamics, we can aggregate the subsystems, assuming them to be always in steady-state relative equilibrium, and consider only the movements of the aggregated system. This amounts to treating each subsystem as a "black box," whose inputs and outputs, but not its internal structure, are of interest.

In order, however, for the aggregation of a nearly decomposable system to be possible, the system must satisfy two strong conditions:

1. There is one characteristic root in each subsystem whose real part has a magnitude significantly smaller than that of all other roots in the same subsystem. We will call such a root the *primary root* of the subsystem and all the others *non-primary roots*.

2. The absolute value of the real part of the primary root of each subsystem must be smaller than that of any non-primary root of any subsystem [Courtois (1977)].

It is possible to generalize the above result by relaxing the first condition, as follows:

Let $\lambda_{1_i}, \ldots, \lambda_{n_i}$ be the eigenvalues associated with the *i*th submatrix. Without loss of generality, we will assume that these eigenvalues are arranged in ascending order of the absolute values of their real parts. For a given value $\lambda_0 > 0$, we can partition this set of eigenvalues into two subsets, one containing those whose real part has a magnitude less than or equal to λ_0 and one containing the rest of the eigenvalues. Let m_i be the number of eigenvalues belonging to the first subset is

$$\{\lambda_{1_I}, \lambda_{2_I}, \cdots \lambda_{m_I}\},$$

where $|\text{Re}(\lambda_{i_I})| \leq \lambda_0$ for $i = 1, \ldots, m$, and the second subset is

$$\{\lambda_{1+m_I}, \lambda_{2+m_I}, \ldots \lambda_{n_I}\},$$

where $|\text{Re}(\lambda_{i_I})| > \lambda_0$ for $i = m+1, \ldots, n$. We will refer to the eigenvalues in the first subset as the *significant roots* and those in the second subset as the *insignificant roots*.

After the contributions of the insignificant roots vanish, the long-run behavior of the *i*th subsystem can be described approximately with only m_i ($\leq n_i$) significant roots. In fact, one can define for each subsystem m_i aggregate variables such that the values of the original variables $x_{1_I}, x_{2_I}, \ldots, x_{n_I}$ can be expressed, after some time, as linear combinations of the aggregate variables.

For example, we can define aggregate variables $y_{1_I}, \ldots, y_{m_I}$ for the *i*th subsystem as follows:

$$y_{i_I} = e^{\lambda} i_I \quad \text{for} \quad i = 1, \ldots, m.$$

Then, the values of the original variables $x_{1_I}, \ldots, x_{n_I}$, can be expressed, after some time has passed, as

$$x_{1_I} = z_{1_I 1_I} y_{1_I} + z_{2_I 1_I} y_{2_I} + \cdots + z_{m_I 1_I} y_{m_I} \quad \text{for} \quad i = 1, \ldots, n.$$

Thus, the entire structure can be redescribed in terms of these aggregate variables. The resulting aggregate structure will have fewer degrees of freedom than the original one.

There is another way of looking at the situation that is instructive. When we model a complex system, we carry our modeling only down to some level of components. Above that level, structure and the interrelations of components are explicit. Below that level, the components are black boxes, each with inputs and outputs but no detailed internal structure. Suppose that we determine the causal structure of the model, but decide subsequently that some part of the model must be elaborated in greater detail. Will the new model, incorporating this elaboration, have the same causal structure as the more aggregated model, or do we have to reexamine the causal ordering from the beginning?

If we assume that the system is hierarchical, hence nearly decomposable, then the characteristic roots associated with the component we have decided to elaborate will be large compared with the characteristic roots of the aggregated system. If we ignore very short time periods, the structure of the component can be summed up in the elements of the eigenvector associated with its largest root. These elements will be constants that, for purposes of examining behavior in the longer run, can be treated as exogenous. They determine the internal relations of the parts of the component with each other. Hence, we can add to our causal diagram a new set of causal arrows, one for each element of the eigenvector, pointing to the component. In all other respects, the causal ordering will remain the same.

We conclude that for hierarchical, nearly decomposable systems the causal ordering in not sensitive to the "grain size" of our analysis. At any level in the hierarchy, the causal ordering that relates to the relative movement of the variables *within* any single component is (nearly) independent of the causal ordering *among* components.

In the final section of this paper, we will elaborate upon this conclusion, showing how causal analysis can be carried out on a model that combines static equations (for the mechanisms that are very slow-acting and those that are very fast-acting) with differential equations (for the mechanisms that operate on an intermediate time scale).

11 Causal Ordering in a Mixed Model

Our discussion to this point has provided formal definitions of a self-contained structure and of causal ordering for systems consisting only of equilibrium relations and for systems consisting only of dynamic relations. In practice, however, systems are often described in terms of a combination of static and dynamic equations. In this section, we provide a definition of a self-contained structure for such a mixed system and a definition of causal ordering within the structure. These definitions are natural extensions of those for static and dynamic structures, which can be regarded as limiting cases of mixed structures.

12 A Mixed Approximation to a Dynamic Structure

We first show how a mixture of dynamic and equilibrium equations can arise as an approximation to a dynamic system. We use a slightly expanded version of our agronomic model, introducing some additional variables: R, the amount of rainfall; W, the size of the wheat crop; P, the price of wheat; N, population; and B, the price of bread. The variables are linked by the following causal relations:

1. The rain causes the wheat to grow.

2. An increase in population causes the wheat price to rise, but a large wheat crop causes the wheat price to fall.

3. An increase in the wheat price causes the price of bread to rise.

4. Increase in the amount of wheat produced causes a slow change in the population.

5. Increases in the population and the amount of wheat acreage cause slow changes in the weather.

We express these relations by the following set of differential equations, where the f's are linear functions of their arguments. In each equation, the independent variables represent the causes, and the dependent variable whose derivative appears on the left-hand side has its value causally determined by the mechanism described by that equation. Notice that a variable may appear on both sides of an equation (change in a variable may be influenced by the magnitude of that variable).

(A1) $dW/dt = f_W(W, R)$,

(A2) $dP/dt = f_P(W, P, N)$,

(A3) $dB/dt = f_B(P, B)$,

(A4) $dN/dt = f_N(N, W)$,

(A5) $dR/dt = f_R(W, R, N)$.

In figure 4, showing the matrix of coefficients of this system, we have introduced ε's for the matrix elements $[i,j]$ in each case where the effect of v_j on dv_i/dt is assumed to be very small. For example, the coefficients of N and W in the first row of the matrix are ε's because the population and the size of the wheat crop are assumed to have only a slight effect on the weather. Hence, it will take a long time for the effect to become signif-

Equation		R	N	W	P	B
A5	R'	1	ε	ε		
A4	N'		1	ε		
A1	W'	1		1		
A2	P'		1	1	1	
A3	B'				β	1

Figure 4
Matrix of coefficients for the example

icant, and, at least for the short-run and middle-run behavior of the system, the variable R can be treated as exogenous. The same assumption is made for the effect of the wheat crop upon population.

Where the influence of the variable v_j on the derivative of v_i is assumed to be very large, we denote the matrix element by β. We have introduced a β in the column corresponding to P of the equation for B because the price of bread is expected to change very rapidly in response to the price of wheat. If the change is such as to restore equilibrium between P and B, we can regard this restoration as taking place almost immediately, whenever the equilibrium is disturbed, and replace the differential equation by the equilibrium relation between the variables.

Making such assumptions about the relative speeds of adjustment in these mechanisms amounts to classifying the dependent variables into three categories:

1. variables whose rates of change are influenced only very little by other variables;
2. variables that adjust so quickly that they are always close to relative equilibrium with their independent variables;
3. all other variables.

Then we can simplify the original description of the system by treating the variables in the first category as exogenous and replacing the differential equations for the variables in the second category by the corresponding equilibrium relations. Making these changes, we obtain the following mixed system:

(A1) $dW/dt = f_W(W, R)$,

(A2) $dP/dt = f_P(W, P, N)$,

(A3) $f_B(P, B) = 0$,

(A4) $N = c_1$,

(A5) $R = c_2$.

If the assumptions we have made about the relative speeds of the mechanisms hold, this set of dynamic and equilibrium equations will be a reasonable approximation, for the middle run, of the behavior of the dynamic system. We have already indicated our meaning of "middle run." We now wish to transfer the notion of causal links to the mixed system and to compare the causal structure of the original with the transformed system.

Some notation We need to introduce some notation that will be used throughout the remainder of this section. Let D be a structure consisting of m linear first-order differential equations, $\{D_1, D_2, \ldots, D_m\}$, in m variables $\{x_1, x_2, \ldots, x_m\}$. The equations are assumed to be in canonical form, so that D_i is of the form $dx_i/dt = f_i(R_i)$ where f_i is a linear function of its arguments.

We will write E_k for the equation obtained by setting the derivative in D_k equal to 0: $f_k(R_k) = 0$. Finally, we will write C_k for the equation obtained by setting the variable in the derivative on the left-hand side of D_k equal to an arbitrary constant: $x = c$.

We can now construct a mixed structure, $M(D)$, by replacing some of the equations of D by the corresponding E_k, others by the corresponding C_k, and retaining the remainder. Designate these three sets of equations in $M(D)$ by E, C, and D, respectively. Further, if Q is any one of these sets of equations, designate by $V(Q)$ the set of all the variables that appear in one or more members of Q.

Returning to our example, we began with five differential equations. We converted the third to the corresponding E_3, and the fourth and fifth to C_4 and C_5. Now the set D contains the first two equations, the set E, the third, and the set C, the forth and fifth.

Definition of self-contained mixed structures Let $M(D)$ be a system of n equations in n variables consisting of equations of types D, E, and C.

DEFINITION The set M of n equations in n variables is a self-contained mixed structure iff:

(C1) One or more of the n equations are in D and the rest are in E and C.

(C2) In any subset of size k of D, the first derivatives of at least k different variables appear.

(C3) In any subset of size k of D in which r $(r \geq k)$ first derivatives appear, if the values of any $(r - k)$ first derivatives are chosen arbitrarily, then the remaining k are determined uniquely as functions of the n variables.

(C4) The first derivatives of exactly d different variables appear in D, where d is the size of the set D.

(C5) $C \vee E$, the join of C and E (the variables of D that appear in these equations being treated as exogenous), is a self-contained static structure.

Given a self-contained mixed structure, as just defined, the causal ordering among its variables and derivatives follow the definitions of causal ordering in dynamic and static structures. More precisely:

1. The ordering among n variables and m derivatives in the subset D is given by the definition of causal ordering in a dynamic structure.
2. The ordering among variables (but not their derivatives) in $C \vee E$ is given by the definition of causal ordering in a static structure.

Thus, in the mixed model derived from our agronomic example, W is causally determined by W and R, and P by W, P, and N. In the static segment of the model, B is determined by P, while N and R are exogenous. This is precisely the causal ordering we find in the full dynamic system if we ignore the very weak causal mechanisms that determine R and N. The causal link from P to B remains, but is changed to an "instant" static one.

The conditions for a self-contained mixed structure impose certain limitations on which equations of a dynamic system can be converted to static relations representing "instant" equilibration. Suppose that a dynamic mechanism determining the variable x is not self-regulating—i.e., does not contain x on the right-hand side. Then, by staticizing that equation, we create a causal relation, which did not exist previously, among the independent variables of the dynamic equation. Since, in the original dynamic system, other causal mechanisms determine each of these variables, the partially staticized system will be over-determined, hence will not be a self-contained structure. It can be shown that this difficulty cannot arise if the equation that is staticized is self-regulating (if x appears on its right-hand side).

13 Conclusions

In the first three sections of this paper we reviewed briefly the definition of causal ordering as well as the semantic bases for postulating direct linkages among variables and for postulating that particular variables in a system be treated as exogenous. A sufficient number of postulates of both kinds are required for determining the causal ordering of variables and mechanisms within a system.

In a fourth section we developed the implications of the causal ordering of variables in a system for comparative static analysis, that is, analysis of the displacement of equilibrium under changes in parameters.

In the fifth section, we extended our analysis to dynamic systems described by systems of differential or difference equation. The causal structure of such a system of mechanisms is revealed when we order the variables and equations so that the matrix of coefficients becomes block triangular. If this matrix is then also nearly decomposable, then the system can be described as a hierarchy of components and subcomponents and the causal ordering among components at each level of the hierarchy can be determined independently.

In that section, we also showed how causal ordering can be analysed in systems that include static equations representing variables that are "nearly" exogenous (affected by the other variables only over long periods of time), other static equations for mechanisms that alter the values of corresponding variables "instantaneously," and differential equations that describe the dynamic behavior of the remaining variables. By differentiating among long-term, short-term, and middle-term phenomena in this way, attention can be directed to the dynamics of specific subsystems without dealing with the entire system at one.

Note

This research was supported in part by the Defense Advanced Research Projects Agency under Contract No. F-33615-84-K-1520, and in part by the Personnel and Training Programs, Psychological Sciences Division, Office of the Naval Research, under Contract No. N00014-86-K-0678. Reproduction in whole or in part is permitted for any purpose of the United States Government.

References

Ando, Albert, Franklin M. Fisher and Herbert A. Simon, 1963, Essays on the structure of social science models (MIT Press, Cambridge, MA).

Courtois, P. J., 1977, Decomposability (Academic Press, New York).

Fisher, Franklin M., 1961, On the cost of approximate specification in simultaneous equation estimation, Econometrica 29, 139–170.

Goodwin, Richard M., 1947, Dynamical coupling with especial reference to markets having production lags, Econometrica 15, 181–204.

Puccia, C. J. and R. Levins, 1985, Qualitative modeling of complex systems (Harvard University Press, Cambridge, MA).

Simon, Herbert A., 1952, On the definition of the causal relation, Journal of Philosophy 49, 517–528.

Simon, Herbert A., 1953, Causal ordering and identifiability, in: William C. Hood and Tjalling C. Koopmans, eds., Studies in econometric methods (Wiley, New York) 49–74.

Simon, Herbert A. and Nicholas Rescher, 1966, Cause and counterfactual, Philosophy of Science 33, 323–340.

I.3 Causality and Model Abstraction

(with Yumi Iwasaki)

1 Introduction

In science and engineering, a set of simultaneous equations is usually used to describe the behavior of a system. Fundamental laws of the domain, such as physical laws, are generally stated in terms of equations, also. An important difference between a functional relation expressed by an equation and a causal relation is that the former is usually symmetric while the latter is not. Functional relations between variables are symmetric whenever the function is invertible, for if x is expressed as a function of y, then y can be expressed as a function of x. On the other hand, causal relations are not symmetric because when we say x causes y, then we do not also imply y causes x (or even that $\sim y$ causes $\sim x$).

Knowledge of causal dependency relations among variables is essential in handling a number of practical problems such as diagnosis and prediction. When one is given a set of equations as a model of some system and a variable is observed to have an abnormal value, it is not a trivial task, especially if the number of variables and equations involved in the system is large, to decide what variables could be causing the abnormality, what other variables should be affected, and what other observations are only spuriously correlated to the initial finding.

A number of artificial intelligence systems have been built that make use of causal knowledge to perform reasoning tasks such as diagnosis, prediction, and measurement interpretation, in a variety of domains. All but a few of these systems pre-specify the directions of causality. Such pre-specified causal knowledge is specific to particular situations and, therefore, is less general than knowledge of acausal, functional relations. For example, the knowledge that "an increase in the temperature of the gas will cause the pressure to increase" is applicable when the volume is not allowed to increase as much as the temperature, while another piece of knowledge "an increase in the temperature of the gas will cause its volume to increase" is applicable when the pressure is held constant. In contrast, a statement of the ideal gas law in terms of the mathematical relation,

$$PV = \eta RT$$

applies to both cases. Moreover, the specific causal knowledge can be derived from this general statement of the law given a description of a specific circumstance in which it is applied. The fact that the temperature and the volume are controlled by some external means is an example of such circumstantial information. If a computer program can make use of circumstantial information to reconstruct causal relations from knowledge of mathematical relations, knowledge can be represented in a more general form of equations than when the knowledge of causal relations is pre-coded.

In this chapter, we present the theory of causal ordering that allows one to interpret the causal relations in a set of equations. The information about the context in which individual equations are used is implicit in the choice of equations comprising the set. The operational definition of causal dependency relations provided by the theory makes it possible to construct a program that can reason causally from mathematical relations, in which physical principles are generally stated. Such a program knows much about general physical principles, will recognize the applicable principles in a given situation, and will use the knowledge to perform a given task, such as diagnosis, prediction, design, that requires causal knowledge, or to give an intuitive causal explanation of system behavior.

Causal ordering The theory of causal ordering [2, 3] provides a technique for inferring the causal dependency relations among variables in a set of functional relations. Though the theory originally grew out of concerns with causality in econometrics, the theory's definition of causal relations is useful in generating a causal interpretation of the behavior of any system described by a system of simultaneous equations, including a physical device. Causal ordering was initially defined by Simon for a static system consisting of equilibrium equations [1]. When the situation modeled involves a feedback loop, applying the causal ordering method to an equilibrium model cannot elucidate the direction of causality around the loop. In such a situation, one must look to a dynamic model to know the causal relations. Simon also defined the causal ordering in a dynamic system consisting of first-order linear differential equations [1]. In practice, a description of behavior rarely consists of only equilibrium equations or only differential equations. Instead, a mixture of equilibrium and differential equations is typically supplied as a description. This paper extends the scope of the theory of causal ordering to include such mixed systems of equilibrium and differential equations.

Abstraction When the system under study involves many variables and relations, it becomes too complex to be grasped easily in its entirety. Then, it is necessary to aggregate the model into a more abstract model involving fewer variables and relations, which is easier to reason about. Aggregation is performed by grouping together variables and relations into subsystems, and by redescribing the entire system in terms of these subsystems and their interactions. This must be done in such a way that the act of grouping variables does not affect the causal relations among variables within a subsystem. This paper addresses aggregation in such a manner that the causality in the aggregated system is consistent with that of the original system. We will also examine the close interrelation between causal ordering and model aggregation. For an aggregated model to approximate the original model well, aggregation must be carried out in a manner consistent with the causal ordering in the original model. Moreover, for the method of causal ordering to produce the correct causal structure, all equations in the model must be at the same level of aggregation.

1.1 Related Work

The research described here builds upon much previous work in a variety of fields. One of them is econometrics, in which the theory of causal ordering in a system of equations was initially developed [1]. The recent work on qualitative reasoning and naive physics in artificial intelligence also provided ideas for this research. Causal reasoning is an essential part of qualitative reasoning about the physical world. Most of the model-based reasoning approaches to date have pre-defined knowledge of causal relations among events, and, therefore, causal relations are considered primitives by these programs [4, 5]. Notable exceptions are the work by de Kleer and Brown [6] and that by Williams [7]. In both of these works, a behavior model is given as a collection of functional relations (constraints) among variables, as it is in the causal ordering approach. In their work on qualitative physics, de Kleer and Brown define causality based on the way effects of a disturbance are propagated to other parts of the model through a network of constraints. In their approach, the problem of determining the causal structure of a model is tightly coupled with the problem of predicting the effects (i.e. decrease or increase) of a disturbance on variables in the model. Williams' approach is similar to de

Kleer and Brown's though some of his constraints have a pre-determined causal direction while de Kleer and Brown's constraints do not. In our approach, we separate the problems of determining causal structure and the effects of a disturbance because they are in fact independent of each other, and the causal ordering approach addresses the first, the problem of determining the causal structure. Given this structure, the effects of disturbances can be determined by standard methods of qualitative mathematics. Despite these seeming differences, the method for determining causality based on propagation of disturbances is generally consistent with, but somewhat less general than, the more formal method of causal ordering, thereby providing an explanation of why the propagation methods work [3, 8].

Any theory that attempts to infer causal relations in a model must address the issue of building a correct model if the inferred relations are to bear any relation to our perception of the real-world phenomena being modeled. In constructing a behavior model, de Kleer and Brown postulate a *locality* principle and a *no-function-in-structure* principle to avoid using non-local and teleological knowledge as much as possible and thereby make sure that their model is free from any pre-conceived idea of what its behavior ought to be. In our causal ordering method, each equation in the model must represent a conceptually distinct mechanism corresponding to a specific connection among components. The notion of conceptually distinct mechanisms underlying equations includes, but is more general than, the concept of physical connections on which equations are based in qualitative physics.

The concept of mechanisms that give rise to causality by linking phenomena is similar to the concept of physical processes in the Qualitative Process Theory (QPT) of Forbus [9]. In QPT, a physical process is "something that acts through time to change the parameters of objects in a situation." A process is specified by a set of objects involved, conditions for the process to happen, relations imposed by the process on parameters, and influences of the process on the objects. Given a state description, QPT infers what processes are in progress, and then it predicts what will happen in the future. We have not tried to develop a general ontology of mechanisms.

The latter part of this paper, which discusses model abstraction, also draws much from the work by Ando, Fisher, and Simon on the aggregation of dynamic models of economic systems [10]. In the qualitative reasoning literature, Kuipers uses abstraction by time-scale in order to control the exponential growth of the number of possible courses of behavior in qualitative simulation [11]. Kuipers has a hierarchy of constraint networks of very fast to very slow mechanisms. When simulating a fast mechanism, variables controlled by slower mechanisms are considered constant, and when simulating a slow mechanism, equilibrium among variables controlled by faster mechanisms is considered to be reached instantaneously. This idea of abstraction by time-scale is very similar to the notion of abstraction in the Ando-Fisher-Simon work discussed in this paper. However, Kuipers does not explore the issue of generating such a hierarchy of models from one original model. The aggregation technique discussed in this paper can be used to generate a hierarchy of models of different time-scales.

This research attempts to integrate ideas and techniques, old and new, drawn from several different fields of science, for the purpose of developing a rigorous, foundational scheme for causal, qualitative reasoning about physical systems.

1.2 Organization of the Paper

Section 2 presents the theory of causal ordering as applied to an equilibrium model. The concept of causal ordering among variables in a system of equilibrium equations is described. We present examples of application of the method to physical devices. Section 3 discusses causal ordering in a dynamic system. The definition of causal ordering in a system of differential equations in canonical form is presented. Section 4 generalizes the definition to a system consisting of both equilibrium and dynamic equations in any form. We define causal ordering among variables in such a system and derive mixed models as abstractions of a dynamic model. We present two techniques for producing a more abstract, mixed system from a dynamic system.

In Section 5 we turn to aggregation of a near-decomposable dynamic system. We describe the concept of near-decomposability and the procedure for aggregating a near-decomposable dynamic system. In Section 5.3, we compare the two types of abstraction techniques—those presented in Sections 4 and 5. Then, we discuss the relation between the notion of abstraction hierarchy and causal ordering. We conclude with a discussion of current and future work in Section 6.

2 Causal Ordering in Equilibrium Structures

Causal ordering was initially defined by Simon for an equilibrium structure consisting of equilibrium equations [1]. The theory of causal ordering provides a technique for inferring the causal relations among variables in a set of functional relations. Causal ordering is an asymmetric relation among the variables in a self-contained structure, which seems to reflect people's intuitive notion of causal dependency relations among variables in a system. Establishing a causal ordering involves finding subsets of variables whose values can be computed independently of the remaining variables, and using those values to reduce the structure to a smaller set of equations containing only the remaining variables. The approach offers a computational mechanism for defining a causal dependency structure.

First, we define an equilibrium structure:

DEFINITION 1: SELF-CONTAINED EQUILIBRIUM STRUCTURE A self-contained equilibrium structure is a system of n equilibrium equations in n variables that possesses the following special properties:

1. That in any subset of k equations taken from the structure at least k different variables appear with non-zero coefficients in one or more of the equations of the subset.

2. That in any subset of k equations in which m $(\geq k)$ variables appear with non-zero coefficients, if the values of any $(m - k)$ variables are chosen arbitrarily, then the equations can be solved for unique values of the remaining k variables.

The condition (1) above ensures that no part of the structure is over-determined. The condition (2) ensures that the equations are not mutually dependent, because if they are the equations cannot be solved for unique values of the variables.

The idea of causal ordering in a self-contained equilibrium structure can be described roughly as follows. A system of n equations is called self-contained if it has exactly n unknowns and if all the equations are independent. Given a self-contained system, S, if there is a proper subset, s, of S that is also self-contained and that does not contain a proper self-contained subset, s is called a *minimal complete subset*. Let S_0 be the union of all such minimal complete subsets of S; then S_0 is called the *set of minimal complete subsets of zero order*. Since S_0 is self-contained, the values of all the variables in S_0 can, in general, be obtained by solving the equations in S_0. By substituting these values for all the occurrences of these variables in the equations of the set $(S - S_0)$, one obtains a new self-contained structure, which is called the *derived structure of first order*. Let S_1 be the set of minimal complete subsets of this derived structure. It is called the *set of complete subsets of 1st order*. Repeat the above procedure until the derived structure of the highest order contains no proper subset that is self-contained. For each equation e_i in S, let V_i denote the set of variables appearing in e_i, and let W_i denote the subset of V_i containing the variables belonging to the complete subsets of the highest order among those in V_i. Then, the variables in W_i are said to be *directly causally dependent* on the elements in $(V_i - W_i)$.

In order for the above procedure to produce causal relations in the model that agree with people's notion of causality in the real world, the equations comprising a model must come from an understanding of mechanisms. The term *mechanism* is used here in a general sense to refer to distinct conceptual parts in terms of whose functions the working of the whole system is to be explained. Mechanisms are such things as laws describing physical processes or local components that can be described as operating according to such laws. An equation representing such a mechanism is called a *structural equation*, and every equation in the model should be a structural equation standing for a mechanism through which variables influence other variables. Since this requirement is crucial for the correct application of the method or any other known method for determining causal relations, we will say more about it later.

Causal dependency relations as determined by the above procedure are based on the notion of *manipulability* of a variable by *intervention* into the system [1]. When we say "variable B depends on variable A," which we will write as

$$A \rightarrow B, \tag{2.1}$$

we mean that there exists some mechanism that determines the value of B from that of A, whether it be a physical law, an actual device, or some other kind of communication path between the two variables. Thus, everything being equal, a change in A will necessarily result in a change in B. Furthermore, the existence of this mechanism suggests a possibility for an outside intervention to influence the value of B. In other words, if

(2.1) is the causal structure of our model, then in the context of this particular model and for a fixed A, the only way to manipulate the value of B is to intervene in the mechanism linking A and B to cause a change in some constant or parameter in the equation representing the mechanism.

Note that the method of causal ordering does not require knowledge about the precise functional forms of equations. The only information that the method makes use of is what variables appear with non-zero coefficients in what equations, which in terms of mechanisms translates to what variables are causally linked by each mechanism. Thus, the causal ordering method applies to qualitative as well as quantitative models.

A few words about the computational complexity: Nayak [12] points out the relation between the problems of computing the causal ordering and finding a complete matching for a bipartite graph. He also describes an efficient algorithm for computing the causal ordering based on the graph. The complexity of the algorithm is $O(\sqrt{n}e)$, where n is the number of variables and e is the sum of the numbers of the variables appearing in each equation.

2.1 Example of Causal Ordering in an Equilibrium Structure

This section presents an example of a self-contained equilibrium structure and application of the causal ordering procedure to the structure.

Figure 2.1 shows a circuit consisting of a voltage source and a resistor, whose length can be changed manually. The following set of variables and equations describe the behavior of the system:

V Voltage drop across the resistor

I Current through the resistor

R Resistance across the resistor

L Length of the resistor

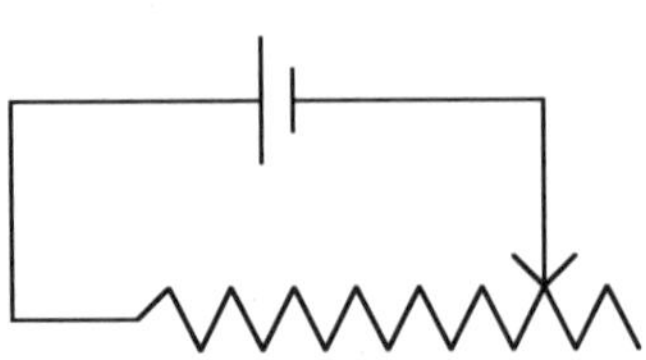

Figure 2.1
A battery-resistor circuit

$$V = IR \tag{2.2}$$

$$R = c_0 L \tag{2.3}$$

$$V = c_1 \tag{2.4}$$

$$L = c_2 \tag{2.5}$$

Equation (2.2) represents Ohm's law. Equation (2.3) represents the relation between the resistance and the length of the resistor, the resistance being proportional to the length. Equations (2.4) and (2.5) represent the assumptions that the voltage and the length are controlled by factors external to the system currently being modeled. Such variables are called *exogenous variables*, and an equation, such as (2.4) and (2.5), that indicates a variable to be exogenous, an *exogenous equation*. Assuming a variable exogenous amounts to putting the mechanism controlling the variable outside the model; thus, exogenous variable assumptions limit the scope of the model. The equation structure composed of the equations (2.2) to (2.5) is self-contained. Applying the causal ordering procedure to this structure will produce the causal dependency structure shown in figure 2.2. The ordering can be interpreted in English as follows:

The amount of the current through the resistor depends causally on the resistance and the voltage. The resistance, in turn, depends on the length of the resistor.

The causal ordering depends very much on the choice of exogenous variables as can be seen by comparing figure 2.2 with figure 2.3. Figure 2.3 is the causal ordering produced when current is assumed to be produced by a current source (such as solar cells) instead of a voltage source (such as a battery). Then, equation (2.4) is replaced by

$$I = c_3. \tag{2.4$'$}$$

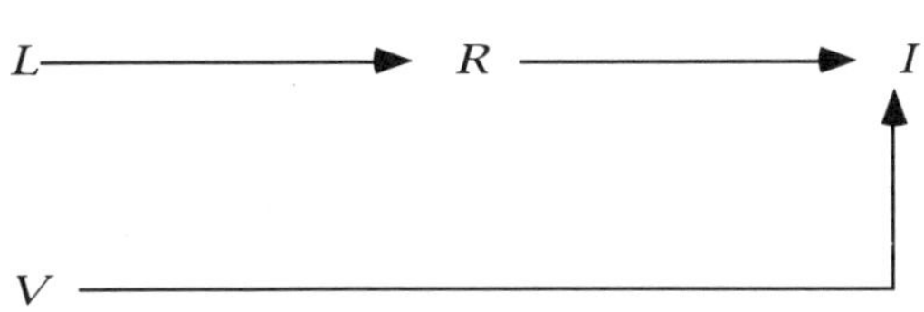

Figure 2.2
Causal ordering in the battery-resistor circuit

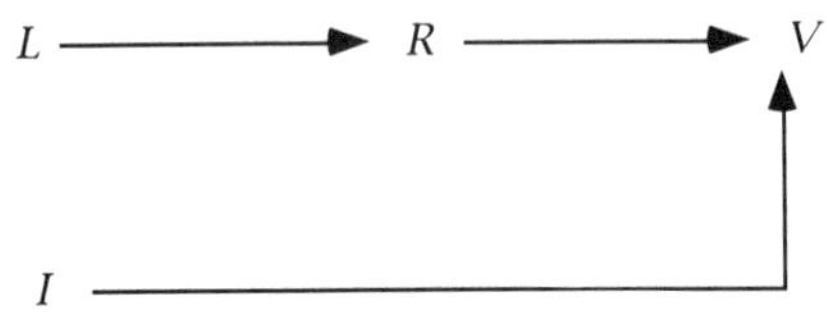

Figure 2.3
Alternative causal ordering in the battery-resistor circuit

The dependency structure can be interpreted in English as follows:

The voltage drop across the resistor depends on the resistance and the current through the resistor. The resistance, in turn, depends on the length of the resistor.

Equations (2.2) and (2.3) can be considered structural equations in this case because the laws that they represent are conceptually distinct. In general, it is not an easy task to decide whether or not a given equation is structural, and there is no formal definition for a structural equation. A counter-example may help clarify the concept. One can combine the two equations by substituting the right-hand side of equation (2.3) for R on the right-hand side of Equation (2.2) to produce the following equation:

$$V = c_0 IL \tag{2.6}$$

Equation (2.6) is not a structural equation because it mixes the conceptually distinct mechanisms represented by Equations (2.2) and (2.3). Whether change in length of the resistor will alter the voltage drop or the current depends on the physical structure of the entire system.

As may be inferred from this example, the concept of structural equation depends on what one takes as *primitive* for a given model. In this sense, the concept of structural equation is relative to the abstraction level of the model. At one level, one may be willing to treat a component with a complex internal structure as a black box and to represent its function with one equation, which will be considered structural at this level. However, in a more detailed model, this equation will not be considered structural because it represents the net effects of several mechanisms that are considered primitives at that level. Since this issue of abstraction levels is critical for model building and also for causal analysis, we will come back to it in Sections 4 and 5, where we discuss model abstraction and its relation to causal ordering.

2.2 Minimal Complete Subsets with Multiple Variables

In the above example, each of the minimal complete subsets of any degree consists of only one variable. However, in general minimal complete subsets can contain any number of variables. While the causal ordering procedure defines ordering between variables in minimal complete subsets of different orders, it does not define any ordering among variables within one minimal complete subset. For example, consider a model G consisting of the following three equations:

$$X + Y = c_1 \tag{2.7}$$

$$X - Y + Z = c_2 \tag{2.8}$$

$$Z = c_3 \tag{2.9}$$

In this model, the only minimal complete subset of zero order is the one consisting of equation (2.9) and Z. After removing Z from the structure, the derived structure of the first order consists of two equations, both of which involve X and Y. Since this structure cannot be reduced any further, the causal ordering procedure halts and the resulting causal structure looks like the following;

$$Z \rightarrow [X, Y].$$

The structure shows that the bracketed variables, X and Y, are mutually dependent and that they jointly depend on Z. In general, when there is a minimal complete subset with more than one variable, the variables are mutually dependent, and the causal ordering method does not assign an ordering among them. Such mutual dependence is due to the existence of some feedback mechanism, and there are no simple, acyclic causal dependence relations among variables. In order to elucidate the causal relations among the variables involved in a feedback loop in detail, it is necessary to examine the dynamic behavior of the system, which is the topic we will discuss in Section 3.

2.3 Equilibrium Model of a Bathtub

Though the causal ordering procedure produces a causal structure that is consistent with the concept of causality based on manipulability, sometimes such a structure does not agree with people's naive notions of causal

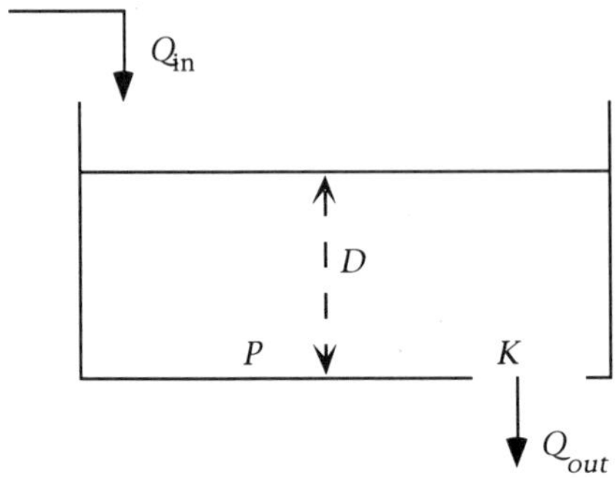

Figure 2.4
Bathtub

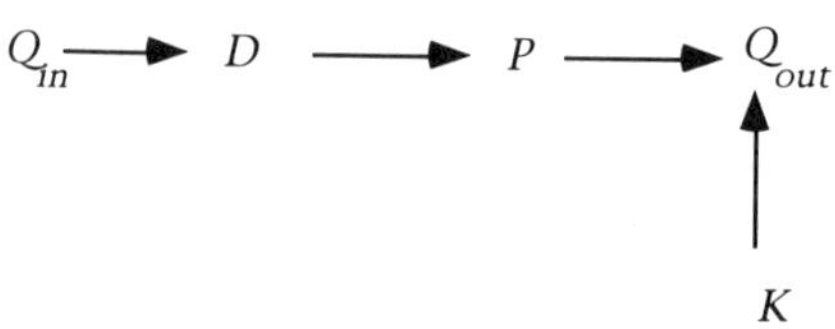

Figure 2.5
"Naive" causal ordering of bathtub

relations in the model. We present one such case to motivate extension of the causal ordering method to dynamic and mixed structures.

The device used as an example is a bathtub as shown in figure 2.4 [13]. There are four variables; the input and output flow rates Q_{in} and Q_{out}, the depth of water in the tub, D, the size of the valve opening, K, and pressure in the bottom of the tub, P.

Intuitively speaking, adding water to the tub increases the depth (D), which increases the pressure (P), which in turn increases the output flow rate (Q_{out}). Figure 2.5 shows this "naive" ordering.

However, the causal ordering structure produced from an equilibrium model of this situation does not agree with this "naive" causal ordering. The equilibrium model can be characterized by the following five equations, where c_1 through c_4 represent positive constants.

$$Q_{\text{out}} = c_1 KP \tag{2.10}$$

The output flow rate is proportional to the pressure.

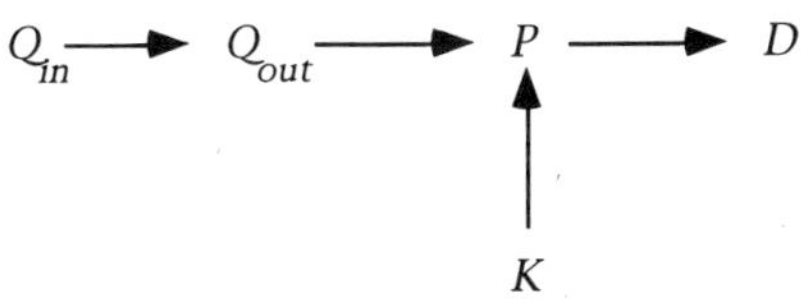

Figure 2.6
Equilibrium causal ordering of bathtub

$D = c_2 P$ (2.11)
The pressure is proportional to the depth of water.

$Q_{\text{out}} = Q_{\text{in}}$ (2.12)
When the system is in equilibrium, the input flow equals the output flow.

$Q_{\text{in}} = c_3$ (2.13)

$K = c_4$ (2.14)
The input flow rate and the valve opening are exogenous (externally controlled).

The causal ordering produced for this bathtub model is shown in Figure 2.6.

The causal structure shown in figure 2.6 shows that the output flow rate depends directly on the input flow rate, the pressure depends on the output flow rate, and the depth depends on the pressure. This causal ordering, at least at first glance, strikes one as being counter-intuitive.

In order to see that the ordering in figure 2.6 is correct with respect to the notion of manipulability, one must recognize that the model describes equilibrium, and variable values represent this equilibrium situation. The equations represent relations that hold in equilibrium; but these relations do not necessarily hold while the system is disturbed from equilibrium. If the system described is dynamically stable, meaning that it will return to equilibrium when disturbed, the equilibrium relations will hold once again after equilibrium is restored but not during the transition period from one equilibrium state to another. In the bathtub example, if the input flow is decreased suddenly, this will cause immediate disturbances in the values of other variables. However, *if the system is dynamically stable*, the output flow must again be equal to the input flow when the system is back in equilibrium. How could we state the relation in the diagram, which shows Q_{out} as cause of P and P as cause of D? We could say that, *in order for* Q_{out} to equalize with Q_{in}, P must maintain an appropriate value, and this requires D, in turn, to hold a corresponding value. The "in order for" makes the causation here teleological, without specifying a mechanism to realize the result, to wit, the mechanism that returns the system to equilibrium when disturbed.

Suppose that the value of K is changed by opening up the valve a little more, then an immediate reaction will be that Q_{out} will increase. However, if the system is stable, when equilibrium is restored eventually, the value of Q_{out} must be equal to Q_{in} (otherwise, the system would not be in equilibrium). Thus, changing K only affects the equilibrium values of P and D but not Q_{out}. The *equilibrium* value of $Qout$ cannot depend on P or D, a fact correctly reflected in the ordering of figure 2.6 but not in Figure 2.5. Nevertheless, it is true that the ordering in figure 2.5 seems more appealing to our intuitive notion of causality in the situation. The reason in this case is that our "intuitive" causal understanding is of dynamic behavior rather than the strictly equilibrium behavior represented by the model of figure 2.6. The method used to analyze the final effects caused by changing one or more parameters but then returning to equilibrium, reflected in figure 2.6, is usually called the "method of comparative statics." In the following Section 3, we will turn to the topic of causal ordering in models of dynamic behavior.

2.4 Qualitative Structures

In this section, we expand the notion of self-contained structures and causal ordering to systems of qualitative equations. We mean by a qualitative equation an equation whose functional form or coefficient values are not completely specified. In modeling a real-world situation, one often does not know the form of the functional relation among variables that is nonetheless known to represent some mechanism. For example, one may know that the gravitational force, F, between two objects is a function of the masses, M_1 and M_2, of the objects, and the distance, D, between them without knowing the exact functional form of the relation. The qualitative equation can be expressed as

$$f(F, M_1, M_2, D) = 0.$$

Sometimes, one may even know the exact functional form but not the actual values of coefficients. In any of these cases, the definition of a self-contained structure in Section 2 cannot be applied directly since the second condition that the equations be solvable for unique values of variables cannot be met without the knowledge of functional forms or coefficient values.

However, if we have reasons to believe that each member in a set of qualitative equations is structural (i.e. represents a conceptually distinct mechanism in the situation), then we would like to be able to talk about the causal ordering in the structure. For this reason, we define the concept of qualitative self-contained structure as a generalization of the definition in Section 2.

First, we assume that for each qualitative equation the exact set of variables appearing in the equation with non-zero coefficients is known even if nothing else is known about the functional relation. Therefore, each equation can be represented as a set of variables. With this assumption, we define a qualitative self-contained structure as follows:

DEFINITION 2: A QUALITATIVE SELF-CONTAINED STRUCTURE A self-contained equilibrium structure is a system of n qualitative (equilibrium) equations in n variables that possesses the following property:

1. That in any subset of k equations taken from the structure at least k different variables appear with non-zero coefficients in one or more of the equations of the subset.

This definition is almost identical to Definition 1 in Section 2 except that the condition 2 is eliminated. Therefore, this definition is a generalization of the definition in Section 2, and the concept of a qualitative self-contained structure is strictly weaker than the concept of quantitative self-contained structure.

Given a self-contained qualitative structure, the procedure described in Section 2 can be used to determine the causal ordering among variables. Furthermore, given a self-contained qualitative structure, we have the following theorems. The proofs are given in Appendix A.

THEOREM 1 All the derived structures of a self-contained qualitative structure are self-contained.

THEOREM 2 The causal ordering of a self-contained qualitative structure is unique.

3 Causal Ordering in a Dynamic System

The previous sections presented causal ordering in equilibrium structures, where all the structural equations were algebraic equations and not differential equations. In this section, we discuss causal ordering in a dynamic system. Since the notion of causality almost always involves something changing (hypothesized or actual), it is important that a method for determining causal relations be able to handle dynamic models. Also, as we saw in Section 2.3, when the situation modeled involves a feedback loop, applying the causal ordering method to an equilibrium model cannot elucidate the direction of causality around the loop, and one must look to a dynamic model to know the causal relations. In our work, we consider causal relations in a model represented as a system of differential equations. In our initial formulation the equations must be first-order, but this does not limit generality, for differential equations of higher order in general can be converted into a set of first order equations by introducing new variables to stand for derivatives. In this formulation, the values of the variables at any moment of time define the state of the system, and the changes in the values of the variables, the first derivatives, are determined by the momentary state.

Following is the definition of a self-contained dynamic structure [14]:

DEFINITION 3: A SELF-CONTAINED DYNAMIC STRUCTURE A self-contained dynamic structure is a set of n first-order differential equations involving n variables such that:

1. In any subset of k functions of the structure the first derivatives of at least k different variables appear.

2. In any subset of k functions in which r ($r \geq k$) first derivatives appear, if the values of any ($r - k$) first derivatives are chosen arbitrarily, then the remaining k are determined uniquely as functions of the n variables.

This definition of self-containment for a dynamic structure is analogous to that for an equilibrium structure. As for the case of equilibrium, the condition (1) above ensures that no part of the structure is over-determined while the condition (2) ensures that the structure is not under-constrained.

Given a self-contained dynamic structure, one can perform elementary row operations on the equations to solve them for the n derivatives. This produces an equivalent system of equations in *canonical form*. A differential equation is said to be in canonical form if and only if there is only one derivative in the equation, and the derivative is the only term appearing on the left-hand side of the equation. A self-contained dynamic structure in n variables, $x_1, \ldots, x_n$, in canonical form is a set of equations of the form

$$\frac{dx_i}{dt} = f_i(x_1, x_2, \ldots, x_n) \quad \text{for } i = 1, 2, \ldots, n.$$

Following the proposal by Simon and Rescher [14], we interpret each of the equations in canonical form to be a mechanism that determines the value of a derivative, hence the "next" value of that variable, as a function of the current state of the system. We then assert that dx_i/dt is directly causally dependent on the variables that appear with non-zero coefficients on the right-hand side of the ith equation.

Let us apply this method to systems governed by Newton's second law:

$$F = ma = m\,\frac{d^2x}{dt^2}$$

We introduce the new variable v, where $v = dx/dt$, and $a = dv/dt$. The canonical system now is:

$$\frac{dv}{dt} = \frac{F}{m} \tag{3.1}$$

$$\frac{dx}{dt} = v \tag{3.2}$$

Given the assumption that F and m are exogenous, the causal ordering of this system is as shown in figure 3.1. The dashed links are due to differential equations. A link marked with I is an integration link to a variable from its derivative. Since it links the derivative of a variable to the value of the variable at the next instant in time, it can be viewed as a causal link from the change in the variable to its new value. For each variable

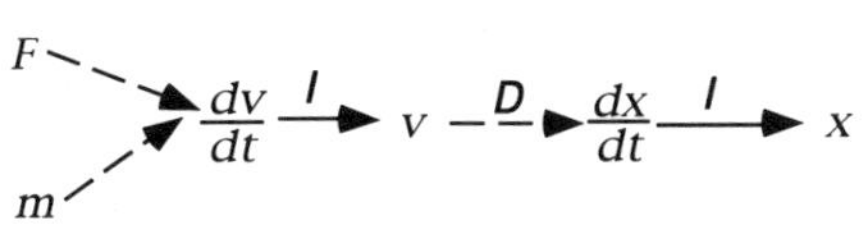

Figure 3.1
Causal ordering in the system of F, M, x, and v

and its corresponding derivative, there will be an (implicit) equation of the form $X = I[dX/dt]$, where I is the integration operator. Equation (3.2) corresponding to the link marked with D in the figure is definitional. In principle, definitional equations can be eliminated from a system description without affecting the content. However, we allow structures to contain definitional equations since it is common to introduce new variables through definitional equations when it is meaningful to do so and the new quantity thus defined facilitates the system description. Since links corresponding to such equations represent only a change in notation, we distinguish them from those representing actual mechanisms.

This system is consistent with our intuitive notions of causality, since by the second equation, change in position is caused by the velocity, while by the first, change in velocity is caused by the ratio of force to mass. As an effect of these changes, we have a new position and a new velocity, and the causal process repeats indefinitely. It is perhaps a little curious to say that "change in position is caused by the velocity" since velocity is defined as the rate of change in position, but at least nothing paradoxical results from using the former locution.

Next, consider the case of a longitudinally vibrating string, whose equation is:

$$a\,\frac{\partial^2 y}{\partial t^2} = \frac{\partial^2 t}{\partial x^2} \tag{3.3}$$

The variable y is the present position of the point on the string that is x units from its origin in the unstretched condition. The second partial derivative with respect to x therefore measures the net force exerted on that "segment" (dy) of the string resulting from its Hooke's Law stress by local extension or contraction. The second partial derivative on the left side is again the acceleration (which we could replace by first derivatives by defining acceleration as the partial of velocity with respect to time, and velocity as the partial of y with respect to time). Hence we are right back to Newton's Second Law and the analysis of the previous example.

3.1 Bathtub: Dynamic Model

Let us now apply this definition of dynamic causal ordering to the example of a bathtub in Section 2.3. Let M_D be the dynamic model of the behavior of the bathtub in figure 2.4 when it is disturbed from equilibrium.

In constructing M_D, we assumed that the speed at which variables return to equilibrium when disturbed is proportional to displacement.[1] M_D consists of the following equations:

$$\frac{dQ_{\text{out}}}{dt} = c_5(c_1KP - Q_{\text{out}}) \tag{3.4}$$

The rate of change of the outflow is assumed to be proportional to its displacement from the equilibrium value c_1KP.

$$\frac{dP}{dt} = c_6(D - c_2P) \tag{3.5}$$

The rate of change of the pressure is assumed to be proportional to its displacement from the equilibrium value, that is, the value determined by the depth of water in the tub.

$$\frac{dD}{dt} = c_7(Q_{\text{in}} - Q_{\text{out}}) \tag{3.6}$$

The rate of change of the depth is proportional to the difference between the inflow and the outflow.

$$\frac{dQ_{\text{in}}}{dt} = c_8 \tag{3.7}$$

The inflow rate is exogenous.

$$\frac{dK}{dt} = c_9 \tag{3.8}$$

The size of the opening is exogenous, also.

Applying the definition of dynamic causal ordering to M_D, and introducing the integration operations, produces the causal structure shown in figure 3.2, which now begins to resemble more closely the "naive" model of figure 2.5 rather than the equilibrium model of figure 2.6. The causal structure can be paraphrased in English as:

> The outflow rate depends on the pressure and the size of the opening. The pressure depends on the depth. The depth depends on the inflow rate and the outflow rate.

The dynamic causal structure shows that there is a feedback loop involving the depth, the pressure, and the outflow rate. If the output rate exceeds (is below) the input rate, the depth will decrease (increase), and therefore

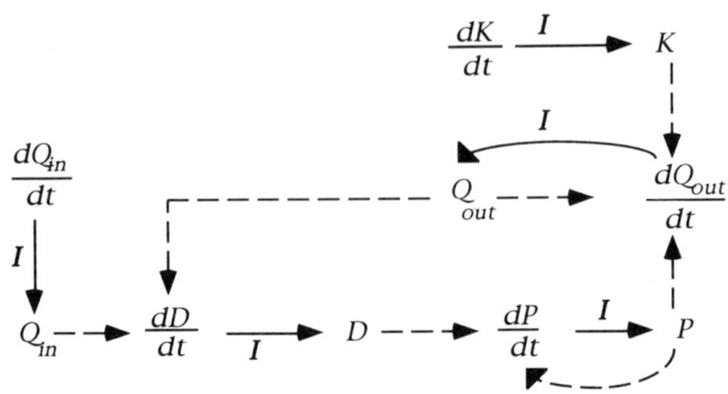

Figure 3.2
Causal ordering in M_D

the pressure will also decrease (increase), whereupon the output rate will decrease (increase). The first part of this loop, in which output rate affects depth, and hence pressure, replaces what we called the teleological causation in figure 2.6. But now a dynamic mechanism has been provided to explain these relations as ordinary causal relations.

3.2 Exogenous Variables in a Dynamic System

In an equilibrium structure, exogenous variables are those that are determined only by factors external to the system under consideration and, thus, do not depend on any other variables within the structure. One can define exogeneity in a dynamic structure analogously. A variable in a dynamic structure is exogenous if its derivative is not dependent on any other variable in the structure. This includes cases where a derivative is only dependent on external factors as well as cases where a derivative is a function of the variable itself but of no other variables. If x_i is an exogenous variable, the *i*th equation in the dynamic structure in canonical form should take one or the other of the two following forms:

Case 1: The derivative is a function of the variable itself only;

$$\frac{dx_i}{dt} = f(x_i) \tag{3.9}$$

Case 2: The derivative is only dependent on external factors;

$$\frac{dx_i}{dt} = c_i. \tag{3.10}$$

3.2.1 Exogeneity and constancy In an equilibrium structure, each exogenous variable constitutes a minimal complete subset by itself. In other words, the structure includes an equation of the form $x_i = c_i$ for each exogenous variable x_i. The purpose of including this equation in the structure in the context of a causal ordering analysis is not to assert that x_i is constant but to assert that x_i is not causally dependent on any other variables. Here, c_i represents all the external factors that x_i depends on but which are outside the scope of the causal analysis. That x_i is not changing is implicit in the structure's being an equilibrium structure, but this does not influence the causal analysis in any way.

In a dynamic structure, if variable x_i is exogenous in the sense of Case 2 above, and if $c_j = 0$, x_i will be constant. However, in general, x_i will not be constant in Case 1 or if $c_j \neq 0$ in Case 2. As in the case of an equilibrium structure, an equation of the form shown in Case 2 means that the derivative only depends on external factors and not that the variable is constant. When there is an external disturbance, the value of such a variable may change. The constants appearing on the right hand sides of the expressions in Cases 1 and 2 represent all the external factors that the derivative depends upon. Both in the equilibrium and dynamic cases, the significance of exogeneity lies in the fact that the variable is not influenced by any other variables within the structure.

3.3 Causal Ordering in Maxwell's Equations

The dynamic causal ordering procedure as presented in this section works for the wave equations that appear, for example, in the physics of sound and for the field equations for vibrations of materials. But now we come to Maxwell's equations, which are a little different. We will sketch out the argument a bit schematically, but all the details can be restored without changing the story in any essential way. We will assume that we have just one spatial and one temporal dimension, so that our equations (in space, no currents) can be written as follows:[2]

$$\frac{\partial E}{\partial x} = a\,\frac{\partial H}{\partial t} \tag{3.11}$$

$$\frac{\partial H}{\partial x} = b\,\frac{\partial E}{\partial t} \tag{3.12}$$

The first of these equations represents Faraday's Law, that a moving magnetic field (the right-hand side) generates a field of electric force. The second equation represents Ampere's Law, that a moving electric field (the right-hand side) generates a field of magnetic force. In both cases, causality runs from the partial derivatives on the right to the field strengths on the left. The standard textbook discussions of these laws assume causality in this direction. Faraday's Law is usually illustrated by the movement of a magnet (hence, of a magnetic field) causing a current in a wire (as a result of the electric force field generated by the movement of the magnet). Ampere's Law is illustrated by a current in a wire (a moving electric field) causing a deflection of a nearby magnet (as a result of the magnetic force field generated by the movement of the electrons).

At first blush the causal direction appears to be strange, for in gravitational theory forces are associated with the positions of bodies and not their movements. However, it is easy to find mechanical examples in which causality operates in just the same direction as in the equations above. If a dam in a river breaks, a moving stream of water will descend, applying force to and accelerating any bodies in its path that are not sufficiently anchored to resist (i.e., to which a sufficient counter-force is not applied). The amount of force will vary with the velocity of the water. Even simpler, a moving billiard ball will impart an acceleration to any ball it strikes; the faster it is moving, the greater the impact (and, therefore, the acceleration).

Now let us carry the analysis a step farther. We differentiate the first equation above with respect to x, and the second with respect to t, obtaining $\partial^2 H/\partial x \partial t^2$ on the right of the first equation and the left of the second. Eliminating the terms in H between them, we have:

$$\frac{\partial^2 E}{\partial x^2} = ab \frac{\partial^2 E}{\partial t^2} \tag{3.13}$$

We again have our familiar wave equation, where the left-hand side can be interpreted as a stress in the electric force field that is causing an acceleration in that field (the right-hand side). However, we may be uneasy about this interpretation, since the left-hand side of our new equation was initially an effect, not a cause, and the right-hand side a cause, not an effect. Let us return to the original equations, and look at them in a slightly different way. There is no fundamental reason why, in some physical systems, time derivatives of variables, like $\partial H/\partial t$ and $\partial E/\partial t$ cannot be exogenous variables. If we look back at figure 3.1, but now take v and m as the exogenous variables (the velocity and mass of the moving billiard ball), then v and m will create (cause) a force F on the ball it strikes. The velocity and mass are now the causes, the force the effect. In the case of Maxwell's equations, we can regard $\partial H/\partial t$ and $\partial E/\partial t$ as generalized momenta, causing by "impact" the strains in E and H, respectively. In Faraday's experiment, the change in the magnetic field is exogenous, corresponding to the movement of the magnet. In Ørsted's experiment, the change in the electrical field, produced by the moving electrons of the current, is exogenous.

The direction of the causal arrow is determined by which forces we take as exogenous. The example that Halliday & Resnick use in Volume 2 of their physics textbook (2nd edition, pp. 39ff [15]) to discuss the propagation of an electromagnetic wave is a coaxial cable connected to a circuit with a switch and battery. With the given arrangement, when the switch is closed, a potential difference is created (a change in the electrical field) between the outer and inner conductors of the cable.

In their words, "if the switch is then thrown ... a potential difference V suddenly appears between these elements. This potential difference does not appear simultaneously all along the line but is propagated with a finite speed c that will turn out to be exactly that of light."

In the first step, we have $\partial E/\partial t$ causing a change in H at the point where the battery is connected to the cable. This change in H, in turn, causes further changes in E, and these changes, at first local, are propagated along the cable. The causal asymmetry is produced by the exogenous event of throwing the switch.

Therefore, we conclude that even though our original definition of dynamic causal ordering produces intuitive causal interpretations in many cases, the restriction that derivatives cannot be causes in not only unnecessary but can lead to counter-intuitive causal interpretations in many cases. Even in dynamics, assumptions only about which quantities are exogenous are sufficient to obtain intuitive causal orderings. In the following section, we present a new definition of dynamic causal ordering that removes this restriction and applies to a wider variety of systems.

4 Generalized Causal Ordering in Dynamic and Mixed Structures

In the previous section, we have provided the formal definitions of a self-contained dynamic structure and of causal ordering for dynamic structures in canonical form. In this section, we present a new definition of dynamic causal ordering, which is more general than the original one in several ways: Since the original definition of causal ordering in dynamic systems required equations to be in canonical form, it is necessary to manipulate the equations algebraically to put them in canonical form if they are not in that form already. Though we considered each equation in canonical form to represent a conceptual mechanism, if putting equations in canonical form requires algebraic manipulation involving more than one equation, thereby combining mechanisms, it is not clear how such manipulation can guarantee that the resulting equations still represent conceptually distinct mechanisms. Furthermore, while restricting the direction of causality to going always from variables to a derivative produces intuitive causal interpretations in most cases, there are cases, such as Maxwell's equations discussed in Section 3.3, which this definition leads to a causal interpretation that is counter to the commonly accepted causal explanation of the phenomena.

The new definition applies not only to systems consisting solely of differential equations but also to systems composed of a mixture of differential and equilibrium equations. When the behavior of a system is described in terms of equations, the description very often consists of such a mixture. We have extended the concepts of self-contained structures and of causal ordering to apply to such mixed systems. This section introduces mixed systems and defines self-containment and causal ordering for such systems as a natural extension of the definitions for equilibrium and dynamic structures. Dynamic structures can be regarded as limiting cases of mixed structures.

Before defining self-containment for mixed structures, we introduce a notation. Let M be a system of n equations in n variables such that some of the equations are equilibrium equations and others are first-order differential equations. Given M, we define Inst(M) as the superset of M consisting of the equations in M and one constant equation for every variable v whose derivative appears in M. A constant equation for a variable is an equation of the form, $v = c$, where c is a constant.

The intuitive meaning of Inst(M) is that it is a snapshot of the behavior, where variables and their derivatives are treated as separate variables. At each instance t, the value of a variable v whose derivative appears in M is caused by the value of $v(t - \varepsilon)$ and $\partial v(t - \varepsilon)/\partial t$, which are outside the scope of Inst(M) at t. Therefore a constant equation for v is added to represent the fact that v is exogenous in Inst(M).

Self-containment for a mixed structure is defined as follows:

DEFINITION 4: SELF-CONTAINED MIXED STRUCTURE The set M of n equations in n variables is a self-contained mixed structure iff:

1. Zero or more of the n equations are first-order differential equations and the rest are equilibrium equations.
2. Inst(M) is a self-contained equilibrium structure when the variables and their derivatives are treated as distinct variables.

A qualitative self-contained mixed structure can be defined in an analogous manner, where Inst(M) in condition 2 must be a qualitative self-contained equilibrium structure.

Given a self-contained mixed structure, as defined above, the causal ordering among its variables and derivatives follows the definitions of causal ordering in dynamic and static structures. As in the definition of the dynamic causal ordering, for each variable and its corresponding derivative, there is an implicit integration equation of the form $X = I[dX/dt]$. The causal ordering in a mixed structure can be determined as follows:

First, determine causal ordering in Inst(M) using the definition of causal ordering in an equilibrium structure, treating variables and their derivatives as distinct variables.

Next, link the derivatives appearing in M to their variables by integration links.

This definition preserves the notion of the original definition that the value of a variable at $t + \varepsilon$ is determined (caused) by the value of its derivative at t (and its own value at t). By transitivity, the variable is causally dependent on whatever other variables the derivative depends upon causally. Furthermore, the definition does not require that the equations be in canonical form, and it allows the possibility of a variable being directly causally dependent upon derivatives other than its own, or of a derivative being dependent upon other derivatives.

4.1 Mixed Model of the Bathtub

Now, we are ready to look at the bathtub example again. Let M_1 be a mixed structure consisting of equations (2.10), (2.11), (2.13), (2.14) and the differential equation (3.6) in place of (2.12);

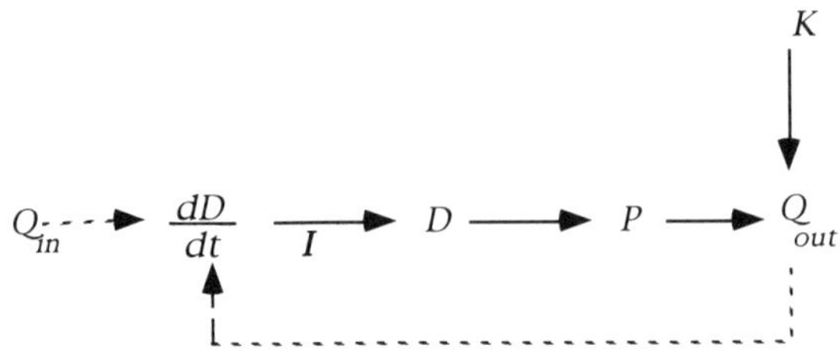

Figure 4.1
Mixed causal ordering of bathtub

$$\frac{dD}{dt} = Q_{\text{in}} - Q_{\text{out}} \tag{3.6}$$

M_1 is a self-contained, mixed structure according to the definition given above. Inst(M_1) consists of equations in M_1 and the following equation (4.1):

$$D = c \tag{4.1}$$

The causal ordering in M_1 is shown in figure 4.1. The causal structure, which indicates the existence of a feedback loop, may be explained informally in English as follows:

> The output flow rate depends on the pressure, which depends on the depth of water in the tub. The rate of change of the depth of water is determined by the input and output flow rates.

The reason for replacing the equilibrium equation (2.12) in the original equilibrium model by the dynamic equation (3.6) while leaving the equilibrium equations (2.10) and (2.11) unchanged is that the equilibrium relations represented by the latter two equations are restored almost instantaneously when disturbed, much more quickly than the relation represented by equation (2.12). Therefore, in a model of a coarser temporal grain-size, it is reasonable to treat (2.12) as taking time but to treat the others as instantaneous. These reasons for going from the dynamic model to the mixed model immediately suggest that mixed models can be regarded as abstractions of dynamic models, and that dynamic models are limiting cases of mixed models. The next section studies this aspect of mixed structures in detail.

4.2 Generating a Mixed Structure from a Dynamic Structure

A mixed structure can be viewed as an approximation to a dynamic structure. When a mechanism in a dynamic structure acts very quickly to restore relative equilibrium, one can regard it as acting instantaneously. Or, when a mechanism acts much more slowly than other mechanisms in the system, so that its effect on the variable it controls is negligible for some long time, the variable may be considered constant. In these cases, the description of system behavior in a dynamic structure may be simplified by replacing the fast mechanism by an equilibrium equation (equilibration) or the slow mechanism by a constant equation (exogenization).

This section discusses generating a mixed structure from a dynamic structure, as an approximation to the latter. Section 4.2.1 presents equilibration as one abstraction technique. Section 4.2.3 presents exogenization as another such technique. Section 4.2.4 compares the two techniques and discusses their differences.

4.2.1 Equilibrating dynamic equations We will use the term *equilibrating* to refer to the operation of replacing a dynamic equation by its corresponding equilibrium equation. Equilibration is performed only on equations representing mechanisms that determine the values of derivatives. Since equilibrating an equation reflects the assumption that the corresponding mechanism restores equilibrium so quickly that it is almost always at equilibrium, equilibration is performed by replacing the dependent derivative by 0. Furthermore, in order to be consistent throughout the structure, all the appearances of the derivative in the rest of the equations are replaced by 0.

A wide range of mixed structures may be produced between the completely dynamic structure and the equilibrium structure, depending on the temporal grain size selected for the model. However, replacing an arbitrary subset of the equations of a dynamic self-contained structure with the corresponding equilibrium equations will not necessarily produce a self-contained mixed structure. Moreover, not every self-contained dynamic structure produces a self-contained equilibrium structure when every equation is replaced by the corresponding equilibrium equation. We demonstrate these points with examples.

In going from the dynamic structure of the bathtub to the mixed structure in Section 4.1, we equilibrated Equations (3.4), (3.5), (3.7), and

(3.8) to produce M_1, which was a self-contained mixed structure. If we equilibrate equation (3.6) in M_D instead of (3.4), we will obtain the following mixed structure, which includes the relation $Q_{out} = Q_{in}$:

$$\frac{dQ_{out}}{dt} = c_5(c_1KP - Q_{out}) \tag{3.4}$$

$$D = c_2P \tag{2.11}$$

$$Q_{out} = Q_{in} \tag{2.12}$$

$$Q_{in} = c_3 \tag{2.13}$$

$$K = c_4 \tag{2.14}$$

This new structure is not self-contained as it does not satisfy Part 1 of the definition of a self-contained mixed structure. This may be explained intuitively by examining the causal structure for the original dynamic structure M_D in figure 3.2. The equation (3.6) states that the equilibrium between Q_{in} and Q_{out} is restored instantaneously. However, since the only causal path from Q_{in} to Q_{out} in the causal structure is

$$Q_{in} \rightarrow \frac{dD}{dt} \rightarrow D \rightarrow \frac{dP}{dt} \rightarrow P \rightarrow \frac{dQ_{out}}{dt} \rightarrow Q_{out},$$

the equilibrium between Q_{in} and Q_{out} cannot be restored before D and P are restored to equilibrium. The fact that equations (3.5) and (3.4) are not equilibrated implies that the mechanisms represented by these equations take longer than (2.12) to restore equilibrium. Therefore, it produces a contradiction to equilibrate equation (3.6) without equilibrating (3.4) and (3.5) at the same time.

4.2.2 Self-regulating variables In the previous section, we saw that equilibrating equation (3.4) produced a self-contained mixed structure, while doing the same with equation (3.6) did not. The two equations are as follows:

$$\frac{dQ_{out}}{dt} = c_1(c_2P - Q_{out}) \tag{3.4}$$

$$\frac{dD}{dt} = Q_{in} - Q_{out} \tag{3.6}$$

The dependent quantities in the equations in the context of the original dynamic structure are the derivatives on the left hand side in both equations. Observe the difference between the two differential equations: the derivative dQ_{out}/dt, which is the dependent quantity in (3.4), depends on the variable Q_{out} through the same equation while this is not the case in (3.6). In other words, in (3.4) the rate of change of Q_{out} directly depends on the current value of Q_{out} itself, while in (3.6) that of D does not. Let us call a variable *self-regulating* if its derivative depends on the variable itself, and *non-self-regulating* otherwise.

DEFINITION 5: SELF-REGULATING VARIABLES AND EQUATIONS A dynamic equation in a self-contained mixed structure is called *self-regulating* if the derivative dv/dt, which is the dependent quantity of the equation, causally depends on v itself through the same equation. Such a variable is called a self-regulating variable. We will sometimes also use the term *self-regulating mechanism* to refer to the mechanism represented by a self-regulating equation.

If a mechanism is self-regulating, replacing the dynamic equation by the equilibrium equation does not remove the variable v, and this variable becomes the dependent variable of the equilibrium equation, leaving the causal ordering unchanged. Thus, as we move from the full dynamic model of the bathtub to the mixed model of Section 4.1, equation (3.4) becomes equation (2.10), dQ_{out}/dt is removed from the system, and Q_{out} is the dependent variable in the new equation. The change alters the causal graph only by eliminating the *I-link* between dQ_{out}/dt and Q, and thereby linking P and K directly to Q (Compare figure 4.1 with figure 3.2.).

If the mechanism is not self-regulating, then replacing the dynamic equation by the equilibrium equation removes the variable and its derivative, changing the causal ordering of the system.

It can be proved that equilibrating any number of self-regulating equations in a qualitative self-contained dynamic or mixed structure will always produce a qualitative self-contained mixed structure (or a qualitative self-contained equilibrium structure if no more dynamic equations remain). However, equilibrating a non-self-regulating equation may produce an over-constrained structure.

Thus, we have the following theorem:

THEOREM 3 Equilibrating any number of self-regulating equations in a qualitative self-contained mixed structure always produces a qualitative self-contained structure.

The proof is given in Appendix B.

4.2.3 Exogenizing dynamic equations In contrast to variables that adjust to changes in other variables very quickly to restore relative equilibrium, some variables change so slowly in response to changes that they can be regarded as independent of the other variables. The equation corresponding to such a variable can be replaced by an exogenous variable equation, which amounts to deleting from the system under consideration the slow mechanism through which other variables influence the variable in question. We will call this operation of replacing a dynamic equation by an exogenous variable equation *exogenizing*. There are two ways to exogenize a variable:

Case 1: If a derivative dx/dt is the dependent quantity in an equation, and it is self-regulating, but the value of dx/dt depends mostly on x itself and very little on other variables, other variables in the equation can be assumed zero to make dx/dt a function of x alone.

Case 2: If a variable is not only unaffected by other variables but changes very slowly, the dynamic equation whose dependent variable is its derivative can be replaced by a constant equation of the variable.

Conceptually, exogenizing is the opposite of equilibrating, because exogenizing a variable assumes it is unaffected by other variables while equilibrating a variable assumes it responds to changes in other variables extremely quickly to restore equilibrium. Exogenizing a variable amounts to deleting a mechanism by placing the mechanism determining the value of the variable outside the scope of the system under consideration, and it is reasonable to do so only when the feedback to the variable from the variables inside the mechanism is negligible over the time period of interest.

In Section 4.2.2, we presented a theorem that equilibrating a self-regulating variable in a qualitative self-contained structure always produces a qualitative self-contained structure, while equilibrating a non-self-regulating variable could produce a structure that is no longer self-contained. On the other hand, exogenizing a variable in a qualitative self-contained structure always produces a qualitative self-contained structure regardless of whether the variable is self-regulating or not. The proof is given in Appendix B.

THEOREM 4 Exogenizing an equation in a qualitative self-contained dynamic or mixed structure always produces a qualitative self-contained structure.

4.2.4 Differences between exogenizing and equilibrating Exogenizing is performed when a variable is hardly affected by other variables within the system over the time period of interest, while equilibrating is performed when a variable, compared to other variables, reacts extremely quickly to changes in those variables to restore equilibrium. For example, given the following dynamic structure of equations, where a and b are positive constants;

$$\frac{dy}{dt} = -ay \tag{4.2}$$

$$\frac{dx}{dt} = b(y - x), \tag{4.3}$$

if x reacts so quickly to a change in y that the equilibrium between x and y is almost always maintained except for a short period of time following a disturbance in y, one may replace equation (4.3) by the following equation:

$$b(y - x) = 0. \tag{4.4}$$

Equations (4.3) and (4.4) imply that

$$\frac{dx}{dt} = 0. \tag{4.5}$$

Equation (4.5) implies that the variable x is constant. This seems to imply that equilibrating and exogenizing are essentially the same thing. However, this is not the case. Equilibrating an equation asserts that the mechanism represented by the equation responds very quickly to a disturbance to restore equilibrium, so that the derivative of the dependent variable in the equation returns to zero very soon after each disturbance. Exogenizing an equation amounts to removing the mechanism from the model, so that the derivative of the dependent variable in the equation is essentially zero, and the integral change is also essentially zero over the whole period of interest.

Equilibrating or exogenizing equations in a dynamic structure amounts to classifying the interactions among variables into three categories; those that are so weak that they can be ignored altogether, those that are so strong that they restore equilibrium among the variables involved very quickly, and the rest. Equilibration generates an abstraction of a dynamic structure by ignoring the short-run dynamics within strongly interacting variables. Exogenization does so by ignoring the very weak interactions that one variable has with others through a slow-moving mechanism. Conversely, if the relative strengths of interactions among variables are known, an equation should not be equilibrated before other equations that represent stronger, faster interactions are equilibrated. This idea of abstracting a structure based on classifying interactions into strong and weak interactions is formalized as a well-known abstraction technique, to which we now turn.

5 Aggregation of Dynamic Systems

Many real world dynamic systems involve such a large number of variables and interconnections that it is difficult to grasp them in their entirety. Abstracting a detailed description to produce a simpler approximation becomes essential in reasoning about a complex system. In Section 4, we discussed a mixed structure as one type of abstraction of a dynamic structure, and we introduced exogenizing and equilibrating operations as means for simplifying a model to produce a mixed structure with fewer differential equations. These abstraction operations are based on qualitative information about the relative speeds at which mechanisms restore equilibrium among variables. In this section, we discuss another, well-known abstraction technique, aggregation of a dynamic system matrix. We will compare the two techniques and show that they are closely related.

The basic idea behind aggregation is this: if variables in a large dynamic system can be partitioned into subsets such that variables in each subset are more strongly connected to each other than to variables in other subsets, one can describe the short-run behavior of each subsystem independently of the other subsystems. Furthermore, one can describe the long-run behavior of the entire system in terms of variables describing these subsets instead of individual variables, treating each subset as a black box. Simon and Ando proved that this was indeed true for the case of a nearly decomposable dynamic matrix with one significant characteristic root for each subsystem [16]. We generalize their result to cases where there are zero or more significant roots in subsystem.

Though the procedures and examples presented in this section are all numerical, the basis for aggregation is the qualitative character of a dynamic system, namely whether it can be partitioned into subsystems in the manner described above. In fact, the purpose of discussing aggregation in this paper is not simply to describe dynamic system aggregation as a numerical abstraction technique, but to show that the same principle can justify model abstraction even in cases where only qualitative information is available.

This section is organized as follows: Section 5.1 presents the concept of near-decomposability of dynamic systems and its implication for their behaviors. Section 5.2 then discusses the construction of an aggregate system from a nearly decomposable system in such a way that the behavior of the aggregate system is a reasonable approximation to the long-term behavior of the original system. In Section 5.3, we will return to the topic of causal ordering and discuss the relation between aggregation, causal ordering, and the qualitative abstraction techniques presented in Section 4.

5.1 Decomposable and Nearly Decomposable Systems

This section formally introduces the concept of a nearly decomposable system and describes the theorems proved by Simon and Ando about the behavior of such systems [16]. Let M^* be a self-contained dynamic system of n equations in canonical form and P^* be the matrix of coefficients in M^*. Thus, M^* consists of equations of the form:

$$\frac{dx_i}{dt} = a_{i1}x_1 + a_{i2}x_2 + \cdots + a_{\mathrm{in}}x_n,$$

and P^* is a matrix of the form:

$$P^* = \begin{vmatrix} a_{11} & a_{12} & \dots & a_{1n} \\ \dots & & & \\ \dots & & & \\ \dots & & & \\ a_{n1} & a_{n2} & \dots & a_{nn} \end{vmatrix}$$

where a_{ij} is the coefficient of x_j in the ith equation of M^*.

P^* is called *completely decomposable* if, by simple rearrangement of rows and columns, P^* can be put in a block diagonal form as

$$P^* = \begin{vmatrix} P_1^* & & & \\ & P_2^* & & \\ & & \ddots & \\ & & & P_N^* \end{vmatrix}$$

where P_I^*s are square submatrices, N is the number of such submatrices in P^*, and all the elements of P^* not in any of the submatrices are zero.

If the matrix of coefficients is completely decomposable, the dynamic system consists of independent components which do not interact at all and which behave independently of each other. The submatrices represent the components.

Now, consider a slightly different, self-contained dynamic system M and its matrix P of the same size as M^* and P^*, such that P has the same diagonal submatrices as P^* but the elements outside of the submatrices are either zero or very small, the magnitudes being less than ε for some given ε. P looks like,

$$P = \begin{vmatrix} P_1^* & & & \\ & P_2^* & \varepsilon & \\ & & \ddots & \\ & \varepsilon & & P_N^* \end{vmatrix}$$

where the elements of P outside of the submatrices are either ε or zero. Then P can be expressed as

$$P = P^* + \varepsilon C,$$

where C is an arbitrary $n \times n$ matrix. A matrix such as P that can be put in this form is called a *nearly completely decomposable* matrix or, for short, a *nearly decomposable* matrix.

The system M whose matrix P is nearly completely decomposable consists of components such that variables within each component interact strongly, but variables from different components interact relatively weakly. The submatrices represent such components and the ε elements outside the submatrices represent weak links among components.

5.1.1 Behavior of a nearly decomposable system For a dynamic system to be dynamically stable, all its eigenvalues must be negative. We will assume that this is the case for all systems we will discuss in this section. Furthermore, we assume that all the roots of the system are distinct. When all the roots are distinct, the time paths of the variables can be expressed as

$$x_i(t) = \sum_{j=1}^{n} z_{ji} c_j \exp(\lambda_{jt}), \tag{5.1}$$

where $\lambda_1, \ldots, \lambda_n$ are the characteristic roots, and $z_{1j}, \ldots, z_{nj}$ is the eigenvector corresponding to the jth root.

If all the roots $\lambda_1, \ldots, \lambda_n$ are arranged in ascending order of the absolute values of their real parts, the contribution of the roots toward the end of the list to the dynamic behavior of the system will be damped rapidly, and will be of importance only to the short-term behavior of the system. For the long-term behavior, we can ignore these roots and treat the system as having a smaller number of degrees of freedom, corresponding to the number of roots we retain.

Let M be a dynamic structure with the corresponding matrix P that is nearly decomposable with N square submatrices. Let m_I be the size of the Ith submatrix, and $x_{1_I}, \ldots, x_{m_I}$ be the variables belonging to the Ith submatrix. Let $\lambda_{1_I}, \ldots, \lambda_{m_I}$ be the characteristic roots belonging to the Ith submatrix. Without loss of generality, we will assume that the roots in each subsystem are arranged in ascending order of the absolute values of their real parts. Therefore,

$$|\lambda_{1_I}| < |\lambda_{2_I}| < \cdots < |\lambda_{m_I}| \quad \text{for } I = 1 \text{ to } N.$$

The time path of each variable in the system can be expressed as follows:

$$x_{h_K}(t) = \sum_{I=1}^{N} \sum_{j=1}^{m_I} z_{jI} h_K c_{jI} \exp(\lambda_{jI}) \tag{5.2}$$

Alternatively, the time path of the entire system can be expressed as

$$x(t) = Z^* \Lambda(t),$$

where $x(t)$ is the column vector of the variables,

$$x(t)^T = \{x(t)_{1_1}, x(t)_{2_1}, \cdots, x(t)_{m_1}, x(t)_{1_2}, \cdots x(t)_{m_2}, \cdots, x(t)_{1_N}, \cdots, x(t)_{m_N}\};$$

Z is the matrix whose columns are eigenvectors corresponding to the eigenvalues, $\lambda_{1_1}, \ldots, \lambda_{m_N}$.

$$
Z = \left|\begin{array}{ccc|cc|c|cc}
z_{1_1 1_1} & z_{1_1 2_1} & \cdots z_{1_1 m_1} & z_{1_1 1_2} & \cdots z_{1_1 m_1} & & z_{1_1 1_N} & \cdots z_{1_1 m_N} \\
z_{2_1 1_1} & z_{2_1 2_1} & \cdots & & \cdots & \cdots & \cdots & \cdots \\
\cdots & \cdots & & & & & & \\
z_{m_1 1_1} & \cdots & & & & & & \\
\hline
z_{1_2 1_1} & \cdots & & z_{1_2 1_2} & z_{1_2 2_2} \cdots & & & \\
\cdots & & & z_{2_2 1_2} & \cdots & \cdots & \cdots & \\
z_{m_2 1_1} & \cdots & & \cdots & & & & \\
\hline
\cdots & & & \cdots & & \cdots & \cdots & \\
\hline
z_{1_N 1_1} & \cdots & & & & & & \\
\cdots & & & \cdots & & \cdots & \cdots & \\
z_{m_N 1_1} & \cdots & & & & & &
\end{array}\right|
$$

and Λ is the column vector of the exponential terms as

$$
\Lambda(t)^T = \{\exp(\lambda_{1_1} t), \exp(\lambda_{2_1} t), \cdots, \exp(\lambda_{m_1} t), \exp(\lambda_{1_2} t), \cdots, \exp(\lambda_{m_2} t), \cdots,
$$
$$
\exp(\lambda_{1_N} t), \cdots, \exp(\lambda_{m_N} t)\}.
$$

Since P is nearly decomposable, the eigenvector z_{j_I} corresponding to the eigenvalue λ_{j_I} ($I = 1$ to N and $j = 1$ to m_I) is such that its elements $z_{k_L j_I}$ are very small for L ($\neq I$). In the above expression for $x(t)_{h_K}$, these small $z_{j_I h_K}$'s represent the effects of the variables outside the Kth subsystem on $x(t)_{h_K}$.

Simon and Ando show that the behavior of such a system may be approximately described in the following four stages [16]:

Short-run dynamics The variables in each subsystem are moving towards their relative equilibrium independently of other subsystems.

Short-run equilibrium The most significant root of each subsystem dominates the behavior of the subsystem.

Long-run dynamics The variables in each subsystem move together towards over-all equilibrium while maintaining relative equilibrium within each subsystem.

Long-run equilibrium Finally, the most significant root of the entire system dominates.

When the behavior of a large system is approximately described in four stages as above, the goodness of the approximation naturally depends on how small the εs are and also how dominant the most significant root of each subsystem is compared to the rest of the roots.

5.2 Aggregation of Variables

It is clear from the expression (5.1) that the behavior of the dynamic system after some time is dominated by the term involving the characteristic root whose real part has the smallest absolute value. We refer to this root as the *most significant root* of the system. Therefore, after some time, the values of the variables can be approximated by the following expression:

$$x_i(t) \approx c_1 z_{1_i} \exp(\lambda_1 \mathrm{t}), \tag{5.3}$$

where λ_1 is the most significant root. This means that we can define a new aggregate variable $y(t)$ such that the values of all the variables can be approximated by linear functions of $y(t)$.

For example, we can define the aggregate variable $y(t)$ for the system to be the sum of all the original variables:

$$y(t) \equiv \sum_{i=1}^{n} x_i(t) \tag{5.4}$$

By differentiating both sides of (5.4) with respect to t, we get

$$\frac{dy}{dt} = \sum_{i=1}^{n} \frac{dx_i}{dt} \tag{5.5}$$

Because of (5.3) and (5.4),

$$y \approx c_1 \sum_{i=1}^{n} z_{1_i} \exp(\lambda_1 t) \tag{5.6}$$

Therefore, each variable has the following approximately linear relations to $y(t)$ after some time:

$$x_i(t) \approx \frac{z_{1_i}}{Z} y(t), \quad \text{where} \quad Z \equiv \sum_{i=1}^{n} z_{1_i}.$$

The goodness of the approximation depends on how dominant the most significant root is compared to the rest of the roots. In cases where the entire system is aggregated into one aggregate variable, the magnitude of the error for each variable can be precisely computed as the following: Let $x_k(t_1)$ and $x_k^*(t_1)$ be the actual value of x_k at time $t_1 \geq 0$ and its value approximated by the aggregate system, respectively. Assume λ_1 is the most significant root of the system. Then, the magnitude of error in $x_k(t_1)$ can be computed as

$$|x_k(t_1) - x_k^*(t_1)| = \left| \sum_{j=2}^{n} c_j z_{j_k} \exp(\lambda_j t_1) \right|, \tag{5.7}$$

where z_{j_k} is the kth element of the eigenvector corresponding to λj.

In the case of a nearly decomposable matrix, one can apply this concept to each submatrix, defining a new aggregate variable for each submatrix. The dynamic structure can be rewritten in terms of these aggregate variables to produce a new matrix of size $N \times N$, which is much smaller and more manageable than the original $n \times n$ matrix. Such an aggregate matrix describes the long-run dynamics of the original system. Each variable in an aggregate matrix represents a separate subsystem in the original matrix, and the values of individual variables in a subsystem can be approximated by a simple linear function of the aggregate variable representing that subsystem.

5.2.1 Procedure for aggregation We now describe the procedure for producing an aggregated matrix from a nearly decomposable matrix in more detail.

M is the nearly decomposable system defined in Section 5.1.1 with N submatrices and M^* is the corresponding completely decomposable system. M and M^* consist of n variables and equations. Each subsystem M_i and M_i^* ($i = 1$ to N) consists of m_i variables $x_{1_i}, \ldots, x_{m_i}$. M_i also consists of equations of the following form:

$$x'_{j_i} = f_{j_i}(x_{1_1}, x_{2_1}, \ldots, x_{m_1}, x_{1_2}, \ldots, x_{m_2}, \ldots, x_{1_N}, \ldots, x_{m_N}) \quad \text{for } j = 1 \text{ to } m_i, \tag{5.8}$$

and M_i^* of the following form:

$$x'_{j_i} = f^*_{j_i}(x_{1_i}, x_{2_i}, \ldots, x_{m_i}) \quad \text{for } j = 1 \text{ to } m_i, \tag{5.9}$$

where f'_{j_i}s and $f^*_{j_i}$'s are linear functions of their arguments.

Let λ_i be the most significant eigenvalue of M_i and let λ_i^* be the corresponding eigenvalue of M_i^*.

Let $z_i^* = \{z^*_{1_i}, z^*_{2_i}, \ldots, z^*_{m_i}\}$ be the eigenvector corresponding to λ_i^*.

We define the aggregate variable y_i for each subsystem M_i to be the sum of all the variables M_i:

$$y_i(t) \equiv \sum_{j=1}^{m_i} x_{j_i}(t) \tag{5.10}$$

The values of the variables x_{j_i} (for $j = 1$ to m_i) of the subsystem M_i after some time can be expressed in terms of its aggregate variable y_i as:

$$x_{j_i}(t) \approx \frac{z^*_{j_i}}{Z_i} y_i(t) \tag{5.11}$$

where $Z_i \equiv \sum_{j=1}^{m_j}$
By differentiating both sides of (5.10), we get

$$y'_i(t) \equiv \sum_{j=1}^{m_i} x'_{j_i}(t) \tag{5.12}$$

Given these aggregate variables, do the following for each subsystem M_i for $i = 1$ to N:

1. Rewrite the equations (5.8) in terms of y's by substituting the right-hand side of (5.11) for x_{j_i}'s. The rewritten equations will look like:

$$x'_{j_i} = g_{j_i}(y_1, y_2, \ldots, y_N) \quad \text{for } j = 1 \text{ to } m_i,$$

where g_{j_i}'s are linear functions of their arguments.

2. Add these m_i equations to produce

$$\sum_{j=1}^{m_i} x'_{j_i} = \sum_{j=1}^{m_i} g_{j_i}(y_1, y_2, \ldots, y_N) \quad \text{for } j = 1 \text{ to } m_i, \tag{5.13}$$

3. Because of (5.12), the left-hand side of (5.13) is equal to y_i, making (5.13) a differential equation of y'_i in canonical form.

The aggregate system consists of the variables y_1 to y_N and the N differential equations thus generated.

5.2.2 Numerical example of aggregation We will demonstrate the aggregation procedure using a numerical example. Let M be a nearly decomposable dynamic system with four variables x_{11}, x_{21}, x_{12} and x_{22}, and the following differential equations:

$$x'_{11} = -50.0x_{11} + 23.0x_{21} + (1.0e-3)x_{12} \tag{5.14}$$

$$x'_{21} = -1.0x_{11} - 0.10x_{21} + (2.0e-3)x_{22} \tag{5.15}$$

$$x'_{12} = (1.0e-3)x_{21} - 47.0x_{12} + 17.0x_{22} \tag{5.16}$$

$$x'_{22} = (3.0e-3)x_{11} - 3.0x_{12} - 0.90x_{22} \tag{5.17}$$

Let P be the matrix of coefficients for the structure M.

$$P = \begin{vmatrix} -50.0 & 23.0 & 1.0e-03 & 0.0 \\ -1.0 & -0.10 & 0.0 & 2.0e-03 \\ 0.0 & 1.0e-03 & -47.0 & 17.0 \\ 3.0e-03 & 0.0 & -3.0 & -0.90 \end{vmatrix}$$

P is nearly decomposable and has the following two 2×2 submatrices, P_1^* and P_2^*.

$$P_1^* = \begin{vmatrix} -50.0 & 23.0 \\ -1.0 & -0.10 \end{vmatrix}$$

$$P_2^* = \begin{vmatrix} -47.0 & 17.0 \\ -3.0 & -0.90 \end{vmatrix}$$

The eigenvalues of P associated with each matrix are as follows:

subsystem	*eigenvalues*
M_1	$\lambda_{11} = -0.52526$
	$\lambda_{21} = -49.535$
M_2	$\lambda_{12} = -2.6170$
	$\lambda_{22} = -47.383$

The eigenvectors of P_1^* and P_2^* corresponding to the eigenvalues λ_{11} and λ_{12} are as follows:

$z_{11}^* = (0.46526, 1)$

$z_{12}^* = (0.38303, 1)$

We will let variables $y_1(t)$ and $y_2(t)$ be the aggregate variables for submatrices M_1 and M_2 defined as the sum of the variables of the respective subsystem. In other words,

$$y_1 = x_{11} + x_{21} \tag{5.18}$$

$$y_2 = x_{12} + x_{22} \tag{5.19}$$

Differentiating both sides of the above two equations with respect to time yields:

$$y_1' = x_{11}' x_{21}' \tag{5.20}$$

$$y_2' = x_{12}' + x_{22}' \tag{5.21}$$

y_1 and y_2 have the following approximate, linear relations to the variables of the submatrices:

$$x_{11} \approx \frac{0.46526}{1 + 0.46526} y_1 = 0.317527 y_1$$

$$x_{21} \approx \frac{1}{1 + 0.46526} y_1 = 0.682473 y_1$$

$$x_{12} \approx \frac{0.38303}{1 + 0.38303} y_2 = 0.2769494 y_2$$

$$x_{22} \approx \frac{1}{1 + 0.38303} y_2 = 0.723051 y_2$$

Substituting these expressions for the variables in (5.14) and (5.15) yields

$$x_{11} = -50.0 \times 0.317527 y_1 + 23.0 \times 0.682473 y_1 + (1.0e - 3) \times 0.2769494 y_2 \tag{5.22}$$

and

$$x_{21} = -0.317527 y_1 + (-0.10) \times 0.682473 y_1 + (2.0e - 3) \times 0.723051 y_2 \tag{5.23}$$

Adding equations (5.22) and (5.23) and dividing both sides by the coefficient of y_1' yields

$$y_1' = -0.565278 y_1 + (1.723047e - 3) y_2 \tag{5.24}$$

Likewise, equations (5.16) and (5.17) yield

$$y_2' = (1.63505e - 3) y_1 - (2.616978e - 3) y_2. \tag{5.25}$$

The variables y_1 and y_2 and equations (5.24) and (5.25) constitute the aggregate structure M'. The aggregate matrix P' is as follows:

$$P' = \begin{vmatrix} -0.565278 & 1.723047e-3 \\ 1.63505e-3 & -2.616978 \end{vmatrix}$$

The time paths of the variables in this aggregate system are as follows:

$$y_1(t) = c_1 \exp(-0.565277t) + c_2(0.839814e-03)\exp(-2.61698t) \quad (5.26)$$

$$y_2(t) = c_1(-0.79692e-03)\exp(-0.565277t) + c_2 \exp(-2.61698t) \quad (5.27)$$

Constants c_1 and c_2 are determined by the initial values of the x_{j_i}'s. They should satisfy the relations (5.18) and (5.19) at $t = 0$.

5.2.3 Conditions for aggregation When the behavior of a nearly decomposable structure is approximated by an aggregate structure, the goodness of approximation will depend on the smallness of the matrix elements outside the submatrices and also on the degree of dominance of the most significant root of each submatrix over other roots. This second condition can be stated more precisely as follows: For a nearly decomposable dynamic matrix to be aggregated as described in this section, the matrix must satisfy the following conditions;

1. There is one root in each submatrix such that the absolute value of its real part is smaller than any others in the submatrix.
2. The absolute value of the real part of the most significant root of any subsystem must be smaller than that of any non-significant root of the other subsystems. In other words,

$$|\mathrm{Re}(\lambda_{1_I}| < |\mathrm{Re}(\lambda_{jJ}| \quad \text{for } I = 1 \text{ to } N,\ j = 2 \text{ to } m,\ J = 1 \text{ to } N.$$

The necessity of the condition (1) above is obvious if the movement of each subsystem is to be represented by one aggregate variable. The second condition is given by Courtois [17]. Courtois showed that the second condition is necessary for the case of stochastic matrices, but that it is also necessary for more general cases can be easily seen as follows: Given a dynamic structure, equation (5.2) expresses the time path of each variable. Without loss of generality, assume that all the characteristic roots λ_{i_j}'s ($i = 1$ to m_j) associated with each submatrix P_j ($j = 1$ to N) are arranged in increasing order of the magnitude of their real parts. Therefore, for each submatrix P_j, λ_{1_j} is the most significant root. Then, equation (5.2) can be expanded as follows:

$$x_{h_K}(t) = S_1 + S_2 \tag{5.28}$$

where

$$S_1 = \sum_{I}^{N} =_1 c_{1_I} z_{jI} h_K \exp(\lambda_{1_I} t)$$

and

$$S_2 = \sum_{I=1}^{N} \sum_{j=2}^{m_I} c_{j_I} z_{j_I h_K} \exp(\lambda_{j_I} t)$$

In aggregating a matrix, one discards S_2 in (5.28). Therefore, if aggregation is to produce a reasonable approximation, the exponential terms in the discarded term, S_2, must diminish before the exponential terms in S_1. In other words, the magnitudes of the real parts of the eigenvalues involved in S_1 must be smaller than those in S_2.

The procedure described so far requires that there be one most significant eigenvalue in each submatrix, and that the most significant eigenvalues of submatrices are more significant than the rest of the eigenvalues of all other submatrices. This procedure can be generalized to apply to a case where a submatrix can have any number of significant roots.

5.3 Aggregation and Causal Ordering

We have so far discussed aggregation as a means of going bottom-up from a detailed description of a system to a description at a higher level of abstraction. There is an alternative, top-down, way of looking at the situation. When we model a complex system, we carry our modeling only down to some level of components. Above that level, structure and the interrelations of components are explicit. Below that level, the components are black boxes with no detailed internal structure. Suppose that we determine the causal structure of the model but decide subsequently that some part of the model must be elaborated in greater detail. Will the new model, incorporating this elaboration, have the same causal structure as the more aggregated model, or do we have to reexamine the causal ordering from the beginning? In this section, we will show that it is not necessary to reexamine the causal ordering of the aggregated structure after elaborating a part of that structure, and we will also compare aggregation and mixed structures as two closely-related abstraction techniques.

5.3.1 Causal ordering in an aggregate structure The aggregation procedure described in the previous section produces a dynamic structure in terms of aggregate variables. Aggregate variables describe the long-term behavior of the subsystems they represent, and the aggregate structure describes the long-term behavior of the entire system in terms of the interactions among subsystems. Since the aggregate structure produced by the procedure is just another self-contained, dynamic structure, its causal ordering can be determined using the definition presented in Section 3.

Consider the nearly decomposable system, M, in the example in Section 5.2.2, consisting of the following equations:

$$x'_{1_1} = -50.0x_{1_I} + 23.0x_{2_1} + (1.0e-3)x_{1_2} \tag{5.14}$$

$$x'_{2_1} = -1.0x_{1_I} - 0.10x_{2_1} + (2.0e-3)x_{2_2} \tag{5.15}$$

$$x'_{1_2} = (1.0e-3)x_{2_1} - 47.0x_{1_2} - 17.0x_{2_2} \tag{5.16}$$

$$x'_{2_2} = (3.0e-3)x_{1_I} + 1.0x_{1_2} - 0.90x_{2_2} \tag{5.17}$$

M was aggregated to produce an aggregated, dynamic structure M' consisting of the following equations:

$$y'_1 = 0.56526y_1 + (1.1112e-3)y_2 \tag{5.24}$$

$$y'_2 = (3.8135e-3)y_1 - 1.2718y_2 \tag{5.25}$$

Figure 5.1 shows the causal ordering in M'. Suppose that after determining the causal ordering in M', one decides to elaborate subsystem M_1 further. Since M is hierarchical, hence nearly decomposable, the characteristic roots associated with the subsystem to be elaborated will have large real parts compared with the characteristic roots of the aggregated system. If we ignore very short time periods, the structure of the subsystem can be summed up in linear combinations of the elements of the eigenvectors associated with its significant roots as in

$$y_1 = c_1 \exp(\lambda_{1_1} t)$$

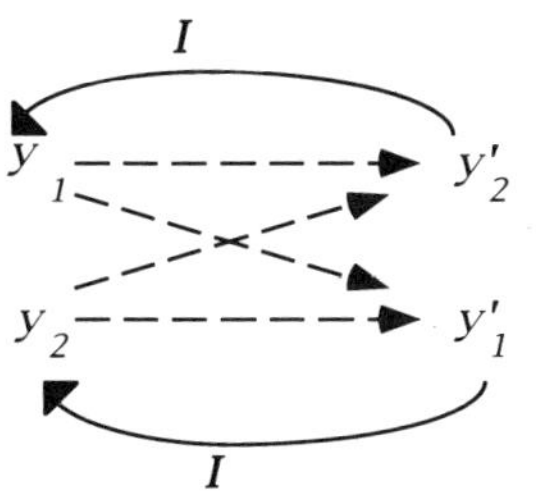

Figure 5.1
Causal ordering in M'

where $-50.0z_{1_1} + 23.0z_{2_1} = \lambda_{1_1} z_{1_1}$,

λ_{1_1} is the most significant eigenvalue associated with M_1, and
z_{1_1} and z_{2_1} are elements of its corresponding eigenvector.

or

$$y_1 = c_1 \exp\left(\frac{(-50.0z_{1_1} + 23.0z_{2_1})t}{z_{1_1}}\right) \tag{5.29}$$

These elements will be constants that, for purposes of examining behavior in the longer run, can be treated as exogenous. They determine the internal relations of the parts of the component with each other. Hence, we can add to M the following constant equations:

$$z_{1_1} = 0.462526 \tag{5.30}$$

$$z_{2_1} = 1.0 \tag{5.31}$$

Let M'' be the structure produced by adding equations (5.29), (5.30), and (5.31) to M'. Then, to construct the causal graph of M'', we simply add to our causal diagram of M' a new set of causal arrows, one for each element of the eigenvectors, pointing to y_1 as shown in figure 5.2. In all other respects, the causal ordering will remain the same.

Alternatively, if one decides to make explicit the internal causal structure within M_1, it can be shown as in figure 5.3. In the figure, the causal structure within M is constructed using Definition 3 of causal ordering in a dynamic structure applied to the component in isolation, i.e. M_1^*.

Note that the additional links (indicated by broken arrows) from the elements of the eigenvector to y_1 in figures 5.2 and 5.3 represent relations

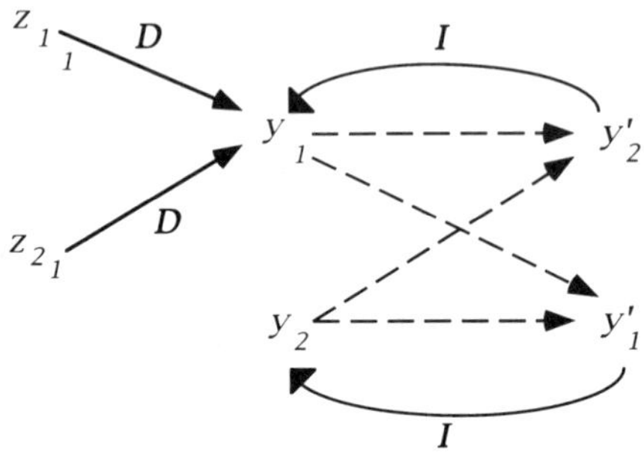

Figure 5.2
Causal ordering in M''

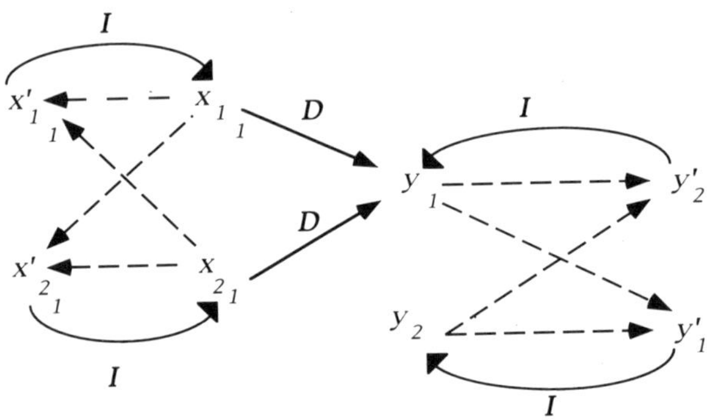

Figure 5.3
Causal ordering in M' with internal structure of M_1

whose nature is somewhat different from that of the causal links we have been discussing up to this point. They are abstraction links connecting variables at one level of abstraction to the aggregate variable that represents their collective long-term behavior at the next higher level of abstraction. Essentially, they represent explanations of the behavior of the aggregate variable in terms of its components.[3] They are causal links in the sense that behavior at a lower level of abstraction is said to "cause" a behavior at a higher level of abstraction, and not in the sense of a one-level causal mechanism, on which structural equations are based. For example, the ideal gas law, $VP = \eta RT$ can be a mechanism in a one-level causal system, while the equations of statistical mechanics provide a lower-level explanation of this mechanism.

Also, note that in figure 5.3, the short-term causal links and long-term ones must be carefully distinguished. The short-term links are the causal links within M_1, and the long-term ones are causal links among components. Introducing these different types of links is necessary in order to show clearly the hierarchical causal structure of a system when causal relations at different abstraction levels are mixed in one diagram.

The above example shows that for hierarchical, near-decomposable systems, the causal ordering is not sensitive to the "grain size" of analysis. At any level in the hierarchy, the causal ordering among components is (nearly) independent of the causal ordering that describes the relative movement of the variables within any single component.

5.3.2 Aggregation and mixed structure as abstraction techniques Aggregation, discussed in Section 5, and the techniques of equilibration and exogenization to produce mixed structures, discussed in Section 4, are two ways for abstracting a complex dynamic structure to produce a simpler description of the system by ignoring its short-term behavior. In fact, the two techniques are closely related [18]. We summarize the relation below:

1. Aggregation

1.1. Decompose the system into components such that variables within a component interact strongly, quickly restoring relative equilibrium among them, while variables from different components interact only weakly.

1.2. Set up aggregate variables for components and redescribe the long-term behavior of the entire system in terms of the aggregate variables.

2. Equilibration

2.1. Choose the equations representing mechanisms that restore equilibrium very quickly so that the equilibrium relations can be regarded to hold instantaneously.

2.2. Replace these differential equations by corresponding equilibrium equations.

The first step of aggregation and equilibration techniques amounts to classifying interactions among variables into two types; strong interactions restoring relative equilibrium among a group of variables very quickly, and weak interactions among different groups that take a long

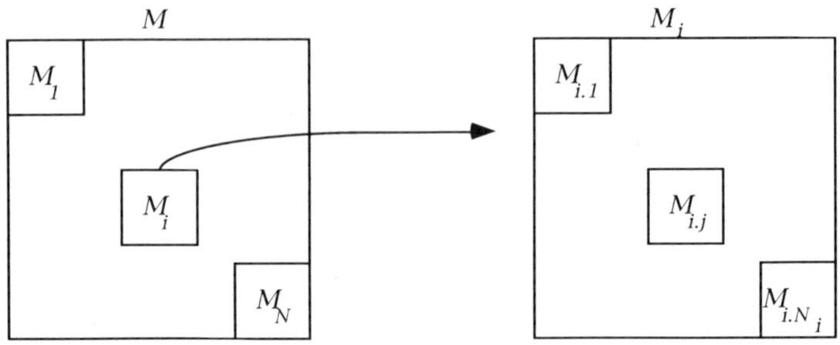

Figure 5.4
Three-level, near-decomposable matrix

time to reach equilibrium. The first step of exogenization classifies weak interactions further into very weak interactions that can be ignored (at least for the time period of interest) and those which cannot be ignored.

Aggregation can also be carried out to any number of levels given a suitably near-decomposable model. The parallel between aggregation and equilibration coupled with exogenization can be illustrated clearly with a three-level, near-decomposable system. Let M be a near-decomposable system with M_1 through M_N subsystems, each of which is also nearly decomposable with N_1 through N_N subsystems respectively. We will denote the subsystems of a subsystem M_i $(1 \leq i \leq N)$ as $M_{i.1} \cdots M_{i.N_i}$. Figure 5.4 shows such a three-level near-decomposable matrix. The system M can be aggregated twice. Let A_1 through A_N denote the aggregate variables of the subsystems M_1 through M_N, and $A_{i.1}$ through $A_{i.N_i}$ the aggregate variables of the subsystems of M_i for $i = 1$ through N. If we are interested in modeling the middle-term behavior of the subsystem M_i, and appropriate model to use will consist of:

1. Equilibrium equations produced by equilibrating the dynamic equations belonging to the subsystems $M_{i.1}$ through $M_{i.N_i}$. These equations represent the fast mechanisms through which variables within each subsystem interact.

2. The dynamic equations of the aggregated version of M_i. These equations represent the middle-term dynamic interaction among the subsystems within M_i.

3. Exogenous variable equations of the aggregate variables A_1 through A_N (except for A_i). These equations represent influences of other sub-

systems of M, which can be considered independent of variables within M_i for the time period of interest.

When groups of strongly interacting variables can be identified in a dynamic system, the theory of aggregation justifies breaking up the system into subsystems and treating the variables within a subsystem as moving together (always maintaining relative equilibrium among them). This type of decomposition requires only qualitative information, namely the relative strength of interactions among variables. Therefore, the theory of aggregation provides a justification for qualitative abstraction techniques even in cases where precise numerical values of the coefficients in the dynamic system are not known. Though Simon and Ando only handle linear systems in their theory of aggregation, its usefulness is not limited to linear systems because it is very common to use piece-wise linear models to approximate the behavior of more complex non-linear systems in engineering problem solving.

The mixed model M_1 of the bathtub system in Section 4.1 implies that the system can be viewed as a nearly decomposable system of the form shown below, where c indicates some non-epsilon coefficients.

	Q_{in}	D	P	Q_{out}	K
Q'_{in}					
D'	ε			ε	
P'		c	c		
Q'_{out}			c	c	c
K'					

In this system, Q_{in} forms one subsystem, and variables D, P, K and Q_{out} form the other subsystem. The εs that connect the two subsystems are the coefficients in Equation (3.6). Q_{out} is an ε influence from the second subsystem to the aggregate system, while dD/dt is an ε input, via the implicit integration equation $D = I(dD/dt)$, from the aggregate system into the second subsystem. Making D exogenous in forming $\text{Inst}(M_1)$ is equivalent to regarding the second subsystem as independent in the short run from the aggregate system.

This view of a mixed system as a nearly decomposable system allows us to state more precisely the restriction on equilibration that we have informally stated in Section 4.2.4: If the structure is nearly-decomposable, we can equilibrate variables within the subsystems, but until we equilibrate these subsystems we cannot equilibrate variables that connect subsystems.

When the qualitative technique of mixed structure is applied to a nearly decomposable system with a set of assumptions about the relative speeds of mechanisms consistent with the way the system is decomposed, the results produced by the two techniques should be consistent with each other. Consider again the dynamic structure M in Section 5.3.1. Suppose that it is known a priori that the mechanism represented by equation (5.14), belonging to the subsystem M_1, acts very quickly to restore relative equilibrium between x_{1_1} and x_{2_1}, and that, likewise, the mechanism represented by equations (5.16), belonging to M_2, restores equilibrium between x_{1_2} and x_{2_2} very quickly. Then, ignoring the long-term effects of the ε terms, we can rewrite the two equations as below:

$$0 = -50.0x_{1_1} + 23.0x_{2_1} \tag{5.14'}$$

$$0 = -47.0x_{1_2} - 17.0x_{2_2} \tag{5.16'}$$

The above two equations, (5.14′) and (5.16′), and equations (5.15) and (5.17) shown below form a self-contained mixed structure.

$$x'_{2_1} = -1.0x_{1_1} - 0.10x_{2_1} + (2.0e - 3)x_{2_2} \tag{5.15}$$

$$x'_{2_2} = (3.0e - 3)x_{1_1} - 3.0x_{1_2} - 0.90x_{2_2} \tag{5.17}$$

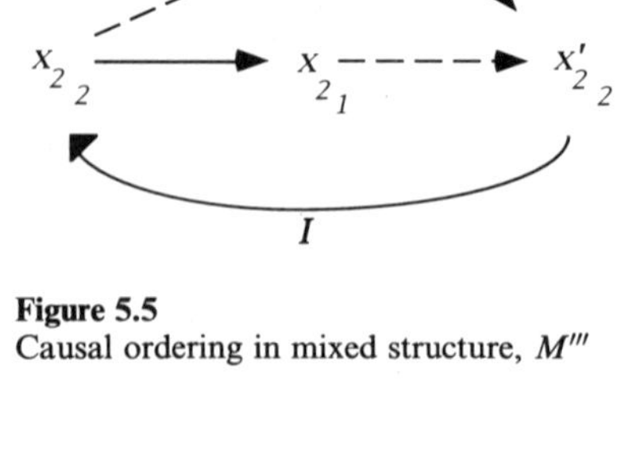

Figure 5.5
Causal ordering in mixed structure, M'''

Let M''' be this mixed structure. Figure 5.5 shows the causal ordering in M'''. Comparison of the diagrams in figures 5.1 and 5.5 reveals that they have basically the same causal structure: There is an internal feedback loop in each subsystem, and there is a feedback loop between the two subsystems.

6 Conclusion

This paper has explored the application of the method of causal ordering to models of physical devices, in the course of which we extended the method to make it applicable to a range of models, from those consisting entirely of equilibrium equations to others consisting entirely of differential equations. We also showed how causal ordering can be analyzed in systems that include static equations representing variables that are nearly exogenous, other static equations for mechanisms that alter the values of corresponding variables instantaneously, and differential equations that describe the dynamic behavior of the remaining variables. The method applies to qualitative models as well as quantitative models.

The causal ordering method provides an operational procedure for inferring causal relations from an acausal, general description of phenomena. Our approach clearly separates the task of determining causal relations from the task of determining effects of a disturbance on the system, thereby producing less ambiguous results than methods relying on constraint propagation in order to determine causal relations.

The paper has also examined the relation between causal ordering and abstraction. We presented several means of generating a more abstract model from a complex dynamic model. None of these techniques require simulating the model's behavior as do the abstraction techniques proposed by other researchers. We showed to what extent the causal analysis of a system is invariant as we pass from a fine-grained description of the system's dynamic behavior to a more coarse-grained description through aggregation or disaggregation, thus providing justification for the standard practice of directing attention to the dynamics of specific subsystems without dealing with the entire system at once.

CAOS The ideas discussed in this paper have been fully implemented as part of a program named CAOS (CAusal Ordering System). The program includes the following modules for reasoning about the behavior of a system: Equation model generation module, causal ordering analysis module, qualitative aggregation module, and numerical aggregation module.

Each of them is described briefly below:

Causal ordering analysis module Implements the method of causal ordering analysis discussed in Sections 2, 3, and 4. Given an equation model, this module applies causal ordering analysis to determine the causal structure in the model.

Qualitative aggregation module Implements the abstraction technique discussed in Section 4.2. Given a dynamic model and a set of equations in the model representing fast mechanisms, it generates a mixed model that is causally consistent.

Numerical aggregation module Implements the aggregation techniques discussed in Section 5. Given a numerical matrix of a nearly decomposable dynamic system, it applies the numerical aggregation procedure to produce an aggregate system.

In addition to these four modules, CAOS also includes the following two modules for performing tasks that are not discussed in this paper but that are nonetheless important in reasoning about system behavior. These modules are:

Equation model generation module Generates an equation model from an explicit representation of flow processes occurring in a component.

Stability analysis module Performs qualitative analysis of a dynamic system matrix. Given a matrix of a dynamic system, tries to determine the dynamic stability of the system using qualitative and quantitative techniques for stability analysis.

Qualitative prediction module Performs qualitative prediction. Given a causal structure of an equilibrium model and an external disturbance, propagates the disturbance along the causal structure to determine the effects on other variables in the model.

We have built a knowledge base of a coal power plant to test CAOS. The knowledge base includes a model of the mass and energy flows in the plant. It is a fairly simplistic model, consisting of five components, and 108 variables.

6.1 Future Directions

The work described in this paper can be extended in several different ways.

Modeling Causality arises when a mechanism links phenomena. A structural equation represents relations (i.e. constraints) imposed among variables by the mechanism, but an equation by itself fails to capture the asymmetry of causality in the underlying mechanism. The causal ordering method, then, is a means to recover the information of causal relations in the mechanisms described by the equations in a self-contained system. Requiring a model to be self-contained forces one to make explicit all the assumptions about the context in which the mechanisms are placed, in the form of equations in the model for exogenous variables.

Since causal ordering depends totally on the choice of equations, how the equations to be included should be selected is a critical question when constructing a model. Unfortunately, this question cannot be given a general, formal answer because it depends on what can be considered mechanisms, which varies widely from domain to domain. Even when one limits the problem to only one domain with a well-known set of mechanisms, the answer still depends on the levels of abstraction and what are considered to be the primitive mechanisms at each level. Determining the mechanisms is not a formal question but one whose answer follows only from knowledge of theory of the domain.

As the types of phenomena of concern vary from domain to domain, the types of mechanisms that are of interest vary also. If the mechanism is a lever, the phenomena are the movements of the bodies resting on its arms. If the phenomena are the weather during a growing season and the size of the wheat crop, then the mechanism is the function that determines the growth of wheat. In the domain of CAOS, the phenomena of interest are mass and energy inputs and outputs, the mechanisms are the processes that produce outputs from the inputs.

A question that naturally arises, then, is, "Why not represent mechanisms?" We, in fact, developed a representation of mechanisms, from which equation models were generated automatically. In this experiment, we limited ourselves to one level of abstraction, and only to modeling mechanisms in the domain of CAOS, which was mainly concerned with flows of energy and matter. This representation of mechanisms as flows worked well in our domain but may not be appropriate for other domains involving very different types of mechanisms, e.g. a domain requiring sophisticated spatial reasoning. Developing a more general representation of mechanisms, and thereby making the concept of structural equations more concrete, is an important research direction.

Forbus proposed a very general representation of physical objects and continuous processes in his work on Qualitative Process Theory (QPT) [9]. Forbus' representation is the basis of the representation of mechanisms used in a program called Device Modeling Environment (DME) developed by Iwasaki and Low [19], which formulates a behavior model from a given device design and simulates its behavior. An important difference between the QPT representation and that of CAOS or DME is that in QPT knowledge of causal relations is given in the definitions of physical processes, which are considered to be the media to transmit causality, while no such commitment is made in the representation of mechanisms in the other two systems.

Aggregation of non-linear systems The numerical aggregation procedure depends on linearity of a structure. It is an obvious and useful extension of this work to devise an analogous aggregation method for non-linear systems since many practical systems in the real world are not linear. Analyzing a system of non-linear differential equations is a difficult problem. Since there is no general technique for analyzing all non-linear systems as there is for a linear case, one would have to restrict oneself to particular classes of non-linear systems, and to develop an aggregation procedure for each class. Sacks developed a program called Piecewise Linear Reasoner, which divides the phase space into regions within which linear equations can be used to describe the system behavior approximately [20] [21]. Nishida et al. also developed a method that emulates expert reasoning and automatically constructs phase portraits [22]. In these approaches, based on piecewise linear approximation, the system's global behavior can be characterized qualitatively in terms of its path through the linear regions. Kalagnanam has extended these approaches further by employing symbolic computation to investigate the analytical properties of the set of differential equations [23]. These approaches may provide a starting point for extending our work on aggregation to non-linear systems.

Applications There are a number of ways in which causal ordering methods can be applied to practical model-based reasoning problems. They include explanation, diagnosis, design, and prediction.

Since the causal ordering theory allows one to generate a causal interpretation of a set of equations, one obvious use of the theory is in generating explanations. DME, the system for model formulation and simulation mentioned above, applies the theory to the behavior models it generates in order to produce natural language, causal explanations of the simulated behavior [24].

In order to diagnose device faults using knowledge of causal relations, the system needs a model consisting of relations among physical parameters, based on physical laws and expected behavior of subcomponents, stated as equations. The program will infer the causal dependency relations implied by a set of such equations together with additional knowledge and assumptions about the domain. Lambert et al. have developed a program called YAKA, which is a combination of diagnostic and knowledge acquisition systems in the domain of an oil refinery [25]. Its model consists of a mixture of equilibrium and dynamic equations. It uses the theory of causal ordering to determine the causal relations among the variables in the model. The knowledge of causal relations is then used to search for the possible causes of a symptom, described as an abnormal value of a variable. The causal knowledge is also used to predict the effects of a hypothesized fault.

The causal ordering method has been used in a similar way in a knowledge compilation system. RWA [26] produces if-then rules for parametric design in the domain of the reaction wheel assembly subsystem of the Hubble Space Telescope. It performs causal ordering analysis of equations describing the thermodynamic aspect of RWA to produce a causal model. It then determines what possible changes can be made to the system in order to achieve a given redesign goal, also predicting side effects of such changes. RWA finally compiles this analysis into if-then rules to be used by a redesign expert system.

Acknowledgment

The authors would like to thank Pandu Nayak and reviewers of the journal for useful feedback on an earlier version of the paper. This research was supported in part by the Defense Advanced Research Projects Agency, Department of Defense, ARPA Order 3597, monitored by the Air Force Avionics Laboratory under contract F33615-81-K-1539, and ARPA Order 8607, monitored by NASA Ames Research Center under grant NAG 2-581. It was also supported in part by NASA Ames Research Center under grant NCC 2-537. Reproduction in whole or in part is permitted for any purpose of the United Sates Government. Approved for public release; distribution unlimited.

Appendix A: Proofs for Theorems 1 and 2

THEOREM 1 The causal ordering of a qualitative self-contained structure is unique.

THEOREM 2 All the derived structures of a qualitative self-contained structure are self-contained.

Proof of theorem 1 Let S be a qualitative self-contained structure.

Suppose that there are two minimal complete subsets s_1 and s_2 in S. Let k_1 and k_2 be the number of equations in s_1 and s_2.

First, we prove by contradiction that an equation cannot belong to two minimal complete subsets (i.e. two minimal complete subsets do not intersect).

Suppose s_1 and s_2 share some equations (i.e. $s_1 \cap s_2 \neq \emptyset$).

Let s_3 be $s_1 \cap s_2$. Let k_3 be the number of equations in s_3 and v_3 be the number of variables in s_3. $k_3 < v_3$ because

1. if $k_3 > v_3$, s_3 violates the condition 1 of Definition 1 contradicting the fact that S is self-contained.

2. if $k_3 = v_3$, s_3 would be a self-contained structure. However, since s_3 is a subset of s_1 and s_2, it contradicts the assumptions that s_1 and s_2 are minimal complete subsets.

The set $s_1 \cup s_2$ contains $k_1 + k_2 - k_3$ equations and at most $k_1 + k_2 - v_3$ variables. Since $k_3 < v_3$, $k_1 + k_2 - k_3 > k_1 + k_2 - v_3$. Therefore, the set $s_1 \cup s_2$ violates the condition 1 of Definition 1, contradicting the fact that S is self-contained.

Therefore, we conclude s_1 and s_2 do not share any equations (i.e $s_1 \cap s_2 = \emptyset$).

Now, we prove by contradiction that there is no variable that belongs to both s_1 and s_2.

Suppose that there is at least one variable that belongs to both s_1 and s_2.

The set $s_1 \cup s_2$ contains at most $k_1 + k_2 - 1$ variables. It also contains exactly $k_1 + k_2$ equations since s_1 and s_2 do not share equations. Therefore, this set violates the condition 1 of Definition 1, contradicting the fact that original structure S is self-contained.

Therefore, we conclude that in a self-contained qualitative structure, if a variable belongs to a minimal complete subset, there is no other minimal complete subset that also contains the variable.

Thus, it is obvious, from the way the causal ordering is determined, that the causal ordering of a self-contained qualitative structure is unique.

Proof of theorem 2 Let S be a qualitative self-contained structure, S' be its derived structure of the first order, S_0 be the set of the minimal complete subsets of the zero order, and k_0 be the number of equations (or variables) in S_0.

We first prove that S' has the same number of equations as variables. Because of the way S' is derived from S, S' has exactly $k - k_0$ variables and at most $k - k_0$ equations. Furthermore, S' could have less than $k - k_0$ equations only if there is an equation e in S such that e does not belong to S_0 and e contains only variables that belong to S_0.

Suppose that there exists such an equation e. The set $S_0 \cup \{e\}$ is a subset of S. This set contains $k_0 + 1$ equations but only k_0 variables, violating the condition 1 of Definition 1. This contradicts the fact that S is a self-contained structure.

Therefore we conclude that S' has exactly $k - k_0$ equations.

Now we prove by contradiction that no subset of S' has more equations than variables.

Suppose that there exists a subset s_1' of S' that contains k_1 equations and v_1 variables where $k_1 > v_1$.

The equations in s_1' could have contained any number of variables belonging to S_0 before S was reduced to S'. Let s_1 be the set of such original equations of s_1'. s_1 contains k_1 equations.

The set $s_1 \cup S_0$ is a subset of S. The set contains $k_0 + k_1$ equations and $k_0 + v_1$ variables. Since $k_1 > v_1$, we have $k_0 + k_1 > k_0 + v_1$. Therefore, this set has fewer variables than equations, violating the condition 1 in Definition x, which contradicts the fact that S is a self-contained structure.

Therefore, we conclude that no subset of S' contains more equations than variables.

Therefore, we conclude S' is a qualitative, self-contained structure.

By induction, we conclude that all derived structures of a self-contained qualitative structure are self-contained qualitative structures themselves.

Appendix B: Proofs for Theorems 3 and 4

In general, given a set S of equations in a set V of variables, if we can find a mapping G from S to V such that

1. $G(s) = v$, where $s \in S$ and v is one of the variables appearing in s, and
2. G is injective (i.e. $G(s_i) = G(s_j) \Leftrightarrow i = j$),

it is clear that any subset of S contains at least the same number of variables as equations. Therefore, to prove that a structure is a qualitative self-contained structure, it is sufficient to prove that

3. the structure contains the same number of variables as equations, and
4. there is a mapping from the equations to the variables that satisfies the above conditions 1 and 2.

Furthermore, it is clear in general that given a self-contained structure, one can find a mapping G that satisfies the above conditions 1 and 2 by letting $G(e_i) = v_i$, where v_i is the dependent variable in equation e_i. Furthermore, G is one-to-one in this case. Let us call such a mapping a *dependent mapping*. When e_i is a member of a minimal complete subset containing more than one equation, one can define $G(e_i) = v_i$ so that v_i is any one of the variables in the subset, v_i appears in e_i, and G is one-to-one.

THEOREM 3 Equilibrating any number of self-regulating equations in a qualitative self-contained mixed structure always produces a qualitative self-contained structure.

Proof Let M be a qualitative self-contained mixed structure of m equations, e_1 to e_m and variables v_1 to v_m. Let l be the number of derivatives appearing in M, and, without loss of generality, we assume v_1 through v_l to be those variables. Without loss of generality, we assume e_1 to be a self-regulating equation and dv_1/dt to be the dependent variable of e_1.

Let G be a dependent mapping from Inst(M) to V, where V is the set of variables in Inst(M), treating variables and their derivatives as distinct variables. Inst(M) consists of the following equations

e_1,

e_2 through e_m, and

Const(M), which consists of constant variable equations for v_1 though v_l.

G maps the equations in Inst(M) to V as follows:

$$G(e_1) = \frac{dv_1}{dt}$$

$G(e_i) = v_i$, where v_i is the dependent variable in e_i. for $2 \leq i \leq m$

$G(e_j) = vj$, where $e_j \in \text{Const}(M)$ and v_j is the variable appearing in e_j. Note one of e_j is the constant variable equation for v_1, and its $G(e_j)$ is v_1.

Let M' be the set of equations $e'_1 \cdots e'_m$ generated by equilibrating v_1 in M. Each e'_i ($i = 1$ to m) is generated by replacing all occurrences of dv_1/dt in e_i by 0. Because of the way equilibration is defined, it is clear that M' satisfies Condition 1 of Definition 4 (i.e. M' contains zero or more first-order differential equations and the rest are equilibrium equations).

To see that the condition 2 of Definition 4 is satisfied by M', observe the following:

- Inst(M) contains $m + l$ equations and variables. Because of the way equilibration is defined, it is clear that Inst(M') contains $m + l - 1$ equations. Also, since Inst(M) contains $m + l$ variables, and M' is generated by removing dv_1/dt from M, it is clear that Inst(M') contains $m + l - 1$ variables.
- The set of variables appearing in Inst(M') is $V - \{dv_1/dt\}$. We can define a mapping G' from Inst(M') to the set of variables appearing in Inst(M') as follows:

$G'(e'_1) = v_1$. Note that since e_1 is a self-regulating equation, v_1 appears in e'_1.

$G'(e'_i) = G(e_i)$ for $2 \leq i \leq m$

$G'(e_j) = vj$, where $e_j \in \text{Const}(M)$ and v_j is the variable appearing in e_j. Note that Const(M') does not contain v_1.

It is clear that G' satisfies the conditions 1 and 2 above.

Therefore, Inst(M') is a qualitative self-contained structure. Therefore, M' is a qualitative self-contained structure.

THEOREM 4 Exogenizing an equation in a qualitative self-contained dynamic or mixed structure always produces a qualitative self-contained structure.

Proof Let M be a qualitative self-contained mixed structure. Since M is self-contained, M has a dependent mapping from M to the set V of variables contained in M. Let G be such a mapping.

Let v_i be a variable in M whose derivative appears in M, and e_i be the member of M such that its dependent variable is dv_i/dt.

Let M' be the structure generated by exogenizing dv_i/dt in M. This can be done by replacing e_i by e_i' of one of the following two forms:

Case 1. $dv_i/dt = c$, where c is some constant.

Case 2. $dv_i/dt = f(v_i)$, where f is some function.

Case 2 is allowed only when e_i is a self-regulating equation, while Case 1 is allowed regardless of whether e_i is self-regulating.

Let V_i be the set of variables appearing in e_i besides v_i. It is clear that each variable v_j in V_i must appear in at least one other equation in M besides e_i because otherwise there would be no equation e such that $G(e) = v_j$. Therefore, the set of all variables and derivatives appearing in M' is the same as that of M. It follows that Inst(M) and Inst(M') contain the same set of variables and derivatives.

Furthermore, if we let G' be a mapping from Inst(M') to the set of variables and derivatives appearing in Inst(M') such that

$$G'(e_i') = G(e_i) \quad \text{and}$$

$$G'(e) = G(e) \quad \text{for all } e \text{ in Inst}(M') \text{ except } e_i,$$

then, it is clear that G' satisfies the above conditions 1 and 2 as G does.

Therefore, Inst(M') is a qualitative self-contained structure. It follows that M' is a qualitative self-contained structure.

Notes

1. This assumption is obviously simplistic except very close to equilibrium and does not reflect the whole reality, but it suffices for the purpose of this discussion.

2. In three dimensions we would have E and H, respectively, on the left-hand sides of these equations, where E is a vector whose three components are

$$\left(\frac{\partial E}{\partial y} - \frac{\partial E}{\partial z}\right), \left(\frac{\partial E}{\partial z} - \frac{\partial E}{\partial x}\right), \text{and} \left(\frac{\partial E}{\partial x} - \frac{\partial E}{\partial y}\right),$$

and correspondingly for H. Our one-dimensional analysis can easily be converted into the three-dimensional one without affecting the conclusions of our argument.

3. Therefore, they have the same status as the definitional link from v to dx/dt in figure 3.1.

References

1. Simon, H. A., *On the Definition of Causal Relation.* Journal of Philosophy, 1952. 49 pp. 517–528.

2. Iwasaki, Y., and Simon, H. A., *Causality in Device Behavior.* Artificial Intelligence, 1986. 29.

3. Iwasaki, Y., and Simon, H. A., *Theory of Causal Ordering: Reply to de Kleer and Brown.* Artificial Intelligence, 1986. 29.

4. Rieger, C., and Grinberg, M., *The Declarative Representation and Procedural Simulation of Causality in Physical Mechanisms.* In *The 5th International Joint Conference on Artificial Intelligence.* 1977.

5. Sembugamoorthy, V., and Chandrasekaran, B., *Functional Representation of Devices and Compilation of Diagnostic Problem-Solving Systems.* In *Experience, Memory, and Reasoning,* J. L. Kolodner, C. K., Riesbeck, Editors. 1986, Lawrence Erlbaum Associates: Hillsdale, NJ.

6. de Kleer, J., and Brown, J. S., *Qualitative Physics Based on Confluences.* Artificial Intelligence, 1984. 24.

7. Williams, B. C., *Qualitative Analysis of MOS Circuits.* Artificial Intelligence, 1984. 24.

8. de Kleer, J., and Brown, J. S., *Theory of Causal Ordering.* Artificial Intelligence, 1986. 29.

9. Forbus, K. D., *Qualitative Process Theory.* Artificial Intelligence, 1984. 24 (1–3).

10. Ando, A., Fisher, F. M., and Simon, H. A., *Essays on the Structure of Social Science Models.* 1963, MIT Press.

11. Kuipers, B., *Abstraction by Time-Scale in Qualitative Simulation.* In *The 6th National Conference on Artificial Intelligence.* 1987.

12. Nayak, P. P., *Automated modeling of physical systems.* 1992, PhD thesis, Department of Computer Science KSL-92-69, Stanford University.

13. Kuipers, B., *The Bathtub Counterexample.* 1987.

14. Simon, H. A., and Rescher, N., *Causes and Counterfactuals.* Philosophy of Science, 1966. 33: pp. 323–340.

15. Halliday, D., and Resnick, R., *Physics.* Second ed. 1966, John Wiley & Sons.

16. Simon, H. A., and Ando, A., *Aggregation of Variables in Dynamic Systems.* Econometrica, 1961. 29.

17. Courtois, P. J., *Decomposability: Queueing and Computer System Applications.* ACM Monograph Series, 1977, Academic Press.

18. Simon, H. A., and Iwasaki, Y., *Causal Ordering, Comparative Statics, and Near Decomposability.* Journal of Econometrics, 1988.

19. Low, C. M., and Iwasaki, Y., *Device modeling environment: an interactive environment for modelling device behaviour.* Intelligent Systems Engineering, 1992. 1(2): pp. 115–145.

20. Sacks, E. P., *Piecewise Linear Reasoning*. In *The 6th National Conference on Artificial Intelligence*. 1987.

21. Sacks, E. P., *Automatic Qualitative Analysis of Ordinary Differential Equations Using Piecewise Linear Approximations*. 1988, PhD thesis, Dept. of Computer Science, Massachusetts Institute of Technology.

22. Nishida, T., Mizutani, K., Kubota, A., and Doshita, S., *Automated Phase Portrait Analysis by Integrating Qualitative and Quantitative Analysis*. In *The 10th National Conference on Artificial Intelligence*. 1991. Boston, MA.

23. Kalagnanam, J. R., *Qualitative Analysis of System Behavior*. 1991, PhD thesis, Dept. of Engineering & Public Policy, Carnegie Mellon University.

24. Gautier, P. O., and Gruber, T. R., *Generating Explanations of Device Behavior Using Compositional Modeling and Causal Ordering*. 1993, Knowledge Systems Laboratory, Stanford University.

25. Lambert, H., Eshelman, L., and Iwasaki, Y., *Using Qualitative Physics to Guide the Acquisition of Diagnostic Knowledge*. In *The Third International Conference on Applications of Artificial Intelligence in Engineering*. 1988.

26. Keller, R., Baudin, C., Iwasaki Y., Nayak, P., and Tanaka, K., *Compiling Redesign Plans and Diagnosis Rules from a Structure/Behavior Device Model*. In *Knowledge Aided Design*, M. Green, Editor. 1992, Academic Press.

I.4 Simulation of Large-scale Systems by Aggregation

Two kinds of difficulties stand in the way of effective simulation of macrosocial systems: system mechanisms may be unknown, or known only imperfectly; and the number of system elements and their interactions may be too great for availablc computing facilities to handle. This paper is concerned mainly with methods for dealing with the latter problem, system complexity; but first I must make some preliminary comments on ignorance of system mechanisms.

1 Modeling the Unknown

Predicting economic fluctuations and predicting the weather have both proved to be very difficult tasks, even when the predictor has at his disposal large modern electronic computers. However, the root of the difficulty is different in the two cases, and consequently we might entertain quite different expectations as to how far accuracy could be improved by providing the predictor with computers that are one hundred times as large and one hundred times as fast as the ones he has now. My confident prediction (made without a computer) is that progress in computer hardware will produce a much greater improvement in weather prediction than in the prediction of economic fluctuations.

In the case of weather prediction, the fundamental physical laws of the atmosphere are fairly well understood. There are, of course, some areas of ignorance—for example, in the theory of turbulent flow—but even in these areas "ignorance" often means that the mathematical and computational problems are intractible, rather than that understanding is lacking of the physical forces at work. The greatest barrier, however, to the effective use of models of the atmosphere for weather prediction is the coarseness of the model grid, a coarseness that is imposed partly by the coarseness of the grid of observations but mainly by limitations on the numbers of interactions that can be handled in real time on existing computing facilities. Whether easing the computing limitations would allow the weatherman to predict the exact times and severities of thunderstorms in Pittsburgh I do not know, but it would certainly improve the accuracy of both his short-term and his long-term forecasts.

Since World War II, modeling of the economic system has progressed from three-equation models, well within the capabilities of desk calculators, to models containing dozens of equations and requiring the help of the largest computers for their computation. It is a matter of debate whether there has been a corresponding increase in the accuracy of economic forecasts. Nor is there any widespread confidence that a further increase in computing power will help matters very much.

The accuracy of model forecasts is limited mainly by the accuracy of the equations describing economic mechanisms that go into the models. Not only is our knowledge of those equations very inexact, but we are faced with serious methodological and practical problems in improving them. Many of the coefficients in the equations purport to describe how economic agents form their expectations, and how they use these expectations about uncertain events to make decisions. Human behavior under uncertainty is not well understood, partly because there is no "one right way" for the rational man to make his decisions when their outcomes depend on the decisions of others who are faced with the same uncertainty. Correct description of the system probably even requires learning equations, for modes of behavior in the face of uncertainty probably change with a society's long-term experience.

We should not expect a model that contains the wrong equations to make the right predictions, no matter how numerous the equations or how large and fast the computer. Hence, we should not expect miracles from modeling and simulation where, as in economics, our ignorance of the mechanisms is extensive. However, even in the face of such ignorance, I do not counsel despair. The questions we want to answer about a system do not always require prediction in detail. If we are interested only in certain aggregated aspects of its behavior, it may be that we can predict those aggregates by use of an appropriately aggregated model. And our knowledge and information may be adequate to supply the mechanisms and parameters of that simpler model, when it could not supply them for the detailed model.

While I would be hard pressed to propose a model that would predict the future populations of each of the large and medium-size cities of the United States, simple (two-equation) models do exist that predict quite accurately the *size distribution*. That is small comfort if our concern is with land planning for Chicago, but may be comfort enough if we are concerned with broad national policies to discourage or encourage urban concentration. I will propose some other examples later where effective solutions to the modeling problem lie in the direction of intelligent aggregation rather than purchasing the services of larger computers.

	1	2	3	4	5	6	7	8
1	x	S	W	M	–	–	W	W
2	S	x	S	W	M	–	W	–
3	M	S	x	W	M	–	–	W
4	M	M	–	x	S	W	W	W
5	W	M	M	S	x	–	W	W
6	W	–	–	W	W	x	S	S
7	–	W	W	W	W	S	x	S
8	–	W	–	W	W	M	S	x

S = Strong; M = Moderate; W = Weak

Figure 1
A nearly-completely-decomposable system (*source*: Simon 1976, p. 512)

2 Nearly-decomposable Systems

In the systems that occur in nature, or are designed by man, not all components interact strongly with other components. Most such systems are, in fact, *nearly completely decomposable*. That is to say, they can be subdivided into blocks in such a way that all strong interactions occur among elements in individual blocks, and only weak interactions between blocks. This kind of hierarchical structure is often recursive, with increasingly weak interactions as we go upward in the hierarchy.

Figure 1 depicts a nearly-completely-decomposable system of three levels. Strong interactions connect the subsystems A = (1 2 3), B = (4 5), and C = (6 7 8). Similarly K = (A B) is connected with interactions of moderate strength, while only weak interactions bind the entire system, S = (K C). By means of parentheses, we can summarize the structure of the hierarchy thus: (((1 2 3)(4 5))((6 7 8))).

Nearly complete decomposability is an almost ubiquitous characteristic of large systems, natural as well as social. The familiar hierarchy from physics and chemistry of elementary particle–nucleus–atom–molecule is an example of near-decomposability, as is the hierarchy of protein–cell–tissue–organism. A social system may be built on the hierarchy of individual–family–community–state, an economic system on the hierarchy of department–firm–industry–economy.

It is not accidental that most natural and social systems are hierarchical. Elsewhere (Simon, 1969, ch. 4) I have outlined the reasons why hierarchy is so all-pervasive. Suppose that complex systems have had to evolve (as they have) from simpler components. The time required for the evolution of a system of n parts, where n is large, will be very long, and will grow exponentially with n, if all n components have to come together simultaneously. However, if the elementary components can combine into small, stable subsystems, and small sets of those subsystems into larger systems, and so on, then the expected time of evolution of the entire system will grow only with $\log n$. Hence, hierarchical systems have an immense evolutionary advantage over those that are not hierarchical, and we may expect that almost all of the large systems we observe in the world will have hierarchical structure—as they do.

What is important and fortunate for our purposes about this state of affairs is that the dynamic behavior of a nearly-completely-decomposable system can be analysed without examining simultaneously all of the interactions of the elementary parts (Simon and Ando, 1961). Suppose that Figure 1 represents the matrix of coefficients of a set of first order linear differential equations. This matrix can be solved for eight eigenvalues that represent the eight frequencies of oscillation of the system. Now, if the coefficients labeled "Strong," "Moderate," and "Weak," respectively, are separated by an order of magnitude or so, then the eigenvalues will have the following structure. Two eigenvalues corresponding to high frequencies will depend mainly on the strong components binding A, one high frequency eigenvalue on the strong components binding B, and two on the components binding C. An intermediate-frequency eigenvalue will depend mainly on the interactions of A with B; a low-frequency eigenvalue will depend mainly on the interaction of K with C; and the lowest-frequency eigenvalue will describe the long-term trend of S as a whole.

In such a structure, the high-frequency eigenvalues can be computed, to a good approximation, for each separate subsystem, without considering the (weaker) interactions with the other subsystems. Moreover, the lower-frequency eigenvalues can be computed on the basis of only aggregated descriptions of the subsystems, and without detailed knowledge of the within-subsystem coefficients. Thus, to understand the dynamic behavior of a system like the one depicted in Figure 1, we need solve only systems of two or three variables (A, B, C, K and S), and not a system of eight simultaneous variables. Since computation time for simultaneous relations increases more than linearly with the number of relations, using the hierarchical structure of a system can greatly simplify its analysis. Moreover, if the system contains symmetries, so that, for example, all the subsystems at the lowest level are identical or belong to a few species, then computation time may increase only with the logarithm of the size of the entire system. A discussion of the application of near-decomposability to the computation of system behavior will be found in Courtois (1977).

The factorability of the behavior of nearly-decomposable systems can be understood in the following way. Elements of each subsystem at the lowest levels of the hierarchy interact strongly at high frequency, hence move rapidly toward internal equilibrium. At progressively higher levels, interactions among components take place at lower frequencies, hence take longer to reach equilibrium when the system is disturbed. Thus, when a hierarchical system is observed over a moderate time span, and with some maximum frequency of observation, we will observe only the equilibrium distributions of the smallest components, for their dynamics will be too rapid to be seen; while the largest components may appear to be stationary, since the time span of observations is too short to detect aggregate change in them. Genuine dynamic behavior will be observed only at the intermediate levels. Altering the frequency and span of observation simply moves the frequency range of the "slit" through which dynamics can be observed.

3 The Need for Simplification

Consider the following, not atypical, modeling problem. We wish to improve the water quality in Lake Erie by reducing eutrophication and algae production, and we propose to construct a computer model that will allow us to assess the impact of alternative control measures (Nelson, 1976). This model will have a large biological component, but an important social one as well. The criteria of tolerable levels of pollution are social, as are the driving functions—the movements of urban population, industry, and agriculture that determine what quantities of pollutants will be produced.

One approach is to construct a complex simulation model of the lake and the adjoining urban and agricultural areas that drain into it—a total area of some thousands of square miles. We impose on this area a grid, and construct equations for each cell to estimate phosphate production (on land) and the metabolic processes of phosphate usage and the growth of algae (in the lake). The grid will need to be quite fine, for there are important spot sources of phosphate (e.g., city sewer outfalls and industrial plants), points of concentration in the lake (e.g., mouths of streams), and complex currents and wind patterns that redistribute materials over large distances.

Accurate data on phosphate sources are not easy to come by—for example, details of agricultural runoff. Nor are the processes of eutrophication at all well understood from a biochemical standpoint. Hence the modeling project, as I have described it, produces an enormous model (tens of thousands of parameters), containing numerous equations that are supposed to represent poorly understood mechanisms, and incorporating large numbers of parameters that can only be estimated very approximately. If the model is conceived as a forecasting tool, so that it operates dynamically over time, it becomes even larger and more complex. In this case, it must incorporate not only a description of the existing distribution of urban population, polluting industry, and agriculture, but also—a much more difficult matter—a regional socio-econometric model to predict the trends in this distributional pattern.

If it be said that I have just constructed a straw man ready for burning, I would answer that I can point to a half dozen current social modeling efforts conceived just as this one was. One of the best known examples, though it was not quite on the scale of the one I have described, was the *World Dynamics* model of the 1972 Club of Rome report (Meadows et al., 1974).

Application of the notions of near decomposability to the Lake Erie modeling problem would lead to vast simplification of the task. First, the long-term changes are sufficiently gradual that a dynamic model is not needed to deal with them; it would be adequate simply to estimate steady-state equilibrium under various sets of assumptions about population of the surrounding area, and to use these equilibria to predict trends. Second, the dynamics of the eutrophication processes are several orders of magnitude faster than the other dynamic components of the system. Since these dynamics are, in any event, very poorly understood, they can be replaced by simple static assumptions that eutrophication varies as some simple function of phosphate input. (This amounts to aggregating the subsystems at the lowest level of the hierarchy.)

Third, in the middle and long run, there will be high intercorrelations of phosphate levels in different parts of the lake, so a fine grid is hardly necessary (a second level of aggregation). Moreover, the policy instruments available for ameliorating the situation (e.g. tertiary sewage treatment, reduction of phosphates in detergents) are sufficiently gross (if powerful) as to make it futile to model system details that cannot be modified independently and in corresponding detail. Finally, ameliorative action can always be taken on an incremental basis with feedback, so that we do not need exact predictions of the magnitude of the effects.

I conclude that the social purposes to be archieved by this modeling can be accomplished with aggregate models of modest size that will not strain even modest computing capabilities, and that will not pretend to an unattainable finesse and accuracy.

This is not an isolated example. In dealing with automotive air pollution, we are faced with a complex technological system of four major components interacting with the socio-economic system that produces and "consumes" the pollutants. There are the relations between automotive design and cost and levels of emissions of pollutants. There are the relations between emission levels and ambient air quality (which depends also, of course, on levels of non-automotive emission). The latter relations have to be combined with meteorological data on wind, precipitation and temperature. There are the relations between air quality and health.

As in the earlier example of water pollution, the impact of these mechanisms depends upon the magnitudes and geographical patterns of the polluting sources. Predicting accurately the pollution levels in, say, a metropolitan area, would require a most detailed model of the social and economic structure of that area, of movements of persons and vehicles within it, and of the dynamics of its change over the coming years. There seems no reason for confidence that a veridical model can be constructed for this part of the system. As a further difficulty, information on the biological effects of pollution is so inexact that it makes no sense to attempt more than order-of-magnitude estimates. Given this degree of crudeness in the medical and socio-economic models, there is no point in modeling the rest of the system in detail (even if it were possible, which it is not). Modeling here calls for little more than back-of-an-envelope estimates (*Air Quality and Automobile Emission Control*, 1974).

4 Sensitivity Analysis versus Prediction

Discussions of simulation of macro-social processes, and the simulation models themselves, generally place a considerable emphasis upon prediction. The World Dynamics models referred to earlier (Meadows et al., 1974) are a good example of this emphasis. These models undertake to predict, for long spans of future years, the values of substantial numbers of demographic, economic, social, and environmental variables. I think no one, including the authors of the models, thinks that we know enough about the underlying dynamic mechanisms to predict anything but broad trends. In fact, the lessons we draw from the models are generally qualitative lessons about the impossibility of sustaining exponential growth indefinitely. These lessons can easily be demonstrated, however, with the aid of much smaller models that are analytically tractible, and hence require no simulation at all. The mass of detail generated by the world dynamics models appears to have no practical use and only an illusory appearance of accuracy.

In general, the emphasis on prediction in macro-social models is a misplaced emphasis. Neither do we have the knowledge of socio-economic mechanisms that would make such prediction possible, nor is it prediction that we need for policy purposes. Our concern is not to *forecast* the future but: (a) to understand the consequences of alternative *possible* futures, and (b) to understand which of these possible futures is associated with particular strategies or policy measures. Moreover, we generally have no important practical interest in the details of the year-by-year path that leads to any future state of affairs. We are more concerned with identifying the region to which the path leads. When this is the case, the method of comparative statics will make much more efficient use of available computing resources than will predictive dynamic modeling.

If our interest, for example, is in the relations among world population, income levels, environmental quality and the drain on resources, perhaps the most useful procedure is to model the steady state of the system for different levels of population and income, and under different assumptions, say, about our energy-producing technology. The computing resource that would be consumed in predicting the step-by-step course of a dynamic model can be used instead, in the steady-state model, to carry out sensitivity analyses and to evaluate alternative population and energy policies. The sensitivity analyses, by determining which variables in the system are of critical importance, can permit us to simplify the model further by focussing on those variables. Whatever computational capacity we recapture through simplification, we can put to work again by detailing the model along other dimensions—by introducing a finer regional breakdown of the data, for example.

There are, of course, situations where prediction is the name of the game. A business forecasting model is necessarily a dynamic predictive model. In a large range of cases, however, detailed prediction is neither possible nor very important. Much more important is an understanding of what are the key variables in shaping system equilibrium and what policy variables can have an effect on that equilibrium. In these cases, we are well advised to devote the computing resources we have available to sensitivity analyses and policy analysis rather than prediction.

5 Conclusion

A general lesson can be learned from the examples of the two previous sections of this paper. In simulation of social systems, we are often interested primarily in aggregative and longer-run effects that can be produced by aggregative, but perhaps robust, policy manipulations. Near-decomposability permits us to ignore the short-term, lower-level dynamic mechanisms of complex systems, treating these systems by the method of comparative statics, and examining the sensitivity of their behavior to changes in specific exogenous variables and policy variables. Hence, we may be able to avoid attempting detailed predictions of the temporal paths of variables under conditions where our ignorance of system mechanisms or where external "noise" impinging on the system makes such prediction infeasible.

No matter how large and fast our computers become, Nature will build systems too large and complex to be simulated in detail. Hence, the theory of simulation must always be concerned with computational efficiency. The exploitation of hierarchy and near decomposability are powerful tools for achieving such efficiency, and hence exploring the properties of extremely large social systems.

References

Air Quality and Automobile Emission Control. A Report by the Coordinating Committee on Air Quality Studies, National Academy of Sciences and National Academy of Engineering, Vol. 1, Summary Report, U. S. Government Printing Office, September 1974, ix. 130p.

Courtois, P. J., *Decomposability: A Queuing and Computer System Application*, New York: Academic Press, 1977.

Meadows, D., et al., *Dynamics of Growth in a Finite World*, New York: Wiley and Sons, 1974.

Nelson, R. J., 'Structure of Complex Systems' in Frederick Suppe and Peter D. Asquith (eds.), *Proceedings of the 1976 Biennial Meeting of the Philosophy of Science Association*, Volume 2, 523–542, East Lansing, Michigan: Philosophy of Science Association, 1976.

Simon, H. A., and Ando, A., 'Aggregation of Variables in Dynamic Systems', *Econometrica* 29: 111–138, April 1961.

Simon, H. A., 'How Complex are Complex Systems?' in Frederick Suppe and Peter D. Asquith (eds.), *Proceedings of the 1976 Biennial Meeting of the Philosophy of Science Association*, Vol. 2, 507–522, East Lansing, Michigan: Philosophy of Science Association, 1976.

Simon, H. A., *The Sciences of the Artificial* (Karl Taylor Compton Lectures), Cambridge: M.I.T. Press, Chap. 4, 1969.

I.5 Prediction and Prescription in Systems Modeling

Modeling is a principal—perhaps the primary—tool for studying the behavior of large complex systems. Forty years of experience in modeling systems on computers, which every year have grown larger and faster, have taught us that brute force does not carry us along a royal road to understanding such systems. Nature is capable of building, on the scale of microcosms or macrocosms or any scale between, systems whose complexity lies far beyond the reach of our computers and supercomputers, present or prospective. Even in environments as artificial and constricted as the game of chess we are faced with numbers on the order of 10 raised to the 120th power. The combinatorics of such numbers are almost beyond our imagining, and certainly beyond our capabilities for computation.

Modeling, then, calls for some basic principles to manage this complexity. We must separate what is essential from what is dispensable in order to capture in our models a simplified picture of reality which, nevertheless, will allow us to make the inferences that are important to our goals. It is optimistic to suppose that principles can be laid down that are so general as to apply to the whole range of modeling tasks. In numerical analysis, we have already developed many classes of algorithms that are specific to particular computational domains and fields of application. Nonetheless, it may be worthwhile to look at the broader aspects of modeling, and to see whether there are some useful things that can be said at a more general level.

I have organized my comments around the notions of prediction and prescription. When we model systems, we are usually (not always) interested in their dynamic behavior. Typically, we place our model at some initial point in phase space and watch it mark out a path through the future. We may do this with a number of different ends in view: we may wish to see if the model will settle down to a position of stable equilibrium; we may wish simply to predict future events (the weather); or we may wish to examine the prospective effects of policy decisions. I will not have much to say about the first of these goals; the second and third are what, in the title of this paper, I call prediction and prescription, respectively.

Chaos and Its Problems

From the beginning of human efforts to model systems—long before the computer era—linearity has dominated the computational scene, not because anyone believed that the systems of interest were truly linear, but simply for reasons of computational tractability. In a few cases, (which, fortunately, covered many of the simpler situations required by field theories in physics) nonlinear systems could be handled computationally, at least for idealized boundary conditions. But the centrality of computational tractability even in physics is marked by the large number of *theories*—for example, theories of the atomic nucleus—that are really proposals for retaining certain terms in approximations to more complete, but uncomputable, models and omitting others.

For the first three-quarters of this century, theories of nonlinear dynamics focused on two and three variable systems, which could be explored graphically, at least for their qualitative properties. If we look at a standard textbook like Andronov and Chaikin (1949), we see that the main interest was in characterizing the positions of stable and unstable equilibria of such systems and their limit cycles.

Although we knew full well that, at certain boundaries in phase space, paths could diverge that originated at points very close to each other, we chose usually to ignore these phenomena as *rare*. As a consequence, such topics as turbulence had to be handled wholly pragmatically, with empirical *Reynolds Numbers* and other parameters, and without much aid from mathematical modeling. Physical modeling, of course, was possible.

The rapid rise, in the last decade, of chaos theory, with its associated ideas of bifurcating systems, solitrons, strange attractors, and fractals, has changed all of this.[1] It has not, of course, taught us how to predict the paths of divergent systems. Rather, it has shown the fundamental reasons why such prediction may be impossible, now and forever. Furthermore, it has led us to consider that some of the important systems we should like to understand, including the weather and the economy, may be essentially chaotic.

On the other hand, the new mathematics of chaos has had some important positive messages for us. It has taught us to ask a set of different questions about dynamic systems. What are the *magic numbers* that govern bifurcation and hence, the transition, for example, from the smooth flow of liquids to turbulence? How can we renormalize fractal-like systems so that we can understand their behavior on different temporal or spatial scales? What are the shapes of the strange attractors that will bound the final, if chaotic, motions of such systems? How can we explain the curious *anti-entropic* structures, solitrons among them, that are created by the dynamics of many simple nonlinear systems? These questions, and some of their answers, are the valuable gifts that the theory of chaos has brought us, to console us for the loss of our powers of prediction.

The implications of these developments for the modeling of large socio-economic systems, environmental-energy systems, or ecological systems have hardly begun to be digested. One implication, for systems that we have reason to suspect are divergent or chaotic, is that we must give up prediction as the primary goal of modeling. Of course, chaos is essentially a statistical condition. It does not imply that *anything goes*. We may, for example, despair of tracing the future course of business cycles without renouncing the goal of making statements about the long-run development of an economy. For instance, we might make perfectly sound statements about the upper limits on per capita GNP without being able to say how closely, or when, these limits will be approached.

With these preliminary remarks about our new glimpses of chaos, and more generally, our new awareness of the wealth of possibilities that can emerge from nonlinearity, I will turn to the use of models for predictions.

Prediction

It is obvious why we are so fascinated by prediction of the future—whether achieved through horoscopes or otherwise. The future is *our* future, or at least the future of our children and their children. It bodes well or ill for us. Moreover, if we could forecast it, perhaps there are some actions we could take to alleviate its ill effects and enhance its favorable ones. If rain is predicted, we can carry an umbrella, and if sunshine, we can plan a picnic or an excursion to the beach. Notice, as in the example of the weather, that we may predict without being able to influence the predicted event. In fact, this is the simplest and commonest kind of prediction.

Much of what is called *analysis* in engineering design also comes under the heading of prediction. When we analyze the stresses in an airplane wing, we look for unstable roots that predict that the wing would sooner or later break off. Here, we are not interested in the time path, but in the possibility or likelihood of an event. A great deal of the power of engineering analyses, and their computational feasibility, resides in the fact that we do not have to track dynamic paths in detail, but only discover the stable and unstable equilibria of the system.

Modeling that undertakes to predict the time paths of large systems does not have an unmitigated record of success. Demography is a discipline that has had sobering experiences in the prediction of future populations. I need hardly mention dynamic economic models, which are regarded as admirable if they can do a little better than chance for a year or two into the future. And no one is making claims for the predictive accuracy of the Club of Rome report (Meadows et al. 1972), now a decade and a half old.

The Club of Rome report is an interesting case, which deserves a little more examination. Nowadays, it is often used as evidence that prophecies of gloom and doom are wholly misleading—which is surely the wrong conclusion to draw from it. Economists have complained that the Club of Rome model had the wrong equations in it, not derived from assumptions of the maximization of subjective expected utility. That also is surely a wrong-headed reaction because those assumptions are known to bear little relation to the real world.

The core of the Club of Rome model was a set of nonlinear dynamic mechanisms, including mechanisms that cause population and capital to increase as functions of present population and capital, and which, insufficiently damped by other constraints, cause exponential growth not only of these variables but of other system variables. One does not have to run such a model very many hours on a large computer—in fact, one does not need to run it at all—in order to conclude that, for many ranges of values of its parameters, such a system will sooner or later explode, at least in the sense of producing large limit cycles of booms and busts of population and other variables (such as per capita income). The basic idea was demonstrated many years ago with simple two-equation models of prey/predator relations (for example, the rise and fall of lynx and rabbit populations).

Nor is the exact time of the explosion a very interesting datum. The fundamental conclusion drawn from the model, that exponential growth cannot be sustained indefinitely, is entirely true, has enormous import for public policy, and could have been inferred from textbook treatments of dynamic systems without any computation.

I am not saying that the Club of Rome model should not have been run. Perhaps it required the actual plots of the time paths of the variables, however speculative, to attract and briefly focus public attention upon the dangers of a world having unconstrained growth of population and energy use. If so, then every dollar spent on computing these time paths was well spent, and the inaccuracy of the predictions was irrelevant to the significance of the message conveyed.

Leaving aside for thc moment questions of political impact, one could argue that the Club of Rome model represents a misapplication of computational resources. The lesson the report aimed to teach could have been taught with a three-equation model computed (if we insist on looking at time series) on a pocket calculator. The computation thus saved could have been used for other purposes, which I will outline later.

There may even be positive harm, other than use of expensive computers, in carrying out such a modeling exercise when the data and equations of the model are only approximately accurate at best. It may give sceptics entirely too much ammunition for questioning even the conclusions that can be drawn validly from the model. Something of this sort happened to the Club of Rome report, but the modeling of nuclear winter provides an even better example.[2]

The basic data that are available for modeling the atmospheric and climatological effects of a nuclear exchange are very crude. The available theories of the dynamics of the atmosphere are equally inadequate to the problem at hand. Given these limitations, it was a heroic effort to construct a possible scenario of the aftermath of nuclear warfare. In the course of building the models, all sorts of assumptions had to be made about the probable values of the parameters concerned. The behavior of the models was a sensitive function of the superposition of these estimated values. In the modeling, some effort was exerted, quite creditably, to examine the robustness of the results under variations in the values of the parameters.

The result, as we know, was rather indeterminate. For some ranges of assumptions (read *for some scenarios of nuclear exchange*) the consequences for the weather, and hence, for human survival, were serious. Within other ranges of assumptions, the consequences were much milder—it appeared that the species might well survive! But the lesson that was drawn from these results by a large segment of the public, and especially by those who were previously unconvinced of the need for nuclear disarmament, was that Doomsday was not guaranteed. And if not guaranteed, Doomsday might not come. The nuclear winter issue rapidly lost political force and disappeared from the public view.

Was this the correct conclusion to draw from the analyses, and did the form of the analyses influence the form of the conclusion? My own answer to the first question is "no," and to the second one, "yes." Kahneman, Slovic and Tversky (1982) have taught us that the response of a patient to the statement, "You have a twenty percent chance of dying during this operation," is very different from the response to the statement, "You have an eighty percent chance of surviving the operation." (The latter statement is interpreted much more optimistically than the former.) From this we can conclude that the response to the statement, "Humanity is more likely than not to survive the climatological effects of a nuclear exchange," will be more optimistic than the response to, "There is a distinct chance that humanity will suffer enormous casualties from the climatological effects of a nuclear exchange."

Let me describe one other example of *iffy* modeling where the response to the findings surprised the modelers. A few years ago, a couple of experiments were run on seeding the clouds of a hurricane (far from the coast) to see if this treatment would reduce the strength of the winds. A decision tree analysis was performed on the data, gathered from two hurricanes over a period of a day or two for each. The decision tree analysis of these very noisy data showed that, even for rather conservative values of the priors, seeding the hurricane would probably produce decidedly beneficial consequences. When these data were presented to a knowledgeable and responsible group of scientists (mostly physicists: it was the U.S. President's Science Advisory Committee), they voted, I think unanimously, that seeding should not be used *for real* until additional data were obtained.

Expected values cut no ice with this group. I think you can guess some of the thoughts running through their minds. If we seed a hurricane just off New Orleans, and as a result it is redirected to Mobile, who will sue whom? There is a strong belief in our culture and in our legal system that nonfeasance is less heinous than misfeasance or malfeasance. Even apart from the courts of law, we feel greater responsibility for our action than for our inaction.

It appears, then, that there is a good chance that the findings derived from *iffy* predictive modeling efforts will be ignored, or if not ignored, misinterpreted. One could take this as a reason for not modeling under circumstances where the results are not likely to be definitive. I would draw a slightly different conclusion: that we should redesign our modeling efforts, as far as possible, to focus them on the questions that we *can* answer more or less definitively.

In the case of the nuclear winter, perhaps the question to be asked should have been: Is it at all possible that a nuclear exchange will cause widespread death and suffering through its climatological effects? In the case of the cloud-seeding study, perhaps the question to be asked should have been, How much additional experimental data, and what kinds of studies on legal liability do we need before we can make a serious decision about seeding hurricanes?

Before we leave the topic of prediction, I must mention one final malady that plagues predictive models of social systems. Such systems have numerous feedback loops, but that, in itself, is not the problem. We constantly model with success engineering systems that are full of passive feedback loops. But the feedback loops in social systems are not passive but predictive. Each of the participants may be trying to forecast the behavior of other actors and of the system in order to adapt his or her own behavior advantageously.

The von Neumann and Morgenstern (1944) theory of games was the first large-scale systematic attempt to deal with this problem, although as early as Cournot economists have been aware of it. The most recent attempt at a solution is the Muth–Lucas theory of rational expectations (Lucas and Sargent 1981). What these impressive theories have provided us with is not so much a solution of the problem as a demonstration of its deep intractability.

More than forty years of intensive research leaves us with the rather firmly established conclusion that there is no unequivocal definition of rationality under conditions of mutual outguessing. Lacking such definition, we have no way, a priori, of postulating expectational or reactional equations for models of social systems, and precious little relevant empirical data for postulating such equations a posteriori. The theorems of game theory and rational expectations have added a new hazard to be faced by designers of social and economic models aimed at prediction.

The difficulties loom especially large for models of competitive, confrontational situations, that either are zero-sum, or are regarded by the participants as being so. For example, models of mutual deterrence, and other models of international relations are exquisitely sensitive to assumptions about the formation of expectations and reactions to the behavior of other parties. Here again, it may be impossible to obtain answers to our predictive questions, and we may be well advised to ask a different set of questions instead.

If we change the questions that we seek to answer in our modeling, then it is also probable that we will want to change the models and our methods of analyzing them. It is to this question that I would like to turn next.

Prescription

Generally, modeling serves policy. We construct and run models because we want to understand the consequences of taking one decision or another. Predictive models are only a special case where we seek to predict events we cannot control in order to adapt to them better. We do not expect to change the weather, but we can take steps to moderate its effects. We predict populations so that we can plan to meet their needs for food and education. We predict business cycles in order to plan our investments and production levels.

Of course, our models may, and frequently do, contain policy variables. Our demographic models may contain variables that represent birth control policies or the effects of public health measures. (Usually, we simply incorporate these in the estimates of birth and death rates.) Our economic models may contain variables that represent government fiscal and monetary policies. Our model of the eutrophication of a lake may include the quantities of phosphates we drain into it. When we include such variables in models, our intent in modeling changes from simple prediction to prescription.

When our goal is prescription rather than prediction, then we can no longer take it for granted that what we want to compute are time series. We do not care what the water quality will be in the lake next year or the year after that. What we care about is how much the phosphate input needs to be reduced to eliminate the unwanted eutrophication. Moreover, given the crudity of our data and the approximate nature of our model of the eutrophication process, we are interested mainly in orders of magnitude. This means that we can greatly simplify our calculations, possibly with the result that the back of an envelope will suffice.

Given my fondness for computers, I always find it a bit regrettable when I reach that conclusion: that I don't need a computer, but only an envelope and a pencil. But facts must be faced. Intelligent approximation, not brute force computation, is still the key to effective modeling.

Let me return to the Club of Rome problem, viewing it now, not as a problem of prediction but as one of prescription. What are the important questions to be answered by the modeling? The important questions, I submit, are: What is the steady-state population that can be sustained on Earth at a reasonable standard of living, and the steady-state rate of energy production that can be sustained without serious damage to the environment? These questions, of course, engender others: What is a reasonable standard of living? What are the alternative sustainable energy sources, and what are their relative advantages and disadvantages? What are the feasible ways of disposing of the wastes produced by people, by production, and by energy generation?

If these are the right questions, or a reasonable approximation thereto, then we probably do not care about a predictive model that tells us, for each point in time, just where we stand. What we want is a model of the steady state, a model of an acceptable world where all constraints on resources and environment are met, more or less permanently. If we can define such an acceptable world, then it will be time to consider the paths we must follow to reach it. Nor will it be important, even at this second stage, to map these paths in detail. Good attention to feedback and correction will get us to our goal even without specific temporal plans.

Let me provide just one more example of the utility of steady-state analysis. A national decision has just been reached that nuclear wastes will be buried in a depository in Yucca Mountain in Nevada. The wastes must be retained for some 10,000 years, and there are some large uncertainties as to what will happen to them over that enormous period, but that is not my concern here. Rough figures are available on the rate at which plutonium wastes are accumulating in the United States at present levels of nuclear power generation. We know also the size of the proposed depository.

Using these three numbers (storage time, rate of production, and size of depository) we compute on the back of the envelope the number of such depositories that are necessary in the steady state. The approximate number is 50 to 70 for the United States alone. I do not propose to draw any policy implications here from this number. I simply present it as an interesting, and possibly significant, fact and as an illustration of the utility of steady-state analysis.

Our practical concern in planning for the future is what we must do *now* to bring that future about. We use our future goals to detect what may be irreversible present actions that we must avoid, and to disclose gaps in our knowledge (for example, the feasibility of fusion energy) that must be closed soon so that choices may be made later. Our decisions today require us to know our goals, but not the exact path along which we will reach them.

Analyzing the conditions for a steady state may require a rather detailed model of the interactions of the variables. One could think of linear programming as a possible framework for such a model, but perhaps that formulation is too restrictive. But however we formulate it, we can devote our computational resources to studying the steady-state interactions rather than plotting time paths in which we have no real interest, and which certainly will have no reality. Redeploying our computational resources in this way, we will be in a position to explore many alternative scenarios and to examine the robustness of our results and their sensitivities to changes in our assumptions or in policy.

I should not like to argue that we are *never* interested in making predictions of time paths. But if we take the goal of our modeling to be prescriptive rather than predictive, we will at least examine that issue at the outset, rather than taking for granted that temporal prediction is the name of the game. We will also consider carefully what aspects of the situation can be modeled at a level of certainty and accuracy that is commensurate with the decisions we are trying to make. We will not run the computer simply because it is there.

Aggregation

I have proposed one way in which the computational demands of modeling can be brought within acceptable bounds. Are there other ways in which we can cope with complexity? I am sure that there are a number, but I would like to focus on a particular one that is familiar to me. The complexity of our models of a system can often be reduced greatly if we are willing and able to limit the frequency range of the dynamics that interest us.

Elsewhere, I have made the argument that the systems, both natural and manmade, in which we are interested are almost always hierarchical (Simon 1981). That is to say, they have a boxes-within-boxes architecture. Quarks combine to form protons, protons and neutrons form nuclei,

nuclei and electrons form atoms, small groups of atoms form radicals and similar components of molecules, and these components form molecules, and so on, through another half dozen levels of biological structure, and social structure above that.

The important property, for our purposes, of such hierarchical systems is that the behavior of the units at any specific level can be described and explained without the need for a *detailed* picture of the structures and behavior at the levels below. That is why we have been able to suspend, from skyhooks, the entire structure of biology, chemistry, and physics while awaiting the appropriation of 12 billion dollars for a supercollider that will tell us what the fundamental particles, those that quarks are made of, are really like.

The hierarchical structure of the world enables us to understand it from the top down (or from the middle out), and in fact to study it one layer at a time with only moderate concern for the layers immediately below and above. Only gross, aggregate features of the layer below show up in the next layer above. Thus, for many purposes of celestial mechanics, we can treat the planets and their satellites as massive points, without extension or structure. For many purposes of genetics, we can treat DNA as a string of nucleotides, without further internal chemical or geometric structure.

From a mathematical viewpoint, hierarchical structures can be represented as nearly-completely-decomposable dynamic systems (Simon and Ando 1961). That is to say, when we examine the matrix of coefficients that represents the dynamics of such a structure, we find that the variables can be grouped in clusters, with high average rates of interaction among variables belonging to a single cluster, but much lower rates of interaction between clusters. Taking into account different orders of magnitude in the rates of interaction, we may find this pattern repeated at many levels—the boxes-within-boxes structure mentioned earlier.

It is easy to show that under these conditions the dynamic behavior of the system can be factored into different frequency ranges, each corresponding to a particular level of interaction rates. When we are studying high frequency interactions, hence short-term behavior, we need consider only the interactions within the smallest clusters, treating each cluster as independent of the others. We can then aggregate, replacing the detail of each cluster by a few aggregate properties (for example, in the astronomical example, its total mass, its center of mass, and the location and velocity of that center). Using these aggregates, we can then examine the behavior of the clusters at the next higher level over a somewhat longer span of time. The process can be repeated indefinitely, as long as the property of near decomposability is present at the appropriate level. Physicists will recognize this as the trick that underlies renormalization.

Symbolic Models

Thus far, I have been writing as if numbers were the natural stuff of which models are created. If we were to take a census of all the computer models that have been created in the past forty years, that assumption would surely appear to be correct. Following up our success of the past three hundred years in using real numbers (and occasionally imaginaries) to represent the world, we have mostly programmed our computers to make numerical calculations.

In fact, until quite recently, many computer users, even quite sophisticated ones, supposed that numbers were the only symbols that computers could process—that somewhere in the bowels of computer memory were great globs of binary symbols that could only be interpreted as numbers. We are all now aware that that is false. Computers can process symbols of all kinds, including symbols that represent natural language or diagrams (Simon 1981).

Human beings are great users of natural language, and much less frequent users of numbers. It is not at all obvious that the best way to model human behavior is to describe it numerically. Of course, if we are modeling an economic system, prices and quantities of goods and services are quite natural symbols to use. But what about a political system? What are the units of power? Of persuasion? Of patriotism and nationalistic fervor?

For some years now, researchers in artificial and cognitive science have been exploring the capabilities of nonnumerical models. The best developed, perhaps, are models of human problem solving (Newell and Simon 1972). In many of these programs, not a single real number appears. I cannot, in this paper, describe the ways in which situations are described nonnumerically, but I can give one example of this kind of modeling.

Jaime Carbonell (1979) constructed a program, often referred to as "The Goldwater Machine," that undertakes to predict how a specific political figure will respond to a specific public event. The program is given information about the political views and values of a public figure (Goldwater was used for debugging purposes), and is also provided with some inference processes that can reason about these views and values and apply them to particular states of affairs. The program is then given information about a particular event (a development in Middle East politics, say), and asked to predict what the public figure who is being modeled will say about the event.

I will leave the matter with this single tempting example. So far there are not a great many others. Here is an exceptionally promising direction for modeling social behavior, not only of individuals, but of groups and societies as well.

Conclusion

There is no single moral that I should like to draw from my discussion of modeling unless it be the commonplace moral that we will do a better job if, before we begin, we ask what our goals are—what questions we are trying to answer. In modeling, as in any other human activity, there is a certain amount of historical inertia. Predictive models bulked large in the early history of modeling, and especially in our enthusiastic efforts to explore the potential of computers when they first became available to us. Moreover, again for historical reasons, we tended to conceptualize our computer as a number cruncher, and we did not immediately see its potential for qualitative and symbolic modeling that did not use numbers.

Before we begin a modeling task, we need to ask whether we need temporal detail, and if so, what amount of it can be supported by the kinds of data and theories that we have available. We need to ask whether a good understanding of steady states may be more important to us than a tracing of time paths. We need to ask whether we can simplify the systems we are modeling by making use of their hierarchical properties to aggregate, or in other ways. And we need to ask whether there are aspects of the situation of interest that are better modeled symbolically, in words or pictures, rather than numerically.

We need to ask these questions because, at best, the situations we wish to model are orders of magnitude more complex than the most elaborate models that supercomputers of the present and future will sustain. We need to apply keen intelligence, whether of people or computers, to make sure that we capture in our models the aspects of the would's systems that are important to us.

Notes

1. Cvitanovic (1984) gives an excellent introduction to chaos theory and reprints many of the original sources.

2. On nuclear winter, see National Research Council, Committee on the Atmospheric Effects of Nuclear Explosions (1985).

Acknowledgment

This research was supported by the Office of Navel Research under contract N00014-86-K-0768 and by the Department of Defense under ARPA order 3597, monitored by the Air Force Avionics Laboratory under contract F33615-81-K-1539. This paper was given by invitation at the 15th Anniversary Conference that took place in June 1988 at the International Institute for Applied Systems Analysis, Laxenburg, Austria.

References

Andronov, A. A., and C. E. Chaikin. 1949. *Theory of Oscillations*. Princeton University Press, Princeton, New Jersey.

Carbonell, J. G. 1979. *Subjective Understanding: Computer Models of Belief Systems*. Yale University, Department of Computer Science, New Haven, Conn. Distributed by the Defense Technical Information Center.

Cvitanovic, P. (ed.) 1984. *Universality in Chaos*. Adam Hilger, Bristol, England.

Kahneman, D., P., Slovic and A. Tversky (eds.) 1982. *Judgment Under Uncertainty: Heuristics and Biases*. Cambridge University Press, Cambridge, England.

Lucas, R. E., and T. J. Sargent (eds.). 1981. *Rational Expectations and Economic Practice*. University of Minnesota Press, Minneapolis, Minn.

Meadows, D. H., et al. 1972. *The Limits to Growth: A Report for the Club of Rome's Project on the Predicament of Mankind*. Universe Books, New York.

National Research Council, Committee on the Atmospheric Effects of Nuclear Explosions. 1985. *The Effects on the Atmosphere of a Major Nuclear Exchange*. National Academy Press, Washington, D.C.

Newell, A., and H. A. Simon. 1972. *Human Problem Solving*. Prentice-Hall, Englewood Cliffs, N.J.

Simon, H. A. 1981. *The Sciences of the Artificial*, 2nd ed. The MIT Press, Cambridge, Mass.

Simon, H. A., and A. Ando. 1961. Aggregation of Variables in Dynamic Systems. *Econometrica* **29**, 111–138.

von Neumann, J., and O. Morgenstern. 1944. *Theory of Games and Economic Behavior*. Princeton University Press, Princeton, N.J.

II THE ADVANCE OF INFORMATION TECHNOLOGY

Strictly speaking, Chapter II.1 does not belong to the topic of this Section, for it is not concerned with information technology. But it *is* concerned with technological change, and this seems a convenient place to put it. Stimulated by a paper by Artle, Humes, and Varaiya, it takes a second look at the model of Chapter III.1 in volume 1, which analyses the rural to urban population shifts produced by the agricultural and industrial revolution. The present chapter aims at showing that, used appropriately, the method of comparative statics (which I employed in the original paper) and the method of excess demand analysis (employed by Artle and his colleagues) are equivalent and give the same results.

Like the chapters of Part I.B, the remaining chapters of Part 2 come out of my concerns with questions of public policy (in this case, policies relating to computers and electronic communications) rather than out of my technical research. They are correspondingly informal in approach. To my mind, futurology does not often lend itself to highly sophisticated methodologies, and in any event, before formal methods can conceivably be applied, we must take care that we have represented the problems correctly.

Therefore, I will not apologize for the fact that Chapters II.2, II.3, II.4, and II.5 represent some of my thinking-aloud about the present and prospective effects of the computer and the new information technology on organizations and management, hence on the behavior of the business firm. I have not studied the effects in any formal way, but I have been intimately associated with these developments for nearly forty years, and have taken some pains to construct a frame of reference for thinking about them. These papers mainly communicate that frame of reference. They supplement and bring up to date my earlier writings on these matters in *The New Science of Management Decision* and elsewhere.

The first half of Chapter II.2 is devoted to showing that, with the advent of electronic technology, information is, in a very real sense, no longer scarce. What is now scarce is human time to attend to information. The implications of this fact for the structure of organizational information systems are then examined. The second half of the chapter looks at another part of the picture: the impact of modern information systems on the relations among human beings in the workplace and on the human (or inhuman) qualities of the workplace. When the chapter was written, the Worldwide Web was not a reality. Whether it is yet a reality in any practically significant sense is a debatable question, but in any event, we have not had nearly enough experience with it to permit me to revise the views that are expressed in this chapter to take account of the extensive electronic networking of the world's organizations and populations that appears imminent.

There is one comment, however, about Web-like developments that I can make with some confidence. The Web is, in an important respect, fundamentally different from the Internet with which some of us in computer science have been living for more than two decades and which provides us with our electronic mail (whether we want it or not). In the Internet, the initiator of a message selects one or more targets ("recipients" might be a more neutral term) and transmits the message to them, willy-nilly. For this reason, it is intrinsically insensitive to the scarcity of human attention. All too readily, it pollutes the ether with information.

In the Web, on the other hand, the initiators of information simply store it (providing the storage themselves) and make it accessible to anyone who wishes to use it (and is clever enough to find it). Its model is the library rather than the postal system. Unlike the Internet, it respects the scarcity of attention, but to be useful, it requires the development of sophisticated artificial intelligence systems to assist in searching for information that is wanted. The uncertainties about the Web center on how we will provide these intelligent search mechanisms, and on various issues about the control and financing of the whole system.

Chapter II.3 identifies the ubiquity of present and potential computer applications (comparable to the ubiquity of applications of mechanical power) as the basic reason why information technology has genuinely revolutionary implications for society. The "ubiquity" depends, of course, on what work now done by humans will in time be doable by machines. The chapter argues that computers, like other artifacts, are neither good nor bad. Their net positive or negative value to society will depend on how we shape the social institutions that use them. It then goes on to discuss briefly the scope (now and in the future) of computer capabilities, and draws conclusions from this discussion about the present and prospective contribution to the processes of education.

Chapter II.4 returns to the theme of an information-rich world in which the time available to people to attend to information is very scarce. It draws lessons (reinforced by the history of management information systems) for the design of information systems, and surveys the current state of the art in artificial intelligence, with comments on its future prospects.

Chapter II.5 takes a somewhat broader view of the relations of human beings to their organizations, considering, but not limiting itself to, the effects of information technology. It asks how current changes in the workplace are affecting individual initiative, satisfaction with work, and employees' attachment to or alienation from the organizations to which they belong. These questions frame, in turn, the issues that are dealt with in Part 3, where we turn our attention to the nature of business organizations, and the relation of organizations to markets.

The Crystal Ball

Chapter II.5 was written in 1978, just after I published a revised edition of my *The New Science of Management Decision*, a book that surveys many of the topics that are discussed in Chapters II.2 through II.5. Before writing the present lines, I looked back at that book, as well as the chapter, to see how ill-aimed and out-of-date were my predictions made almost two decades ago (before the advent of personal computers, if you can remember that ancient day). With a bit of surprise but considerable gratification, I found a high level of consistency of what I wrote then with developments up to the present.

In my judgment, none of the technological or social changes that have taken place in the ensuing years call for any important revision in the conclusions that are drawn in either the chapter or the book. We still hear a great deal about the "underclass" that is being created in our society, and there is little doubt that income inequality has increased in the past two decades. But attributing this shift, or the persistence of undesired levels of unemployment, or the high unemployment rate among the least educated to the burgeoning of information technology seems to me wholly unfounded in either fact or theory—for reasons that are addressed in the chapter and at greater length in *The New Science of Management Decision.*

In the introduction to Part III of Volume 1 of *Models of Bounded Rationality*, I indulged in a bit of boasting about my track record as a forecaster of technological change (especially in the domains of automation and nuclear power). I believe I can claim that the record continues to be good; we shall see how it fares in the future.

To turn from boasting to analysis, it may be instructive to ask what makes it possible to predict major effects of exceedingly rapid technological changes. A number of factors deserve mention.

The state of the art First, you must be thoroughly informed about the current state of the art, both in practice and in research, including the "first derivatives"—the current rates of change. This kind of information allows you to push a little distance into the future (five years?) without danger of great error. No technology that has not yet appeared on the horizon is likely to have a great effect on the world before five years have passed.

Scarce factors Second, you must think long and hard about what are the key factors, and especially the key scarce factors, or bottlenecks, that pace the rate of change. In predicting the advance of computers and information technology, the key factors have been (1) advances in size and speed of computers, and the accompanying decline in computation cost, (2) advances in software, especially for artificial intelligence applications, and (3) the growing imbalance between our capacity for producing information and our capacity for absorbing it. Too exclusive attention to item (1) has been responsible for overoptimistic predictions about the rate of introduction of new computer applications.

Too generalized a treatment of item (2) can cause errors in both directions. Of crucial importance for prediction have been the very different rates of progress in (a) "routine" numerical computation, (b) artificial intelligence applied to mental tasks (e.g., medical diagnosis, engineering design) and (c) artificial intelligence applied to robotics—sensory and motor processes. We can see continuing rapid expansion of computer usage in domain (a), a very recent initiation of rapid expansion in (b), and much slower progress to date in (c), but with substantial recent acceleration. Good knowledge of the state of the art, and perhaps more important, of the opportunities and problems that govern the specific rates of progress in these different directions, permit reasonably accurate predictions to be made of their relative rates of advance.

Inattention to item (3), the scarcity of the time people have available for absorbing information, has had and continues to have unfortunate consequences for the design of information systems. There has been, and continues to be, a rather consistently repeated problem with respect to

(3): new systems are designed principally by computer experts (hardware and software experts), sometimes assisted by accountants or others familiar with the system inputs. These system designers are seldom experts on the needs of system users.

So we have had management information systems that supply managers with information without asking what decisions the managers make and what information would be useful in making them. We have had computer-aided instruction systems that exploit all the glamour and color of monitor displays ("virtual reality" and all that) without asking how people extract information from displays and use it to draw inferences, and without ascertaining the rates at which people can do these things. This is an old weakness in engineering design, not peculiar to computers: we become fascinated with out technical capabilities and design sophisticated hammers which go around looking for nails that are shaped so as to be hammerable by them.

Predicting dates A third factor underlying successful prediction is to pay more attention to relative rates of change than to the dates when particular developments are going to occur. Of course, predicting without dates can be a cheap cop-out—predicting, for example, that at some time our Sun will burn out. But there is a middle ground. As I suggested earlier, we are frequently less interested in the specific date when something is going to happen than in what we must do to facilitate (or prevent) its happening. Near-future forecasts and forecasts of near-future rates of change are the only forecasts of critical importance, for it is to these that we must react. Forecasts for the more distant future can more profitably take the form of scenarios of prospective steady states that can be modified by changing policy variables, and thereby examining alternative futures.

My most serious "failure" in prediction, which wasn't actually a failure, occurred in 1958, when Newell and I picked four advances in artificial intelligence that we predicted would occur within ten years. All of them have occurred, or are about to occur (a computer program as the World's chess champion is the one that remains), but we missed the timing of that last one by a factor of about four. We can debate whether that is good or bad predicting, but it provides an obvious target for the naysayers who like to remonstrate against "hype" (which sometimes comes to mean predictions they don't agree with).

Why Predict?

It might be asked why a scientist should be motivated to predict the directions in which events are going to move in his or her area of expertise. The answer seems obvious: large social consequences may hang upon these movements and on our success in anticipating and modifying them. The scientist, who is better qualified than others to carry out sound predictive analysis in his field of expertise, may well feel a sense of social responsibility for providing assessments of the changes likely to take place. The predictions may turn out to be wrong—they are almost certain to be wrong in detail—but if made with care, they are less likely to be wrong than the predictions of those who have little knowledge of the field. A great sufficiency of the latter kind of predictions are always forthcoming.

There is, of course, the well-known fact that preoccupation with a field generally produces optimism about it and a consequent positive predictive bias. But fear and ignorance also produce predictive biases, usually with the opposite sign. The best safeguard we have against biases, and the best basis for interpreting and correcting the predictions others make, comes from full disclosure of interest and conflict of interest, matters in which our society has acquired considerable sophistication in recent years.

References

Simon, H. A. (1977). *The new science of management decision* (rev. ed.). Englewood Cliffs, NJ: Prentice-Hall.

Simon, H. A. & Newell, A. (1978). Heuristic problem solving: The next advance in operations research. *Operations Research*, *6*, 1–10.

II.1 The Rural–Urban Population Balance Again

1 Introduction

The economic determinants of the rural-urban population balance are of considerable interest both for the economic history of the industrialized part of today's world, and for the urbanization processes that are now going on in the developing nations. Some 35 years ago (1947), I published a paper on these topics, and quite recently (1977, 1979), Artle, Humes and Varaiya have returned to the same questions, proposing a new method of analysis and extending my earlier results.

It is my purpose here to examine further the relation between my original analysis and that set forth in the first paper by Artle et al., both with respect to the methods of analysis employed in these two papers, and with respect to one of their substantive findings. In particular:

1. Artle et al. (1977, p. 186) state that in the case where there is an improvement in productivity in only one sector (say, manufacturing) and not in the other (say, agriculture), 'no definite conclusion about the change in the division of labor can be made for this case, within the framework of Simon's paper, unless a different method of analysis is used.'
2. These authors (1977, p. 187) also state that the method of analysis they use 'provides sufficient information to draw fairly general conclusions about the direction of the flow of labor from one sector to the other. In particular, it will be shown that Simon's proposition about the effect of equal rates of productivity increase and Baumol's case of "unbalanced growth" follow as special cases of a more general result.'

In the second and third sections of the present paper, I shall undertake to show that the method of analysis I used in my 1947 paper (comparative statics) and the method of analysis used by Artle, Humes and Varaiya (1977) (excess demand analysis) are in fact equivalent and lead to precisely the same conclusions. In particular, I will derive their result in the case where there is a productivity improvement in only one sector using my method of comparative statics.

In the fourth section of the paper I will consider the economic meaning of the Theorem 4.2 of Artle et al. (1977, p. 191) which states that: "In the case of unbalanced growth, labor migrates towards the progressive (non-progressive) sector if the demand for its output is elastic (inelastic) to its own price."

The analysis of these last two sections will remind us of some classical relations, discussed many years ago by Henry Schultz, among the different price and income elasticities that can be defined for models of the sort considered here.

2 Comparative Statics and Neutral Technological Change

The two papers under discussion postulate identical models of a two-sector economy, with equilibrium determined by constrained maximization of consumer utilities and producer profits. My analysis (comparative statics) was carried out by introducing changes in the productivities of one or both sectors, and then comparing the new equilibrium with the original one, in order to ascertain the changes that would take place in prices, quantity of output of each sector, and employment in each sector. Artle et al. compute the shifts in the prices that will prevent a shift of labor between the two sectors (i.e., prices that will equilibrate the new marginal values of product with the labor costs), and use these prices to compute the resulting excess demands for goods.

In order to show that the two methods obtain the same results, it is necessary for me to summarize my model briefly. Both methods of analysis require about the same amount of algebra to reach their conclusions, so I will employ my original procedures, and retain most of my original notation.

Consider commodities A and M of which the quantities q_a and q_m are produced with quantities x_a and x_m, respectively, of labor:

$$q_a = \xi(x_a), \qquad q_m = \eta(x_m). \tag{1}$$

The total supply of labor is fixed:

$$x_a + x_m = X = \text{constant}. \tag{2}$$

The utility of consumers is given by an index, $\phi = \phi(q_a, q_m)$. The profits of producers of A and M, respectively, are

$$\pi_a = q_a p_a - x_a, \qquad \pi_m = q_m p_m - x_m. \tag{3}$$

where p_a and p_m are commodity prices, while the wage rate is taken as unity. Then total money product is

$$I = q_a p_a + q_m p_m. \tag{4}$$

The conditions for equilibrium with utility and profit maximization are

$$\phi_a p_m = \phi_m p_a \quad \text{where} \quad \phi_Z = (\partial\phi/\partial q_Z), \tag{5}$$

$$p_a\xi_x = 1, \qquad p_m\eta_x = 1 \quad \text{where} \quad \xi_x = (\partial\xi/\partial x_a), \quad \eta_x = (\partial\eta/\partial x_m). \tag{6}$$

Sufficient conditions for maximization are given in equations (7) and (10) of my 1947 paper. They are

$$\phi_{aa} - 2(p_a/p_m)\phi_{am} + (p_a^2/p_m^2)\phi_{mm} < 0, \quad \text{and} \tag{7}$$

$$p_a(\partial\xi_x/\partial x_a) < 0, \qquad p_m(\partial\eta)x/\partial x_m) < 0, \tag{8}$$

where the ϕ_{xy} are second partial derivatives: $\partial^2\phi/\partial x\,\partial y$.

We now suppose that a technological advance occurs in both sectors. We designate by $\bar{q}_a$, $\bar{q}_m$, etc., the new values of the variables, and we suppose the new production function to be of the form:

$$\bar{a}_a = (1+\rho)\xi(\bar{x}_a), \qquad \bar{q}_m = (1+\sigma)\eta(\bar{x}_m), \quad \rho,\sigma > 0, \tag{9}$$

The other equations are unchanged in form.

Next, we calculate the changes in the equilibrium values of the variables, defining

$$\delta q_a = \bar{q}_a - q_a, \qquad \delta q_m = \bar{q}_m - q_m, \quad \text{etc.} \tag{10}$$

Now by straightforward, if tedious, algebra we can express δx_a as a function of ρ and σ [equivalent to equation (22) of Simon (1947)]:

$$\delta x_a = [p_a p_m/(\gamma + p_a p_m \varepsilon)][-\rho(q_a\beta + \phi_m p_a) + \sigma(q_m\alpha + \phi_a p_m)], \tag{11}$$

where

$$\alpha = (p_a\phi_{mm} - p_m\phi_{am}) < 0, \beta = (p_m\phi_{aa} - p_a\phi_{ma}) < 0, \quad \text{and}$$
$$\gamma = (p_m\beta + p_a\alpha) < 0; \quad \varepsilon = (\phi_m p_a^2\xi_{xx} + \phi_a p_m^2\eta_{xx}) < 0,$$

where the inequalities follow from the conditions for stability of equilibrium.

The denominator of (11) is negative, but in the numerator there are both positive terms $(-\rho q_a\beta, \sigma\phi_a p_m)$ and negative terms $(-\rho\phi_m p_a, \sigma q_m\alpha)$, so that the sign of δq_a is indeterminate.

In Simon (1947, eqs. (24)–(30)), it was shown that the ratio of income elasticities of demand for M and A, hence the ratio of changes in quantities demanded when relative prices are fixed is: $\beta q_a/\alpha q_m$. If the income elasticity of demand for manufactured goods is more than the income elasticity of demand for agricultural goods, then this ratio will be greater than unity.

Now consider the numerator of (11) in the special case where $\rho = \sigma$ (neutral technological change). Up to a positive multiplier, it becomes

$$-q_a\beta + q_m\alpha - \phi_m p_a + \phi_a p_m. \tag{12}$$

The third and fourth terms cancel, by (5), while the first dominates the second, under the assumption just made that their ratio exceeds unity. Hence, under the assumptions of neutral technological change and greater income elasticity of demand for manufactured goods than for agricultural goods, δx_a will be negative—agricultural employment will decline with rising productivity. This is the result derived in equation (34) of Simon (1947).

3 Non-neutral Technological Change

Artle et al. (1977) show that, under certain assumptions about price elasticities, agricultural employment will decline even if there is technological advance in manufacturing alone. They further claim that the method of excess demand analysis is essential for the derivation of this result. I shall derive the same result by the method of comparative statics, and then will examine the meanings of the price elasticities that are postulated.

From (4), and remembering that I is fixed, since the wage rate is the numeraire, we have

$$0 = p_a\delta q_a + q_a\delta p_a + p_m\delta q_m + q_m\delta p_m \tag{13}$$

and from (5),

$$\phi_a\delta p_m + \phi_{aa}p_m\delta q_a + \phi_{am}p_m\delta q_m = \phi_{ma}p_a\delta q_a + \phi_{mm}p_a\delta q_m + \phi_m\delta p_a. \tag{14}$$

Solving (13) for δq_m, substituting this value in (14), and simplifying—remembering our previous definitions for α, β, and γ, we obtain

$$\gamma\delta q_a = (p_m\phi_m - \alpha q_a)\delta p_a - (p_m\phi_a + \alpha q_m)\delta p_m. \tag{15}$$

Taking p_a and p_m as our independent variables, we can read off the price elasticities of demand for agricultural goods:

$$(p_a/q_a)\partial q_a/\partial p_a = [p_a(p_m\phi_m - \alpha q_a)]/[q_a\gamma], \quad \text{and} \tag{16}$$

$$(p_m/q_a)\partial q_a/\partial p_m = -[p_m(p_m\phi_a + \alpha q_m)]/[q_a\gamma]. \tag{17}$$

By symmetry, we have also

$$(p_m/q_m)\partial q_m/\partial p_m = -[p_m(p_a\phi_a + \beta q_m)]/[q_m\gamma] \tag{18}$$

Now suppose the absolute value of the price elasticity of demand for *M* is greater than unity, while the corresponding elasticity for *A* is less than unity:

$$(p_a/q_a)(\partial q_a/\partial p_a) > -1, \qquad (p_m/q_m)(\partial q_m/\partial p_m) < -1, \tag{19}$$

The first of these relations is, by (16), equivalent to

$$p_a p_m \phi_m - p_a\alpha q_a < -q_a p_m \beta - q_a p_a \alpha, \quad \text{or} \tag{20}$$

$$-p_a\phi_m - q_a\beta > 0. \tag{21}$$

In the same way, from (18) and (19), we get

$$p_m\phi_a + q_m\alpha > 0. \tag{22}$$

If we now return to (11), we see that (21) and (22) guarantee that the numerator will be positive, hence that ∂x_a will be negative. Moreover, if $\rho = 0$, we require only the second inequality in (19), while if $\sigma = 0$, we require only the first inequality. But these results encompass Theorems 4.2 and 4.3 of Artle et al., showing that the theorems can be proved by the method of comparative statics—and by essentially the same path as with the method of excess demand analysis.

4 Interpretation of the Price Elasticities

How are the inequalities in (19), and especially the second one, to be interpreted? Using (4) and (5), first let us calculate the effect that a change in real income, *I*, would have upon the consumption of *A*, holding prices constant:

$$\delta I = p_a\delta q_a + p_m\delta q_m, \tag{23}$$

$$(\phi_{aa}p_m - \phi_{ma}p_a)\delta q_a = (\phi_{mm}p_a - \phi_{am}p_m)\delta q_m. \tag{24}$$

Substituting for δq_m in (24) and simplifying, we get

$$\beta\delta q_a = (\alpha/p_m)(\delta I - p_a q_a), \text{ or} \tag{25}$$

$$\partial q_a/\partial I = \alpha/\gamma \quad \text{and, since} \quad \partial I/\partial p_a = q_a, \tag{26}$$

$$\partial q_a/\partial p_a = \alpha q_a/\gamma. \tag{27}$$

But the right-hand side of (27) is essentially the second term in the numerator of (16). Hence this term measures the *income effect* of a change in price of A.

Again, using (4) and (5) let us calculate the effect of price changes in both A and M, of such magnitude as to hold I constant. In this case, from (13) and (14), we get

$$p_a\delta q_a = -p_m\delta q_m, \tag{28}$$

$$\beta\delta q_a + \phi_a\delta p_m = -\alpha(p_a/p_m)\delta q_a + \phi_m\delta p_a \quad \text{from which} \tag{29}$$

$$\partial q_a/\partial p_a = p_m\phi_m/\gamma. \tag{30}$$

But the right-hand side of (30) is the first term in the numerator of (16). Hence this term measures the effect of a *compensated change* in price of A (i.e., a change in the relative prices of A and M that does not alter real income).

Thus, by (27) and (30), we have decomposed the total elasticity of demand of A with respect to its price [eq. (16)] into the sum of a compensated relative price elasticity, (30), and an income elasticity, (27), respectively.

Now the assumption that the total elasticity of demand of one of the commodities, say M, be greater than unity in absolute value is seen to imply that the first term in (22), which is positive, dominates the second term, which is negative. We see that these terms are identical with those that appear in the numerator of (17). That is to say, they are the components of the cross-elasticity of demand for A with respect to a change in price of M. The first term, $p_m\phi_a$, represents the decrease in demand for A produced by a (compensated) decrease in price of M; while the second term, $q_m\alpha$, represents the increase in demand for A produced by an increase in income (the income effect of the reduced price of M). Thus, that the total demand elasticity for M be positive is equivalent to the cross-elasticity of demand being negative—a decrease in the cost of producing M causing a decrease in the consumption of A.

The question of whether these assumptions are likely to be satisfied in a real economy is, of course, an empirical one, which cannot be decided by theory or debate. If A and M were close substitutes, it would be a plausible assumption. However, in the case of the aggregates of manufactured and agricultural goods, respectively, it seems an excessively strong assumption to postulate that a reduction in price of manufactured goods will cause such a great substitution of manufactured for agricultural products that—in spite of the contrary income effect—the consumption of agricultural goods would actually decrease. This would seem especially unlikely to be the case in underdeveloped countries where foodstuffs, available at not much above the subsistence level, are the principal product of agriculture.

If we do not make this assumption, however, how do we account for the apparent fact that urbanization goes forward in some economies where agricultural efficiency appears not to change while manufacturing technology is advancing? Several alternative conditions can produce this scenario. One of these is disguised unemployment in agriculture, where the marginal productivity of labor in agriculture is essentially zero. Another, and probably more significant one, is that most of the economies we observe are not closed, but engage in international trade on a significant scale. Under these circumstances, a reduction in manufacturing costs could lead to increased export of manufactures in exchange for increased food imports. This kind of shift appears to have occurred at various points in history in the cases of Japan, India, and China, for example, and earlier, in the classical case of England.

5 Conclusion

In this paper I have explored further the economics of the rural–urban population balance. Using the method of comparative statics, I have confirmed the results obtained by Artle and his colleagues (1977) with excess demand analysis, thus demonstrating that the two methods of analysis are equivalent.

The formulas obtained by the method of comparative statics permit an interpretation of total elasticity of demand for a product as compounded of an income effect and a (compensated) price effect, respectively. This interpretation, in turn, allows some assessment of the plausibility of assuming, under various conditions, that the total demand for a commodity aggregate like manufactured goods will be elastic. It can be seen, in fact, that this is a very strong, and perhaps even unrealistic, assumption, for it requires that the substitution between the two aggregates be so great as to overcome the income effects on their consumption.

References

Artle, R., C. Humes, Jr. and P. Varaiya, 1977, Division of labour—Simon revisited, Regional Science and Urban Economics 7, 185–196.

Schultz, H., 1938, The theory and measurement of demand (University of Chicago Press, Chicago, IL).

Simon, H. A., 1947, Effects of increased productivity upon the ratio of urban to rural population, Econometrica, 15, 31–42.

Varaiya, P., R. Artle and C. Humes, Jr., 1979, Division of labor and the distribution of income, Regional Science and Urban Economics 9, 71–82.

II.2 The Impact of Electronic Communications on Organizations

Introduction

In the summer of 1969, Walter Goldberg was instrumental in organizing a conference at Aspenås, Sweden, on modern developments in organization and management. For that conference, I prepared a paper that undertook to analyze some of the consequences of the new technologies of computation for the memories, or data banks, of organizations. Now fifteen years have passed, a period during which both the character of computers and the extent of their application to the work of organizations has changed enormously. It is time for a new look at the impact of computers and electronic communications on organizations; and this time, I will not limit my discussion to organizational memories but will address a broader range of questions.

Computers today are orders of magnitude larger (in terms of memory capacity), smaller (in terms of the physical space they occupy and the power they consume), faster, and cheaper (in terms of operations per dollar) than they were fifteen years ago. Even though computers, with all of these changes, retain almost the same von Neumann architecture they have had from the beginning, quantitative changes of these magnitudes cannot fail to have qualitative effects. These qualitative effects, in turn, are vastly multiplied by the concomitant increases in the technical and economic feasibility of wide-band information transfer among computers through electronic communications networks.

The quantitative effects to which I refer are the great increases in breadth and sophistication of the applications of computers to the work of business and governmental organizations. What the increases in speed and size and the decreases in cost have meant is that all kinds of information processing capabilities can be, and have been, developed to form the basis for these applications. It is not simply a matter of running faster the programs we had written a decade ago, but of implementing entirely new kinds of programs, and even of programming languages, which we could conceive of at an earlier time but could not implement practically with the technology we then had available. Under this heading come, for example, the graphics capabilities of computers that underlie modern computer-aided design; the list-processing programming languages that are required in the construction of expert systems and other applications of artificial intelligence; powerful systems for understanding spoken language; flexible systems for interactive communication on wide-flung computer networks that link many different kinds of computers; and sensory and motor systems for the robotic devices.

The ubiquity of new applications of this technology is obvious enough. But the applications are mostly of such recent date that we have not had time to accumulate much experience about their implications for the structure and operation of organizations. These implications may even extend far beyond the boundaries of individual organizations. In Paris, for example, there has been founded the Centre Mondiale de Informatique et Ressource Humaine, one of whose missions is to see what contribution computer technologies of these sophisiticated kinds can make to the economic and social development of the Third World nations.

In the absence of extended objective data about the impact that these developments are having, or are about to have, on organizations, we have to rely on anecdote or ethnographic observation.[1]) On a modest scale, some sophisticated computing systems and computer networks have now existed for more than a decade. As a member of the computing community at Carnegie Mellon University, which, in turn, is a node in the national ARPA communications network, I have lived within such a system for the past dozen years of my professional life. If I do not have data of a systematic sort, I can at least provide my ethnographic report on what life has been like in such a system. Much of the "data" reported in this paper will come from this very personal source. I hope that in time it will be joined by the reports of other observers, as well as by data gathered in a thoroughly systematic way with due attention to the requirements of sampling.

It will not always be easy to interpret the significance of these personal observations. For example, it would be interesting to know what effects, if any, the new computing environments will have upon people's leisure time activities. I can report that, among the graduate students and faculty in my environment there is a very high interest in outdoor activities of many kinds, including, hiking, backpacking, spelunking (cave exploration), skiing, hang-gliding, navigating hot-air balloons, and sports. Interest in television appears low (a poor competitor with computer games?).

Now these are rather interesting facts, if they are facts, but it is not clear what they mean for the societies of the future. Perhaps they mean that computing and electronic communications attract people with certain personality traits that predispose them to these kinds of leisure activities. perhaps all they mean is that computing communities today are inhabited largely by young academic people, who do the things that young academic people like to do. I am afraid that a large part of the information we have at this time about the social systems of computerized environments is of this iffy kind.

The Design of Communications

In order to have a framework for our discussion, it may be well to consider first some of the considerations that need to go into the design of electronic communications systems that are to be installed in organizations. The question to be addressed here is not how such systems actually *are* designed, but rather what considerations *ought* to govern their design. These can sometimes be quite distinct questions.

Capacity Limits

A communication network consists of nodes, or processors, and links, or communications channels. The processors can be human beings or computers; usually there are both kinds in a network. Links transmit messages from one node to another. Nodes input messages, operate upon them, store information extracted from them, and output new messages.

Each node in a communication network is characterized by its capacity to handle the messages that are input to it, and by the volume and characteristics of the messages it outputs. The capacity of a node, in turn, depends on the processing it is expected to do on the messages it receives, and on what messages it is expected to output. When the capacity of a node is exceeded by the load of input messages imposed on it, and/or its responsibilities for producing output messages, the quality of its performance will degrade. The degradation may be graceful or catastrophic. Degradation can take the form of processing incoming and outgoing messages less completely and thoroughly than before, or assigning priorities to tasks and ignoring those of low priority.

For example, laboratory studies of an early-warning station in an air defense organization showed clearcut degradation in the processing of radar information and information received from other nodes in the system whenever the total number of planes under surveillance increased. On a few occasions, in the face of extremely high loads, the degradation was catastrophic: the system simply failed to keep track of flights in its area. In most cases, however, as load increased, the flights associated with the radar blips were classified as safe or potentially dangerous, and only the flights in the latter category were tracked. This particular system had a built-in (human) component that, by application of rules of priority, regulated the amount of information it processed, sometimes successfully, but sometimes at the expense of quality of performance.

On a less formal basis, most of us are aware of priority schemes that we apply to our own everyday agendas. Some kinds of matters are handled immediately; others are set aside to be taken care of "when there is time". Many tasks may be handled with considerable care whenever the total load is light, but in much more cursory fashion as the load increases.

Early management information systems were typically designed in terms of the criterion of "making more information available to the manager." The decisions as to what information was to be provided, and when, largely resided in the hands of the system and its designers. The main filtering device left to the manager was to ignore information received when it exceeded capacity or seemed irrelevant to needs. The idea of balancing the volume of information transmitted against the capacities of recipients to absorb it was not a common feature of such designs; nor were notions of priority as between different kinds of information.

With the development of the information technology, these grave defects in management information systems, while they have not been fully corrected, are being somewhat ameliorated. System design now includes the concept of an information bank that does not shovel information at users, but can be accessed when and if users perceive the need for information. Of course, the indexing of data banks must be sophisticated, so that potential users can know what information is available, and can access it with ease.

As the techniques of artificial intelligence are applied to the architecture of information systems, another possibility emerges that has not yet been much exploited: to provide such systems with the intelligence that will permit them to participate in the filtering process. For example, the system itself, if sufficiently intelligent, may call to the attention of managers information that is of potential relevance to them, and may take over a large part of the task of indexing information automatically, and even of analysing it.

In all such systems, maintaining the balance between the production and consumption of information remains a central design criterion. I have always thought it a good rule of thumb that no new automatic component should be introduced into an information system unless the volume of information it absorbs is at least an order of magnitude greater than the volume it produces.

Networking and Capacity

The same questions of capacity that arise in information systems and data banks arise in the design of electronic communication networks. Design has too often been based on the simple premise that more communication is better than less. That assumption is just as questionable when applied to networks as it is when applied to information systems.

Most human white-collar organizations in developed nations are already networked electronically: the network is a telephone system. To anyone accustomed to a phone system of high reliability and good voice quality, trying to operate in an environment that lacks such a system is highly frustrating. But what implication does the presence of the system have for the loads imposed on its nodes?

The load-creating capabilities of a telephone system are limited by one important feature: placing a call imposes a time-load on the caller that is as heavy as the load placed on the receiver. However, the choice of recipient and of time of calling are entirely in the hands of the caller. For this reason, persons who are likely to be the targets of many calls generally require the protection of a filter—a secretary, or nowadays sometimes an automatic answering device.

Phone communications may also increase loads in another way. Many people find it easier to pick up a phone than to write a letter, and will call on occasions where they would not trouble to write. However, I don't know whether anyone has gathered data to determine whether the recipient of a phone inquiry typically spends more or less effort in responding than the recipient of the same inquiry in the form of a letter. Two opposing forces are at work here. On the one hand, people find it far easier to generate an oral stream of words than a written one, hence are likely to answer inquiries in more detail orally than in writing. On the other hand, the oral stream can also be produced much more rapidly than the written one. I should not like to hazard a guess as to where the balance lies.

As experience has accumulated with telephones, a consensus has evidently been reached that they make a net positive contribution to the functioning of an office, for we see phones on virtually every desk, and relatively simple human filtering systems (e.g., secretaries) to manage them. The introduction of automatic calling systems with taped or synthesized messages creates, or will soon create, an entirely new problem, for it is likely to produce a massive, and strongly resented, imbalance between callers and receivers. It will surely call for stronger filtering measures than are now usually employed.

In the electronic communications systems that are now coming into being, the telephone is supplemented with an electronic mail facility. What are its characteristics? Does it differ in any significant respects from the telephone, and if so, what are the implications of the differences? The obvious and important difference is that sender and receiver don't have to be synchronized. The recipient need not be present or available at the time the message is transmitted, nor the original sender at the time of the reply. This provision of a memory to unhitch sender and recipient eliminates, first of all, the frequent sequences of phone calls that must be placed between people who are only intermittently free, hence seldom simultaneously available. At the same time, it hardly delays the message turnaround time (and, in my experience, usually reduces it).

The second important difference between the telephone and the network message system is that the latter does not require real-time response to inquiries or requests, but provides respondents with the opportunity to gather their wits, or even to seek out additional information before replying. One of the most useful pieces of advice that my father gave me was never to sign in the presence of the salesman. That advice is easier, and more gracious to follow with a network mail system than with a telephone system. On the other hand, the message system does not permit the kind of interactive interchange that characterizes human conversation. More cycles may be required to detect and correct errors of interpretation, and context must be regenerated on each round of the discontinuous exchange.

The sound, if bland, conclusion one might draw is that telephone and message systems are complementary rather than competitive commodities, and that organizations possessing both—as will soon be the case for most large organization—will find message systems gradually playing a larger and larger role in relation to phone systems.

Networks and Hierarchies

Traditional organizations, including those we work in today, are hierarchical in form. Hierarchy has two aspects in organization: the familiar pyramid of authority, and a pattern of communications that matches the pattern of departmentalization. By the latter I mean that if we record the frequency of communication between different nodes, we find that the pattern is not uniform but highly structured. There are clusters of nodes with very high rates of inter-node communication, and much lower rates between clusters than within clusters. There are many levels of such clusters, with a drop in communication rate as we proceed from each level to the next above. In fact, the pattern of communication frequencies reflects, approximately, the pyramid of authority. In the technical literature, communication networks with this hierarchical structure are called "nearly decomposable."

There are some very good reasons why organizations are hierarchical; some of these reasons are discussed in the last chapter of my book, *The Sciences of the Artificial*, Cambridge, Mass.: MIT Press, Second edition, 1981. Above all else, hierarchy has a complexity-reducing effect that vastly simplifies the operation of large systems with multiple, heterogeneous tasks. There is nothing in the new technology of electronic communication that removes these functions and advantages of hierarchy. Hence, when we think about "networking", we should not imagine an even flow of messages from all nodes of the network to all others, but instead the highly patterned flow that is characteristic of nearly decomposable structures. In the design of networks, the pattern of flow that is anticipated will be reflected in the band widths of different linkages. Small work groups will have a high level of internal communication, not necessarily among the human members, but especially with data sources that are accessible by all members of the group. Other, less frequently accessed common facilities will be shared by larger units of the organization, made up of sets of the first-level groups. The network hierarchy, then, will parallel the hierarchy of organizational units. Up to the present, relatively little research has been done on the design of such hierarchical networks, and the topic is in urgent need of attention.

The Need to Know

The problems of information-processing capacity need also be addressed in making decisions about where information should be stored in organizations. Who needs to know what facts and to have access to what data? To answer these kinds of questions, we must scrutinize the meaning of "to know."

In a non-literate society, people know something when they have that something stored in their heads and can access it on demand. In such societies, there is no place to store information other than in human heads. Of course, even in a non-literate society, knowing can be delegated. The king can dispense with knowing certain things if he can be sure that the knowledge is stored in the head of an accessible advisor. Thus, knowledge can be social as well as individual.

With the introduction of written documents and reference books, the situation changes radically. A great deal of knowledge continues to be carried in human heads, for in literate societies we see even highly skilled and professional personnel carrying on their work with only occasional reference to books. Nevertheless, the books are there, containing most, if not all, of the collective knowledge of the society, and ready to supplement or replace the fallible human memory at the cost of some reduction in speed of access.

The availability of rapid communication networks again tilts the balance between storing in the head and storing in external memories in favor of human storage, for now knowledge becomes available to anyone who has a good index of, and access to, the experts in whose heads the knowledge is stored. When data banks become part of the communication networks, the balance is shifted once more. Now the data bank, adequately indexed, can aspire to the roles of both human memory and reference book. Now we have to re-examine the question of what human beings need to know, but also open the question of what information should exist in "hard copy" rather than in computer memories.

Neither data banks nor networks have yet reached such a stage of development that we have moved much from our traditional attitudes and modes of behavior with respect either to human knowledge or to books. But the questions are being raised more and more frequently. I can cite only a few illustrative examples, mostly pertaining to the so-called "expert systems" that are now being created by research in artificial intelligence.

Several systems have been created that do a credible, professional-level job of medical diagnosis in their domains of competence. One of these is the CADUCEUS system developed by Myers and Pople at the University of Pittsburgh. Another is the MYCIN system developed by Shortliffe and his associates at Stanford University. Most of the information that finds its way into these systems is derived from medical textbooks, with some supplementation from the experience of expert human diagnosticians. Some fraction of this information is also stored in the head of every person who has gone through medical training.

The question we will be asking with increasing urgency and frequency is whether and in what form such information needs to be stored in the heads of the next generation of medical students. (Since the advent of hand-held calculators we have been asking a similar question about the storage of addition and multiplication tables in the heads of schoolchildren.) I do not have an answer to the question, but I am certainly not prepared to predict that the informational content of medical education will be the same in a decade as it is today. Already, we have begun to make minor modifications and adjustments in other curricula. For example, calculus courses place less emphasis than they did a decade ago upon students' learning large numbers of specific integrals.

Computer systems themselves are interesting testbeds for the study of alternative forms of information storage. When does a computer user consult a hard-copy manual, and when an on-line "help" message? Of course the answer depends on some crucial technical details—the relative accessibility and comprehensibility of the two information sources, as well as the problem to be solved. But it is clear that in the Carnegie Mellon system the balance is swinging steadily and inexorably from hard-copy to on-line information.

Good contemporary examples of such shifts in the realm of business are the on-line systems that provide information on stocks and bonds to security brokers, replacing hard-copy, frequently revised reference sources. Most of the substitution to date has been a replacement of reference books and other hard-copy sources by on-line data banks. There has as yet been no substantial replacement of information that is stored in human memories. If that is to take place on an important scale, it will have to await the further development of expert systems.

One prediction is easy to make: that a larger and larger part of society's information will be stored in electronic memories. As we have seen, it is much harder to predict what changes this implies for the information that will be stored in books and in human heads. The library continues to play its traditional role at Carnegie Mellon, and members of the community continue to find it more convenient, on many occasions, to consult the local human experts than to use on-line "help" facilities. But it is no new thing for there to be a high level of duplication and redundancy in information sources. For the near future, that redundancy is likely to increase as computer memories duplicate information already available in other memories.

Removing People From the Loop

Thus far we have been proceeding under the assumption that communication takes place ultimately between human beings, the electronic system serving only as some kind of mediator. This assumption must be reexamined.

The following account is not fiction, but a description of actual events. A certain sum of money was to be transferred from an account in a bank in a European city to another person's account in a bank located in a midwestern American city. (That decision was made by human beings.) The decision was communicated to the computer of the European bank, which sent notice of the transaction to the computer of its American correspondent bank. The correspondent bank's computer created a new message, in two parts, which was transmitted to the computer of the New York branch of the midwestern American bank. One part of the message contained the bare fact of the transfer of funds; the other part gave the details of the account in which they were to be deposited. The New York branch bank's computer, receiving the two parts of the message at different times, failed to connect them. It set up an account for the money received, pending the receipt of information about its disposition. After several days, still lacking this information, it notified the correspondent bank's computer that it was returning the funds. An account was set up to hold them, and a message prepared returning them to the originating European bank. The story might have gone much further, but at this point it was interrupted by some humans who, wondering what had become of the money, traced the transactions and put matters back on the track.

This story is not recounted as a piece of evidence for the superiority of human intelligence over computer intelligence. I am sure that such comedies of errors did not originate in the computer era; human beings are fully as capable as computers of creating them. The story's purpose is simply to point out that there are whole realms of business today in which sequences of communications take place wholly within computing systems—or sets of mutually communicating computing systems—without human intervention. That being the case, we must not conceive of the network design problem as one of facilitating communication between human beings, but as one of facilitating decision making and the communication of decisions through networks of nodes, each of which may be a computer or a human being.

The only place where the design of such a network can begin is with an analysis of the decisions that have to be made and the transactions that have to be carried out to do the system's work. Working back from the load of decisions and transactions, we can consider the allocation of that load to people and computers, and the communications that are necessary to implement and support the allocation. This is a quite different design process from taking as given the set of human tasks and creating a system of computers and communication links to support the human actors.

Communications and Human Interaction

A question that constantly arises, and should arise, in relation to the new information technology is the impact of that technology on human life in organizations. In some human minds, the words "machine" and "automation" have strong associations to words like "dehumanization" and "alienation." What precautions must we take to prevent the introduction of electronic systems from causing a deterioration in the human qualities of organizational life?[2])

The Human Workplace

We human beings have very ambivalent attitudes towards the artifacts that we create and among which we live. A few generations past, the ambivalence was much less: except for a few Thoreau-like outliers, the term "civilized" had positive valence for most people, and the term "primitive" negative valence. Nowadays, the number of people who are aware of the costs associated with the benefits of civilization is large. Moreover, most of us are able to conjure up vivid pictures—sometimes based on experience—on insults to the environment and of inhuman workplaces that are products of contemporary industrialization.

Our ambivalence will defy analysis until we are able to define with some care, and some degree of operationality, just what we mean by "civilized" and "primitive", and by a human, or humane, work environment; and unless we understand something about the causes of alienation. When we stigmatize the factory assembly line as an inhumane workplace, we seem to have at least four things in mind: the boredom of routine, repetitive work, the subservience of the human worker to the pace and conditions set by machines, the suppression of meaningful human contact and interaction, and the lack of participation of the worker in the decision-making process in the work place. Of course, many of these same stigmata apply to the work of hoeing a potato field or hollowing a dugout canoe, or doing many of the other arduous, and sometimes, repetitive, tasks, that occupy much time and effort in other, simpler societies.

But the question is not whether boredom, isolation, and lack of independence of action are good for human beings. Most of us would agree that they are not. The important question is whether, and to what extent, they are necessary concomitants of work in a modern automated factory or office environment. How can we design jobs for such an environment so that they will not be excessively repetitive, will not prevent social interaction, and will not destroy autonomy?[3])

One thing we notice immediately in the automated office and the highly automated factory is that the people who operate the system are mostly not linked to it on a second-to-second basis. In contrast to the traditional, and old-fashioned, assembly line, their work and responses do not have to be synchronized with the movements of machinery. Rather, their interventions are aperiodic, and often associated with assigning tasks to the machines and monitoring output. The environment in which the work is done is usually physically comfortable, and noise levels are low enough to permit conversation. People interact with machines, but they often also interact with each other.

This description fits some environments better than others, and I do not wish to idealize a less-than-ideal reality. But as a generalization, we have been more successful in automating the routine than the non-routine components of work, and we have largely released the worker from the moment-to-moment grasp of the machine that characterized the most objectionable forms of the assembly line. What this shows is not that the work environment produced by the introduction of electronic communications will inevitably be a humane environment, but that there are wide possibilities to design it deliberately to be so.

Social Interaction by Network

Although our experience with organizations linked by electronic networks is still not extensive, certain phenomena have already emerged in such settings, and have been commented upon. While the evidence is anecdotal, there is considerable consistency in the observations that have been made in different settings.

First, the availability to organization members of a computer with which (whom?) to communicate, does not appear to reduce communication with other human beings. Nor does the interpersonal communication take place mainly through computer messages. The computer science department in which I have lived for many years is a highly "social" group of people. The amount of face-to-face social interaction among its members appears to me at least as great as in any other university department of which I have been a member. There are numerous departmental social affairs, as well as shared hobbies, political interests and what not.

One way in which the network contributes to this interaction is by providing a means for advertising activities to the group, so that they are well informed about opportunities for participation. Sports teams, cave-exploring expeditions, and many other activities are organized by this means. For many years, there has been a cooperative organization for purchasing cheese, the orders being placed through the electronic network.

These interactions are supported by a system of electronic bulletin boards—files to which messages can be sent, and which can be read by members of the system. Each member specifies which of the bulletin boards will be automatically displayed to him or her at each new login to the system. Items are displayed by title, and the viewers can decide for each item whether they wish to read the entire message. There is a general bulletin board, and specialized boards for many different special interest groups. For example, the cognitive science bulletin board transmits messages about seminars and other events of interest in the general domain of cognitive psychology and artificial intelligence.

The bulletin boards exercise a socializing influence not only in keeping people informed about events of many kinds, but also in acquainting them with their fellow members, whose messages they see displayed on the boards. If they read, from time to time, the "opinions" bulletin board, they come to know the views on many subjects of the members who provide messages to that board.

One phenomenon that was not predicted when these systems where installed, but that has been observed in a number of different systems, is "flaming." Members of a system who are angered by something that has occurred (perhaps by some "anti-social" use or misuse of the system) transmit messages of protest, often expressed in quite hostile and extravagant language, to the bulletin board. The messages are considerably more violent in expression than would be messages transmitted in hard-copy writing or in a face-to-face encounter. The "impersonality" of the medium evidently allows expressions of hostility that would be unacceptable under other conditions.

The consequences of flaming for the solidarity of the social groups is hard to assess. It is my impression that, once the phenomenon has become familiar, the violence of expression is discounted (like the rhetoric of political speeches), and has no long-term effects. However, flaming deserves more careful study than it has had. It, in any event, counters the idea that the use of computers for communication will remove emotion from the human interaction.

The mail bulletin board facilities of electronic communications systems create real dangers that members of the system will be overwhelmed with messages. I have already mentioned two kinds of safeguards, against those dangers. First, members may choose which bulletin boards they wish to scan. Second, messages on both bulletin boards and mail files are first presented by title, and the recipient may decide whether or not to read the full messages.

Even these safeguards may prove to be insufficient, and may have to be supplemented by more intelligent filters. It is easy for anyone on the system to create small or large mailing lists for messages, so that mail messages can be sent broadcast. On occasion, this capability has led to systems being flooded by messages, and even brought to their knees by the overload. However, networks also develop and enforce norms of "good citizenship". Members who are thought to abuse the system are subjected to "flaming" and other social sanctions imposed by their colleagues. A local culture develops that defines proper and improper communication, and the culture is to a very considerable extent self-enforcing.

In our University environment, official administrative interventions have been called for only rarely.

Electronic Communications and Power

There has been much speculation about the implications of electronic communications systems for the distribution of power in organizations. Starting with the unexceptionable proposition that "knowledge is power" much concern has been expressed that those who "control" the electronic systems will control the organizations that they serve. The difficulty with this claim lies in determining who "controls" the electronic system. And the answer to the question of control is surely not independent of the system architecture and mode of operation.

At the outset, I think we can dismiss the idea that electronic systems will be controlled by programming specialists. Systems programmers are technicians, and as with all technicians, their work must be directed and supervised so that it will be meshed with the goals of the organization. But I am not aware that there are any problems of supervising systems programmers that are different from the problems of supervising other kinds of experts. Their role is much like that of the staffs that maintain and operate the telephone system: they have little to say about the content of the messages that go out over the wires.

The Technical Possibilities

Our task is not to *predict* how electronic communications will affect the distribution of power, but to *design* electronic systems that will deal with power in the ways we think desirable. To oversimplify vastly, we can decentralize power by creating numerous sophisticated work stations with strong capabilities for acquiring and analysing information, or we can centralize power by creating centralized data banks with carefully controlled access.

Undoubtedly, we will want both to centralize and to decentralize. We will want both to provide wide access to information and to control access. The computer science profession has already been addressing for many years the technical issues involved in making this kind of differentiation possible. Personal computers and work stations, combined with networks having capabilities for broad-band information transmission, provide a technology for decentralization. Security systems, involving passwords and other means for restricting access, provide a technology for maintaining control over information and securing personal privacy.

I do not mean that the social and technical problems are easy to solve, or that the solutions will be perfect. But I urge that we not limit our system designs on the supposition that they cannot be solved.

Design Criteria

The balance between centralization and decentralization of information and decision-making must be evaluated in terms of effects on control, on the quality of decisions, and on the costs of information transmission. The question of control is heavily laden with values—with our beliefs as to which organization members should participate significantly in the making of which sets of decisions. There is no technical "right answer" to these questions. In a society like Sweden or the United States, where participation is regarded by many as a desirable social goal, per se, a different answer will be reached than in a totalitarian society.

With respect to the quality of decisions, it is often claimed that cheap means for transmitting information will inevitably make more centralization attractive. There is some historical evidence for this claim—for example in the changed and diminished role of ambassadors after telegraphic communication appeared on the scene.

Cheap information transfer can be interpreted to imply that *all* the relevant information can be transmitted to a central decision point, and that such a central point cannot help but make better decisions than decentralized units that are only partially informed. But the conclusion rests on a dubious technical assumption—that *all* or most of the relevant information can be transmitted through the electronic system, and the even more dubious assumption that the human members of the system have nothing to contribute in the way of analysis. Finally, it rests on the assumption that is easier to transmit information required for decision to central points than to transmit the goals and criteria that are to govern decision to the decentralized locations where the information about immediate circumstances is available.

To justify centralization, it is not enough that all of the information can be centralized; it is necessary that all of the expertise be centralized also. (Ambassadors have been known to point this out when decisions are taken out of their hands.) If cheap communication makes it easier to centralize information, it also makes it easier to transmit centralized information to decentralized decision points. Messages can flow in both directions on the telegraph wire equally well.

Thus, the increasing capabilities of electronic communications systems offer no simple answers to the question of centralization versus decentralization. System designers will have to begin with the nature of the decisions that have to be made; the sources of information and expertise for making them; the relative ease of transmission of the various kinds of relevant information; the kinds of decision-making processes that are available to man and machine. In any foreseeable future, we will surely see in our organizations a distributed decision-making system that will not seem wholly strange to us in terms of our previous experience.

Conclusion

In talking about the future of a technology as radically new and powerful as electronic computers and networking, one is continually torn between the temptation to predict a wholly new (and brave?) world, and the temptation to predict that all will go on exactly as before. The faint image on the crystal ball will hardly refute either prediction. And in any event, all depends upon the time horizon one selects. In a sufficiently short time, nothing will change, and in a sufficiently long time, everything.

For this reason, I have been less concerned in this paper with predictions than I have with proposing points of view that may be helpful in understanding and planning for the new development. In the first part of the paper, I have pointed out that we must shift from a view that focuses upon the availability of information to a view that focuses upon the availability of capacity for attending to information. That has seemed to me, for some years, to be a very obvious point, but it still does not receive the attention it deserves in the design of information systems.

In the second part of the paper, I asked whether we have reason to expect that the workplaces of the future will be more or less congenial to human beings than those of the present. On balance, I arrived at a rather optimistic answer—again not in the form of a prediction, but in the form of an assertion that we can determine the outcome by the way we design our systems.

Finally, in the last part of the paper, I have asked what implications the new information technology has for the distribution of power in our organizations. My answer to this, as to the previous, question is that the decision lies in our own hands. The technology offers a wide range of possibilities; we must decide how they will be exploited.

In sum, then, I do not see a single future ahead of us that is inexorably determined by technological forces. I see an exciting new technology coming into being, and that technology presenting us with a wide range of options. The past history of our species shows us absorbing a large number of technologies—from stone tools to the steam engine—with results that have been both good and bad. On balance, I do not have any urge to return to the life of the happy savage, and I suspect that most of my readers do not either. So we must hope, with a modicum of historical support for the reasonableness of that hope, that the benefits we will derive from these new electronic possibilities will outweigh their costs. But "hope" is not enough. Technology creates the possibilities, but it is we, through our plans and decisions, who determine which of them will be realized, and what the consequences will be for human welfare.

Notes

1. The more dignified term is "ethnography." Sherry Turkle, in *The Second Self*, New York: Simon and Schuster, 1984, uses the term to characterize her own observations of the computer culture, which differ rather widely from mine. But this would not be the first time that two ethnographers have seen different things in the same culture.

2. A reader of an earlier draft observes that I do not mention unemployment as one of the dangers to be guarded against. In my *New Science of Management Decision*, Englewood Cliffs, N.J.: Prentice-Hall, Revised edition 1979, Chapter 4, I explain why I do not think there is any particular relation between computerization—or automation in general—and unemployment.

3. In another place, I have discussed the issue of worker participation in decision-making. See my *What is Industrial Democracy? Statsvetenskaplig Tidskrift*, No.2, 78–86, 1979.

II.3 The Steam Engine and the Computer: What Makes Technology Revolutionary

It may seem absurdly anachronistic to be reflecting about the steam engine in a conference devoted to the role of computers in higher education. But it's often been said that computers have triggered a second industrial revolution, so perhaps there are some lessons to be learned from the First Industrial Revolution, the one that was triggered by the steam engine—lessons that might have some bearing on what we can and should do with computers and on what computers might do to and for us.

The First Industrial Revolution

We think of revolutions as being sudden events, producing far-reaching changes in a very short period of time. But the revolution launched by the steam engine took, by any reasonable account, 150 years. The invention that started it was Thomas Newcomen's "atmospheric" steam engine, which appeared in about 1711. Newcomen developed his engine primarily because his coal mines were being flooded and he needed more powerful pumps than were currently available to get the water out of the mines. James Watt made some important improvements on the engine in 1769, in the course of trying to repair one of Newcomen's engines. Two generations had already gone by, and one could hardly speak of a revolution yet. The aims and aspirations of these "revolutionaries" were distinctly limited.

In order for the steam engine to produce genuinely revolutionary change, there had to be a whole series of subsequent inventions, none of which were—or could have been—contemplated by its originators, and these took still another generation, reaching well into the 19th century. The steam engine was adapted for use in transportation, giving us the steamboat and the steam locomotive, and in industry, the power loom. Perhaps even more important were a number of complementary inventions that were initially quite independent of the steam engine but that were harnessed to it to produce further changes. The most notable of these was the dynamo, which used the steam engine to generate electricity. (To convince you of how long this revolution took, let me remind you that there were many rural areas in the United States that didn't have electrity until about 50 years ago.) Then there was another series of what it is fair to call "derivative" inventions—the internal combustion engine, the automobile, the electric light bulb, the airplane, the telephone. The point is that when technology reshapes society, it is not the result of a single invention but of a host of additional, completely unanticipated inventions, many of them of the same order of magnitude as the first one in the chain.

Conversely, what we sometimes call technological change actually permeates society, affecting it in far more than merely "technological" ways. Before the automobile, one of the most important skills of a physician, certainly the one he used the most, was the skill of driving a horse. For a while, that was replaced by the less time-consuming activity of driving an automobile. Now, physicians don't even have to do that; their patients come to them. We don't ordinarily think of the steam engine as changing medical practice, yet it did; it certainly altered the physician's time budget. The creation of the suburbs is another example. And—though again it seems surprising at first—one of the largest migrations in human history was brought about by air conditioning, which transformed what many people thought of as uninhabitable parts of our country into the very attractive Sunbelt. The invention of air conditioning is usually dated at about 1911, and no one at that time could have anticipated that, as a result of it, a large part of the American population was going to move from one part of the country to another. As one more example, the burning of coal to produce steam for the generation of electricity had a number of adverse consequences, leading us to look for other fuels that could be used for the purpose. As a result, we opened that Pandora's box known as nuclear power.

I've already alluded to one lesson to be drawn from all of this, and that is the lesson of unpredictability. There are no crystal balls that can tell us what the consequences of a fundamental technological change are going to be. A genealogical chart of the First Industrial Revolution would encompass about six generations. Parents all come to understand the impossibility of foretelling how their children are going to turn out; how much more futile it would be for them to try to imagine what their great-great-great-great-grandchildren will be like.

A second lesson, also alluded to, is the extent to which the ramifications of any one technological change depend upon the stimulation it provides to other inventions, and the links that are made from it to inventions that may be independent of it, as steam was linked to electricity.

A third lesson is the importance of what we might call "education by immersion." Most Americans, after all, did not learn to drive automobiles in driver-education classes. Instead, they learned to drive because there was a Model T on the farm, or maybe a tractor, and there was something or someone that had to be moved from here to there—so they got in their cars and figured out what all those levers and pedals did, and they also learned, out of necessity, how to take the car apart and put it together again. None of this was planned ahead of time, nobody sat down and figured out the kinds of courses that would be needed in order to teach people how to use these new contraptions. We educated ourselves about them because we had to, and it was easy to do because they were all around us.

A final lesson to be drawn from this history is the lesson of generality. In the last analysis, the reason that the steam engine and the associated inventions proved to be revolutionary is that they didn't do anything specific. Rather, they allowed us to move in innumerable directions. They replaced and augmented human and other forms of animal muscle by the muscle of engines, thereby completely transforming the nature of that major input into everything we produce—energy. No single-purpose device is going to bring about a revolution, however convenient or useful it may be. Revolutionary significance lies in generality.

Potential of the Computer

How are these lessons applicable today? If we were to make a genealogical chart for the second industrial revolution, it would of course be far less elaborate than the one for the first, because computers have been around for only about 40 years. Though there have already been a number of derivative inventions, most of them are still fairly closely related to the original conception of the computer, whether it is solid-state hardware, time sharing (now almost outmoded), higher-level languages or methods of non-numerical computation of various sorts, primarily means of making the computer faster and more powerful. At most, there have been two generations so far. It is true that people in the hardware business like to say that they are now in the fifth generation, but that's a little like asking us to accept child marriage. I think it's more accurate to say we're now in the third generation, and even that one is at most in its adolescence.

This third generation is identified by several elements. One is the appearance of minicomputers and microcomputers. Their significance is not in the opportunity they give us to play games at home or to keep the family accounts, but in the fact that they open up the possibility of computer education by immersion. Today, for the first time, we can say that a very large proportion of the American population has had hands-on experience with a computer (and the event is recent enough to be still very vivid in the minds of most of us). Another element is the development of computer graphics and of new kinds of workstations. Still another is computer-aided instruction. Of course, computer-aided instruction has been around in some form for almost as long as computers have been. We have had an instructional management game in operation at the business school of Carnegie Mellon University since at least 1960. Nevertheless, computer-aided instruction is still rather primitive and has had only a very modest effect on the way education takes place in this country or anywhere else. Robotics, expert systems, and cognitive science are also part of the third generation of the second industrial revolution. And finally, computers are beginning to form links with other parts of technology, in particular with our systems of communications and information transfer. Networking is one example of this—the creation of a system in which computers no longer stand alone but can talk not only to us as individuals, but also to each other, in a great variety of ways.

Surely, the second industrial revolution is just as unpredictable as the first one was—and the second has barely begun. We are closer in time to the first computer than James Watt was to Thomas Newcomen. There is a lot of solemn talk about what computers can't do—there's even a book by that name (1967)—but that's not a very interesting subject. Computers today are doing a lot of things they were "known" to be unable to do a while ago, and what they can't do today they may very well be doing tomorrow. (The author of that book has already had to get out several revised editions.) Besides, our task is not to decide what computers can't do but to look ahead for the very short distance that we are capable of and to think about what we can get computers to do, what we would like them to do that they can't do right now. Each year we see more impressive computer systems for handling natural language. Still, most of them are limited to particular domains of discourse. I know of no computer program today that can enter into a general conversation with you about anything you want to bring up. There is plenty of room for developments of that kind without worrying about whether there are ultimately some things that computers will never be able to do.

It is sometimes said, by way of demonstrating the superiority of human beings, that computers cannot be imprecise, even when the situation demands imprecision. I'm not sure that this is a shortcoming—how much have humans really gained from their ability to be imprecise?—but anyone who has had much experience with computers is not likely to believe that they cannot be imprecise. More and more, we are using computers in tasks where the exact course of action is not determinate at each moment. A problem solving program, an expert system, is an organized but highly flexible way of making use of information that is incomplete and imperfect and that comes to it in a variety of forms and sequences. A capability for imprecision no longer marks the boundary between what computers can and cannot do.

Human beings are also said to possess "intuition." That's a term we use when someone looks at a problem and doesn't at first know the answer, but a minute or two or even just a few seconds later, does know the answer, and knows it without any awareness of the process by which the answer was found. When we see someone coming down the street, we may not know who it is at first, but if it's a friend we are likely to know it long before we know how we knew it. But if that's what intuition is, then it can be said that computers have it, too. An important part of the anatomy of an expert system is a database, indexed by a set of cues that the system can recognize. When one of those cues appears, the system retrieves relevant information from its database. A medical diagnosis system, for example, can be presented with a few symptoms, and it will "intuit" what the ailment is. Of course, like any prudent diagnostician, it doesn't entirely trust its intuition, so it goes on to request that certain tests be made, and with the additional information, it confirms or refines or alters the diagnosis. Unless we deliberately want to make a mystique out of human thinking, and sometimes it seems that we do because it makes us feel better about ourselves, we have to conclude that what's going on in such a system is exactly what we call intuition when a human being does it. Once again, the supposed contrast between what people can do and what computers can do doesn't fit the facts of computation in the modern world.

When we're especially impressed by an intuition, we are apt to call it "insight," and beyond that we begin to talk about "creativity." Here too, however, there are computer programs that can do things that would be regarded as "insightful" and "creative" if they were done by humans. Theorems in mathematics and logic have been discovered and proved by computers unaided by human hands or minds. Some of my associates and I have been working for six or eight years on a program that we call BACON. We have given it, for example, the data that Kepler had available to him at the time he made his discovery of the third law of planetary motion or that Joseph Black had available when he proposed his theory of specific heat, and we found that the program is able to rediscover the law or the theory (1986). We can conclude that we don't have to postulate any kind of mysterious processes, any kind of fundamentally unknown—much less unknowable—processes to account for what in humans we like to call creativity. Hence, we can't establish the creative process as an Iron Curtain that limits what computers can do.

Computing by Immersion

The first computer we acquired at Carnegie Mellon was an IBM 650. When we got it, in about 1958, we didn't have any idea what we were going to do with it. The electrical engineers didn't want to be associated with it because they were afraid they would have to maintain it; the mathematicians didn't want to be associated with it because it seemed beneath their dignity. So we put it in the basement of the business school, but we were very careful not to put a lock on the door. What happened was that the students swarmed all over it, just as previous generations had swarmed over the Model T. It was then that the faculty began to learn about it, to save themselves from embarrassment. What was happening was education by immersion.

The same phenomenon could be seen in industry. In those early days, a business executive would decide that his company ought to have a computer, often merely because one of his colleagues at another company had just gotten one and he wanted to be progressive and up-to-date. On occasion, I was called in to advise in such situations, and my advice was usually, "Before you buy a computer, decide what you intend to do with it, and then plan your installation around those intended uses." That was terrible advice, and I probably ought to return the fees I got for giving it. Fortunately, my advice often wasn't taken, because the motivation for getting the computer was not to use it but just to have it. But then it arrived, and when I observed what happened afterward, I realized that the best advice was, in fact, just to have one around, for that's the only way a company or a university, or anybody else, is going to learn what to do with it. You have to make friends with it, talk to it, let it talk to you. Hit the keys and see what happens. The computer will tell you about itself, and it tells you probably better than the instruction book. Immerse yourself in the technology. I don't mean we shouldn't have classes about computers—after all, I work for a university—but they are not going to be the major educational force. One of the most impressive things about a computer is its capacity, by virtue of its power and the flexibility of its responses, to be its own instructional device.

Besides helping us learn about themselves, computers can play a role in helping us learn about other things as well. On that subject, I bring to your attention a very information and thoughtful article by Derek Bok of Harvard in a recent issue of the EDUCOM Bulletin (1985). Among its other virtues, it is mercifully free—or almost so—of smug remarks about what computers can't do. We are indeed a long way from knowing what they can do for education. In our university, we certainly don't have a detailed blueprint for what our campus is going to look like with a network, or with all the things a network will bring about. We are engaged in an exploration, an adventure.

At Carnegie Mellon today, we have a computerized campus mail system. It's a great convenience, and I think students find it so, too. I'm much more accessible to them now than I was ever able to be before. They can write me a note, without having to go through a secretary, and what's more, I often answer it, promptly, because it's so easy to do. A fair amount of my correspondence is conducted that way now. It has obvious advantages even over the telephone, because you don't have to be there when the call is made, and the sender doesn't have to be there when you return the call, so information is actually transferred more quickly than is often possible by phone. That's the kind of modest change computers have brought so far to our campus. Change of this kind is hardly revolutionary.

A Revolution in Education?

Before the computer and all the associated devices can have any great impact on the educational system, there have to be major developments in our understanding of what the educational process is. Up to now, particularly at the university level, we have operated on what I call the "infection theory" of learning. This theory holds that if you assemble a large number of people in a room and spray a large number of words at them, some of those words will be infectious and will stick with some of those people and perhaps affect their future behavior. (Another form of the theory is that people are infected if they spray themselves with words from a large number of pages of print.)

A different theory might be called the "Mr. Chips" theory, according to which students learn by being treated with tender loving care. But, while tender loving care may be as important for students as it is for patients in a hospital, it is no more adequate as a theory of learning than it is as a theory of curing disease. The "Mark Hopkins and a log" theory is a variant of the Mr. Chips theory, a peculiarly useless one in view of the fact that we wouldn't have enough logs to accommodate 6,000 students—and Carnegie Mellon is far from being a large university.

Technology has helped to implement the infection theory in a modest sort of way. It has provided the means for broadcasting the words, using microphones and loudspeakers or headphones, and for putting the professors on film. (Sometimes I think it's only the economic self-interest of professors that demands that they be there live at all.) Though some people believe that technology actually interferes with Mr. Chip's ministrations, I think the contrary is true, as I've already suggested in describing our campus mail system. The idea that having a lot of screens and boxes around makes human beings less interested in talking to each other, or doing all the other kinds of things that human beings do, just isn't borne out by the facts. At Carnegie Mellon, the Computer Science Department has been saturated with networked computers for a dozen years, yet it is the most social and sociable department on campus, both at work and at play.

On the other hand, an improved technology of infection still does not amount to a revolution in education. If computers are to have real educational significance, there will have to be a major advance in what's now called cognitive science. We must gain a much deeper understanding of what it is that a student learns, what it is that a student should learn in order to become capable of exercising particular skills, and how that learning comes about. The theory we need does not so much concern the electronics we have available as it does the human component in the system that does our thinking and our learning. A good deal of progress has been made toward that theory, or at least its foundations, in the past 30 years. Now we are just getting to the point where researchers are beginning seriously to apply it to actual educational procedures.

It seems equally obvious to me that computers will not revolutionize education until there are massive changes in the organizational and administrative structure of the educational system as well. There must first of all be a redefinition of the teacher's role. Perhaps we'll never reach the point of having a completely professor-free university, but at least the professors will have to abandon the theory of infection. Secondly, we have to develop new conceptions of the production and marketing of software. There is no more sense in having each university prepare all its own instructional programs than there would have been in having each one publish its own textbooks. In general, for every megabuck we spend in hardware and systems software, we will need to spend another megabuck for research on effective learning and development of modern learning environments in the schools.

By way of conclusion, let me say that, as I hope the examples of the steam engine and the computer make clear, new technology is simply new knowledge; and as such, it resides not in machines but in the human brains that invent them, develop them, and use them. Even though the machines can help us learn about their characteristics by our use of them, still, in the last analysis, we have to think about technology in terms of human knowledge.

Knowledge confers capabilities, but capabilities, like knowledge itself, can be used for good or ill. Prometheus brought us indispensable knowledge, while Pandora brought us mischievous knowledge. Yet, without denying all the problems that we face in contemporary society, some of which are admittedly an outgrowth of our knowledge, I think that most of us would rather be living in the 20th century than in the 13th. Technological revolutions are not something that "happen" to us. We make them, and we make them for better or for worse. Our task is not to peer into the future to see what computers will bring us, but to shape the future that we want to have—a future that will create new possibilities for human learning, including, perhaps most important of all, new possibilities for learning to understand ourselves.

References

Bok, D. (1985). Looking into education's high-tech future. *EDUCOM Bulletin*, 20, 2–10, 17.

Dreyfus, H. L. (1967). *What Computers Can't Do*. New York: Harper & Row, (Rev. edition, 1979).

Langley, P., Simon, H. A., Bradshaw, G., & Zytkow, J. (1986). *Scientific Discovery*. Cambridge, MA: MIT Press.

II.4 Managing in an Information-Rich World

We often hear our society described nowadays as an "information" society. It is said that tangible products, like steel and wheat, have been replaced in the world's economy by information and by devices for displaying, transmitting, and manipulating information. There is a measure of truth in that description, although the death of manufacturing and agriculture has perhaps been exaggerated—the great bulk of the world's employed population is still engaged in cultivating plants and animals or manufacturing products made of wood, metal, fiber, and plastic.

Perhaps, then, it would be better to speak of an "information-rich" society, a society in which information is produced and flows at rates unprecedented in world history. Our society is surely "information-rich" in this sense. We are bombarded by information, engulfed in it. It pours out of our newspapers, our books, the television set, the telephone—to say nothing of our traditional human conversational partners, who are still a vital part of our personal communication system. I almost forgot to add the computer as one of our new information sources—in many ways, I will argue, the most important.

If Information Is Plentiful, What Is Scarce?

Plenty and scarcity are relative terms. At Easter time, new rabbit pets appear in some homes, and then in some yards. And those rabbits tend to multiply, as rabbits do. Then we discover that wherever rabbits are plentiful, grass is scarce. A rabbit-rich society is also likely to be a grass-scarce society. The abundance of one resource causes a scarcity of another. What is scarce when information is plentiful? I think we all know the answer from personal experience: when information is plentiful, time to attend to it is scarce. Attention is the scarce factor in an information-rich society.

When Abraham Lincoln was a young man, he had access to very few books. It was worth his while to walk long distances to borrow books. (Remarkably, he also walked long distances to return them!) Time for reading was plentiful relative to the scarcity of good books. Fortunately, he found a few very good ones, and he studied them with great care. Nowadays we would be skeptical that someone could educate himself or herself, as Abraham Lincoln did, with a dozen books.

Because our basic attitudes are rooted in a culture where time could be plentiful, but information was scarce, we sometimes think that we must pay attention to information just because it is there—like the mountain-climber Mallory, who said that was why he climbed mountains: they were there. If the newspaper is delivered, we must read it (some academicians even think they must read the *Sunday New York Times*). If the telephone rings we must answer it.

A Rational Information Strategy

In this information-rich world, it is instructive to ask oneself what would constitute a rational strategy toward information. Let's begin with the daily newspaper—whichever one you are addicted to. In the first place, most of what you find in today's newspaper was in yesterday's—some of the lead paragraphs excepted. The world does not change very much in one spin of the globe: Nicaragua, Afghanistan, Ireland, Sri Lanka, axe murders, Irangate were with us yesterday, are with us today, and will be with us tomorrow.

In the second place, most of the tiny incremental changes that take place from one day to another can be predicted. There will be one new political scandal, one new corporate takeover attempt, a few cases of aggravated assault, and so on. Of course, the names of the actors will change, but almost all of them are strangers to you anyway.

In the third place, how often it is efficient to update your information store depends on what use you are going to make of that information. What do you intend to do about Afghanistan? About axe murders? About corporate takeovers? And do you need to have today's or yesterday's news in order to do it?

Having carried out this exercise myself, I quickly concluded that I could dispense with the daily newspaper, and turn to the weekly news magazines instead. Applying the same analysis to them, I progressed next to monthlies. Then I discovered a wonderful little book, *The World Almanac*, which reviews and updates the world's history annually. The savings of time and attention have been colossal.

But, you will object, important things do happen in the world from time to time: Presidents are elected; wars are declared. Certainly you need to know about those. Indeed you do; and if you go to lunch with a few friends each day, you will learn about them at lunch, at the very latest. As a bonus, you will acquire a reputation as a good listener.

I hope that you do not think I am prejudiced against newspapers. What I have said applies equally well to radio and television. All are dispensable, and when dispensed with, the time available for reading informative books is increased enormously.

Why do I exempt books? Because books (the right books!) contain information that is not as transitory and ephemeral as the information in periodical sources. If you want to understand contemporary China, the least efficient way is to take a brief trip to China, without knowledge of the language. The next least efficient is to read everything that is printed about China in any newspaper. The most efficient is to spend a much shorter period of time reading a few authoritative books on Chinese history, Chinese culture, and the contemporary Chinese government and economy. That is the cost-effective way to gain knowledge in an information-rich world.

Applying the Strategy to Management

The same analysis we apply to our personal information-ingesting habits can be applied to information-processing in business organizations. The fact that information can be created is not a sufficient reason for creating in, nor the fact that it can be distributed a sufficient reason for distributing it, nor the fact that it is available for reading a sufficient reason for reading it.

A few years ago, the State Department faced a problem in its communications between embassies around the world and Washington. Whenever a crisis occurred anywhere in the world, a great flood of messages flowed into Washington, not only from the embassy at the site of the crisis, but from all of the embassies in nations that were directly or indirectly affected by it—that is, almost all embassies. The teletypes in Washington could not handle the message load, and great backlogs developed in which were buried, with all the others, the few critical messages that really needed to get through.

Information processing experts were consulted. Their solution was to replace the teletypes with line printers that had adequate capacity to keep pace with the message flow. So the information flooded in—to be read by whom? The capacity bottleneck in the printers was simply replaced by a capacity bottleneck in the foreign service officers who were supposed to read their output. A typical outcome, you may say, of a technological fix that does not draw the boundaries of the system broadly enough.

This incident cannot be dismissed as an isolated example. Our capacities for duplicating information—by printing, xeroxing, or distributing it via a computer bulletin board—have exploded; while our capacities for absorbing information have not increased at all. The history of so-called "Management Information Systems" illustrates how costly this mismatch between sending and receiving capacities can be.

Management Information Systems were hailed as opening a new era of informed management. What the first generation of these systems accomplished, for the most part, was to inundate managers' desks with irrelevant reports that they had neither time nor desire to study. As a result, MIS is in generally bad repute, and has been replaced by new buzzwords like "Management Decision Aids." The change in label, if accompanied by a corresponding change in viewpoint, is a notable advance.

The first generation of MIS was designed mostly by experts in accounting and computing who observed that a great deal of information lies around in most companies—information about costs and revenues, about production and sales and inventories—and that the powerful new technology of computers could assemble this information into reports that analyzed it from every conceivable angle. How the reports could or would be used was little considered. The designers of the systems were simply not knowledgeable enough about what it is that managers do, what decisions they make, and what information would be relevant to these decisions.

If a corporate information system is to be useful for management, then its design must begin with an analysis of the jobs of managers. What decisions do managers, in different locations within the organization, in fact make or participate in making? What kinds of information would help to make these decisions better? When these questions are asked, and the jobs of managers are studied carefully, certain important facts about the decision-making process begin to emerge.

First, a great deal of the information that would aid decision making does not originate inside the company at all, but outside. It is information about customers, about competitors and the industry, about trends in the economy in the short and long runs, about developments in international economic affairs. It is especially true as we move toward the top of the executive ladder that the information managers need for their decisions is external information, information about the outside world, rather than internal information about the company.

Top executives do not simply look inward, managing company internal affairs; they are the principal "interfaces" of the company with the outside world, discovering the needs for change and innovation that arise from external opportunities and threats. A management information system for top management has to be based at least as much on information obtained from the outside as information derived from company records. Organization units have to be created that can produce this information, or it has to be purchased.

Second, the bulk of the information that would aid decision making is not numerical information, but information written in natural language—the language of newspapers, trade journals, correspondence, and books. A computer system that is to aid managerial decision making cannot simply crunch numbers; it must be equally adept at processing words, extracting their meanings, filtering them, analyzing them.

In short, if managerial decision aids are to make good their promises, they must draw on the full resources of artificial intelligence to provide computer programs that (1) have access to information originating outside the company, (2) have sophisticated capabilities for filtering and analyzing such information, and (3) have natural-language capabilities as extensive and powerful as their numerical capabilities.

In its original forms, MIS showed how to produce information. It did not show how to absorb it. The challenge today is to produce systems that can analyze vast amounts of information with such sophistication that they output for human consumption only a small part of what they receive. A good rule of thumb for a computer system is that it should not be installed unless it inputs several orders of magnitude of information more than it outputs to its human users.

The idea of "filtered" or "analyzed" information creates concerns. How will we be sure that the system will give us access to the information that is really important? Won't we miss something? These concerns miss the point of my central argument: that as long as information is in long supply and attention is in short supply we will necessarily "miss something." We are capable of absorbing only a trivial fraction of the information that is around. It is essential that we attend to the most important information and ignore the less important. Computer systems, properly programmed, can make that selection for us. Their selection will not be perfect, but it will be more effective than the hit-or-miss selection we can make ourselves or with only human help.

Artificial Intelligence and Experts

The practicality of introducing computers as intelligent assistants in selecting and analyzing information hinges on our current understanding of intelligence and our abilities to program computers to exhibit it. An assessment of these capabilities best begins with an account of what we know about human experts, and then proceeds to the design of expert systems for computers.

The problem-solving and decision-making processes of human experts have been studied intensively by psychologists for the past thirty years. From that study, important generalizations have emerged. We know that expertise is based on extensive knowledge. Typically, the expert has at least 50,000 "chunks" of knowledge about his or her special domain. This knowledge is organized in a particular way: It is "indexed" so that when the expert finds himself faced with a problem, he will notice cues in the situation that will recall to him the relevant knowledge he has stored. The number 50,000 does not seem so large when we remember that our natural-language vocabularies are larger than that.

We know also that it takes a long time to acquire this indexed memory—not less than ten years for world-class performance. In nearly a dozen fields of human performance that have been studied, the biographies of world-class experts show without exception a period of intense training and development over at least a decade. Not all experts are world class, but the intensiveness of the training required reminds us of the immense investments in human experience we have in all of our business organizations.

The way in which the expert knowledge is organized explains why experts can solve many problems and respond to many situations "intuitively"—that is, very rapidly, and often without being able to specify the processes they have used to reach their answers. Intuition is no longer a mystery. It is simply the capacity to recognize familiar cues in the situations that arise, and to use these cues to retrieve information. It is not a special faculty, but the inevitable by-product of the acquisition of knowledge, and its storage in this form.

The numerous expert systems that have been built and are now being built as applications of artificial intelligence are based squarely on the understanding we have gained of human expertise. There are now many examples of expert systems that are capable of performing at a good professional level. Among the best known of these are medical diagnosis systems like Caduceus and Mycin.

Of more direct relevance to management are expert systems that can perform financial analysis. As long ago as 1960, Geoffrey Clarkson had built a system capable of making investment decisions for portfolios of trust funds. The system's decisions matched closely with those of a trust investment officer of a bank. More recently, Marinus Bouwman has shown how expert systems can diagnose the health of companies by automatic analysis of their financial statements—again, at a good professional level of quality.

The Future of Artificial Intelligence

We might ask what the boundaries are beyond which AI cannot penetrate. If there are such boundaries, it is not at all clear where they lie. Nor is it too profitable to ask where the present boundaries are, for they are moving rapidly. Hence, probably the most fruitful inquiry is to determine what are the most essential and the most promising directions of motion. (The most essential and the most promising need not be the same.)

Natural language The processing of natural language by computer is a research direction that has both great importance and great promise. Its importance for communication between people and computers is obvious. The progress to date has been considerable. Today we have systems that can understand natural-language descriptions of problems and program themselves to try to solve the problems (UNDERSTAND). We have programs that can read physics problems, written in English, interpret these problems, convert the interpretations into algebra, and go to work on the solutions (ISAAC). We have programs that can analyze very simple stories sufficiently to determine the plot, the motivations of the characters, and so on.

All of these programs understand English, but only with severe restrictions on vocabulary and the domain of interpretation. We may say that we have a grasp of some of the principal mechanisms required for handling language, but have a long way to go to achieve the generality that characterizes human use of language.

Originality Programs have now been written (DENDRAL, AM, BACON, and others) that can search for regularities in data, and thereby discover scientific laws. The BACON program, for example, has been able to (re)discover Kepler's Third Law of planetary motion, Ohm's Law of electrical currents, Black's Law of temperature equilibrium, and many others, by careful, highly selective induction from the original data. These programs, and others like them, provide a decisive answer to claims that programs cannot go beyond the skills of their programmers.

Learning A variety of learning schemes for computers have been devised and are under study. One of these, adaptive production systems, allows the computer to learn a skill like solving algebra equations by examining worked-out examples of solutions—like those presented in standard textbooks. The adaptive production system analyzes each step in the solution, finds what action has been taken, detects a cue that can be used to recognize the relevance of the action (hence signal when it should be taken), and builds these insights into new instructions that can solve equations. Learning is an exceedingly active domain of research in artificial intelligence today.

Sensing and acting Robotics, the construction of systems that can sense the situation in the real world around them and act to change that situation, have proved to be the most difficult challenge to AI research. The human eye and ear, and the limbs whose actions they can guide, have proved to be very sophisticated organs—much more sophisticated than the "new brain" that does our high-level thinking. While steady progress is being made, we are much farther from building computer sense organs that come close to matching their human counterparts than we are to building problem-solving components that can think like engineers, businessmen, or professors. We may be closer to automating the skills of a manager than the skills of a bulldozer driver.

Natural language, originality, learning, and robotics are some of the main areas of artificial intelligence research and progress today. As our capabilities in these areas grow, the applications of AI will grow correspondingly. In cooperation with people and computers, the division of labor will continue to change.

Artificial Intelligence and Cognitive Science

I have emphasized the use of computers to perform tasks requiring intelligence, thereby broadening the domains for the automation of skills. But computers have equal importance as tools for gaining a deeper understanding of, and thereby enhancing, human performance. The main body of intelligence in our society resides (and will for a long time continue to reside) not in computers but in human heads. We can improve our productivity by enlisting computer intelligence to augment human intelligence. But we may be able to improve it even more rapidly by improving the quality of human intelligence. There are several domains in which this might be done: education, business decision making, and the formation of public policy.

A large fraction of the human resources in our society are engaged in education. I am not referring to the teachers, but to the students. A third of our lives are spent in educating ourselves so that we can spend the next two thirds productively. Yet, the theories that underlie the practice of education are primitive and shallow. They amount to little more than a theory of infection: that if you spray people with lots of words, some of them may be catching.

As we begin to understand the nature of learning processes (as in the adaptive production systems I mentioned earlier), we should be able to improve our educational processes. Even a twenty percent increase in their efficiency could support an increase of ten percent in lifespan working time. As our population ages, that ten percent could become crucial to maintaining even our present levels of per capita productivity.

The improvement of managerial decision making, and the improvement of the quality of our public policy making are other goals that research on human thinking may help us to attain. Today, we are faced with the worldwide problem of finding a sustainable source of energy that is compatible with a livable environment. There is little use in solving just one facet of the problem (energy or environment) without solving both. We are going to need all of the resources of intelligence we can muster to find viable alternatives and to understand the global consequences of those we find.

But in dealing with the difficult problems that face us, we need not rely exclusively on either human intelligence or machine intelligence. The most promising direction is to harness them together—to design cooperative man-machine systems that can carry out analysis that neither component by itself could sustain. Computers today can share the work of thinking with us, and there is plenty of work—and will continue to be—for both of us.

Understanding Ourselves

To some people, the idea that we are learning how human beings think, that we are gaining an understanding of the workings of the human mind, is a little threatening. It threatens, in particular, the uniqueness of that mind—its separation from the rest of nature. In the same way, Copernicus threatened the uniqueness of our location in the universe, and Darwin threatened the uniqueness or our origins as a species.

Perhaps there is no threat at all. Perhaps uniqueness is not the touchstone of human worth. Today, we have seen our fragile planet as viewed from space. We have learned that humankind must live in peace on that planet. The task is not to show how we are unique and set apart from nature. The task is to show how we can live in harmony with, and as a part of nature. The study of human thinking, the achievement of a deeper understanding of our minds as part of ourselves, can help us find that harmony.

II.5 On the Alienation of Workers and Management

Many cultures, including our own, cherish a myth of an earlier Golden Age, in which life was delightful and free from dangers and problems, and men and women were happy. The story of the Garden of Eden is such a tale. During the 18th century, the Age of Reason, such myths flourished, generated in the minds of political philosophers who were inspired, perhaps, by romantic travelers' tales of the idyllic existence of the Indians of the New World.

Jean Jacques Rousseau, especially, romanticized about the noble savage, sought the causes for his fall from grace, and proposed a civilized alternative to the state of nature. "Man", he said, "was born free, but everywhere he is in chains."

The ideal of a Golden Age did not die with the 18th century. In our own day, we cast nostalgic eyes on the past, imagining that we see there simpler and happier times that have been taken from us by the complexities and confusions of our present industrial society. Somehow, the homes and the workplaces of that earlier time had charms that are missing from our modern life.

My purpose tonight is to examine some of our present discontents—those that centre on the workplace—to assess their severity, and to ask how far they differ from the discontents of the past. Only by such an assessment can we reach sound judgements as to which of our problems are genuine and which illusory, which have remedies, and which are necessary accompaniments to the human condition.

The simplest way to put my question is this: Are our modern factory, office and shop fit places for human beings, working out and living out their days? In particular, are the changes taking place in the workplace—changes resulting from the continuing advance of technology, or from rising levels of education in our society, or from our responses to the problems of resource scarcities and environmental pollution—are these changes improving the quality of life in the workplace, or causing it to deteriorate?

Of course, these questions may not have a uniform answer. The conditions of some people may have ameliorated, of others deteriorated. We may have to say something different about the life of the executive and the life of the blue-collar or clerical worker. Moreover, the quality of life has many dimensions. We may observe progress along some of them, regress along others. In my remarks tonight, I want to focus on one of those dimensions: the levels of work satisfaction, people's attachment to or alienation from their work. I will begin with executive work, which I think differs enough from blue-collar and clerical work to deserve a separate answer.

The Work of the Executive

Twenty years ago we learned a new phrase, "the Organization Man." We learned it from William H. Whyte, who wrote a widely circulated book of the title;[1] it has since become a part of our language. Like all words of the living language, it has changed its meaning over the years, out of the control of its originator. Whyte meant the term as a pejorative: the Organization Man was an executive who had sold his soul to the Corporation. He dressed as it wanted him to, married as it wanted him to, and thought as it wanted him to. But most important for Whyte, the Organization Man was a member of a group. He was loyal to the group, conformed to the group norms, and made his decisions and did his work through group processes. It was no part of his role to express his individuality, to innovate in solitude, or to dissent from the group consensus.

Whyte's argument has been widely interpreted, and often applauded, as an attack on modern business institutions and modern industrial society. It was no such thing. It was an expression of nostalgia for an individualistic ethic—the Protestant ethic, as it is often called—which Whyte thought was rapidly being displaced by a Social Ethic (*ibid.*, p. 7): "By social ethic I mean that contemporary body of thought which makes morally legitimate the pressures of society against the individual. Its major propositions are three: a belief in group as the source of creativity; a belief in 'belongingness' as the ultimate need of the individual; and a belief in the application of science to achieve the belongingness." By "science," he meant specifically social psychology as applied to human relations.

Many of us (I can speak for myself) share Whyte's sympathy for the rugged individualists of the past—the Henry Fords and the Andrew Carnegies. But there are several things we must remember about them. First, there was generally room enough for only one of those individualists in any single company. Henry Ford could be an individualist because he could hire as many organization men as he wanted to work for him. Organization men with a difference—they did not make decisions in groups; they were seldom allowed to make decisions at all.

Second, we must not imagine that there is no place for individualists in the business and industrial world today. Their main opportunities arise, as they have always done, in the spawning of new industries. I can think, offhand, of a dozen examples in the electronics industry alone—men like William Hewlett of Hewlett–Packard, or Pat Haggerty of Texas Instruments. Moreover, these contemporary individualists seem often to have acquired a managerial style that allows them to work effectively with others. They seem to have absorbed at least some elements of the social ethic. But perhaps we would find that that was also true of men of the past, like Carnegie, if we examined their careers carefully.

So we are left with the question of whether Whyte, in his portrait of the Organization Man, was revealing a genuine trend in our society, or whether he was just rediscovering the fact that most people, most of the time, need a supportive social environment—need to "belong"—and are capable, at most, of only modest bursts of creativity, whether in isolation or in groups. Whyte himself is quite cautious in his claims and proposals. He speaks of a needed balance between the individualist ethic and the social ethic, and argues only that the balance, in recent years, has moved too far toward the latter.

Let us accept the premise that the social ethic describes—if with a bit of exaggeration—the ways of thought and action of most business executives today. What does this say of their satisfactions, of the quality of life in the executive workplace, of their attachment to it, or alienation from it?

First, I hope that I have at least raised doubts in your minds that there has been any massive shift during the past few generations in the nature of the executive's work or of his social environment. Conformity to social pressure is not an invention of our generation. Nor should we go to the other extreme and assume that ours is peculiarly an age of nonconformity. The solid ranks of blue jeans I see in my classes disabuses me of that idea. What kind of nonconformity produces this coincidental convergence on blue jeans, beards, and informal living arrangements?

Man is not a solitary savage but a social animal. Most human beings are not productive, or even comfortable, when placed in isolation and asked to solve vague, complex, unstructured problems. We cannot conclude that the office, which provides them with social support and social interaction, is an inhumane environment for them.

How then are we to account for the boredom and lack of satisfaction that many executives experience in their jobs? If the workplace is humane, why do many persons express their alienation from it, and why do they seek their satisfaction outside it? There is a considerable body of research—much of it due to the late Daniel Berlyne at the University of Toronto[2]—that describes the conditions under which activities can hold people's interest and attention. In simplest terms, the conditions are that the activities be sufficiently complex to continue to present elements of novelty, but sufficiently simple to be understandable, so that pattern can be discerned in them.

The level of complexity of a task does not, of course, remain constant. Experience with it gradually reduces its complexity, so that in time almost any task can become routine, uninteresting, boring. Nor is the complexity of a task the same for all persons. What is incomprehensible to some may be banal to others.

Observation teaches us that in most organizations most of the time the average level of complexity of executive tasks is somewhat lower than we would wish it if our main aim were to maximize job interest and job satisfaction. But of course that is not, and cannot be, our main aim. The goals of successful company operation have to take priority over the goals of immediate work satisfaction for executives. Put in simplest terms—which apply to all kinds of work and not just to executive jobs—there are lots of dull tasks that have to be done in the world each day, and to each of us falls a larger or a smaller share of them. Some of these dull tasks, particularly those requiring mechanical effort, we have passed off to machines, but more than enough remain for the human beings in almost all occupations.

When a person's job is unrewarding, for this or other reasons, he looks for his main satisfactions to other parts of his life, and we say that he is alienated. Again, this is not a peculiarity of contemporary life. The novels and letters of Stendhal complain constantly of the tedium of executive life in the French army and government a century and a half ago.[3] Samuel Pepys writing his diary in England three centuries ago, gives us only glimpses of the work of his office at the Admiralty, because, apart from periodic political crises that affect it and endanger his position, he finds his life outside the office so much more interesting.[4] The testimony of these witnesses is especially interesting, in that both were reputedly effective executives, and both were intensely interested in, and curious about, life, even though their curiosity was more often satisfied outside the workplace than in it.

How has the introduction of computers into business changed this picture? To date, the impact of the computer on executive work has been very modest, particularly at the higher levels of the executive ladder. In some middle-management areas (e.g., scheduling and inventory control) the computer has assumed responsibility for routine, repetitive decisions that managers had previously made. Here, the consequence has been to transfer the manager's attention to somewhat longer-run concerns, and to the management of people.

At higher executive levels, even these kinds of effects have not been visible. To a limited extent, the computer has affected the top executives' jobs by changing and improving the flow of information to their decisions—the information that is available to them, for example, when they are engaged in collective bargaining, about the cost of particular provisions in the labor contract.

Changes of this sort, however, have little significance for the human quality of the executive's job. They do not change the nature of his interactions with his associates or his subordinates. Of course, we cannot be sure that this will continue to be the case—that later developments in the computer revolution will not impinge on the manager's job in more fundamental ways. Nothing we have seen up to the present time allows us to predict with any confidence what the shape of such developments might be, or their consequences for alienation or for the balance between the social ethic and individualism.

What I have said should not be taken as an argument against making the executive workplace a more challenging and humane environment. Use of the computer to automate routine work is one possible direction of improvement, although we should remember that the human jobs left behind after the automation may sometimes be simpler instead of more complex than those they replaced. Other possibilities for work enrichment may be found in more frequent lateral transfer of executives from one responsibility to another.

In arguing that I see no evidence of strong trends toward increased alienation of executives from their work, I have presented no systematic evidence—no statistics, and no experiments. Instead, I have relied on anecdotes and appeals to your own personal experiences for support of my position. I should like to turn now to a domain where at least a modicum of objective evidence is available to discipline our personal viewpoints. In the rest of my remarks, I should like to talk about work satisfactions and alienation of blue-collar and clerical workers, and particularly about the impacts on work satisfaction of factory and office automation.

Work before Industrialization

Golden Age myths do not all describe a happy uncivilized savage. There is also a Golden Age of preindustrialized society, inhabited by happy craftsmen and even (though they are less mentioned) happy peasants. The contrast of this Golden Age with the bleak realities of life in factory and mine during the early Industrial Revolution provides a central topic for nineteenth century social criticism. The theme of alienation finds a clear voice in the writings of Karl Marx. The *Communist Manifesto*[5] provides a succinct statement:

> Owing to the extensive use of machinery and to the division of labor, the work of the proletarians has lost all individual character, and consequently, all charm for the workman. He becomes an appendage of the machine, and it is only the most simple, most monotonous, and most easily acquired knack that is required of him.

One hundred years after the publication of the *Communist Manifesto* the same fears were expressed with respect to the introductions of the computer to automate factory and office work. Two charges, then, have been leveled: that the Industrial Revolution dehumanized work, and that the appearance of the electronic computer has dehumanized it further.

Again, few statistics are forthcoming that would settle these questions in any definitive way. We know that, prior to the Industrial Revolution, almost all people were poorer in material goods than they are in the industrialized nations today. Perhaps, however, they were poor but happy. Perhaps they have given up their pleasant and challenging occupations for the potage of a goods-filled unsatisfying leisure.

An English writer, Alasdair Clayre, in his book, *Work and Play*,[6] hit upon the ingenious idea of searching out what the preindustrial workers in England themselves said about work. Of course, there was much more written *about* workers and peasants than there was *by* workers and peasants. Nevertheless, he was able to find a little diary material, some reasonably concrete reports by observers, and, most important, the evidence of poems and work songs that were current among the people. Here is a typical example of what he found, part of a poem written about 1730 by one Stephen Duck (*ibid*, p. 93):

Week after Week we this dull Task pursue, / Unless when winn'wing Days produce a new; / A new indeed, but frequently a worse, / Thc Threshall yields but to the Master's Curse: / He counts the Bushels, counts how much a Day, / Then swears we've idled half our Time away. /

The evidence is wholly consistent. Work—whether on farm or at sea—is described as difficult and wearisome. After work is done there may be time for pleasure. As Clayre sums it up (*ibid.*, p. 134):

It is not often, in the whole body of traditional songs, that we find a reference to work as an activity valued in itself, independent of love, of the chances of interruption by girls, of play, or of rewards.

We cannot, then, even enter a Scottish verdict of "not proven." Though the evidence is less full then we might wish, the weight of it is clearly opposed to the reality of a Golden Age of work that was destroyed by the machine and the factory. We should not go to the other extreme of supposing that the Industrial Revolution was itself a Golden Age. We know too much about the brutalities of the first century of the factory system to fall into that error. But my concern this evening is with alienation in the twentieth century, not in the nineteenth.

Automation and Alienation

The computer appeared on the scene at the end of the Second World War. It did not begin to find substantial application in business and industry, except in scientific and engineering calculation, until the middle 1950s. Hence, we are now only about two decades into the computer revolution. There seems to me no doubt that it is a revolution of the most profound kind, which has only begun to run its course. The computer provides mind, in the same sense and with the same generality that the steam engine provided muscle. Productive processes operating entirely automatically, untouched by human hands or brains, are no longer science fiction but fact—even if, as yet, rather uncommon fact.

Because the computer is such a recent innovation, we do have some reasonably reliable and comparable data on levels of work satisfaction before its introduction and today. We also have evidence from a few careful studies of the changes experienced by workers at the time computers were introduced into their factories and offices.

For more than fifteen years, various national public opinion polling organizations have been conducting job satisfaction surveys of national samples of workers. Data are now available from at least fifteen such surveys. The evidence they provide is unequivocal: there are no signs of decline in the average levels of job satisfaction reported by respondents in these surveys. Fifteen or twenty years ago, most workers (80 to 90 per cent) said they were "satisfied" or "reasonably satisfied" with their jobs. About the same percentage say the same things today.[7]

Of course we must be careful how we interpret these findings. A man who says he is reasonably satisfied with his job may not be especially happy in it. He might have a long list of things he would like to see changed. He might not even be particularly pleased with his choice of occupation, and might wish that he had entered another. We do not have good measuring sticks for absolute levels of satisfaction. But what we *can* conclude from the findings of the polls is that, however high or low the absolute levels of satisfaction, there has been no discernible trend in those levels since computers began to be used by business and industry on a large scale. Automation, as far as it has gone to date, has not produced new alienation.

A person whose conception of automation was formed by viewing Charlie Chaplin's *Modern Times* might understandably be puzzled at these poll results. The dehumanizing effects of machines appear so blatant that is would seem that workers could not fail to notice them, unless they were numbered by their work experiences (as has occasionally been suggested by critics of the factory system). But of course *Modern Times* is a caricature, and it is a caricature of a form of mechanization that is becoming increasingly outmoded. To get a more factual picture of the meaning of automation for workers, we must examine the automated workplace itself and study its characteristics.

A substantial number of studies have now been published describing factories and offices operating at one or another level of mechanization and automation, including before-and-after studies of the installation of new computing systems. Let us review briefly what they have found.

First there are studies of the short-term, transient effects of introducing computers, like the observations reported by Ida Hoos.[8] In these studies, we see considerable evidence of psychological trauma produced by the changes. Workers are often fearful of the new technology, and express feelings that their work has been dehumanized. They worry about the prospects of their being displaced by the computer, and about their abilities to cope with their altered jobs.

That such reactions to computerization have frequently occurred cannot be doubted, but their proper interpretation is more problematic. Are they, in fact, reactions to computers and a computerized workplace; or may they be, instead, reactions to change? And even more particularly, may they be reaction to the particular ways in which change was introduced and implemented?

Writers on human relations have been pointing out for years that the way in which an innovation will be received by the members of an organization will depend critically upon the way in which the innovation is presented to them. Change may be feared and resisted, or change may be accepted as a welcome challenge. There is nothing in human nature that is inherently hostile to change, for human beings seek out novelty as often as they flee it. Whether their reaction to it will be positive or negative appears to depend in large part on the nature and extent of their participation in the change process.

In simplest terms, people usually react positively to actions that they perceive as being done *by* them, and negatively to those they perceive as being done *to* them. It is not change, but feelings of anxiety and helplessness in being subjected to change over which they have no control or influence that causes malaise and opposition.

We cannot be sure, therefore, whether studies that show negative attitudes towards a computerized workplace, measured shortly after the new technology has been installed, reflect characteristics of the technology or are simply the consequences of a clumsy, poorly managed change process. We know that managements in the past have frequently been guilty of failing to consult workers and secure their participation, in all sorts of changes, most of them unconnected with mechanization. We know that these failures in communication quite consistently produce exactly the sorts of reactions that have been observed in the before-and-after computer studies. Hence, we are left with two different possible causes for these reactions, and no basis for disconfounding them. For further enlightenment, we mush turn to other sorts of studies.

Nearly fifteen years ago, Robert Blauner carried out an important series of case studies which he reported in his book, *Alienation and Freedom: the Factory Worker and his Industry.*[9] Blauner's idea was that "technology" is much too broad a term to use in explaining the psychological impact of industrialization upon the worker. There are many forms of manufacturing technology—the assembly line is only one of them—and different forms might have quite different psychological significance. Some of them might be severely dehumanizing and alienating, and others less so or not at all.

Blauner looked at companies using four different technologies: a printing concern, a textile manufacturer, an automobile assembly plant, and a continuous process chemical manufacturing plant. He found substantial differences in the levels of satisfaction or dissatisfaction of workers in these four situations. Some of the diversity of attitudes could be attributed to differences in the ethnic and social origins of the workers, but even when allowance was made for this factor, large differences remained. Worker satisfactions were relatively high in the printing concern and the chemical plant, relatively low in the textile mill and the auto assembly plant.

With a little imagination, we can conjecture some of the reasons for these findings. Printing was, at least at the time of Blauner's study, a relatively traditional technology employing skilled craftsmen. The textile mill and the assembly line fit more closely to the "Modern Times" stereotype. Most of the jobs in these factories were highly routine and repetitive, and the human work was paced by the rhythm of the machines.

The finding that job satisfaction at the chemical plant was relatively high requires a little more consideration. It was a modern, highly automated plant, in which humans found themselves primarily in a backup role—not operating the process but monitoring it, and intervening only in the case of malfunctioning. In addition to monitoring the ongoing operation, the human staff had, of course, the responsibilities for maintaining the plant and making repairs. Some parts of the engineering staff were continually engaged in the longer-term concerns of improving and expanding the plant, and introducing new operations into it. A relatively large fraction of the jobs associated with the plant called for a high level of skill, and few of the jobs were paced by the tempo of the manufacturing processes themselves. The man supervised the machine, maintained the machine, designed and modified the machine, but was not driven by the machine. His pace did not have to be matched, from moment to moment, to its pace.

It is the chemical plant, and not the textile mill or the auto assembly line, that most nearly typifies the direction in which highly automated and computerized factory and office work are moving. It is of great significance that the newer technology appears to be substantially more congenial to its human operators than the technology that was typical of an earlier phase of the Industrial Revolution. The current and continuing trend toward high levels of automation is eliminating some of the routine and boredom of semi-automated technologies.

Another series of studies that deserves attention was carried out by Thomas L. Whisler in a score of insurance offices.[10] Like Hoos, Whisler was interested in the comparison of attitudes toward work prior to and subsequent to the computerization of large-scale clerical operations. The difference between Whisler's studies and those of Hoos is that Whisler examined the offices, not immediately after the change had been introduced, but some years later. He did not observe strongly negative attitudes of the sort that Hoos had reported. On average, the clerical workers reported that their jobs were now more demanding—a higher level of accuracy and reliability was expected of them. At the same time, they reported that their jobs were no less pleasant or more boring than they had been before. Evidently the higher demands of the jobs produced as much challenge as tension.

A striking feature of Whisler's findings is that all of the changes in attitude he found were very small in magnitude, and often in opposite directions in different firms. A rather radical alteration of the data processing technology had produced only small, almost insignificant, changes in the perceived human quality of the work environment.

We need many more studies like those of Blauner and Whisler before we can be satisfied that their results may safely be extrapolated to the whole spectrum of manufacturing and clerical operations that are now being automated. However, the findings should be surprising only to persons who have not examined in detail the new technology—who still view it as if it were in a direct line of descent from the traditional mechanized factory, instead of representing a quite distinct and different line of evolution.

Systems Effects of Automation

To understand the effects of automation upon job satisfaction, it is not enough to observe the direct impact of automation upon the factory or office where it takes place. The purpose, and economic justification, of automation is to save human labor. After automation, fewer persons will be employed for a given level of output than before. This increase in productivity means that there will be shifts in the distribution of the labor force among occupations and industries. Under present conditions, and those of the foreseeable future, these shifts are bringing about a relative decline in the fraction of the labor force that is engaged in manufacturing and routine clerical occupations, and an increase in the fraction engaged in service occupations, a change that has already been going on for a generation and is likely to continue into the indefinite future.

This shift raises the important question of whether service jobs tend, on average, to be more or less satisfying than jobs in manufacturing industries or large clerical offices. The data from opinion polls do not show large differences in satisfaction among these categories, but the categories are too gross to allow us to reach conclusions with any great assurance. In particular, "service occupations" is a most heterogeneous category that includes schoolteachers, cosmetics salesmen, department store clerks, and innumerable other groups. Unless we know which of these occupations are going to be most expanded, we cannot easily decide whether work is going to become, on average, more pleasant or less pleasant.

Probably, on average, service occupations are not less routine than occupations in factories and offices. On the other hand, most service occupations appear to afford more-than-average human contact in their performance. This is generally considered a positive and humanizing aspect of a job, and a majority of people probably regard it as so.

We arrive at the conclusion that automation, by producing a net shift in the employment spectrum towards the service occupations, may make a small contribution toward increasing job satisfactions and the humaneness of the workplace, and almost surely is not deleterious in its effects. In all of this discussion, the assumption has been made implicitly that the levels of employment and unemployment are independent of how much automation has been introduced into the economy. Most economists would accept that assumption, and I have given the arguments for it in Chapter 5 of my *New Science of Management Decision*.[11]

Conclusion

In the preceding pages, I have surveyed the evidence for and against the existence of a trend toward the alienation of executives and workers from their jobs. I have considered the possibility both of a long-term trend, having its beginnings with the Industrial Revolution, and a short-term trend over the past twenty years, resulting from the widespread introduction of the computer into factory and office.

The evidence for either trend is almost wholly absent. There was no Golden Age of work prior to the Industrial Revolution—or at least, the workers themselves seemed unaware that they lived in one. Similarly, it appears that workers are about as satisfied or dissatisfied with their jobs today as they were twenty years ago.

A similar conclusion can be reached about the satisfaction of executives. The Organization Man and his discontents are not a phenomenon that is peculiar to our generation. Our attention has simply been called to, and a name provided for, a "social ethic" that has probably been the rule of executive behavior rather than the exception as long as we have had organizations.

Denial of trends in alienation does not mean that alienation is not extensive in all of the industrialized nations—Communist as well as Western. The main cause for it is not that work has been industrialized, but that man must work to live, and that, on average, jobs are not as complex as they would have to be to enlist the deep interest of those who fill them.

There is no reason for great optimism that the problem of alienation from work will ever be solved—that we will be freed entirely from the curse of the Apple. Some degree of alienation is probably an integral part of the human condition.

But there is no reason, also, why we should not search as diligently and intelligently as we can for ways to reduce the level of alienation in our society—ways that will make the workplace a more frequent locus for important life satisfactions to a larger fraction of the people who spend so many of their waking hours there.

Although modern trends toward automation have not, so far, had a visible impact on worker alienation, yet, the highly automated workplace appears to be a more humane environment than the typical workplace of earlier forms of manufacturing. We may therefore legitimately hope that automation will in time make a modest contribution to the solution of the important human problem we have been addressing.

Notes

1. N.Y.: Simon and Schuster, 1956.

2. *Conflict, Arousal, and Curiosity*. N.Y.: McGraw-Hill, 1960.

3. *To the Happy Few: Selected Letters of Stendhal*. N.Y.: Grove Press, 1952.

4. *Diary and Correspondence of Samuel Pepys, F.R.S.* London: George Bell and Sons, 1875, 4 vol.

5. Chicago: Charles H. Kerr & Company, n.d.

6. New York: Harper & Row, 1974.

7. Robert P. Quinn and Linda J. Shepard, *The 1972–73 Quality of Employment Survey*, Ann Arbor: Survey Research Center, Institute for Social Research, University of Michigan.

8. *Automation in the Office*, Washington, D.C.: Public Affairs Press, 1961.

9. Chicago: University of Chicago Press, 1964.

10. *The Impact of Computers on Organizations*. New York: Prager, 1970; and *Information Technology and Organizational Change*. Belmont, Cal.: Wadsworth, 1970.

11. Revised edition, Englewood Cliffs, N.J.: Prentice-Hall, 1977.

III MOTIVATION AND THE THEORY OF THE FIRM

The papers of Part III represent an effort to rethink the role of organizations in a modern economy and the reasons for the size and power of business firms. In *Administrative Behavior* (1947), I devoted a good deal of attention to what I called, interchangeably, organizational loyalty and organizational identification as a motivating force for organizational behavior. What I did *not* do in that book was to reconcile what I perceived to be the critical role of the organizational identifications of managers and employees with the belief, widely accepted in economics and in popular thought, that human behavior is basically selfish. I simply accepted the observed phenomena of identification as facts without asking how they were rooted in the architecture of human motives. The "new institutional economics," which I will discuss in a moment, attempted to account for organizational behavior on the basis of the common economic assumptions that people are motivated exclusively to gain income or wealth, and without appeal to a motive like loyalty or identification. I did not find that account convincing or consistent with what I perceived to be the empirical facts.

Working my way through this conundrum has been the greatest challenge in my economic research in the past two decades. It has produced an interesting, and I think important, explanation of organizational identification in terms of evolutionary mechanisms that support extensive altruism in human behavior. Organizational identification, thus motivated, provides an explanation, in turn, for the viability of the large business organizations that share with markets the ordering of a modern economy.

Group identification provides an explanation, also, for the wide variety of ethnic, national, religious and other loyalties that play a central role in human affairs, and that account for the presence of the large organizations (national, religious, and so on), other than business organizations, that populate the social landscape. However, I will have little to say in this volume about these other ramifications and implications of identification. I mention them because the existence of these many and complex loyalties adds additional credibility to the altruism-rooted theory of identification that I introduce here.

Markets and Organizations

The fall of communism in the Soviet Union and the other states in Eastern Europe has been hailed as a clear demonstration of the superiority of the market system over central planning, and perhaps it is. Of course, events of the recent past in Russia and adjoining areas have made the demonstration much less conclusive than it was previously thought to be. But, even if we had been spared this rather unpleasant sequel to the initial optimism, it would be safer to qualify the phrase "central planning" and replace it by "central planning at the level of the national state." For when we examine the so-called market economies, we find that the major part of the human economic activity in them takes place, not in markets, but inside the walls of large aggregates of people called business firms. And within those walls there is a great deal of central planning that uses criteria other than market prices.

Markets have not displaced organizations; indeed the latter have experienced unparalleled growth over the past several centuries. And currently we see that a good deal of the economic malaise in Eastern European countries (and probably also in China) can be attributed to the failure of these societies to acquire all of the skills needed to make large industrial organizations operate effectively. It would appear that successful market economies are actually organization-and-market economies.

The New Institutional Economics

Within economics there has been a resurgence of interest in organizations that has mainly taken the form of the "new institutional economics" spearheaded by Oliver Williamson. The development has some roots in the behavioral theory of the firm (and even older roots in the writings of John R. Commons and Joseph Schumpeter), but is largely a quite recent development (see Chapter IV.6).

In seeking to explain the corporation and its role in an organization-and-market economy, the new institutional economics has adhered rather closely to the assumptions and analytic methods of neoclassical theory—too closely for my tastes. It has argued that the boundaries between markets and organizations in economic affairs are determined by the transaction costs associated with different kinds of contractual relations (including the employment relation) and the costs of enforcing the terms of contractual agreements (including the protection of the employment contract against "shirking" and "opportunism" by those who are supposed, by contract, to act as agents of the interests of others).

Organizational Identification (Loyalty)

Transaction costs and opportunism provide an inadequate explanation for the central role played by large organizations in modern economies. In particular, we observe an enormous amount of behavior at all levels in organizations that is directed toward achieving the organization's objectives—an amount far beyond any capabilities that managements actually possess for detecting and punishing shirking, allocating credit for superior performance, or generally, measuring the marginal contributions of participants and rewarding them accordingly. (I recommend to my academic colleagues that they look around their own universities before deciding whether I am exaggerating. Everyday observations there provide an exceptional opportunity to get first-hand empirical data, including data on one's own behavior, about human motivations in organizations.)

I do not wish to claim that human beings, inside or outside organizations, are not mainly guided by selfish motives, but rather that "selfishness" (if that is what it is) frequently takes a special form in organizations, the form we call "organizational loyalty" or "organizational identification." It requires organizational identification, as well as sticks and carrots, to direct behavior toward achieving organizational objectives, and in highly effective organizations, the former plays the dominant role. To state the matter in classical terms, if members of organizations are maximizing their utilities, then organizational goals must constitute major parts of their utility functions.

In large part, the chapters in this section are devoted to developing the thesis stated in the previous paragraph. As I mentioned above, the thesis was advanced long ago, in Chapter 10 of *Administrative Behavior*, and it has been generally accepted by organization theorists but has received little attention from economists, leaving the prominence of organizations in economic affairs something of a mystery for them. What is specifically new in the present account is a Darwinian explanation of the bases for altruistic behavior and of the consequent close link between organizational identification and altruism.

Altruism and Loyalty

Chapter III.1 sets the foundations for a theory of organizational identification derived from the mechanism of altruism working in conjunction with bounded rationality. I initially undertook the inquiry that provided these foundations in an effort to get a better understanding of the neo-Darwinian claim that altruism in humans (except altruism to close kin) could not survive the processes of natural selection (Dawkins, 1976). This is a very precise formal claim, based on the fact that altruists (almost by definition of altruism as sacrifice of self's fitness to enhance the fitness of others) would be less fit (would produce, on average, fewer progeny) than non-altruists, hence would ultimately disappear from the population. Given the premises, the mathematical argument is impeccable, and is accepted by essentially all modern population geneticists. It has even found a place in elementary college biology textbooks.

As it seemed to me that fitness-sacrificing behavior was rather often observable in humans, I set out to find a chink in the argument that denied this possibility. Two assumptions, both with strong empirical support, provide the basis for an alternative model in which altruists can survive and flourish within the formal framework of neo-Darwinism. The first assumption is that people are boundedly rational; the second is that most of our beliefs are acquired, not by independent verification of the facts in the real world, but from social sources regarded as legitimate. "Legitimate" sources mean sources that are regarded as competent to deliver the truth (as far as it is known) in specified domains and as motivated to be objective in these domains.

Initially, the young child's mother and father are such sources for most topics. Gradually, the child becomes receptive to other channels of social communication (school, books, peers, doctors, and other experts in special domains), and builds up a large body of socially legitimated knowledge and belief for use in making decisions. We avoid cholesterol because our doctor (and the mass media) has told us to, not because we could, from medical evidence that we have reviewed directly and from our own knowledge, show it to be harmful.

This receptivity to legitimized social communications I have called "docility" ("instructability" might be a preferable term, without the overtones of passivity that "docility" carries). Docility (or instructability) brings with it a very large bonus in fitness, for the docile individual can learn not to touch stoves without first being burned. For a creature of bounded rationality, reason joined with docility in a benign social environment can achieve a much higher level of fitness than the unaided reason of the loner. In fact, few infants or children would survive to adulthood without a generous endowment of docility. For this reason, evolution would select strongly for it, and presumably has done so.

Now the fitness advantage that docile individuals possess can be "taxed" by the society by convincing or persuading or advising those individuals to engage in certain behaviors that may *not* contribute to fitness (enlisting in the armed forces, for example), but that are advantageous to the society—i.e., are altruistic. As rationality is bounded, this advice is about as likely to be accepted as any other advice received through social channels. As long as the load of altruistic behaviors society is able to impose on the docile individual does not exceed the bonus of fitness conferred by docility, the docile individual will be fitter than the non-docile. Bounded rationality prevents docile individuals from judging with any reliability when the social advice they are receiving will actually contribute to their fitness and when it will detract from it. Hence they pay the "tax" willingly in the form of altruistic behavior.

Again, this argument can be formalized rigorously within the neo-Darwinian framework. That formalization is set forth in Chapter III.2, and I will not say more about it here. But the conclusion that people can, and sometimes will, act altruistically has very important consequences. One form that altruism visibly takes is the substitution of the goals of a group (family, nation, teenage gang, business organization, ethnic or religious group, and so on) for individual "selfish" goals. The cost of this substitution in terms of lowered individual fitness may be small or large, but the substitution is clearly advantageous to the group. In this way, we can see how organizational loyalty or identification can play a major role in enhancing the effectiveness of groups over that of isolated individuals. We find a mechanism, in addition to, and substantially more powerful than, those proposed by the new institutional economists, that motivates behavior in support of organizational goals.

As we shall see, the mechanism of organizational identification is not merely motivational but has an important cognitive component as well. This cognitive component also derives from bounded rationality and the consequent need of individuals to simplify their decisions by adopting a representation or frame of reference reflecting the environment that impinges upon them. Again, I will leave the discussion of this cognitive mechanism to the chapters of this part.

Chapter III.2 draws conclusions from the altruism-identification argument for the respective roles of organizations and markets in a modern organization-and-market economy. Chapters III.3 and III.4 restate the altruism argument in an economic context and develop further both the motivational and cognitive aspects of the identification mechanism. It is time to create a "new-new" institutional economics which incorporates this mechanism and its powerful effects.

References

Dawkins, R. (1976). *The Selfish Gene*. New York, NY: Oxford University Press.

Simon, H. A. (1947). *Administrative Behavior*. New York, NY: Macmillan (4th edition, 1997).

Williamson, O. E. (1975). *Markets and Hierarchies*. New York, NY: The Free Press.

Williamson, O. E. (1985). *The Economic Institutions of Capitalism*. New York, NY: The Free Press.

III.1 A Mechanism for Social Selection and Successful Altruism

Within the framework of neo-Darwinism, with its focus on fitness, it has been hard to account for altruism, behavior that reduces the fitness of the altruist but increases average fitness in society. Many population biologists argue that, except for altruism to close relatives, human behavior that appears to be altruistic amounts to reciprocal altruism, behavior undertaken with an expectation of reciprocation, hence incurring no net cost to fitness. Herein is proposed a simple and robust mechanism, based on human docility and bounded rationality, that can account for the evolutionary success of genuinely altruistic behavior. Because docility—receptivity to social influence—contributes greatly to fitness in the human species, it will be positively selected. As a consequence, society can impose a "tax" on the gross benefits gained by individuals from docility by inducing docile individuals to engage in altruistic behaviors. Limits on rationality in the face of environmental complexity prevent the individual from avoiding this "tax." An upper bound is imposed on altruism by the condition that there must remain a net fitness advantage for docile behavior after the cost to the individual of altruism has been deducted.

It is of no little moment for the human future whether people are necessarily and consistently selfish, as is sometimes argued in population genetics and economics, or whether there is a significant place for altruism in the scheme of human behavior. Do centrally important institutions like business and government depend entirely on motivating participants through their selfish interests in order to operate successfully? Is reciprocal altruism (actually a form of self-interest) the only kind that can survive?

In recent years there have been many attempts to derive theoretical answers to these questions from the first principles of natural selection (*1*). Most of the answers give a central, almost exclusive, role to self-interest, and, apart from altruism to close kin, leave little room for genuine, as distinct from reciprocal, altruism.

The proposal in this paper can be read as an "even if" argument. Even if we accept the genes of individual persons as the controlling sites for natural selection—the assumption most antagonistic to altruism—a mechanism can be described that selects for altruistic behavior well beyond altruism to close kin and beyond support from expected reciprocity or social enforcement. The mechanism will select for behavior that reduces the fitness of the altruist while increasing average fitness in the society.

The argument does not deny the existence of social mechanisms for transmitting behavior traits; in fact, socially learned behavior is central to the theory. Nor is it concerned with the many forms of behavior usually called "altruistic" that are unrelated to biological fitness. The argument shows that even though altruistic behavior, strictly defined, is penalized, altruism can still be positively selected.

Essentially, the theory accounts for altruism on the basis of the human tendency (here called docility) to learn from others (more accurately, the tendency to accept social influence)—which is itself a product of natural selection. Because of the limits of human rationality, fitness can be enhanced by docility that induces individuals often to adopt culturally transmitted behaviors without independent evaluation of their contribution to personal fitness.

Altruism

By altruism I mean behavior that increases, on average, the reproductive fitness of others at the expense of the fitness of the altruist. Fitness simply means expected number of progeny. An exchange in which both parties are compensated for what they initially cede does not count as altruism but as enlightened self-interest (sometimes called soft or reciprocal altruism). Still, the boundaries are tricky, as we shall see.

Notice that "altruism" and "selfishness" in genetics bear no close resemblance to these terms in everyday language. Presumably, Don Juan was fitter than Croesus or Caesar. From a genetic standpoint, the amassing of wealth or power does not count at all toward fitness, only the amassing of progeny. By the same token, liberality with wealth or willingness to cede power do not constitute genetic altruism. Altruism means forgoing progeny.

We could debate at some length whether, either at the present time or earlier in the history of our species, wealth and power have or had any strong connection with genetic fitness. If the connection is weak, then the evolutionary argument that people are essentially selfish in the everyday sense of that word—is correspondingly weakened. Under those circumstances, there could be any amount of altruism, in the usual sense of that term, without any behavior that would qualify as altruistic in a genetic sense.

In this article, I am concerned with fitness, altruism, and selfishness only in the genetic meanings of those terms. In the concluding section I will return briefly to desire for wealth and power as human motives. In any event, our goal is not to establish how much or how little altruism, in either case, there is in human behavior, but rather to show that altruism on a substantial scale is not inconsistent with the strictest neo-Darwinian assumptions.

The Neo-Darwinian Analysis

The acceptance by many modern geneticists of the axiom that the basic unit of selection is the "selfish gene" quickly led to the production of population models that left little room for the survivability of altruistic behavior (*2*). If altruism incurred any cost in fitness, that is, in reduced potential or reproduction, then it could not compete against selfishness.

To be sure, it was recognized that altruism was viable under several specific (and rather narrow) conditions. First, altruism toward close relatives could increase fitness through the genes shared with those relatives. But the closest relatives (except identical twins) have only half their genes in common, and this fraction drops by a factor of two with each step of distance in the relationship. Consanguinity can account for altruism only toward close kin (*3*).

The second qualification is that, if several mixed societies (trait groups) contain varying fractions of altruists and non-altruists, then (i) the groups with the larger fractions of altruists may outbreed the groups with smaller fractions, (ii) as a result, the fraction of altruists in the entire population may increase for some time, (iii) even though the fraction of altruists in each separate group will necessarily decrease (*4*).

Of course, if the groups inbreed, then, in the long run, as the least altruistic (and least successful) groups became extinct or nearly so, the number of altruists in the entire population would begin to decrease, and altruism would ultimately become extinct. If, however, the population members periodically mixed thoroughly for purposes of reproduction, then the fraction of altruists in the total could continue to increase indefinitely.

All of these results can be formalized with relatively simple mathematical models. I will borrow heavily from these mathematical formulations, but my assumptions will be different from those in the model just described (*5*).

In addition to the models mentioned above, several explicit theories analyze the co-evolution of culturally transmitted and genetically transmitted traits. Among the most prominent of these are the theories of Cavalli-Sforza and Feldman, Lumsden and Wilson, and Boyd and Richerson (*6–8*). I will discuss them after I have presented my own model.

A Simple Model of Altruism

Consider a population consisting of n individuals, of two types, A and S, in proportions p and $1-p$, respectively. The individuals of type A are altruistic, while those of type S are selfish. Each A expresses a behavior that contributes b offspring to members of the population (including himself), the recipients being chosen at random. The cost of this altruistic behavior is that each A has c fewer children than he or she otherwise would have. The average number of offspring, F_A and F_S, of each A and S will be: $F_A = X - c + bp$, and $F_S = X + bp$, where X is the number of offspring in the absence of altruistic behaviors, the same for both types of individuals. All individuals, including altruists, can serve as recipients to the np altruists, and selfish S individuals incur no cost of altruism. Since c is positive, selfish individuals always have more offspring than altruistic ones. To the degree that the behaviors are heritable, selfish individuals will therefore be found with greater relative frequency in each succeeding generation.

Notice that the total contribution of each altruist to the population is b, assumed independent of the size of the population. Under an alternative assumption, which does not affect our main conclusions, each altruist contributes b to the fitness of each member of the population, thereby making the total contribution of the altruist bn, where n is the size of the population. In this latter case, the contribution is a "public good"—its consumption by one member does not decrease the amount available to others. (An attractive garden visible to passersby is an example.)

As was mentioned earlier, if there are a number of groups instead of one, and if the groups are segregated during most of their life cycle but intermingle thoroughly while reproducing, then altruists may have greater net fitness than non-altruists and may grow in numbers at the expense of the latter. Systems with this property are called "structured demes," and mathematical models of them are examined in considerable detail by Wilson (*4*).

Social Learning and Altruism

With only a single change of assumption, which I will now motivate, my simple model can be converted into one in which altruists are fitter than selfish individuals even within a single self-contained population that is not a structured deme. In this system, altruism will not only survive, but will gradually permeate the entire population (*9*).

The human species is notable, although not unique among animals, in requiring for survival many years of nurture by adults. In most human societies, the survival and fitness even of adults depends on the assistance, or at least forbearance, of other adults. Leaving aside active hostility from others, even access to food and shelter cannot be ensured in most societies without the consent of others.

The human species also has a notable ability to learn, and especially to learn from other people, particularly with the help of language. We will use the term "social learning" to refer to learning from others in the society.

Social learning makes two major contributions to an individual's fitness. First, it provides knowledge and skills that are useful in all of life's activities, in particular, in transactions with the environment. Second, goals, values, and attitudes transmitted through social learning, and exhibited in the speech or behavior of the learner, often secure supportive responses from others. For brevity, we will call the knowledge and skills of the first kind "skills," and those of the second kind "proper behaviors."

Learning of both kinds obviously contributes to fitness. We will use the term "docile" (in its dictionary meaning of "disposed to be taught") to describe persons who are adept at social learning, who accept well the instruction society provides them. Individuals differ in degree of docility, and these differences may derive partly from genetic differences. There are differences in intelligence (cognitive ability to absorb what is taught) and in motivation (propensity to accept or reject instruction, advice, persuasion, or commands).

Docile persons tend to learn and believe what they perceive others in the society want them to learn and believe. Thus the content of what is learned will not be fully screened for its contribution to personal fitness. This tendency derives from the difficulty—often an impossibility—for individuals to evaluate beliefs for their potential positive or negative contribution to fitness. For example, many of us believe that less cholesterol would be beneficial to our health without reviewing (or even being competent to review) the medical evidence. Hundreds of millions of people believe that behaving in a socially acceptable way will enhance the probability of enjoying blissful immortality.

Belief in large numbers of facts and propositions that we have not had the opportunity or ability to evaluate independently is basic to the human condition, a simple corollary of the boundedness of human rationality in the face of a complex world. We avoid most hot stoves without ever having touched them. Most of our skills and knowledge, we learned from others (or from books); we did not discover or invent them. The contribution of docility to fitness is enormous.

Guilt and shame, although perhaps genetically independent of docility, also serve most people as strong motivators for accepting social norms. Guilt is particularly important because it can operate independently of the detection of nonconformity.

In analogy with earlier simple models, I assume a population made up of two kinds of people: those who are docile, D, and those are not, S. We assume that both kinds of people are identical in fitness, except that docile people, because of the skills and proper behaviors they have acquired, produce on average d more offspring than the others. Thus, $F_D = X + d$, while $F_S + X$. Clearly, docile people will increase in relative number in the society.

Now if the society coexists in its environment with other societies, we may also compare the relative rates of growth of these societies. As in the models of qualified altruism that we have already examined, there may be certain altruistic behaviors that, although costly to the fitness of the individual who exhibits them, have more than a compensating advantage for other individuals in the society.

A society that instilled such behaviors in its docile members would grow more rapidly than one that did not; hence such behaviors would become, by evolution at the social level, a part of the repertory of proper behaviors of successful societies. Societies that did not develop such a repertory would be less fit than those that did, and would ultimately disappear. But could the altruism ultimately survive within the more successful societies?

To answer this question, I add altruism acquired by social learning to the model and see how docile-altruistic individuals fare relative to selfish ones. I will now simply call docile-altruistic individuals "altruistic," F_A, as in the previous models: $F_A = X + d - c + b(c)p$ and $F_S = X + b(c)p$. Again, p is the percentage of altruists in the population; X is the number of offspring in the absence of altruistic behaviors; d is the gross increase in A's offspring due to A's docility; c is the net cost to A, in offspring, of altruistic behavior acquired through the docility mechanisms; $b(c)$, which replaces the b of the previous model, is the number of offspring contributed to the population by A's altruistic behavior. I express this number as a function of c, because the amount of altruism exacted from A, and its corresponding contribution of fitness to others, depend on the society's definition of proper behavior, itself subject to cultural evolution.

Under these assumptions, an individual who is docile, enjoying the advantage (d) of that docility, will consequently also accept the society's instructions to be altruistic as part of proper behavior. Because of bounded rationality, the docile individual will often be unable to distinguish socially prescribed behavior that contributes to fitness from altruistic behavior. In fact, docility will reduce the inclination to evaluate independently the contributions of behavior to fitness. Moreover, guilt and shame will tend to enforce even behavior that is perceived as altruistic. Hence the docile individual will necessarily also incur the cost, c, of altruism.

Now, unlike the previous model, in this case, because $F_A - F_S = d - c$, the fitness of altruists will actually exceed the fitness of selfish individuals as long as d exceeds c, that is, as long as the demands for altruism that society imposes on docile individuals are not excessive compared with the advantageous knowledge and skills acquired through docility. If this condition is satisfied, the proportion of altruists will increase.

Suppose there are decreasing marginal returns from altruism, so that $d^2b/dc^2 < 0$. In the short run (that is, for fixed p), it will be optimal for the society to fix c at the level where $db/dc = 1$, but the long-run optimal strategy will be to demand less altruism initially so as to increase the absolute number of docile individuals as rapidly as possible, that is, to set $p(db/dc) = 1$. For small p, this implies that db/dc will be large, hence that c will be small or even zero [if $(dc/dc)_0 < (1/p)$]. As p grows, social demands on the altruists can be increased correspondingly—the greater the fraction of altruists in the society, the more altruistic it can be.

In this scheme of things, altruism is a relative matter, for only a subset of the altruist's behaviors reduce fitness. Moreover, the altruist is rewarded, in advance, by the "gift" of docility; altruism is simply a byproduct of docility. Docile persons are more than compensated for their altruism by the knowledge and skills they acquire, and moreover not all proper behaviors are sacrificial. (Learning to drive in the right lane is a proper behavior, but not sacrificial.) The term "altruism" applies only to the sacrificial subset of the behaviors engendered by docility.

If docility were something the individual deliberately chose, one might even rename the accompanying altruism "enlightened selfishness." But docility (at least its genetic component) is bestowed, not chosen, and with the bestowal goes the propensity to adopt proper behaviors, including altruistic ones. By virtue of bounded rationality, the docile person cannot acquire the personally advantageous learning that provides the increments, d, of fitness without acquiring also the altruistic behaviors that cost the decrement, c.

Three final observations: first, altruism includes the effort individuals spend to induce and enforce learning and proper behavior in others. The docility mechanism will work only if there are providers of skills and knowledge as well as recipients. But nurturing and enforcing behaviors will be learned as an essential component of the proper behaviors of altruism. In enforcement are included carrots as well as sticks—praising and nurturing others who exhibit proper behavior, as well as frowning on, shunning, or otherwise punishing those who do not.

Second, the fitness advantage of altruists would be decreased if individuals could feign proper behavior without detection. (They would be motivated to do so only when they knew the behavior was altruistic.) There are probably severe limits, however, as to how far deception will be successful (*10*).

Third, the effectiveness of the docility mechanism would be impaired if individuals could discriminate perfectly proper behaviors that were "for their own good" from those that were altruistic. But people can discriminate only very imperfectly between beneficial and altruistic behaviors.

Moreover, much of the value of docility to the individual is lost if great effort is expended evaluating each bit of social influence before accepting it. Acceptance without full evaluation is an integral part of the docility mechanism, and of the mechanisms of guilt and shame.

Comparison with Alternative Models

I return now to the models of Cavalli-Sforza and Feldman, Lumsden and Wilson, and Boyd and Richerson and compare their mechanisms for altruism with the docility mechanism.

Cavalli-Sforza and Feldman (*6*, fn. 6), examining the interaction between cultural and genetic transmission of traits (*6*, pp. 102–107 and pp. 133–143), show that a selectively disadvantageous trait can spread to a whole population, where by a disadvantageous trait they mean "a maladaptive social custom (for example, one creating some degree of danger to life that is not compensated for by other advantages in Darwinian fitness) or a custom decreasing fertility ..., or an infectious disease" (*6*, p. 106).

They do not consider, however, traits that, while maladaptive to individuals, confer net benefits on the population (altruistic behaviors); nor do they explain why negative selection of maladaptive social customs does not remove them, either by positive selection of those individuals who reject them, or by selection or social norms, or both. Many sociobiologists would therefore regard their model as incomplete, holding constant things that evolutionary forces would change in the long run. The mechanism I have proposed avoids both of these difficulties.

Lumsden and Wilson provide no mechanism for altruism other than altruism toward close kin and reciprocal or "soft" altruism (*11*).

Boyd and Richerson (*8*, chap. *7*, fn. 6) introduce a mechanism that produces altruism by "conformist transmission," which is, essentially, preferential selection of the behaviors individuals encounter most frequently. Conformist transmission has something in common with the docility mechanism, but differs from it in several crucial respects.

Degree of conformism, in the initial version of the Boyd and Richerson model (8, pp. 206–213) depends solely on frequency of exposure, without individual differences between conformers and defectors. If such differences are introduced for traits that are individually disadvantageous, there will be negative selection of conformers and positive selection of rejecters until the traits disappear.

The authors recognize this difficulty (*8*, p. 213) and introduce the possibility of individuals rejecting individual culturally transmitted traits. They then show that for rather special circumstances (involving migration among groups living in varying environments) conformist transmission (hence altruism) could be stably maintained.

But the docility mechanism I have proposed accounts for altruism even in a homogeneous environment, and does not depend on the frequency with which a trait is encountered. Finally, it is considerably simpler and more robust than conformist transmission, depending only on a couple of system parameters.

This review of these alternative theories of altruism shows that altruism based on docility provides a simpler mechanism, valid under a wider range of conditions, than the others.

Implications for Economics and Politics

The existence of heritable docility, and the consequent possibility for a society to cultivate and exploit altruism, has very strong implications for social theory, including economics, and the theories of political institutions and other organizations. I will mention just a few such implications as examples.

First, goals like gaining wealth and power might become very strong motivations even if they made no direct contribution to genetic fitness. If it were advantageous to the success of a society for people to seek wealth or power, then these could be taught and rewarded as proper behaviors. The dangers of early assassination (and consequent deficit of offspring) to those who exercise power could be absorbed in the term c, among the costs of altruism. In particular, the desire for glory becomes, in this framework, an understandable human motive.

Motives like wealth, power, and glory would be difficult to sustain if associated with major costs to fitness. They are readily sustained if they are both useful to the society and nearly neutral for individual fitness. Power motives might have net value to the society by providing leaders who enhance the society's ability to organize to exploit resources or defend against enemies. Wealth-amassing motives might be useful if they created more wealth than was drawn off by those who strove for gain.

Consider next an example from politics. It has been difficult to explain what self-interest leads many people to go to the polls on election day. Any single vote is unlikely to change an election outcome, so it should seem pointless to a rational person to exert effort to vote. Even a small opportunity cost of casting a ballot is too much. But a society that includes voting among the proper behaviors can, at a minute cost to the fitness of altruists, secure their participation in elections.

Many other troublesome issues of public goods can be explained in the same way—contributions to charity and volunteer work being important examples. Of course other motives may also help to cause these behaviors. People may volunteer in order to make useful acquaintances. There are many possibilities, but no reason to rule out altruism as an important motivation.

Finally, many people exhibit loyalties to organizations and organization goals that seem wholly disproportionate to the material rewards they receive from the organization or its success (*12*). In particular, few people (including top executives) receive rewards from business firms that are proportional to the profits. Yet executives and other employees seem often to make decisions in terms of their expected effects on the firm's profitability. And empirical evidence suggests little difference in the relative efficiencies of profit-making and non-profit firms in the same industry (for example, health care, water supplies, education) (*13*). With profits or without, people often identify with organization goals and organizational survival.

All these topics deserve a more thorough treatment than they are given here. Mentioning them suggests what a wealth of possible behaviors opens up when we admit docility as a major mèchanism of social transmission.

As a final caution, I repeat that what I have called altruism, a partial sacrifice of genetic fitness, may be very different from the forgoing of wealth and power that is called altruism in common discourse. Nothing in the model predicts that we will not see people attending to their economic, interests in most of their everyday behavior; or for that matter, that we will not see them giving away a large part of the wealth they have taken great pains to amass.

In our century, we have watched two great nations, the People's Republic of China and the Soviet Union, strive to create a "new man," only to end up by acknowledging that the "old man"—perhaps we should say the "old person"—self-interested and concerned with his or her economic welfare or the welfare of family, clan, ethnic group, or province, was still alive and well. It will be important to reexamine this striking historical experience, not in terms of oversimple models of the "selfish gene," but in a framework that acknowledges that altruism, either as defined socially or as defined genetically, is wholly compatible with natural selection and is an important determinant of human behavior.

References and Notes

1. G. C. Williams, *Adaptation and Natural Selection: A Critique of Some Current Evolutionary Thought* (Princeton Univ. Press, Princeton, 1966); R. D. Alexander, *Annu. Rev. Ecol. Syst.* 5, 325 (1974).

2. R. Dawkins, *The Selfish Gene* (Oxford Univ. Press, Oxford, 1976).

3. W. D. Hamilton, *J. Theor. Biol.* 7, 1 (1964).

4. D. S. Wilson, *The Natural Selection of Populations and Communities* (The Benjamin-Cummings Press, Menlo Park, CA, 1980).

5. The reader who wants to pursue the mathematics further will find Wilson's book (4, footnote 4, pp. 23–32) indispensable.

6. L. L. Cavalli-Sforza, M. W. Feldman, *Cultural Transmission and Evolution* (Princeton Univ. Press, Princeton, NJ, 1981).

7. C. Lumsden and E. O. Wilson, *Genes, Mind, and Culture* (Harvard Univ. Press, Cambridge, MA, 1981).

8. R. Boyd and P. J. Richerson, *Culture and the Evolutionary Process* (Univ. of Chicago Press, Chicago, IL, 1985).

9. The docility mechanism described in this section was introduced less formally by H. A. Simon, *Reason in Human Affairs* (Stanford Univ. Press, Stanford, CA, 1983).

10. This issue has been examined by R. H. Frank, *Passions Within Reason* (Norton, New York, NY, 1988).

11. C. J. Lumsden and E. O. Wilson, *Promethean Fire* (Harvard Univ. Press, Cambridge, MA, 1983), pp. 30–32.

12. H. A. Simon, *Administrative Behavior* (Macmillan, New York, 3d ed., 1976).

13. B. A. Weisbrod, *Science* 244, 541 (1989).

14. I am very grateful to a number of geneticists and others who have contributed to my education on this subject by reading and commenting upon earlier drafts of this paper, including D. T. Campbell, J. F. Crow, R. C. Lewontin, D. S. Wilson, and E. O. Wilson. Supported by the Personnel and Training Programs, Psychological Sciences Division, Office of Naval Research, under contract N00014-86-K-0768.

III.2 Organizations and Markets

In classical and neoclassical economic theory, markets are at the center of the stage. The actors in these markets are workers and consumers (sometimes combined into households), firms, owners of resources, governments, and perhaps others. The economic world of the neoclassical textbooks is a world of transactions, and these transactions typically involve an exchange of goods, services, and/or money that both parties to the transaction find advantageous to achieve these goals. Along with consumption, work and leisure are important components of the utility functions of households. Often, profit is assumed to be the sole objective of firms and their owners.

The description of the parties who participate in these transactions is minimal. However, as soon as firms are elaborated to become more than simple nodes in a network of transactions, to be producers—transformers of "factors" into products—difficult and important questions arise for the theory. A large part of the behavior of the system now takes place inside the skins of firms, and does not consist just of market exchanges. Counted by the head, most of the actors in a modern economy are employees, who either do not spend their days in trading, or if they do (for example, if they are salesmen or purchasing agents) are assumed to trade as agents of the firm rather than in their own interest, which might be quite different.

This raises the question of why there are firms at all. Why are not all the actors independent contractors? Why do most of them enter into employment contracts, selling their labor for a wage? What determines the make-or-buy decisions of firms, hence the boundaries between them and markets? When will two domains of activity lie within a single firm, and when will they be handled by separate contracting firms?

A second set of questions asks how the employees of firms are motivated to work for the maximization of the firm's profit. What's in it for them? How are their utility functions reconciled with those of the firm? In the employee's utility function, work is usually assumed to have negative utility and leisure (including loafing and working lackadaisically) to have positive utility. Why do employees often work hard?

The simple (neoclassical) answer to the motivational question derives from the employment contract, under which workers maximize their utility by accepting the authority of the firm; that is, by agreeing to accept orders from the profit maximizers in charge. But this answer leads to the new question of how the employment contract is enforced by the employer. In particular, how are employees induced to work more than minimally, and perhaps even with initiative and enthusiasm? Why should employees attempt to maximize the profits of their firms when making the decisions that are delegated to them?

These questions about the scope of activity and operation of firms have spawned a vigorous cottage industry, a branch of which is sometimes called "the new institutional economics," which tries to explain when activities will be carried out through the market and when they will be carried out within the skins of firms, and tries to explain also how it is possible for firms to operate efficiently. In the literature of the new institutional economics, two ideas that play a major role in the explanations are "transaction costs" and "opportunism" (for example, Williamson 1975, 1985). Sometimes the explanations are couched in terms of "information asymmetry" or "incomplete information" (Ross, 1973; Stiglitz, 1974). In other writings these topics are subsumed under agency theory, which treats the employment contract as an optimal contract between principal and agents, and studies how contractual arrangements can deal with shirking and other motivational problems.

The idea behind these ideas is that a proper explanation of an economic phenomenon will reduce it to maximizing behavior of parties who are engaged in contracting, given the circumstances that surround the transaction. The terms of the contract will be influenced by the access of the parties to information, by the costs of negotiating, and by the opportunities for cheating. Access to information, negotiation costs, and opportunities for cheating are most often treated as exogenous variables that do not themselves need to be explained. It has been observed that they even introduce a sort of bounded rationality into the behavior, with the exogeneity of the limits of rationality allowing the theory to remain within the magical domains of utility and profit maximization.

A fundamental feature of the new institutional economics is that it retains the centrality of markets and exchanges. All phenomena are to be explained by translating them into (or deriving them from) market transactions based upon negotiated contracts, for example, in which employers become "principals" and employees become "agents." Although the new institutional economics is wholly compatible with and conservative of neoclassical theory, it does greatly multiply the number of auxiliary exogenous assumptions that are needed for the theory to work. For example, to explain the presence or absence of certain kinds of insurance contracts, moral risk is invoked; the incompleteness of contracts is assumed to derive from the fact that information is incomplete or distributed asymmetrically between the parties to the contract. Since such constructs are typically introduced into the analysis in a casual way, with no empirical support except an appeal to introspection and common sense, mechanisms of these sorts have proliferated in the literature, giving it a very *ad hoc* flavor.

In general, the new institutional economics has not drawn heavily from the empirical work in organizations and decision-making for its auxiliary assumptions. (For introductions to that literature, see March and Simon, 1958; Cyert and March, 1963; Kornai, 1971; Simon, 1979). Nevertheless, it is appropriately subversive of neoclassical theory in that it suggests a whole agenda of microeconomic empirical work that must be performed to estimate the exogenous parameters and to test the theory empirically. Until that research has been carried out (and the existing literature on organizations and decision making taken into account), the new institutional economics and related approaches are acts of faith, or perhaps of piety.

The Ubiquity of Organizations

A mythical visitor from Mars, not having been apprised of the centrality of markets and contracts, might find the new institutional economics rather astonishing. Suppose that it (the visitor—I'll avoid the question of its sex) approaches the Earth from space, equipped with a telescope that reveals social structures. The firms reveal themselves, say, as solid green areas with faint interior contours marking out divisions and departments. Market transactions show as red lines connecting firms, forming a network in the spaces between them. Within firms (and perhaps even between them) the approaching visitor also sees pale blue lines, the lines of authority connecting bosses with various levels of workers. As our visitor looked more carefully at the scene beneath, it might see one of the green masses divide, as a firm divested itself of one of its divisions. Or it might see one green object gobble up another. At this distance, the departing golden parachutes would probably not be visible.

No matter whether our visitor approached the United States or the Soviet Union, urban China or the European Community, the greater part of the space below it would be within the green areas, for almost all of the inhabitants would be employees, hence inside the firm boundaries. Organizations would be the dominant feature of the landscape. A message sent back home, describing the scene, would speak of "large green areas interconnected by red lines." It would not likely speak of "a network of red lines connecting green spots."

Of course, if the vehicle hovered over central Africa, or the more rural portions of China or India, the green areas would be much smaller, and there would be large spaces inhabited by the little black dots we know as families and villages. But the red lines would be fainter and sparser in this case, too, because the black dots would be close to self-sufficiency, and only partially immersed in markets. But let us, for the present, restrict our attention to the landscape of the developed economies.

When our visitor came to know that the green masses were organizations and the red lines connecting them were market transactions, it might be surprised to hear the structure called a market economy. "Wouldn't 'organizational economy' be the more appropriate term?" it might ask. The choice of name may matter a great deal. The name can affect the order in which we describe its institutions, and the order of description can affect the theory. In particular, it may strongly affect our choice of the variables that are important enough to be included in a first-order theory of the phenomena.

How does the economy look when it is viewed as an organizational economy, with market relations among organizations? I have already suggested some of the more prominent features.

First, most producers are employees of firms, not owners. Viewed from the vantage point of classical theory, they have no reason to maximize the profits of firms, except to the extent that they can be controlled by owners. Moreover, profit-making firms, nonprofit organizations, and bureaucratic organizations all have exactly the same problem of inducing their employees to work toward the organizational goals. There is no reason, a priori, why it should be easier (or harder) to produce this motivation in organizations aimed at maximizing profits than in organizations with different goals. If it is true in an organizational economy that organizations motivated by profits will be more efficient than other organizations, additional postulates will have to be introduced to account for it.

Second, the system is nearly in neutral equilibrium between the use of markct transactions and authority relations to handle any particular matter: that is to say, very small changes in the situation can tip the equilibrium one way or the other. It is hard to explain degrees of integration of economic activities. In many instances, transaction cost analysis is not applicable, and even where it is, there often remains considerable latitude for different degrees of integration. For example, why are auto dealerships not a part of auto manufacturing companies, rather than having contractual relations with them?[1] Why did General Motors manage its own tool design for many years, but recently decide to contract most of it out? Under constant returns to scale and reasonably competitive markets, which characterize many manufacturing situations, make-or-buy decisions become ambiguous. The possibility of using internal division-by-division balance sheets, and internal pricing in negotiation between components of an organization further blurs the boundary between organizations and markets.

Without the introduction of very particular ad hoc assumptions, unbuttressed by empirical evidence, neoclassical theory provides no explanation for the repeated appearance of Pareto distributions of business firm sizes in virtually all situations where size distributions have been studied (Ijiri and Simon, 1977; Simon, 1979). (In a Pareto distribution, the logarithm of the number of firms above any given size decreases linearly with the logarithm of the size.) These observed distributions are difficult to reconcile with any notions that have been proposed for optimal firm size, but are easily explained by simple, plausible probabilistic mechanisms that make no appeal to optimality.

In sum, an organizational economy poses the questions of why the larger part of a modern economy's business is done by organizations, what role markets play in connecting these organizations with each other, and what role markets play in connecting organizations with consumers. Moreover, the boundary between markets and organizations varies greatly from one society to another and from one time to another. What mechanism maintains the highly fluid equilibrium between them? Until these questions are answered, it will be difficult to draw conclusions about the relative efficiencies of different forms of ownership and control of organizations, or the relative efficiency of markets versus central planning.

Motivation and Efficiency in Organizations

There are three different questions of social organization that are usually confounded, but which need to be considered separately. The first is the question of the relative efficiency of markets and organizations. The second is the question of the consequences of having a society's organizations owned by profit-making organizations, by nonprofit organizations, or by public organizations, respectively. The third is the question of the consequences of using central planning instead of markets to regulate relations among organizations. At present, our concern is only with the first question: what makes organizations work as well or badly as they do?

In particular, for whom is profit the motive? Adolf Berle and Gardiner Means posed the problem very sharply in their famous book, *The Modern Corporation and Private Property* (1933), by showing that even at the top executive levels of the modern corporation there is a great gap between ownership and control, and a correspondingly great opportunity for discrepancy between the goal of owners (profit) and the goals of managers (career status, wealth, a quiet life, and so on).

Demsetz and Lehn (1985) have contested the argument of Berle and Means on the ground that even large corporations show considerable concentration of ownership. Typically, a half dozen owners (or fewer) own 10 or 20 percent of the shares, enough to retain controlling power. Often, these owners are also the active top executives. But the objection does not hold water. If a company has an executive bonus plan, and if an executive's percentage share in bonus awards is greater than his or her percentage share of dividends, then it pays that executive to divert earnings from dividends to bonuses. Most companies have executive award systems that make this conflict of interest very real. Golden parachutes and leveraged buyouts are other significant examples of transactions where the interests of shareholders and executives may diverge strongly.[2]

If even top executives may be conflicted in their motives, the problem should be still greater for employees who are not owners at all, or only insignificantly. Principal-agent theory, on which the new institutional economists often rely, assumes that agents within firms will shirk unless their actions contribute directly to their own economic self-interest. It is only via monitoring combined with contracts that appeal to their self-seeking nature that such shirking may be mitigated. But the assumption that executives (and perhaps other employees) would choose to advance their own careers and wealth and consumption, rather than pursuing organizational goals like maximizing profit, is not prescribed by neoclassical theory, which leaves the specification of the utility function completely open.

Why not assume that maximizing the firm's profit is precisely what maximizes the utilities of executives and other workers? In a society of robots, an owner would not settle for less. But most of us would think this an unrealistic assumption to make for a human society. An organization theory with an unspecified utility function is not a theory at all. And one with an unrealistic utility function does not provide a basis for understanding real organizations. Instead, we should begin with empirically valid postulates about what motivates real people in real organizations. I shall argue that such postulates can be derived from four organizational phenomena whose roles are amply documented in the literature on organizations: authority, rewards, identification, and coordination.

Authority: The Employment Relation

The employment contract is an example of what is now sometimes called an "incomplete contract;" that is to say, some of its terms are unspecified. Employees agree to do, over the life of the contract, what they are ordered to do; but the orders will not be issued until some time after the contract is negotiated (Simon, 1951; Williamson, 1975).

The usual argument (within the neoclassical framework) for the existence of incomplete contracts is that in a world of uncertainty actions will have to be taken as the situation calls for them, without time for negotiation. The employee is rewarded, in the level of the wage, for willingness to bear the brunt of this uncertainty as to what actions will be chosen, and to do, when the time comes, whatever the employer thinks the situation calls for. This argument does not imply that uncertainty is replaced by complete certainty at the time of decision. On the contrary, taking decisions under conditions of uncertainty may be one of the important skills demanded of the decision maker. The essential point is that the uncertainty for the employer is decreased by delaying the commitment to specific actions from the time employment begins until the time when action is called for.

An employment contract contains all sorts of implicit (and explicit) limitations that set boundaries to the range of actions the employee will be directed to perform. These boundaries define the "zone of acceptance" within which an employee can be expected to obey orders. The zone of acceptance is also sometimes called a "zone of indifference," for the choice among alternative behaviors, while of major importance to the employer, may be of little or no concern to the employee. A secretary, for example, usually has little or no preference for typing a letter to one of the company's customers rather than another, and little interest in the content of the letter. Even a factory manager will accept, within wide limits, whatever mix of products the factory is ordered to produce in a given month.

The combination of uncertainty on the part of the employer (as to what will need to be done in the future) and broad acceptance of the employee (of what he or she will be ordered to do) makes the employment contract a very attractive bargain for both parties. The new institutional economics finds that employment achieves great savings in transaction costs—the costs of negotiating separate contracts for each action.

But this theory of the employment contract must be elaborated. Authority in organizations is not used exclusively, or even mainly, to command specific actions. Most often, the command takes the form of a result to be produced ("repair this hinge"), or a principle to be applied ("all purchases must be made through the purchasing department"), or goal constraints ("manufacture as cheaply as possible consistent with quality"). Only the end goal has been supplied by the command, not the method of reaching it. The mechanic must apply all kinds of knowledge and skill to repairing the hinge. The section chief must initiate purchases of supplies needed for the work of that section; however, the company's standard procedures must be taken as ground rules for the way the purchases are made. The factory manager must control manufacturing cost and quality.

Employees, especially but not exclusively at managerial and executive levels, are responsible not only for evaluating alternatives and choosing among them but also for recognizing the need for decisions, putting them on the agenda, and seeing to the generation of possible actions. Doing the job well is not mainly a matter of responding to commands, but is much more a matter of taking initiative to advance organizational objectives.

Commands do not usually specify concrete actions but, instead, define some of the premises that are to be used by employees in making the decisions for which they are responsible (Simon, 1947). Hence, seeing that commands are obeyed is not simply a matter of observing behavior, but of affecting the thought processes and the decision premises of employees. Further, it is usually difficult or impossible to ascertain what these decision premises have been without reviewing the whole decision—thus causing an almost complete loss of the economy that was sought in delegating it in the first place.

The command an employer might like to issue is: "Always decide in such a way as to maximize company profit!" But that would simply reintroduce the question of how the extent of obedience to the command is to be observed without losing the benefit of delegation. Even if the employees were robots, whose loyalty could be guaranteed, the problem would not be solved. For giving each robot complete discretion would surrender large efficiencies usually attainable from specialization in decision-making work. We need to delegate within guidelines, which creates the problem of monitoring the observance of guidelines without recentralizing what has just been delegated.

If authority is used to transmit premises for making decisions rather than commands for specific behaviors, then many different experts can contribute their knowledge to a single decision. Information and policy rules can flow through the organization along many channels, serving as inputs—decision premises—for many organizational behaviors.

The accounting department gathers cost data, which it supplies to the head of the blast furnace department to help make operating decisions in that department. At the same time, the blast furnace manager is receiving instructions from metallurgical specialists on the technical aspects of the operation. The faint blue lines that our visitor from Mars saw within the green areas were not just streams of orders, but flows of all kinds of decision premises (constraints and information as well as orders) from one point in the organization to another.

This explication of the employment contract and authority takes us back to the question of motivation. For the organization to work well, it is not enough for employees to accept commands literally. In fact, obeying operating rules literally is a favorite method of work slowdown during labor-management disputes, as visitors to airports when controllers are unhappy can attest. What is required is that employees take initiative and apply all their skill and knowledge to advance the achievement of the organization's objectives.

We should not assume without evidence that organizations *do* work well. But "well" is a relative term. In most organizations, employees contribute much more to goal achievement than the minimum that could be extracted from them by supervisory enforcement of the (vague) terms of the employment contract. Why do employees not substitute leisure for work more consistently than they do? Why do they often work so vigorously for the welfare of the organization?

Rewards as Motivations

One obvious answer to the motivational question is that employees may be motivated to accept authority by giving them material rewards, promotion, and recognition for advancing the organization's goals as defined by management. Such rewards certainly provide motivation, but they only operate satisfactorily when certain conditions are met. The most important condition is that the employee's contribution to the organization's goals must be measurable with reasonable accuracy. For example, salesmen are frequently compensated (at least partly) on a commission basis. Blue-collar employees are sometimes compensated on a piecework basis, albeit in a continually decreasing number of situations. Executives, and sometimes others, receive bonuses that are supposed to be related to their contributions to profits.

But such reward systems are effective only to the extent that success can be attributed accurately to individual behaviors. If the indices used to measure outcomes are inappropriate, either because they do not measure the right variables, or because they do not properly identify individual contributions, then reward systems can be grossly inefficient or even counterproductive. Where output quantities are measured with inadequate attention to quality, response to rewards will cause quantities to grow at the cost of lowered quality. Where compliance with company policies that constrain action is not measured, constraints will be ignored and violated. Salesmen may misrepresent the product, workmen may ignore safety rules, managers may buck difficulties to other departments.

In general, the greater the interdependence among various members of the organization, the more difficult it is to measure their separate contributions to the achievement of the organizational goals. But of course, intense interdependence is precisely what makes it advantageous to organize people instead of depending wholly on market transactions. The measurement difficulties associated with tying rewards to contributions are not superficial, but arise from the very nature and rationale of organization.

Many large U.S. corporations attempted to respond to this problem in the years after World War II by slicing their organization into components that were relatively self-contained. Then, separate balance sheets could be maintained for each division, and these balance sheets could be used to evaluate results and to compute rewards.

Of course, divisionalization can be successful only to the extent that the divisions are actually self-contained. If one division operates mainly as a supplier of parts to other divisions, then policies have to be laid down for setting the prices for items "sold" by the one division to the others, and for determining under what conditions a division may go outside the company to purchase items at a lower price. For these and similar reasons, divisionalization can only be carried a short distance down the structure of a typical corporation, and solves the problem of attributing outcomes to individuals only at the higher levels, if at all.

Although economic rewards play an important part in securing adherence to organizational goals and management authority, they are limited in their effectiveness.[3] Organizations would be far less effective systems than they actually are if such rewards were the only means, or even the principal means, of motivation available. In fact, observation of behavior in organizations reveals other powerful motivations that induce employees to accept organizational goals and authority as bases for their actions. We turn next to the most important of these mechanisms: organizational identification.

Loyalty: Identification with Organizational Goals

Pride in work and organizational loyalty are widespread phenomena in organizations (Simon, 1947). These traits are more strongly evident among skilled and managerial employees than among employees engaged in very routine work. (The latter are also more easily supervised, and can sometimes be rewarded on a piecework basis.) In part, these attitudes can be attributed to the linkage between an organization's overall success and the personal careers and monetary rewards it can provide its employees. But this explanation ignores the problem of the commons—of benefits that are jointly gained and shared by all, non-contributors along with contributors—and the consequent possibilities for free-riding. The quality and success of an organization depends very little on the energy of any single employee (except possibly an executive at or near the very top). Why will employees work hard if they can gain almost as much by loafing?

Of course free-riding can be observed in organizations. The elimination of free riding is generally thought to be the principal reason for the success of the Chinese agricultural reforms after 1980, when responsibility and reward for agricultural production were transferred from the commune to the family. The question is not whether free riders exist—much less employees who exert something less than their maximum—but why there is anything *besides* free-riding. Why do many workers, perhaps most, exert more than minimally enforceable effort? Why do employees identify with organizational goals at all?

Contemporary evolutionary theory has cautioned us against postulating altruistic motives for people. In models of natural selection, nice guys generally aren't fit; they don't multiply as rapidly as their more selfish brethren. The argument from natural selection has often been used, explicitly or implicitly, to fill the utility function with selfish personal goals. But models of natural selection do not actually provide strong support for the idea that people will only pursue selfish personal economic goals. In fact, such models in no way foreclose the possibility (indeed, the probability) that people will be strongly motivated by organizational loyalty, even when they can expect no "selfish" rewards from it (Simon, 1983; 1990).

First, it should be emphasized that what natural selection increases is fitness, the number of progeny of the successful competitor. But in modern society, the attainment of wealth or other selfish rewards is not directly connected to number of progeny. In fact, first-world societies generally display a negative correlation between income level and size of family. But let us waive this point, as distracting us from the main argument, and suppose that attainment of the goals usually described as selfish (especially personal economic goals) contributes to evolutionary fitness.

We come then to the second point: each human being depends for survival on the immediate and broader surrounding society. Human beings are not the independent windowless Leibnitzian monads sometimes conjured up by libertarian theory. Society is not imposed on humans; rather, it provides the matrix in which we survive and mature and act on the environment. Families and the rest of society provide nutrition, shelter, and safety during childhood and youth, and then the knowledge and skills for adult performance. Moreover, society can react to a person's activities at every stage of life, either facilitating them or severely impeding them. Society has enormous powers, enduring though a person's lifetime, to enhance or reduce evolutionary fitness.

What kinds of traits, in addition to personal strength and intelligence, would contribute to the fitness of this socially dependent creature? One such trait, or combination of traits, might be called docility. To be docile is to be tractable, manageable, and above all, teachable. Docile people tend to adapt their behavior to norms and pressures of the society. I am not satisfied that "docile" conveys my meaning precisely, but I know of no better word.

That fitness is derivable from being docile becomes evident when we consider the opposite of docility: intractability, unmanageability, unteachability, incorrigibility. The argument is not that people are totally docile, nor that they are totally selfish, but that fitness calls for a measured but substantial responsiveness to social influence. In some contexts, this responsiveness implies motivation to learn or imitate; in other contexts, willingness to obey or conform. From an evolutionary standpoint, having a considerable measure of docility is not altruism but enlightened selfishness.

To survive as a trait, docility must contribute on average to the fitness of the individual who possesses it. Yet it may still lead to self-injurious behavior in particular cases. Thus, docile individuals may do better at earning a living, but loyalty to the nation may lead them to sacrifice their lives in wartime. Once docility is present, society may exploit it by teaching values that are truly altruistic; that is, which contribute to the society's fitness, but not to the individual's. The only requirement is that *on balance* and on the average the docile individual must be fitter than the one who is not docile.[4]

Of course, showing that a configuration of traits or genes would contribute to fitness, if they existed, does not prove they exist. But ample empirical evidence shows that most human beings are gifted with a considerable measure of docility. The purpose of the present argument is to show that this docility and the altruism it induces is wholly consistent with the premise of selection of the fittest. In fact, the theory of natural selection strongly predicts the appearance of docility and altruism in social animals.

Docility is used to inculcate individuals with organizational pride and loyalty. These motives are based upon a discrimination between a "we" and a "they." Identification with the "we," which may be a family, a company, a city, a nation, or the local baseball team, allows individuals to experience satisfactions (to gain utility) from successes of the unit thus selected. Thus, organizational identification becomes a motivation for employees to work actively for organizational goals. Of course, identification is not an exclusive source of motivation; it exists side by side with material rewards and enforcement mechanisms that are part of the employment contract. But a realistic picture of how organizations operate must include the importance of identification in the motivations of employees.

The strength of organizational identifications will depend upon the extent to which a society uses the docility mechanism to inculcate them, and this appears to vary considerably from one society to another. For instance, it would probably be agreed by ethnographers that in Chinese society greater pressure is exerted to induce identification with the family than with employing organizations, while the reverse is true of Japanese society. Such conjectures can be tested, for example, by examining practices of nepotism, and attitudes toward it, in the two societies.

The strength of the organizational loyalties of employees is not to be attributed only to motivation induced by docility. There is also an important cognitive component. The bounded rationality of humans does not allow us to grasp the complex situations that provide the environments for our actions in their entirety. The first step in rational action is to focus attention on specific (strategic) aspects of the total situation, and to form a model of the situation in terms of those aspects that lie in that focus of attention. Rational computation takes place in the context of this model, rather than in the response to the whole external reality.

One dimension of simplification is to focus on particular goals, and one form of focus is to attend to the goals of an organization or organization unit. Having defined that unit as the "we," actions are evaluated in terms of their contribution to the unit's objectives. The ubiquity of this narrowing of attention is easily demonstrated. As one example, Dearborn and Simon (1958) presented a group of business executives with a description of the current situation of a large company, and asked them to identify the most serious problem facing the company. In their own companies, some of the executives were responsible for manufacturing, others for sales, others for finance. In almost every case, the "most serious problem" identified by the executive lay in the domain of his or her own department—manufacturing problems for manufacturing executives, sales problems for sales executives, and so on.

It is a commonplace of organizational life that a person's organizational identification will shift with his or her position, although the motivational basis for the shift is perhaps more widely recognized than the cognitive basis. But a shift in organizational position exposes the employees to new "facts" and phenomena, to a new network of communications, and to new goals. A different model is inevitably formed of the decision-making situation, a model that emphasizes local components of the environment and local goals. Behavior is very much a function of position.

Because of cognitive limits, the precise form that goals take may depend on what can be measured in the situation. In business organizations, the accounting statements provide stylized measurements of profits, size, growth, market share, and so on. Even if these measurements are only rough approximations of the things they are supposed to be measuring, they are likely to replace the "real" unmeasured concepts in the decision-making process.

Willingness of employees at all levels to assume responsibility for producing results—not simply "following the rules"—is generally believed to be a major determinant of organizational success. This discussion implies that acceptance of responsibility will be affected both by the reward system and by the strengths of organizational identifications. Here again, large intercultural differences may exist. The recent establishment of a substantial number of international joint ventures, with managements and employees recruited from different cultures, provides an excellent research environment for studying these differences and their effects upon organizational efficiency.

Since the developments are quite new, little information is yet available about them. But one example where data are available is the joint venture between Toyota and General Motors in northern California (Krafcik and Womack, 1987). Here Toyota took over a former General Motors plant, equipped it with standard state-of-the-art machinery, rehired employees mainly from the previous work force and accepted the same union. They have been able to produce automobiles with about 45 percent fewer labor hours than an entirely comparable GM plant that uses American managers and management methods, and about 30 percent fewer hours than a new GM plant having more modern "hitech" equipment, and only about 15 percent *more* labor hours than a comparable Toyota plant in Japan.

The causes for these enormous differences in efficiency have almost nothing to do with the classical physical production function. They also appear to have little to do with cultural differences at the blue-collar level.[5] They seem to have nothing to do, either, with material reward structures, which are not significantly different in the various plants. They must be attributed in large part to differences in management practices (for example, quality control practices, and inventory policies), perhaps bolstered by differences in management attitudes and motivations.

Coordination

This examination of authority and organizational identification should help explain how organizations can be highly productive even though the relation between their goals and the material rewards received by employees, if it exists at all, is extremely indirect and tenuous. In particular, it helps explain why careful comparative studies have generally found it hard to identify systematic differences in productivity and efficiency between profit-making, nonprofit, and publicly-controlled organizations (Weisbrod, 1988, 1989). Also, it explains why Demsetz and Lehn (1985) found no difference in profits between corporations that were managed or controlled by owners and those with diffuse stock ownership.

But to understand the relative advantages of organizations and markets, and the circumstances under which one would operate more effectively than the other, one further component must be added to our description of organizations. Organizations, through the authority mechanism, provide a means for *coordinating* the activities of groups of individuals in ways that are not always easily achieved by markets.

Coordination is a rather slovenly word, often abused in organizations. An experienced executive cringes when he or she learns that someone has been appointed to "coordinate" a set of activities, since calling for coordination without specifying just what it means is simply a lazy way of passing off problems to someone else. I will try to make the concept more precise by using it to designate a specific kind of activity.

The theory of games has sharply underscored that decisions are usually indeterminate when each party in a situation is uncertain about the actions of the others. This result is quite independent of whether their goals are complementary or competitive. One simple example of this indeterminacy is that it is rational for a motorist to drive on the *same* side of the road as other drivers headed the same direction, whichever that may be. There is no question of correct behavior in relation to the environment, but only of coordinating the behaviors of all the actors. Such rules of the road, or standardization, can greatly improve the performance of systems in those (ubiquitous) situations where the correctness of an action depends on what the other actors are doing.

A more complex example of coordination is provided by a university. Conceive of a university that consisted only of some rooms, some teachers, and some students. Students and teachers would "simply" negotiate to meet at certain times and places for their classes. The resulting chaos would probably be resolved by inventing the institutions of a registrar's office and a class schedule. While it would be extravagant to urge that class schedules provide the raison d'etre for education by universities, rather than by contractual tutoring arrangements negotiated through markets, nevertheless, the coordinating function of schedules is not trivial.

A major use of authority in organizations is to coordinate behavior by promulgating standards and rules of the road, thus allowing actors to form more stable expectations about the behavior of the environment (including the behavior of other actors). Since organizations provide a mechanism (authority) for establishing rules of the road, which markets do not, one might even expect organizations rather than markets to be the environments in which the behavior called "rational expectations" would be most often observed.[6]

In a book on central planning during World War II, Ely Devons (1950) raised the question of why prices are supplanted by government plans, expressed as quantity goals for production and allocation, as coordinating mechanisms during wartime. The usual argument for markets, as in the well-known 1945 paper of von Hayek, is that they simplify the decision process by reducing the need of each actor to know what the other actors are doing or what situations confront them. To the extent that markets and prices perform this simplifying function, we would expect them to replace centralized decisions when a situation becomes more complex—for example, during the rapid changes that take place in shifting from a peacetime to a wartime economy. Yet, as Devons points out, it is just at such times that central planning tends to increase. Is this irrationality, or are there valid reasons for the shift?

The answer is rather obvious. Prices perform their informational function when they are known or reasonably predictable. Uncertain prices produced by unpredictable shifts in a system reduce the ability of actors to respond rationally. This point is often made by economists in arguing the costs of unexpected inflation, but its implication for the choice between organizations and markets is less often noted. Nor is it often noted that many kinds of uncertainties other than price uncertainties may make coordination through organizational procedures advantageous.

The difficulty that economics has had in giving a good account of organizations and their predominance is traceable in no small part to the fascination of economists with systems in equilibrium. Analysis under assumptions of perfect knowledge and certain expectations has little relevance, surely, for such issues of economic organization as explaining how an economy is structured between organizations and markets. Prices provide only one of the mechanisms for coordination of behavior, either between organizations or within them. Coordination by adjustment of quantities is probably a far more important mechanism from a day-to-day standpoint, and in many circumstances will do a better job of allocation than coordination by prices. For example, inventory control systems record the amounts of inputs for the organization's activities, and place orders when quantities fall below specified levels. The orders, recorded by the control systems of suppliers, initiate the scheduling of new production and are used to adjust aggregate production levels as well.

From a conceptual standpoint, it is entirely feasible to construct economies in which prices are based on costs and final demands are limited wholly by budget constraints, with demand vectors that are otherwise insensitive to prices. Quantities of goods sold and inventories, not prices, provide the information for coordinating these systems. The Leontief input-output models, with exogenous vectors of final demands, are examples, and the Hawkins-Simon theorem (1949) states the conditions under which such systems have non-negative solutions. They possess the same information-conserving virtues as price-regulated systems (von Hayek, 1945). Each actor need only know his or her own business.

Many observers of business scheduling and pricing practices have claimed that (with the possible exception of the agricultural and mining sectors) models that use quantities as signals approximate first-world national economies more closely than do models in which prices are the principal mechanisms of coordination. I don't wish to argue that point here: but simply observe that quantity adjustments play a very large role in the real world in equilibrating the operations of different organizations and different parts of organizations.

The stylized market exchanges of neoclassical economic theory generally involve only prices and quantities, which is the foundation for their parsimony in information. But actual contracts negotiated between business firms—putting consumer products aside, for the moment—usually specify far more than prices and quantities. Contracts for construction of a building or of a product of engineering (like a generator or an airplane) specify in enormous detail the specifics of the product to be delivered. They require a massive exchange of information in both negotiation and execution. The red market traces that our Martian visitors observed from space are not narrow tracks along which only money and goods flow, but broad highways to accommodate a vast flow of detailed information as well.

Thus, the assertion that markets permit each firm to do its business with little knowledge of its partners is a fiction. In construction, in heavy industry, in manufacturing involving high technology, and in other areas, contracting partners carry on communication at a level comparable to the levels observed between departments of a firm. When products are manufactured to specifications, a great deal of information must flow among the various groups of people involved in the manufacture. But the widespread use of subcontracting in the automobile and construction industries, just to mention two, demonstrates that it is often quite feasible to transport this information across organizational boundaries, so that vertical integration is unnecessary. From this perspective, the distinction between market communications and internal communications, and the criteria for choosing between the two alternative arrangements, become correspondingly vague.

The choice between prices or quantities to coordinate the activity levels of different organizations or parts of organizations does not by itself dictate the respective roles of organizations and markets. Prices may be used to coordinate the activities of different parts of single organizations, provided that some way can be found to determine what the market prices should be, and quantity adjustments can be made between different organizations as well as within them.

There is one important difference in the operation of coordination mechanisms within and between organizations. Coordination between organizations depends almost wholly on economic motivations and rewards, and becomes seriously imperfect wherever major externalities are present that cannot be removed by enforceable contract arrangements. Within organizations, on the other hand, identification is a powerful force for combatting externalities produced by attachment to subgoals, by virtue of the loyalty it can produce to the goals of the whole system. A department will be less likely to skimp on quality to cut costs if its members identify with the final product. In particular, identification becomes an important means for removing or reducing those inefficiencies that are labeled by the terms "moral hazard" and "opportunism."

These observations nudge us toward the conclusion that organization size and degree of integration, and the boundaries between organizations and markets, are determined by rather subtle forces. The wide range of organizational arrangements observable in the world suggests that the equilibrium between these two alternatives may often be almost neutral, with the level highly contingent on a system's history. A traditional arrangement may be preserved until its inefficiencies become overwhelming—or even beyond. The same conclusion is suggested by the constant flux of mergers and spinoffs in the business world, many of these transformations being governed by considerations quite unrelated to productive or allocative efficiency, and many having consequences for efficiency that even those involved in them cannot evaluate.

Over a span of years, a large fraction of all economic activity has been gathered within the walls of large and steadily growing organizations. The green areas observed by our Martian have grown steadily. Ijiri and I have suggested that the growth of organizations may have only a little to do with efficiency (especially since, in most large-scale enterprises, economies and diseconomies of scale are quite small), but may bc produced mainly by simple stochastic growth mechanisms (Ijiri and Simon, 1977).

But if particular coordination mechanisms do not determine exactly where the boundaries between organizations and markets will lie, the existence and effectiveness of large organizations does depend on some adequate set of powerful coordinating mechanisms being available. These means of coordination in organizations, taken in combination with the motivational mechanisms discussed earlier, create possibilities for enhancing productivity and efficiency through the division of labor and specialization.

In general, as specialization of tasks proceeds, the interdependency of the specialized parts increases. Hence a structure with effective mechanisms for coordination can carry specialization further than a structure lacking these mechanisms. It has sometimes been argued that specialization of work in modern industry proceeded quite independently of the rise of the factory system. This may have been true of the early phases of the industrial revolution, but would be hard to sustain in relation to contemporary factories. With the combination of authority relations, their motivational foundations, a repertory of coordinative mechanisms, and the division of labor, we arrive at the large hierarchical organizations that are so characteristic of modern life.

Conclusions

The economies of modern industrialized society can more appropriately be labeled organizational economies than market economies. Thus, even market-driven capitalist economies need a theory of organizations as much as they need a theory of markets. The attempts of the new institutional economics to explain organizational behavior solely in terms of agency, asymmetric information, transaction costs, opportunism, and other concepts drawn from neoclassical economics ignore key organizational mechanisms like authority, identification, and coordination, and hence are seriously incomplete.

The theory presented here is simple and coherent, resting on only a few mechanisms that are causally linked. Better yet, it agrees with empirical observations of organizational phenomena. Large organizations, especially governmental ones, are often caricatured as "bureaucracies," but they are often highly effective systems, despite the fact that the profit motive can penetrate these vast structures only by indirect means.

This theory of organizations calls for reexamining some of the classical questions of political economy. The primacy of profit as the enforcer of organizational efficiency is replaced by organizational goals, combined with organizational identifications and with material rewards and supervision, all of which motivate employees to work toward these goals. This framework makes it necessary to reopen the question of when profit-making, nonprofit, and governmental organizations should be expected to operate well, and when market competition is needed to discipline organizations to perform efficiently.

The reopening of these questions is important for both capitalist and socialist economies. On the one side, capitalist economies are actually mixed economies, faced with a multitude of problems of regulation and deregulation, of socialization and privatization. On the other side, many socialist economies have had mediocre success in maintaining the efficiency of their organizations, and are experimenting with the reintroduction of markets, often while trying to avoid extensive privatization. Good answers to the policy questions that face all industrialized societies depend on having empirically sound theories of the behavior of large organizations. Such theories cannot be developed from the armchair. They call for fact-gathering that will carry researchers deep into the green areas, the organizations, that dominate the terrain of our economic systems.

Notes

1. Williamson's explanation—actually, Alfred P. Sloan's explanation (see Williamson, 1985, p. 10)—that employees could not be supervised adequately in their offers for used cars, is not convincing. Dealerships are also organizations, and their salesmen are employees.

2. Demsetz and Lehn (1985) cite evidence to show that corporations where ownership is widely distributed have, on average, profits as large as those with concentrated ownership. This fact does not undermine the argument of Berle and Means for conflict of economic interest; on the contrary, it raises the question—which I will undertake to answer below—of why executives with small stakes as shareholders do appear to work for company profits.

3. Everything said here about economic rewards applies equally to privately owned, nonprofit, and government-owned organizations. The opportunity for, and limits on, the use of rewards to motivate activities toward organizational goals are precisely the same in all three kinds of organizations. For sophisticated discussions of motivation and efficiency in profit-making and nonprofit organizations, see Weisbrod (1988, 1989).

4. This is not the place to describe in detail how docility and altruism induced through the docility mechanisms can be incorporated in a formal model of evolution by natural selection. I will simply sketch the general idea. Let k be the average number of offspring of an individual in the absence of docility or altruistic behavior; $d > 0$ the gross increase in offspring due to docility; $c > 0$ the cost to a docile individual in offspring of the socially induced altruistic behavior; p the percentage of individuals in the population which are docile and hence altruistic; and b the number of offspring added to the *population* by an individual's altruistic behavior. Assume further, that the parentage of offspring contributed by altruism is distributed randomly through the population. Then it is easy to show that the difference between the net fitness of altruists and non-altruists (non-docile individuals), respectively, will equal $d - c$. Hence, provided that d is larger than c, altruists will be fitter than non-altruists. Moreover, a society will grow more rapidly the greater the fraction of altruists in it, the increase in average fitness being $(d - c + b)p$.

5. These two statements should be qualified slightly. With regard to the first, components imported by the Toyota plant from Japan may be more uniform in quality than components purchased by the other GM plants. With respect to the second, applicants interviewed for employment in the Toyota plant were screened for problem solving attitudes and skills. Note that both of these factors, whether important or not, are matters of management practice. Finally, I would not wish to claim that the factors I have mentioned were the only ones affecting the comparison.

6. Of course, perfectly competitive markets do provide stable expectations of prices at least in equilibrium, and thereby permit Pareto optima to be achieved in principle. But prices are only one of many dimensions along which uncertainty of expectations may complicate rational decision making.

References

Berle, A. A., and Means, G. C., *The Modern Corporation and Private Property*. New York: Macmillan, 1933.

Cyert, R. M., and March, J. G., *A Behavioral Theory of the Firm*. Englewood Cliffs: Prentice-Hall, 1963.

Dearborn, D. C., and Simon, H. A., "Selective Perception: the Identifications of Executives," *Sociometry*, 1958, *21*. Reprinted in Simon, *Administrative Behavior*, chapter 15.

Demsetz, H., and Lehn, K., "The Structure of Corporate Ownership: Causes and Consequences," *Journal of Political Economy*, 1985, *93*, 1155–1177.

Devons, E., *Planning in Practice*. Cambridge: Cambridge University Press, 1950.

Hawkins, D., and Simon, H. A., "Note: Some Conditions of Macroeconomic Stability," *Econometrica*, 1949, *17*, 245–248.

von Hayek, F. A., "The Use of Knowledge in Society," *American Economic Review*, 1945, *35*, 519–530.

Ijiri, Y., and Simon, H. A., *Skew Distributions and the Sizes of Business Firms*. Amsterdam: North Holland, 1977.

Kornai, J., *Anti-Equilibrium*. Amsterdam: North-Holland, 1971.

Krafcik, J., and Womack, J. P., "Comparative Manufacturing Practice: Imbalances and Implications," Appendix A., working paper, International Motor Vehicle Program, MIT, May 1987.

March, J. G., and Simon, H. A., *Organizations*. New York: Wiley, 1958.

Ross, S., "The Economic Theory of Agency: the Principal's Problem," *American Economic Review*, 1973, *63*, 134–139.

Simon, H. A., *Administrative Behavior*. New York: Macmillan, 1947; 3rd edition, 1976.

Simon, H. A., "Rational Decision Making in Business Organizations," *American Economic Review*, 1979, *69*, 493–513.

Simon, H. A., "A Formal Theory of the Employment Relationship," *Econometrica*, 1951, *19*. Reprinted in Simon, H. A., *Models of Bounded Rationality*, Vol. II, Chapter 5.2. Cambridge: MIT Press, 1982.

Simon, H. A., *Reason in Human Affairs*. Stanford: Stanford University Press, 1983.

Simon, H. A., "A Mechanism for Social Selection and Successful Altruism," *Science*, 1990, *250*, 1665–1668.

Stiglitz, J. E., "Incentives and Risk-Sharing in Sharecropping," *Review of Economic Studies*, 1974, *41*, 219–255.

Weisbrod, B. A., *The Nonprofit Economy*. Cambridge: Harvard University Press, 1988.

Weisbrod, B. A., "Rewarding Performance that is Hard to Measure: The Private Nonprofit Sector," *Science*, May 5, 1989, *244*.

Williamson, O. E., *Markets and Hierarchies*. New York: The Free Press, 1975.

Williamson, O. E., *The Economic Institutions of Capitalism*. New York: The Free Press, 1985.

Winter, S., "Economic 'Natural Selection' and the Theory of the Firm," *Yale Economic Essays*, 1964, *4*.

III.3 Altruism and Economics: A Summary Statement

In this paper, I shall consider how far altruism in human behavior is reconcilable with neo-Darwinian and with neo-classical economic theory, and explore some of the consequences for economic theory of the presence of substantial altruism in behavior. To anticipate my conclusions, I will show that altruism is wholly compatible with Darwinism, that altruism has large consequences for economic behavior, especially the behavior of managers and employees, and that extensive empirical research is needed today to establish the place that altruistic values hold in the human utility function.[1]

The parallelism between Darwinian evolutionary theory, on the one hand, and classical and neoclassical economics, on the other, has often been noted and exploited [Hirshleifer, 1977]. It is argued that, just as those species that produce more surviving progeny will outgrow those that produce fewer (are less fit), so those firms that are more profitable will outgrow those that are less profitable. Survival of the more profitable has been put forward, in turn, as a basis for believing that profit-maximizing firms will predominate in a competitive economy. In this paper we will be concerned mainly with a somewhat different question about the relation of evolutionary theory with economics, that is, with the role of altruism in individual behavior, not in the behavior of firms. However, at the end of the paper, I will return to the question of what our analysis implies for the goals of firms.

The Definition of Altruism

Neo-Darwinian theory rests on the nearly tautological postulate that only fitness counts—that in the long run, those species will populate the earth that have produced the most progeny. Since the environment provides many quite different niches calling for different forms of adaptation, many species can co-exist, but only by specializing to occupy particular niches.

Altruism is defined in evolutionary theory as behavior that sacrifices one's own production of progeny, one's own fitness, to enhance the fitness of others. Let F_S be the fitness of selfish individuals, and F_A the fitness of altruists. Then F_S will be equal to some base value, X, for the species, plus a benefit, bp, contributed by the altruists, where b is a parameter, and p is the percentage of altruists in the total population. On the other hand, F_A will be equal to X plus bp, minus c, where c is the cost to fitness of the altruistic behavior [Simon, 1990].[2] Clearly, under these assumptions, selfish individuals will be fitter than altruists, and altruism will ultimately disappear, however beneficial it might be for the growth of the population as a whole. In barebones form, this is the case that neo-Darwinian theory makes against altruism. There are two important qualifications to this simple argument: Darwinian selection is compatible with altruism to close kin (siblings, parents, children), and in so-called "structured demes" [D. S. Wilson, 1980]. But these very special cases are not of great import to modern societies. I will return to the neo-Darwinian theory again a little later to show that under slightly different assumptions from those employed above quite different conclusions can be drawn about the viablitity of altruism.

In everyday life, and in most of the literature of the social and behavioral sciences, altruism is defined very differently than it is in evolutionary theory. Altruism is sometimes formally defined as behavior that sacrifices the altruist's utility, measured by his or her utility function, for the utility of another. Using this definition (call it Definition AI), it is obvious that a neoclassical utility maximizer cannot exhibit altruism. But Definition AI is not the one we usually employ, especially when applying economic reasoning to such topics as organizational behavior or public choice. In discussing these topics, we generally treat behavior as altruistic if it sacrifices wealth or power for the wealth or power of another, and selfish if it seeks to maximize wealth and/or power. Call this Definition AII.

Using Definition AII, altruism can now be reconciled with utility maximization by incorporating Other's satisfactions in Self's utility function. As Gary Becker once put it, "I decide whether to turn out my reading lamp in bed by comparing the utility of my pleasure in reading with the amount of utility *I* receive from my wife's being able to sleep." This is quite legitimate—a wholly utility-maximizing behavior—for the postulates of neoclassical theory say absolutely nothing about what values the utility function contains. We will call the abstract neoclassical definition of utility, Definition UI. There is no inconsistency, then, between altruism, using definition AII, and maximization of utility, using Definition UI.

However, in the literature of institutional economics and public choice we also do not usually employ this free-floating definition, UI, of utility. Much more often, we postulate (often implicitly) that *Own's* wealth and power are prominent (sometimes exclusive) components of the utility function. Call these definitions UII(W) and UII(P), respectively. If Own's wealth is the sole component of the utility function, then behavior is altruistic (AII) that sacrifices Own's wealth for the wealth of Other. And if power is the sole component of the utility function, then behavior is altruistic that sacrifices Own's power for the power of Other. With this view, the utility function is no longer an empty box, to be filled with whatever the individual chooses to value. Instead, it is assumed (a very strong empirical assumption) that it is filled only with wealth and/or power.

It is important to notice that altruism (sacrificing wealth and/or power) is consistent with utility maximization if we use Definition UI for utility, but not if we use Definition UII. Definition UII, with its much stronger assumption about the content of the utility function, rules out altruism completely under utility maximization. Hence, the common use of Definition UII rather than Definition UI in the applications of neoclassical reasoning to real-world affairs has strong consequences.

Of course there are no limits on the number of variants we can construct of Definition UII, simply by filling the utility function with different contents. We might, for example, allow combinations of wealth and power in the function, or add a "glory" component. These three components are especially attractive because the quantities they refer to are fungible: wealth, power, and glory can usually be exchanged for others of the World's goods, hence can be thought of as surrogates for other utilities, or even as a sort of numeraire.

In some kinds of worlds, these goods can be exchanged for fitness: the wealthy, powerful, or famous can have more progeny than those who lack these goods. In such worlds, but not necessarily in others, there is a close link between the evolutionary and the social definitions of altruism.

Neo-Darwinian Altruism

With these questions of definition out of the way, it is time to reconsider the compatibility of fitness with altruism within the neo-Darwinian framework. I begin with two assumptions, which I believe have unimpeachable empirical support (but I do wish also to emphasis that they *are* empirical assumptions).

ASSUMPTION I Docility. Human beings who are genetically disposed to docility are, ceteris paribus, fitter than human beings who are not docile.

Docility, here, means a tendency to accept knowledge and advice that is transmitted through social channels.[3] In this context, docility connotes disposition to be taught or to believe, but not necessarily to be tractable or passive. Docile people learn readily in a social setting, and tend to acquire socially approved behaviors and beliefs in matters both of fact and value. Docility may have both a cognitive and a motivational component.

On the cognitive side, docility implies belief legitimated by social processes (information received from "qualified" sources), rather than belief based on self-evaluated empirical evidence. On the motivational side, docility means acceptance on the basis of social legitimation and approval rather than acceptance on the basis of individual drives and motives that were not socially acquired.

ASSUMPTION II Bounded Rationality. Because of limits of knowledge and computational power, people are frequently unable to judge whether particular beliefs are true, and whether particular behaviors will contribute to their utility (wealth, power, or whatever it may be).

The hypothesis of bounded rationality is crucial to the explanation of human behavior not only in the context of docility, but in virtually all real-life situations, for human beings are never even remotely in a position to know all available alternatives of action, or to evaluate the consequences of each. Limits on knowledge and computation are central to the human condition. But I well not elaborate upon bounded rationality in general, a theme I have been emphasizing in season and out since 1947 [Simon, 1947, 1979, 1986]. Our concern here is with the implications of bounded rationality for altruism.

Altruism Revisited

Let us now incorporate our assumptions of docility and bounded rationality in the simple (or simplistic) Darwinian model that was presented earlier [Simon, 1990]. We assume that docile individuals receive an increase in fitness, *d*, as a result of the skills they acquire from the social environment and the advantages they gain by exhibiting socially sanctioned behavior. The society can now impose a "tax" on this bonus to fitness by influencing docile persons to engage in some behaviors that contribute to the net fitness of the society but that are, in fact, fitness-reducing to the individual. Society can influence individuals, for example, to be brave soldiers or to limit the sizes of their families. Call this "tax" t, so that the net contribution of docility to an individual's fitness will now be $d - t$. We count in the "tax" only behaviors that could not be enforced effectively by society in the absence of docility. Hence we rule out what is usually called reciprocal altruism—behavior contributing to others on the expectation that it will be reciprocated in some way, or on the expectation that failure to contribute will be punished.

Under these assumptions, we recalculate the relative fitness of selfish persons and altruists. F_S will now equal $X + bp$, where, as before, X is a base level of fitness, b is a positive contribution made by each altruist, and p is the percentage of altruists in the population. However, F_A will now equal $X + (d - t) + bp$. As long as d is larger than t, so that $(d - t)$ is positive, altruists will be fitter than selfish persons, and will gradually dominate the population.

Why do clever altruists not avoid the "tax", t? Primarily because they are not aware that they are being taxed. Limits of knowledge and computational ability prevent them from seeing that some of the behaviors in which society persuades them to engage are inimical to their fitness. They are persuaded, for example, that limiting family size is "for their own good." Bounded rationality may be further reinforced by the mechanisms of guilt and shame. If these mechanisms have a genetic component, and if docility makes a net contribution to individual fitness, then since persons who experience guilt and shame will be more docile than others, there will also be positive selection for these traits. Beliefs about rewards and punishments after death, which are present in one form or another in most religions, provide an important example of the support of altruism by docility combined with bounded rationality. Independently of whether any particular such belief is true or not, its truth or falsity is not something that a human being can establish easily, if at all. Hence, such beliefs are strongly influenced by the surrounding culture. They often promise rewards for behavior that is altruistic, i.e., fitness-reducing. It must be emphasized that d can be a very large term in the expression for fitness. As the current population of the Earth and its rate of growth demonstrate, human beings in modern civilized societies, especially those enjoying the benefits of current medical technology, are much fitter than humans in primitive hunting and fishing, or even agricultural, societies. If

d is a large term, t can be correspondingly large. In a modern high-tech society there is room for a lot of altruism.

Wealth, Power, and Glory

Before we leave the Darwinian fitness model, one more complication should be introduced. Consistent with our earlier Definition UII of utility, wealth, power, and glory appear to be prominent objects of human desire in virtually every society that has been studied. How do we explain the ubiquity of these components of the utility function? There would seem to be at least three possible explanations, not mutually exclusive. For simplicity, I will speak of wealth, but the argument applies to any or all of the three values, certainly to power, but probably also to glory.

First, there could be genetic selection of a desire for wealth. It is not clear that under contemporary conditions wealth contributes to fitness (i.e., to number of progeny), but it certainly did in many, if not most, early societies, where wealth gave access both to food and to mates. Even if wealth does not now contribute to fitness, too few generations have elapsed since the time when it did to remove from the genome any genetic component of these drives that had become established.

Second, because of its fungibility, wealth might well become a value for any adaptive system, even one of severely bounded rationality, that had some sensitivity to the future. Then, whatever the system's specific values, wealth would come to be desired for its exchangeability with other goods. Fungibility would be particularly valuable under conditions of uncertainty, a feature that is not absent from our world.

Third, if the presence of a certain number of wealthy individuals enhanced the fitness of a society, the duty of striving for wealth, of substituting saving and investment for consumption (on a scale beyond that compensated by the rewards for waiting) could become one of the "taxes" that the society placed on its docile members. In such a society, striving for wealth would be a form of altruism; Andrew Carnegie's "gospel of wealth" was an expression of such a doctrine.

We have here an embarrassment of riches. There is no dearth of mechanisms that would predispose members of a society to seek wealth (or power, or glory). Of course the mechanisms are not mutually exclusive; they might well reinforce each other in promoting people's urges to acquire these goods.

The Role of Altruism in Society

We have seen that neo-Darwinian theory says little about what valucs can appear in the utility function; altruism is quite as acceptable as selfishness, provided that docility, net of its altruistic deduction, makes an overall contribution to fitness. We have also seen that human beings appear quite generally to hold (if in widely varying degrees) wealth, power, and glory as being valuable, a preference that may or may not include a genetic component or be tied directly to fitness.

Loyalty and Group Identification

There is one other human value that needs special mention because of its central role in economic behavior: group loyalty. Human beings exhibit a strong tendency to behave in ways that contribute to the achievement of the goals of the groups to which they belong: not only the family, but larger groups like tribes, ethnic groups, nations, and—especially important for our purposes—organizations. They frame situations in terms of a "we," whose interests may conflict with the interests of "they." And the "we" shifts from time to time with shifts in the focus of attention; at one time it is the individual, at another the family, at still another a religious, language, or racial group, at others an organization or a nation. Thus, people may speak of (and work toward) the economic well-being of themselves or their family. But they may equally speak of (and work toward) the economic well-being of their city, or their company, or their ethnic group, or their nation. They are attentive to such indicators of the condition of the groups with which they identify as the average rate of unemployment (in their city or state, in their profession, in their race or age group), or total or per capita income. They are particularly attentive to indicators of the well-being of the groups with which they identify *in comparison with* other groups, and to the trends of these indicators over time.

Group loyalty often expresses itself in altruistic behavior, and that is why the altruism mechanism is so central to our concerns. Without altruism, group loyalty could persist only so far as it could be enforced by rewards and punishments. "Reciprocal altruism," which is not altruism at all, would be possible, but not pure altruism.

There are unanswered empirical questions here of the utmost importance for economics, in particular, questions of the balance between reciprocal altruism and true altruism in the behavior we observe in human political and economic organizations. Lacking detailed evidence to answer these questions, I will have to rely on the anecdotes provided to all of us by our everyday experiences. Such anecdotes are not a permanent substitute, of course, for real evidence, but they will have to suffice until the systematic empirical work has been done. In engaging in such casual empiricism, I will at least not be departing from the customary practices of contemporary economic theorizing.

There are also unanswered empirical questions about the forces and mechanisms that secure the identification of an individual with one group rather than another. Under what circumstances will loyalty to family take precedence over loyalty to company, and vice versa? When will people measure their well-being by the average well-being of the ethnic group to which they belong? What determines the scope of an identification? (Are we Croats or Southern Slavs or Slavs?) Is identification a kind of "imprinting" process? When are people sensitive to such imprinting and when can they alter it? Here is a huge unknown (or almost unknown) continent of empirical social inquiry.

Motivation in Organizations

The account given of business firms and other organizations in the new Institutional Economics rests on such imperfections of human rationality as transaction costs, opportunism, asymmetries of information, and unenforceability of agreements [Williamson, 1985]. In the theory of the business firm in that literature, the assumption is strongly present (but often implicit) that the economic actors desire wealth and power, and that they are selfish with respect to these specific values. Observation of behavior in real-world organizations undermines this assumption of total selfishness (however much it supports the other neo-institutional assumptions of bounded rationality). In real-world organizations, employees, from executives to blue-collar workers, frequently make decisions to advance the goals of the organization even when these decisions may cost them something in terms of their personal values. They identify with the goals of the organization, thereby exhibiting organizational loyalty [Simon, 1976, Chapter X]. They do not usually "work to rule," confining their production and contributions to the minimum laid down in the regulations.

The whole possibility of delegating most decisions to managers and supervisors located at various levels in the organization depends on the delegates' accepting the organizational goals as their decision premises. And the delegation would be wholly ineffective if each decision had to be checked again in detail at higher levels to make sure that it did in fact implement these goals. Without organizational loyalty substantial delegation would be impossible. This is particularly true at middle and higher management levels where there is, and for effectiveness must be, extensive delegation of initiative, i.e., of responsibility for searching out problems and opportunities and finding promising new courses of action to deal with them.

Organizational loyalty and selfishness often make conflicting demands on the individual, and neither one consistently dominates. The point is not that individuals always sacrifice their own interests for those of the organization—clearly they don't—but that they sometimes do. A major reason why they do is that they perceive the organization's goals as *their* goals—which is precisely what identification means. "We" and "they" are fundamentally important pronouns in the language, and an individual's conception (varying from one time to another) of who "we" are defines his or her frame of reference in making decisions.

Since I have developed this point in a recent article [Simon, 1991], I can be brief about it here. If people commonly identify with organization goals, then personal reward and profit cease to hold the unique position in motivating individuals that they would otherwise have. In particular, the differences in executive and employee motivations that are often supposed to exist between government and privately owned organizations or between profit making and non-profit organizations may be small or even nonexistent. We will need to examine carefully the evidence on the relative efficiency of these different forms of social organization, for if organizational identification is common, efficiency cannot be inferred from theoretical first principles, but must be determined empirically.

Understanding motivations in organizations is particularly urgent at this moment in history when many nations are asking fundamental questions about the forms of their social and economic organization. What is the role of prices and markets in motivating socially efficient decisions? What effect does the form of ownership—private profit-making, private non-profit, cooperative, governmental—have upon motivation and choice of goals? Sound understanding of motivations is critical for finding the right answers to these questions. For example, recommending the replacement of central planning with markets says little or nothing about how organizations operating in a market system can be reinvigorated or how ownership should be arranged.

Natural Selection of "Correct" Motives

Reference was made earlier to the argument of Hirshleifer and others that selection of the fittest (of the most profitable) among business firms will guarantee that the surviving firms will be profit maximizers. If we could be sure of that outcome, then the motivations of individuals might be of little importance to economics at the level of markets or of the whole economy. But is the argument valid? Darwinism implies only "survival of the fitt*er*" and not "survival of the fitt*est*. Competition can only select among organisms or organizations that have been "invented" and have come into being. If there are no profit-maximizing firms, then evolution can only favor those among the existing firms that come closest to this norm. "Closest" may not be very close, especially when there are many factors in the external environment, some of them changing rapidly, that alter the firm's abilities to make profits and the effectiveness of its current procedures [Cyert and DeGroot, 1987].

Moreover, if there is a mechanism causing firms to increase fitness in response to competition [Nelson and Winter, 1982], this mechanism will be a hill-climbing process that seeks local maxima. Only in the simplest of worlds does local maximization guarantee anything even approaching global maximization. The maximizer will more likely end up on top of the Sears Tower than Mount Everest. The Darwinian equilibrium of the Australian fauna was seriously displaced with the importation of rabbits, which Nature had not previously "invented" in Australia. In an economic world where new technologies and social inventions are continually being introduced, there is no reason why the organizations that are viable at any given time should be optimizers if, indeed, this term can be defined in such a context. Hence, we may expect that organizations will displace others that are much less fit (profitable) than they are, but not that the selection process entails profit maximization. A theory of the firm based on natural selection will be concerned primarily with continuing change through innovation rather than with an illusory equilibrium at an optimum [Nelson and Winter, 1982].

The history of this kind of evolving system may be highly sensitive to the order in which innovations are introduced. Success to date of a particular technology may influence strongly the resources devoted to its continuing development, hence its success in the future in competition with alternative technologies. As David [1988] has shown, the victory of alternating-current over direct-current technology in the history of electrification was not pre-ordained by the superior efficiency of the one over the other, but resulted from a whole complex of circumstances, including the exact dates of introduction of various components of the technology: transformers, ac-dc converters, and others. The final choices of specific ac frequencies were even more contingent on short-run, but irreversible, considerations.

Any remaining illusions that the behavior of firms, or of the economy, can be explained in terms of a stable, optimizing equilibrium, are challenged by the discovery that even simple Walrasian market mechanisms may produce chaotic regimes [Grandmont, 1987; Day and Shafer, 1987], so that small changes in initial conditions produce widely diverging paths. In the theory of the firm, and in the interactions of that theory with the theory of markets, we will necessarily deal with the dynamics of a non-linear economic system, and these dynamics are unlikely to be simple.

Motivations in Politics

Introducing the mechanisms of group identification into our model of human decision making also has profound consequences for our understanding of political institutions. Within the current literature of public choice, the standard assumption is that actors are striving to maximize wealth or power, or some combination of these. This assumption makes paradoxes or mysteries out of familiar phenomena.

For example, individuals have essentially no selfish motive for voting—a single vote is unlikely to change the outcome of an election in a city, much less a nation. Yet millions of people do vote, even though comparable numbers may stay at home. Altruism, in the form of identification with the political entity, the city or nation, provides a motivation for voting, and for other pro-social behavior where public goods are involved, that selfishness does not.

The experiences in this century of the peoples of Russia and China can be interpreted (and have been interpreted) as showing that economic self interest is the only reliable motive for powering an economy. But such an interpretation does not separate out the effects of central planning from the effects of forms of ownership, or of motivation. Nor does it explain the frequent eclipse of issues of efficiency by struggles for ethnic autonomy—for political self-determination of an abstract *we*.

In the presence of group identifications, of which ethnicity is an instance, even the notion of selfish economic motivation becomes ambiguous. How do people judge whether one party or another will advance their economic interests? By the recent history of their family income? By trends in per capita GNP? By the economic gains or losses of their ethnic group? By their own employment or unemployment, or by that of some group (factory workers, white collar workers, farmers) to which they belong or with which they believe their economic prospects are joined?

This array of possibilities banishes the idea that we can predict political behavior from the axioms of utility maximization—or even these axioms conjoined with assumptions about human economic motivation and selfishness. To predict behavior, we must have empirical information about the motives that guide people, about their knowledge and beliefs concerning the operation of the economy and the social system, and about the particular subset of values, knowledge and beliefs on which their attention is currently focused by the events around them.

There is no *a priori* source for this information. It can be won only by painstaking observation of human behavior in the marketplace, in the home, and in organizations. Until economics has paid its dues, very expensive ones, of empirical study and experimentation, it has no chance of arriving at veridical theories of human political behavior. There are no Three Laws of Motion that can substitute for the study of actual human behavior.

Conclusion

In this chapter, I have reexamined the question of whether Darwinian selection is compatible with altruism, and have shown that, contrary to prevailing doctrine, the two are indeed compatible. The analysis starts with two assumptions: first, that docility contributes to human fitness, hence will be selected for; second, that by reason of the limits on their rationality, human beings must accept many things as true without being able to test their validity independently. Society uses this bounded rationality to "tax" docility, inducing individuals to engage in many behaviors that increase average fitness in the society but decrease the net fitness of thc altruist.

One especially important form of altruism is loyalty to (identification with) groups to which the individual belongs. The shape of this loyalty, and the nature of the groups to which it attaches in a particular society go far toward determining the institutional structure of that society and its social processes. In particular, identification with organizations, especially by employees, allows organizational effectiveness to reach far higher levels than could be attained by rewards and punishments alone in the face of wholly selfish motivation.

Given the viability of altruism, even such traditional "selfish" goals as wealth, power, and glory receive a possible new interpretation. They may have little to do, at least under modern conditions, with individual fitness. Instead, they may be socially induced motives that contribute to average fitness in the society—in short, a form of altruism. This, of course, is a speculation which needs to be tested empirically. The willingness of people sometimes to provide public goods also becomes understandable once altruism is admitted into the set of effective human motives. And even "selfish" political behavior must be reexamined in the light of its dependence on the group identifications that members of the polity form and that exercise a strong influence on their behavior.

Introducing this more complex and realistic picture of the motives of human actors in the economic and political arenas requires us to abdicate any belief that human behavior can be inferred from a rational model without painstaking empirical inquiry into peoples' specific values, beliefs, and foci of attention. It calls for a reassignment of priorities in economics and in the education of economists toward this empirical inquiry and toward the techniques of experimentation and observation that must be mastered to carry it out.

The tools of contemporary econometrics are wholly inadequate to the task. Economists, even empirically oriented economists, can no longer screen themselves from the world behind banks of statistical data, data that are frequently noisy and barely relevant. They will have to venture out into the world itself, like anthropologists who learn the languages of the natives, speak with them, and observe them. But how this can be done must be left to another article.

Notes

This research was supported by the Personnel and Training Programs, Psychological Sciences Division, Office of Naval Research, under Contract No. N00014-86-K-0768; and by the Defense Advanced Research Projects Agency, Department of Defense, ARPA Order 3597, monitored by the Air Force Avionics Laboratory under contract F33615-81-K-1539. Reproduction in whole or in part is permitted for any purpose of the United States Government. Approved for public release; distribution unlimited.

1. I will speak throughout this chapter about "utility functions." I do not really believe that people have utility functions that assure consistency of choice; and the empirical evidence is squarely on the side of disbelief. My alternative to utility functions is sketched in Simon [1955] and [1956], reprinted as Chapters 7.2 and 7.3 in Simon [1982]. However, my argument will not depend in any critical way on whether people have global utility functions or systems of values organized in some other, presumably less mythical, way. Hence, I will use the usual economic terminology as a convenient label.

2. I will apologize in advance for referring in this chapter largely to my own publications, as the main aim of the Chapter is to bring together into a coherent picture arguments that I have made separately, on the topics of bounded rationality, organizational motivations, public choice, and altruism.

3. I am not wholly satisfied with the term, "docility," which carries overtones of passivity, but there does not seem to be a wholly satisfactory alternative in English. "Socializability" would be a possibility if it were not so awkward. For the present, I will stick with "docility."

References

Cyert, R. M. and DeGroot, M. H. *Bayesian Analysis and Uncertainty in Economic Theory*. Totowa, NJ: Rowman and Littlefield, 1987.

David, P. A. The Economics of Gateway Technologies and Network Evolution: Lessons from Electricity Supply History. *Information Economics and Policy* 3, no. 2 (1988): 165–202.

Day, R. H. and Shafer, W. Ergodic Fluctuations in Economic Models. *Journal of Economic Behavior and Organization*, September 1987, 339–61.

Grandmont, J-M., ed. *Nonlinear Economic Dynamics*. Boston: Academic Press, 1987.

Hirshleifer, J. Economics from a Biological Viewpoint. *Journal of Law and Economics*, April 1977, 1–52.

Nelson, R., and Winter, S. *An Evolutionary Theory of Economic Change*. Cambridge: Harvard University Press, 1982.

Simon, H. A. *Administrative behavior*. New York: Macmillan, 1947, 1957, 1976.

———. A Behavioral Model of Rational Choice. *Quarterly Journal of Economics*, February 1955, 99–18.

———. Rational Choice and the Structure of the Environment. *Psychological Review*, March 1956, 129–38.

———. Rational Decision Making in Business Organizations. *American Economic Review*, September 1979, 493–513.

———. *Models of Bounded Rationality*. 2 vols., Cambridge: MIT Press, 1982.

———. Rationality in Psychology and Economics. *Rational Choice: The Contrast Between Economics and Psychology*, edited by R. M. Hogarth and M. W. Reder. Chicago: University of Chicago Press, 1986.

———. A Mechanism for Social Selection and Successful Altruism. *Science*, 21 December 1990, 1665–68.

———. Organizations and Markets. *Journal of Economic Perspectives*, Spring 1991, 25–44.

Williamson, O. E. *The Economic Institutions of Capitalism*. New York: The Free Press, 1985.

Wilson, D. S. *The Natural Selection of Populations and Communities*. Menlo Park, NJ: Benjamin/Cummings Publishing Company, 1980.

III.4 Altruism and Economics: Social Implications

Altruism is an elusive concept. To pin it down, I must begin with population genetics, distinguishing altruism's technical meaning there from its everyday meanings in social and economic affairs. Then I will examine the role of altruism in the operation of the economy.

I Altruism in Neo-Darwinian Theory

The key concept in modern evolutionary theory is *fitness*: the number of progeny an individual produces or, for species, the average number of progeny of members of the species. If several species inhabit the same niche, the fittest will eliminate the others; and species will evolve with the appearance of mutants having greater fitness than the original genotype. The speed with which one genotype or species will replace another is determined by the ratios of their average reproduction times and fitnesses.

One can speak of the fitness of an individual or the average fitness of a group to which the individual belongs. If several groups compete for the same niche, the one having the highest average fitness will survive.

In evolutionary theory, altruism means behavior that reduces the actor's fitness while enhancing the fitness of others. If the total contribution of the altruist to the fitness of others is greater than the fitness lost by the altruist, altruism will increase the prospects of the group's surviving in competition with other groups.

Altruistic genes will thrive only under rather special circumstances. Altruism to close kin (siblings and children) can survive if it makes a sufficient contribution to their fitness, since they share a large fraction of the genes of the altruist and will propagate them. However, altruism to others with whom the altruist does not share a large fraction of genes is unlikely to survive, even if it enhances the fitness of the group as a whole—for while the whole group is growing, the altruists in it will gradually vanish, reducing and then eliminating the group's initial advantage. There are a few other cases where altruism can survive and flourish (e.g., so-called structured demes), but only one of them is important in the present context. Indeed, it is of supreme importance for the human species.

II Bounded Rationality and Altruism

Human beings (and other creatures) do not behave optimally for their fitness, because they are wholly incapable of acquiring the knowledge and making the calculations that would support optimization. They do not know all of the alternatives that are available for action; they have only incomplete and uncertain knowledge about the environmental variables, present and future, that will determine the consequences of their choices; and they would be unable to make the computations required for optimal choice even if they had perfect knowledge. I will not make the argument here for bounded rationality, for it is widely accepted today. I will simply take it as an axiom: *human beings are capable only of very approximate and bounded rationality*.

Because of bounded rationality, docility contributes to the fitness of human beings in evolutionary competition. By "docility" I mean *the tendency to depend on suggestions, recommendations, persuasion, and information obtained through social channels as a major basis for choice*. Most of us who restrict our consumption of fats do so, not because our own experience and research has provided convincing evidence that a fatty diet is unhealthy, but because we have been told, on reliable authority, that such a diet is harmful. "Reliable authority" is a term describing a social system and interpersonal relations within it.

In large measure, we do what we do because we have learned from those who surround us, not from our own experience, what is good for us and what is not. Behaving in this fashion contributes heavily to our fitness because (a) social influences will generally give us advice that is "for our own good" and (b) the information on which this advice is based is far better than the information we could gather independently. As a consequence, *people exhibit a very large measure of docility*. On average, it contributes to their fitness and hence drives out nondocility in evolutionary competition.

Since docile persons depend heavily on socially provided advice and orders, they often make choices that reduce their own fitness under social advice to do so. They are often unable to judge independently that a recommended choice is actually disadvantageous to them as individuals. This inability is a necessary consequence of their bounded rationality, the same bounded rationality that makes docility, on average, enhance their fitness.

Consequently, society can "tax" docile individuals by sometimes persuading them to take altruistic actions that decrease individual fitness. So long as the cost of the altruism to them is less than the gain obtained from improving their other choices, docile individuals will remain fitter than nondocile ones. If the cost to individual fitness is less than the value of these altruistic acts in enhancing the average fitness of members of the society, then the society will gain from the altruism in competing with other societies. It follows that societies that induce altruism in docile individuals will survive in competition with those that do not.

Of course societies as abstractions do not "tax" their members. Those who advise altruistic behaviors are responding to the same social influences as those advised: they are also docile and behaving in a manner socially defined as appropriate. At the social level, the gradual change and selection of culture traits are producing patterns of information, advice, and resulting behavior that enhance the average fitness of members of the society; and because of docility, social evolution often induces altruistic behavior in individuals that has net advantage for average fitness in the society. Altruism includes influencing others to behave altruistically.

III Intelligence and Altruism

Recently, I published a simple model formalizing these arguments, which demonstrates that extensive altruism will appear in populations characterized by bounded rationality and docility (Simon, 1990). I present here a modified version of the model that meets an objection raised by Oded Stark (pers. comm.): that with differences in intelligence among docile individuals, the more intelligent could discriminate better between advice useful to fitness and advice recommending altruism, and this difference in discrimination would extinguish altruism. I will show here that the intelligent altruists, though less altruistic than the unintelligent altruists, will be fitter than both unintelligent altruists and selfish individuals.

The following equations determine the net fitnesses of intelligent altruists (fI), selfish persons (fS), and unintelligent altruists (fU), respectively:

$$\mathrm{fI} = \mathrm{fn} + \mathrm{fd} \cdot \mathrm{dI} + \mathrm{faI} \cdot \mathrm{qI} \cdot \mathrm{cI} + \mathrm{faU} \cdot \mathrm{qU} \cdot \mathrm{cU} - c \cdot \mathrm{cI}$$

$$\mathrm{fS} = \mathrm{fn} + \mathrm{faI} \cdot \mathrm{qI} \cdot \mathrm{cI} + \mathrm{faU} \cdot \mathrm{qU} \cdot \mathrm{cU}$$

$$\mathrm{fU} = \mathrm{fn} + \mathrm{fd} \cdot \mathrm{dU} + \mathrm{faI} \cdot \mathrm{qI} \cdot \mathrm{cI} + \mathrm{faU} \cdot \mathrm{qU} \cdot \mathrm{cU} - c \cdot \mathrm{cU}.$$

The f's are fitness coefficients: fn is normal fitness; fd · dI and fd · dU are increments in fitness for docility; faI and faU are increments in fitness from others' altruism; cI and cU represent the extent to which I and U are altruistic; dI and dU denote the abilities of I and U to benefit from docility; qI and qU are the percentages of I and U altruists in the population. The cost of altruism is c.

I assume that everyone benefits equally from the altruism of the altruists. Intelligent altruists benefit more from docility than do unintelligent altruists (dI > dU). Intelligent altruists are also less altruistic than unintelligent altruists (cI < cU). Under these assumptions, the fitness of intelligent altruists will exceed that of unintelligent altruists (fI > fU). On the other hand, as long as $\mathrm{fd} \cdot \mathrm{dI} > c \cdot \mathrm{cI}(\mathrm{fd} \cdot \mathrm{dU} > \mathrm{c} \cdot \mathrm{cU})$, the fitness of intelligent (unintelligent) altruists will exceed the fitness of selfish persons, $\mathrm{fI} > \mathrm{fS}(\mathrm{fU} > \mathrm{fS})$.

I now ask how the relative populations of intelligent altruists, unintelligent altruists, and selfish persons would change over 30 generations if the following values are assigned to the fitness and cost parameters: $\mathrm{fn} = 1.01$; $\mathrm{fd} = 0.02$; $c = 0.005$; $\mathrm{faI} = 0.01$; $\mathrm{faU} = 0.005$; $q_0\mathrm{I} = 1/3$; $q_0 S = 1/3$; $p_0\mathrm{U} = 1$; $\mathrm{dI} = 2$; $\mathrm{cI} = 0.8$; $\mathrm{cU} = 1$; $\mathrm{dU} = 1$.

Starting with equal numbers in the three groups, in 30 generations the intelligent altruists will have become a majority (53 percent), and the selfish persons will be disappearing rather rapidly (18 percent), while the unintelligent altruists disappear more slowly (29 percent). The survival of altruism only requires that even intelligent persons cannot discriminate perfectly between fitness-enhancing and altruistic behavior. Because they benefit from their docility, intelligent altruists will be fitter than intelligent selfish individuals. Since the boundedness of rationality is ineradicable, altruism will survive.

IV Social Meanings of Altruism and Selfishness

Neoclassical economics assumes that people maximize utility but postulates nothing about what utility is. With only this assumption, it is impossible to distinguish altruism from selfishness. One might call altruistic any choice that decreased the utility of the chooser while increasing the utility of others; but such a definition is useless. With the appropriate utility function, a person whose utility derived from giving to other people could selfishly give away millions of dollars.

In contrast, if one defines altruism as sacrifice of fitness, it becomes possible to determine empirically (in principle) which choices are selfish and which are altruistic. Whether giving away a million dollars is selfish or altruistic depends simply on the effect of the gift upon the number of progeny of the donor. This surely departs from everyday definitions of selfishness and altruism.

In actual applications of utility theory to concrete economic behavior, utility is commonly neither left unspecified nor equated with fitness. Most often, it is equated with income or wealth or (for the firm) profit; maximizing utility is identified with maximizing economic reward. That economic actors desire only economic gain is a far stronger assumption than that they maximize utility. It is also empirically false.

Furthermore, fitness arguments do not imply that desire for economic gain is the dominant human motive. Perhaps in earlier centuries wealth was a major contributor to fitness, and one could regard desire for economic gain as adaptive during that period. There is no such connection today. Population increase is generally far more rapid in the third world than in the first. Within economies like our own, there is also a negative correlation between income level and reproduction rate. The statistics show the poor to be fitter than the rich.

Suppose, more realistically, that human choice is driven by a number of motives, not limited to economic gain, that are based on anticipated consequences (pleasure and pain) for the chooser. Then one can call behavior "altruistic" to the extent that it is influenced by expectations of pleasure and pain for other persons. This definition also has problems (e.g., how do we deal with empathetic pleasure?), but it comes close to everyday commonsense definitions of altruism. It includes economic gain among the selfish motives but does not restrict selfishness to it alone.

Although wealth is not closely linked to fitness, another human characteristic, docility, is so linked. Human beings are born today even more helpless than in the past. They require extensive nurturing and education to survive and reproduce. The complexities of modern life increase the rewards for acceptance of social influence and, consequently, altruism.

What motivates human choice is an empirical question, and neoclassical conclusions that derive from the dubious assumption that economic motives dominate must be reexamined. In several areas of economics, current doctrines will have to undergo severe revision as motives other than economic gain (and especially altruistic ones) assume their appropriate place in theory.

V Group Loyalty as Altruism

Current events in former Yugoslavia, in the former Soviet Union, in Ireland, in India (the list is endless), bring home vividly the strength of ethnocentrism as a human motive. Ethnics can define themselves in many ways, among them religion, language, and history. Ethnicity calls for decisions that are "good for the group," but "good" is highly ambiguous, having economic, territorial, and cultural components (e.g., the right to use a particular language or practice a particular religion). It would be impossible to demonstrate any close connection between the decisions made by members of ethnic groups and the economic well-being (much less biological fitness) of those members. Ethnicity thrives on altruistic behavior, often taking the form of risky violence against outsiders.

Knowing a person's ethnic loyalties goes only a short distance toward predicting attitudes and behavior. The ethnic will strive for economic gains for the group, but (as history shows) often more vigorously for political gains even at considerable economic sacrifice. Bounded rationality creates an immense gap between knowing that ethnics desire to improve the condition of their group and predicting what policies they will support. To know the latter, one has to know their economic and political theories. Different theories lead to different rankings among policies.

Ethnic loyalties compete with many other loyalties, thereby making the prediction of choice further dependent on empirical investigation rather than a priori postulation. Marx thought that ethnic loyalties were dominated by class loyalties, and so they were for a time in revolutionary Russia and China. Nothing in theory indicates when loyalties will be attached to an ethnic group, when to an economic or social class, and when to some other social entity (e.g., women's liberation).

From ethnic groups and social classes, one can descend to more microscopic groups, like the family. Much of the "corruption" that troubles Chinese economic reform today derives from dominance of family loyalty over loyalty to the business firm or the nation. Theory cannot predict this; only empirical study of particular cultures can.

Nations, even those of mixed ethnicity like the United States, sometimes command strong loyalties. A few people attach their loyalties to even broader groups: the European Community, the United Nations, humankind. One cannot predict whether their numbers will grow or shrink, or what policies their loyalties will lead them to. These are all empirical questions, not consequences of theory. Loyalties to groups provide perhaps the most important basis for altruism.

Among the most important loyalties in modern society is loyalty to organizations: business corporations, universities, armies, voluntary associations, and their components. Since organizations are principal players in modern economies, identification of employees and executives with goals of companies and subunits plays a major part in economic motivation (Simon, 1991).

Group loyalties, have not only a motivational but also a cognitive component. They define the boundaries of the group over which "goods" are to be summed, and they cause particular variables and simplified world models to govern the thinking of group members. Nowhere is this more evident than in organizations. Promotion of a person from section chief to department head greatly alters his or her preferences. The consequences of that person's decisions are now summed over the whole department instead of the section. Moreover, decisions are now made within the new environment of information in which the department head resides. There are not only different goals, but also a differently experienced reality in which these goals are to be achieved.

Perhaps, in the previous position the principal reality was the factory floor and vendors of raw materials and parts. Now, all sorts of new information from salesmen or accountants or research and development units redescribe the situation that the executive faces. The composite of goals and structured information that surrounds the head and members of an organizational unit produces powerful loyalties and definitions of the situation that are called *organizational identifications*.

Most of the economy's work goes on inside organizations, influenced heavily by information that is internal to them. Regrettably, the "new institutional economics," (Oliver E. Williamson, 1985) mostly ignores organizational identification as a powerful altruistic force conditioning both participants' goals and the cognitive models they form of their situations. Appropriate attention to altruism, especially organizational identification, substantially changes the theory of the firm and, consequently, theories of the economy.

VI Public Choice

Like the classical theory of the firm, the theory of public choice assumes that behavior is governed predominantly by desire for economic gain or power, ignoring altruistic motives and bounded rationality (Simon, 1985). I will mention two examples of the difficulties caused by these misconceptions.

First, the voting "paradox" (the fact that people vote) is only a paradox if there is no altruism. When the door opens, even a crack, to altruism, voters can behave in ways approved by societal opinion. Second, we cannot predict voting behavior from the assumption that voters are interested in economic welfare, unless we know how they believe the economy operates and with what groups they identify. Assuming self-interest, whether limited to economic goals or not, will not do the trick.

Beyond public choice, economics has ventured into other social domains, for example, the family. Again, the theories assume that human behavior is motivated by economic gain (Simon 1987), leaving no room for altruism or bounded rationality. They baselessly try to settle by postulate what can only be determined by careful empirical study.

VII Conclusion

Economic theory has treated economic gain as the primary human motive. An empirically grounded theory would assign comparable weight to other motives, including altruism and the organizational identifications associated with it.

The theory would recognize that human motives change over time, responding to experience and the surprises of history. Individuals do not form their preferences in isolation from other individuals, but in response to both public events and information that is widely broadcast. Theory must make room for tulip crazes, responses to oil shocks, or the unexpected rise of ethnicity.

Instead of political science or history as derivative of economic analysis, there is a need for economics based upon the facts of history and political and social life. Such an economics will have little to say a priori but will reason from numerous painfully gathered facts. It will have the merit of describing the world in which we actually live. Altruism, especially altruism derived from group and organizational loyalties, will play a major role in it.

References

Simon, Herbert A., "Human Nature in Politics: The Dialogue of Psychology with Political Science," *American Political Science Review*, June 1985, *79*, 293–304.

———, "Rationality in Psychology and Economics," in R. Hogarth and M. Reder, eds., *Rational Choice*, Chicago: University of Chicago Press, 1987, pp. 25–40.

———, "A Mechanism for Social Selection and Successful Altruism," *Science*, 21 December 1990, *250*, 1665–8.

———, "Organizations and Markets," *Journal of Economic Perspectives*, Spring 1991, *5*, 25–44.

Williamson, Oliver E., *The Economic Institutions of Capitalism*, New York: Free Press, 1985.

IV BEHAVIORAL ECONOMICS AND BOUNDED RATIONALITY

The chapters in this final Part say something about economics and a great deal about economists: what they have been doing and what I believe they should be doing. Anyone familiar with my previous published work will not be surprised by this theme. In the 1940s and 1950s I undertook to apply to questions in economics the concept of bounded rationality and the related concept of satisficing that had grown out of my research on organizational decision making. These proposals were received by most mainline economists with something less than unbounded enthusiasm. In fact, they were largely ignored as irrelevant for economics (and as probably wrong) for many years.

The indifference to the attempt to reorient the theory of choice used in economics forced me to think hard both about my views and about why they received so little response. In particular, it led me to examine the economic literature to see whether, indeed, it had foundations that were sufficiently solid without bounded rationality to bolster them. The papers of Part VIII, Volume 2, of *Models of Bounded Rationality*, report some of my findings about the weaknesses of those foundations.

At both macro and micro levels, evidence for the facts that would be required to give credence to neoclassical theory was mostly absent. The theory, on examination, required large numbers of auxiliary assumptions that were usually introduced a priori without substantial empirical support. There were other weaknesses, but these were the most striking. I have continued to try to understand the reasons for the reluctance of the profession to undertake the empirical research that would be needed to modify neoclassical theory in the directions of reality—and to see how that reluctance could be countered. The papers of this Part represent my recent efforts to this end. They build on my previous critique of neoclassical theory, but are especially focused on providing concrete and empirically based characterizations of a large number of specific difficulties in current theory, both micro and macro, diagnoses of the roots of these difficulties, and proposals for remedying them.

Harbingers of Change

The rate of change in economics, agonizingly slow at first, has been increasing in recent years, perhaps beginning with the disillusionment associated with stagflation and the demise of the Phillips Curve. Today the movement toward a more behaviorally based theory is accelerating quite visibly. Even introductory textbooks (at least in microeconomics) are beginning to give space to alternatives to neoclassical orthodoxy (e.g., Frank, 1994; Earl, 1995). The Great Wall has been breached, and no longer offers an impervious defense against the incursion of heresies. (At the same time, long stretches of it are still manned by defenders.)

I have no illusion that the current changes are a consequence of anything I have said or done. They are coming about because economists are seeing more and more clearly the failure of neoclassical theory to answer believably the questions that need answers; I and the others who urge the reform serve, at most, as agents of a new Zeitgeist.

The Shape of the Reform

The first nine chapter of Part IV aim at a series of related objectives. Chapters IV.1–IV.4 summarize briefly the central concepts of behavioral economics, including bounded rationality. Chapters IV.5–IV.7 show how neoclassical theory, in its applications to policy, makes essential use of auxiliary empirical assumptions that are seldom subjected to rigorous empirical tests; these chapters then outline the changes in empirical methodology and practice that are required to remedy this state of affairs. Chapters IV.8–IV.9 provide numerous examples of (a) "facts" deduced from neoclassical theory that don't correspond to the real world, (b) diametrically opposing pairs of policy views both stemming from neoclassical theory but employing conflicting auxiliary assumptions that have not been tested empirically, and (c) "explanations" of economic phenomena that are cloaked in neoclassical language, but whose validity depends entirely upon unexpressed and unvalidated empirical hypotheses.

Out of the discussion in these chapters comes a characterization of the kind of economic theory we need and the changes in economic thinking and methodology that are required to bring it about.

1. A veridical economic theory must rest on an empirically valid general theory of human thinking and decision making; it must be a *behavioral theory* (Chapter IV.2).

2. The behavioral theory must incorporate what we know of *bounded rationality*—the limits of human capability to calculate, the severe deficiencies of human knowledge about the consequences of choice, and the limits of human ability to adjudicate among multiple goals (Chapter IV.3).

3. The behavioral theory must provide realistic substitutes for the usually unattainable goal of maximizing utility: it must show how human beings can use their limited capabilities for rationality to find and choose reasonable alternatives: for example, by *satisficing* (Chapter IV.4).

4. The behavioral theory is substantially less deductive, *more inductive*, than neoclassical theory has been. It resembles molecular biology, with its myriads of complex structures and processes, far more than it resembles physics, with its powerful deductions from broad general laws. Consequently its continuing progress will depend on strengthening its empirical methods, relying far less than it has previously on regression analysis of aggregative data, and borrowing and improving upon direct methods of experimenting upon and observing human behavior that have been developed in psychology and sociology (Chapters IV.5–IV.7).

5. Bounded rationality is *procedural*, not *substantive* rationality. Human behavior cannot be predicted from the optimal behavior in a given environment. Behavior depends on how the economic actors perceive and represent the environment, how they define their goals and methods for assessing goal attainment, what facts they know or assume and what strategies they have for problem solving. The economic actors' rationality will be defined by the processes they use in making their decisions rather than the substance of the decisions they reach; and the processes they employ cannot be deduced from the objective description of the problem situation; they can only be determined inductively from empirical observation or inferred from empirically based theories of behavior (Chapters IV.8–IV.9). In particular economic actors will be much influenced by contemporary social beliefs which, in turn, will undergo gradual change with the course of historical events. Behavioral economics, like geology and evolutionary biology, is an historical science (see especially the section on Schumpeterian dynamics in Chapter IV.8, and on attention and representation in Chapter IV.9).

6. Economics must give up those aspects of neoclassical belief that have no *foundation in evidence*: for example, the belief that markets reach equilibrium because of optimizing behavior and marginal calculations of buyers and sellers, that the magnitudes of the exponents in the Cobb-Douglas function fitted to aggregate date reflect the marginal productivity of labor or capital, or that U-shaped short-run cost curves, with their U-shaped long-run envelope, have anything to do with the size

distribution of business firms. All of these unsupported beliefs still make their regular appearance in economics textbooks and literature. They must vanish, because the phenomena they purport to explain either don't exist or have much simpler and better-supported behavioral explanations. (Chapters IV.8–IV.9).

While the reform of economics toward a more realistic description and explanation of economic institutions and how they operate has already led to some major pieces of theory, it is not yet a completed structure. It surely does not possess anything like the completeness of neoclassical theory. But completeness is not an acceptable substitute for veridicality.

The Public Face of Economics

The general public often finds itself bewildered by the conflicting views that are propounded by economists of various persuasions. On several occasions I have addressed this bewilderment. Chapters IV.10–IV.11 give an account of how economists subscribing to the same neoclassical orthodoxy, as most do, can arrive at quite different policy preferences. This divergence from a common theory to conflicting policy recommendations occurs, as we have already seen from the preceding chapters, because the neoclassical theory must be augmented, for actual application, with auxiliary assumptions that are seldom motivated by data, and different economists make different assumptions.

The ad hoc assumptions postulate that economic actors will depart in specified ways from perfect rationality. Depending on exactly where the assumptions depart from the strict neoclassical theory, quite different conclusions can and do follow about how the system will operate. For example, the standard explanations of the economy's departures from equilibrium (unemployment, inflation, business cycles) rest squarely on such unmotivated artifacts.

The Profession's View of Itself

It is not only the general public that is disillusioned with neoclassical theory and the casual empiricism so often associated with it. At economics meetings and on university campuses, one observes a widespread cynicism about the current orthodoxy, and especially its excessive formalism, combined with pessimism about whether anything can be done about it. In my visits to universities, I find this cynicism to be especially strong among economics graduate students who are not yet far enough into the profession to have lost their sense of the unreality of what they are being taught, or to have acquired a mathematical fastidiousness that confuses rigor with truth.

There is something seriously amiss in a science where so many practitioners and postulants have acquired this high level of cynicism about the work and study in which they are engaged. The chapters of Part IV (and Parts III and IV of Volume 2) seek to describe a path to an economic theory that comes closer than neoclassicism to describing economic institutions and economic behavior as they actually are in the world today. It is a long and arduous path, but no longer or more arduous than the paths that scientists are following with great success in such domains as molecular biology or geophysics or any of the other domains where the ratio of validated facts to theoretical generalizations must, by the nature of things, be large.

An Example of Research on Reasoning in Economics

But I do not want to end on such a contentious note. The final chapter, IV.12, provides a tiny positive example of how we can advance our knowledge of economics by studying how people think about it. The research reported in this chapter, carried out in collaboration with Hermi Tabachneck and Anthony Leonardo, is one of a number of laboratory experiments (interpreted by a theory in the form of a computer simulation) aimed at describing and explaining how people deal with information about an economic situation that is presented in various forms: in words, in diagrams, in tables or in algebraic equations. By itself, this study (like the myriad of careful biological experiments reported in *Science* each week) advances economics only an imperceptible fraction of an inch. But thousands (or perhaps tens of thousands) of such studies, designed and interpreted within the framework of a growing theory, will bring us out of our present impasse and to a new level of understanding of the workings of the human mind, and through it, the working of economic processes.

References

Earl, P. E. (1995). *Microeconomics for business and marketing*. Aldershot, England: Edward Elgar.

Frank, R. H. (1994). *Microeconomics and behavior*. Now York, NY: McGraw-Hill.

IV.1 Preface to *Handbook of Behavioral Economics*

The impressive development of classical economic analysis over the past 200 years has been accomplished with the use of extremely simple assumptions about the behavior of the human actors on the economic scene. The consumer maximizes his or her utility; the business firm, its profit. Today we know that powerful results can be obtained from analysis using these assumptions, but we also know something about the limits of those results for explaining the actualities of the economic world.

The limits show up, for example, in the current confusions and uncertainties of macroeconomists about government policies for combating underemployment and inflation. For lack of empirically founded theories of how economic actors actually make decisions in the face of uncertainty and complexity—where the assumptions of global rationality are no longer even approximately valid—neoclassical economics provides us with little help in understanding business cycles or the longer movements of economic development.

At the level of the business firm and the consumer, classical theory gives few hints as to how real human beings make real decisions in a world that rarely provides them with the data and computational resources that would be required to apply, literally, the theory of the textbooks. We need empirically valid theories of how business organizations operate, of how investment decisions are actually made, of how the levels of salaries and wages are determined, and of the growth and sizes of business firms.

In sum, we need to augment and amend the existing body of classical and neoclassical economic theory to achieve a more realistic picture of economic processes as well as a more accurate understanding of the equilibrium toward which these processes move.

Behavioral economics is the name we give to the research enterprise that seeks to meet these needs. It is no new thing. Alfred Marshall of *Industry and Trade* could well have labeled himself a behavioralist. And, of course, behavioral economics can claim John R. Commons, Thorstein Veblen, Joseph Schumpeter, George Katona, and many other distinguished economists of past and recent generations.

But behavioral economics, with its emphasis on the factual complexities of our world, has not always appeared as attractive as the axiomatized certainties of marginal analysis and subjective expected utility. Classical and behavioral economics have stood apart, eyeing each other nervously and suspiciously. They have put off the synthesis that we shall need to fully grasp the economic world around us.

I am encouraged, at the present time, by what I perceive as a strong ground swell of interest in behavioral economics and in closing the gap between behavioral and classical theory. With enough patience and diligence in exploring the empirical realities of economic processes, and enough ingenuity in modeling these processes, we will be able, in time, to return economics to the real world. I welcome this volume as a survey of the work that is carrying us in that direction.

IV.2 Behavioural Economics

Since economics is certainly concerned with human behaviour—with, as Marshall put it, '[the] study of mankind in the ordinary business of life'—the phrase 'behavioural economics' appears to be a pleonasm. What non-behavioural economics can we contrast with it? The answer to this question is found in the specific assumptions about human behaviour that are made in neoclassical economic theory.

Contrast of Behavioural with Neoclassical Theory

The Neoclassical Assumptions

How does human behaviour enter into classical and neoclassical economics? First, human goals and motivations are assumed to be given a priori in the form of a utility function, which allows an individual to make consistent choices among all possible bundles of goods and services. Second, economic actors are assumed always to choose, among the alternatives open to them, that one of the alternatives that yields the greatest utility (Savage, 1954).

These two assumptions—of a given utility function and of utility maximization (rationality)—are usually made explicitly. Other assumptions about human behaviour are often implicit in classical and neoclassical theory, and are not necessarily maintained through all variants of the theory. It is usually assumed that not only the utility function but also the set of available alternatives is given a priori. In search theory, this assumption is replaced by the assumption that new alternatives may be generated by a process of search, but at some cost, which is assumed to be known, as is the expected marginal return to the search.

With respect to the consequences of alternatives, it may be assumed that these are known completely and with certainty, or that what is known is a joint probability distribution of outcomes, although occasionally, forms of 'uncertainty' that are not reducible to probabilities are introduced into the theory. It is almost always assumed in neoclassical theory that, given their knowledge of utilities, alternatives, and outcomes, economic actors can compute which alternative will yield the greatest (expected) utility—although it is conceptually (if seldom practically) possible to incorporate a cost of computation into the theories that is analogous to the cost of generating alternatives in search theory.

Behavioural Departures from Neoclassical Assumptions

With this characterization of classical and neoclassical economics, we can now, by a process of contrast, define rough boundaries for behavioural economics. Behavioural economics is concerned with the empirical validity of these neoclassical assumptions about human behaviour and, where they prove invalid, with discovering the empirical laws that describe behaviour correctly and as accurately as possible. As a second item on its agenda, behavioural economics is concerned with drawing out the implications, for the operation of the economic system and its institutions and for public policy, of departures of actual behaviour from the neoclassical assumptions. A third item on its agenda is to supply empirical evidence about the shape and content of the utility function (or of whatever construct will replace it in an empirically valid behavioural theory) so as to strengthen the predictions that can be made about human economic behaviour.

Thus, behavioural economics is best characterized not as a single specific theory but as a commitment to empirical testing of the neoclassical assumptions of human behaviour and to modifying economic theory on the basis of what is found in the testing process. And not all of the economists who hold a behavioural point of view also hold a common theory, or are all preoccupied with examining the same parts of the economic mechanism.

Directions of Behavioural Research

Accordingly, we can distinguish a number of different foci and directions of inquiry in behavioural economics. Some investigations are concerned with the assumptions of utility and profit maximization, and with replacing these with alternative motivational assumptions that appear to describe human motivations in the marketplace more accurately (e.g. Baumol, 1959).

Another focus of behavioural research in economics is decision making under uncertainty—determining whether economic actors are able to and do maximize subjective expected utility, as called for by neoclassical theory. Here the interest is less in motivation than in the *ability* of human beings to carry out the calculations required to make the optimal decisions—the issues involved are largely cognitive.

The limitation in human ability to deal with uncertainty is just a special case of the numerous cognitive limitations that prevent economic actors from knowing and adopting the optimizing alternative of choice. The term 'bounded rationality' has been proposed to denote the whole range of limitations on human knowledge and human computation that prevent economic actors in the real world from behaving in ways that approximate the predictions of classical and neoclassical theory: including the absence of a complete and consistent utility function for ordering all possible choices, inability to generate more than a small fraction of the potentially relevant alternatives, and inability to foresee the consequences of choosing alternatives, including inability to assign consistent and realistic probabilities to uncertain future events (Simon, 1955).

Conventional Behaviour

At the farthest remove from neoclassical economics are explanations of phenomena that do not rest at all on rationality assumptions. For example, it has been observed that the mean compensation of the top executive in corporations varies with the logarithm of the size of the corporation (Roberts, 1959). To explain this regularity in neoclassical terms one has to show that the marginal contribution of the top executive is proportional to the logarithm of company size; and this proposition implies, in turn, very specific conditions on the distribution of executive abilities (Lucas, 1978).

However, an explanation that requires no assumption about executive abilities can be derived form (a) the empirical observation that most companies are pyramidal, so that the number of organizational levels grows logarithmically with the number of employees; and (b) the empirical observation that most people regard it as 'legitimate' or 'appropriate' for a boss to be paid some multiple (about 1.5 times, say) of the salary of his or her immediate subordinates. The observed regularity in average salaries follows from these two observations (Simon, 1957). We may call this a 'sociological' explanation, since it postulates commonly held social beliefs or attitudes, but not rational calculation.

In the same way, the observed regularities in business firm size distributions (which usually fit closely to the Pareto distribution) follow from the assumption that expected growth is proportional to attained size (the

Gibrat assumption). The assumption, in turn, can be derived from the postulate that access to internal and external investment funds is proportional to size, without postulating rational choice as part of the causal mechanism (Ijiri and Simon, 1977).

As a third example, the empirical observation that the labour share of total product has been nearly constant in the industrialized world during the past century may be explained from the premises: (a) that interest rates are nearly stable; (b) that at all levels of average per capita income, nearly the same fraction of total income is saved, hence the ratio of capital supply to total output is nearly constant (Simon, 1979). But premises (a) and (b) may be accepted as empirical (sociological) regularities that do not derive from assumptions of rationality or from assumptions that marginal costs are equal to marginal benefits.

If, in fact, important social phenomena, like salaries, access to capital for growth, or rates of saving, do not depend on rational calculations, but are conventionally determined, then the corresponding parts of economic theory need to be built on empirical knowledge of socially accepted conventions rather than on derivations from the assumption of rationality. What phenomena are 'conventionally' rather than 'rationally' determined is itself an empirical question, and not one that can be settled by pure reasoning.

It is often possible to rationalize the kinds of behaviour that were described above as conventional, but the real work in such explanation is done by *ad hoc* auxiliary assumptions, which is quite different from inferring the behaviour uniquely from the assumptions of economic rationality alone. For example, almost any observed distribution of executive salaries would be compatible with Lucas's (1978) model provided that appropriate adjustments were made in the assumed (and unobservable) distribution of executive abilities. The proposed sociological explanation for the salary distribution is falsifiable, while Lucas's model is not.

In similar fashion, the historical stability of interest rates and of the saving to income ratio could be attributed in some measure to characteristic of individual utility functions. In this case, again, rationality assumptions play no important role. The argument rests on an unmotivated assumption about human preferences—an empirical assumption.

The 'New Institutional Economics'

Less distant from neoclassical theory than the examples just cited are explanations that incorporate the rationality assumptions, but also invoke limits on the information available to actors or impose 'transaction costs' on their use of information in order to account for specific institutional phenomena. Much of the work of Williamson (1975) falls in this category.

For example, there is a fundamental difference between a sales contract and an employment contract. The former involves an exchange of specific commodities for money, while the latter involves the willingness of the employee to accept authority (i.e. to have his actions determined by the employer) in exchange for money. How can we predict which economic transactions will take the form of sales contracts, and which the form of employment contracts? It can be argued that if the employer has great uncertainty as to what specific duties he will want performed, and the employee is nearly indifferent among various ways of spending his time, then an employment contract will be the rational choice, otherwise a sales contract (Williamson, 1975, chs. 4, 5; Simon, 1951).

Similar rational analyses have been proposed to explain the existence of various kinds of contractual instruments—for example, special forms of insurance and of forward contracting. 'Moral risk', that is, the practical unenforceability of some kind of contract clauses in the face of opportunistic behaviour of the parties, also commonly enters into explanations for the existence or non-existence of particular sorts of contracts. Williamson (1975) invokes the combination of bounded rationality and opportunism as the mechanism for explaining the relative roles of banks, conglomerates, and divisionalized corporations in allocating investment capital.

The body of modern economic analysis that employs concepts like limited information, transaction costs, and opportunism to explain observed economic phenomena is often called the 'New Institutional Economics'. A common feature of these sorts of institutional analyses is that the real 'action' in the derivations comes not from the rationality assumptions, but from the assumptions of informational or other limits on rationality, or from what were in the previous section called sociological postulates. If employers had perfect foresight, or if they could costlessly renegotiate their contracts with employees for each new task to be performed, there would be no rationale for employment contracts. If householders made even roughly correct estimates of flood risk, purchases of flood insurance would rise sharply. Conglomerates can allocate investment funds more profitably than banks, because the former have inside information not available to the latter. And so on.

Moreover, since the institutional analyses usually involve the comparison of two, or a few, discrete alternatives rather than a continuum of choices, it is seldom necessary to evoke the assumption of maximization. Even a satisficing actor can be expected to select the better of two alternatives if the difference in expected outcomes is large. Conversely, if institutional arrangements are compatible with either maximizing or satisficing assumptions, evidence about them cannot be used to choose between these assumptions.

Explanations of institutional arrangements can often be reached by qualitative arguments about what is 'functional' rather than arguments about what is optimal. This reduction in dependence on rationality assumptions cuts two ways. By weakening the assumptions required for the arguments, it raises the prior probability of the explanation; by introducing into consideration a host of different potential auxiliary sociological assumptions, it increases the urgency of testing independently the empirical validity of these assumptions. Casual empiricism is especially inappropriate in these contexts.

It would be a valuable exercise to determine what part of neoclassical economics, and especially the new institutional economics, would survive the replacement of optimizing by satisficing or functional arguments. Presumably, theorems about Pareto optimality and market efficiency would be lost, but not necessarily theorems about stability of equilibrium. And as suggested above, many claims about the functionality of particular institutional arrangements would still be supported by the weaker assumptions.

The 'Utility Function' of the Firm

A good deal of neoclassical economic reasoning does not require any specific assumption about the shapes of the actors' utility functions. Much of the literature on the theory of the firm, however, requires the assumption that firms maximize profit or, in long-term analyses, the present value of stockholders' equity. There are many conceivable alternatives to the profit-maximization assumption, classifiable into three main categories: (a) that the firm seeks to maximize some other quantity than profit; (b) that individual executives strive to maximize their personal utilities, which are unlikely to coincide with the firm's utility; and (c) that executives and other participants identify with the subgoals of the organizational units to which they belong, and work to maximize attainments of these subgoals (Marris, 1964).

An example of the first kind of alternative is Baumol's (1959) proposal that firms strive to maximize revenue rather than profits. Evolutionary arguments have been evoked against this sort of alternative to profit maximizing, but the objections rest on the assumption, much stronger than any in biological Darwinism, that only profit maximizers can survive. Again, it is clear that the issue has to be decided by empirical inquiry. In the biological world at least, many organisms survive that are not maximizers but that operate at far less than the highest achievable efficiency. Their survival is not threatened as long as no other organisms have evolved that can challenge the possession of their specific niches. Analogously, since there is no reason to suppose that every business firm is challenged by an optimally efficient competitor, survival only requires meeting the competition. In a system in which there are innumerable rents, of long-term and short-term duration, even egregious sub-optimality may permit survival.

Nelson and Winter (1982) have examined evolutionary models of business firm growth that dispense with the assumption of profit maximization. Each firm, in their models, may have a different production function, and one that changes through imitation or, stochastically, from investment in R&D. With industry models of this sort, distributions of firm size may be obtained similar to those actually observed.

The second kind of deviation from the profit maximizing assumption—that which rests on considerations of executive behaviour—is perhaps the most frequently advanced. One form it takes is the 'organizational slack' hypothesis of Cyert and March (1963), which suggests that firms will ordinarily settle for 'satisfactory' profits, and that it is only when they fail to achieve these that they search for improved products or methods of operation. Leibenstein's (1976) concept of 'X-efficiency' has a similar flavour. One way to relate such behaviour to rationality assumptions is to postulate that 'comfort' is an important component in executive utility functions, and that there is a trade-off between the comfortable executive life and profits.

Another deviation from the neoclassical assumptions is to view the firm not as a system with a well-defined utility function, but as a coalition of partially cooperating and partially competing interests. The goal-defining process can then be viewed in terms of game theory. The notion of the corporation as a coalition has been developed by Cyert and March (1963) and by Williamson (1975).

Research on organizations has revealed the central importance of the mechanism of *identification*—the tendency of actors in an organization to internalize, and be guided by, the goals of the particular subparts of the organization with which they are most closely associated. In part, identification may be accounted for by systems of reward, but that is almost certainly an incomplete account. Cognitive mechanisms (especially focus of attention) and mechanisms of social motivation (including docility) appear to be at least as important as rewards in determining the criteria of choice that are applied to decisions. For example, departmental executives asked to identify the most important problem facing a company that has been described to them tend disproportionately to select problems in their own domain of expertise—the sales managers, sales problems; the production managers, production problems, and so on (Dearborn and Simon, 1958).

Individual Utility

In analysing the behaviour of consumers and employees, the outcomes often depend heavily on what is assumed about the structure and content of their utility functions. Changes in preferences between work and leisure, for example, will ordinarily produce corresponding changes in the labour supply function. Similarly, changes in social attitudes about women's roles may play a major part in determining the participation of women in the labour force, the number of children, and many other variables important to long-term social and economic development. As Becker (1981) has shown, this does not forestall economic analysis of these phenomena, but it does limit the power of the rationality principle to arrive at conclusions without numerous assumptions about the utility function.

The assumption of utility maximization is sometimes misunderstood to imply that only selfish motives play a role in human behaviour. However, except in the context of evolutionary theories that emphasize selection, the assumption of utility maximization, whether of business firms or of individuals, does not, of course, imply that human beings are selfish, only that they arc consistent. Altruism can be accommodated in the utility function simply by including the well-being of other persons as one of its components. When utility maximization is not postulated directly, but is derived from Darwinian arguments of survival, then altruism, except for 'weak altruism' or 'enlightened self-interest', becomes more difficult to account for. Maximization of Darwinian fitness, as usually formulated, leaves little room for altruistic behaviour towards other who are not close relatives.

It is possible that this difficulty could be removed by closer attention to 'docility' (susceptibility to social instruction and influence) as a trait contributing strongly to fitness (Simon, 1983, ch. 2). Whether docility does, in fact, play a role in shaping preferences is an empirical question to be answered by behavioural research. And to what extent altruism (as distinguished from enlightened self-interest) actually enters into human behaviour is also an issue that must be settled by empirical study.

Decisions under Uncertainty

Of all of the variables affecting, potentially or actually, the economic decision-making process, uncertainty has perhaps attracted the greatest amount of research attention, both theoretical and empirical. We now have substantial knowledge about the relation between actual human behaviour in the face of uncertainty and the behaviour predicted by the subjective expected utility model.

Data from the laboratory shows that, under different circumstances of choice, subjects depart from the predictions of the SEU model in diametrically opposite directions. At times when they view the world as stable or static, they place too much weight on past events in prediction; but when they perceive large structural changes taking place in the environment, they underestimate the significance of past experience for predicting the future.

Extensive studies of decisions to purchase or not to purchase flood insurance (Kunreuther, 1978) reveal behaviour that cannot be reconciled with any model of utility maximization. Specifically, it is found that people tend to ignore (hence, not to insure against) low-probability, high-consequence events, unless they have had rather direct past personal experience of them.

Assumptions about how people deal with uncertainty and predict future events have important consequences for macroeconomic theory. For example, rational expectations theories, adaptive expectations theories and cobweb theories make quite different predictions about the impact of government monetary and fiscal policies. But it can be shown that the bounds placed on rationality, and not the rationality assumptions, account for the main differences in prediction among, for example, leading business-cycle theories. A Keynesian theory of the cycle can be derived from a neoclassical model simply by assuming that labourers suffer from money illusion in their demands for wages; while a rational-expectations theory of the cycle can be derived from the same neoclassical model by assuming that businessmen mistake a general change in the price level for a relative change in the prices of the goods they purchase (another form of money illusion). As in institutional arguments, the real work in these theories is not being done by the rationality assumptions but by auxiliary assumptions about limits on rationality (including limits on the accuracy of information)—assumptions often made on the basis of extremely casual evidence.

Search and Choice Processes

Applications of the concept of bounded rationality to choice situations where uncertainty about outcomes is a dominant factor have been discussed above. Another line of research, mainly in the laboratory, seeks to examine the processes of search that people use, both in the exploration for alternatives and in their use of information about alternatives (Hogarth, 1980; Kahneman, Slovic and Tversky, 1982). A standard experimental paradigm confronts subjects with a number of alternatives, and allows them to obtain additional information about each until they make a choice or the available information is exhausted. Experiments in this paradigm show that decision makers usually satisfice, both in the sense of failing to examine all of the information that is available, and in the sense of choosing an alternative as soon as one has been found that is satisfactory along all the dimensions of concern.

A few studies have been made of situations where subjects must explore for new alternatives and must decide when to terminate the search. For example, a field study of the job search processes of business school students (Soelberg, 1966) showed students using a variety of rules of thumb to limit the list of firms they contacted and to choose among those who made offers to them.

In real-world situations, it is seldom realistic to talk about examining all alternatives or paying attention to all the potentially relevant information. Empirical evidence is still very scanty about the circumstances under which people will pay attention to particular variables in making their decisions (e.g. under what circumstances they will pay attention to the difference between real and nominal prices). Evidence is also very scanty (but see Cyert and March, 1963; Soelberg, 1966) about the circumstances under which people search for new alternatives.

The search for alternatives is, of course, a critical process in understanding entrepreneurial behaviour, decisions to invest in research and development activities, and generally in understanding the ways in which new economic activities and enterprises are spawned (Nelson and Winter, 1982; Winter, 1984). This Schumpeterian view toward economic development has recently been expanded and systematized by Nelson and Winter (1982), who model the growth of industries in which the development of new products and practices plays a major role in competition among firms. They show that in such models, evolutionary selection can replace or complement optimization as a driving force for change.

Methods of Behavioural Research

Within the classical tradition, the principal evidence that has been used to test economic theories empirically has been public statistics, usually aggregated at least to the level of the industry (although limited use has been made, especially in investment theory, of financial data for individual firms). A powerful and sophisticated set of econometric tools has been developed for extracting from such data all the information that they contain. But it becomes increasingly clear that data of these kinds are simply too aggregated and noisy to reveal much about the decision-making processes of the economic actors. In neoclassical theory, those processes are simply postulated, in terms of the rationality assumptions, and never subjected to any really searching direct test.

What is even more troublesome, the typical inputs to econometric analysis provide little information that would be relevant to choosing the appropriate auxiliary assumptions (assumptions about the limits to rationality) that, we have seen, play a major role in drawing inferences from economic theories. In the absence of empirical evidence for choosing these assumptions, they are generally made in a casually empirical, armchair way.

The progress of economics, and especially the prospects for adequate empirical testing of economic theories, would seem to depend, therefore, on finding new kinds of data to supplement the sorts of aggregative evidence now typically employed. One important new kind of data comes from case studies, a second from survey research, and a third from laboratory experiments. Computer simulation models can provide a powerful tool for relating these kinds of data to theory. But successful use of such data will call for new methods for aggregating data that are gathered from individual firms or individual economic actors. Each of these points calls for a brief comment.

Case Studies

A small, but growing, number of case studies have been made of the decision-making process in individual business firms (Cyert and March, 1963; Bromiley, 1986; etc.) and of individuals (Soelberg, 1966; Clarkson, 1962; Bouwman, 1982; etc.). That these studies have had little impact on economic theory must be attributed in considerable measure to the absence of a theory of aggregation that would indicate just how to use them. In general, economists, though willing to engage in casual introspective empiricism, have not been willing to treat the firms whose behaviour has been studied in depth as 'representative firms'.

Survey Research

In the case of survey research, where appropriate sampling methods can be used, there is no such difficulty in relating the survey data to macromodels of industries or the economy. In fact, data on businessmen's expectations have been used, to a limited extent, as inputs into econometric models (Katona, 1975). The main limiting factors here appear to be the small number of economists who are trained to produce and interpret survey data, and the limited resources that have been applied to generating such data.

Experiments

The use of experiments to study economic behaviour is a relatively new, and rather rapidly spreading, development (see, e.g., Smith, 1976; Hong and Plott, 1982). A principal problem here is to produce in the laboratory motivational conditions that can be extrapolated to the real world. A principal limitation on the growth of laboratory experimentation is, again, the limited access of graduate students in economics to training in techniques of experimentation.

Computer Modelling

Computers are widely used in economics, not only to run regressions, but also to model the economic system. Most of the models are aggregative, but there has been a certain amount of investigation of so-called 'micro-models', whose units are samples of individual actors and firms (e.g. Eliasson, 1984; Winter, 1984). In addition, one can point to a few models of decision-making within an individual firm (Bonini, 1963; Bromiley, 1986). Attention has been paid to the aggregation problem in constructing micro-models, but that problem remains a major barrier to acceptance of findings derived from models of these sorts as a part of the main stream of economic theory and knowledge.

Bibliography

Baumol, W. J. (1959). *Business Behavior, Value and Growth*. New York: Macmillan.

Becker, G. S. (1981). *A Treatise on the Family*. Cambridge, Mass.: Harvard University Press.

Bonini, C. P. (1963). *Simulation of Information and Decision Systems in the Firm*. Englewood Cliffs, NJ: Prentice-Hall.

Bouwman, M. J. (1982). The use of accounting information: expert versus novice behavior. In Ungson & Braunstein (Eds.), *Decision Making*. Boston: Kent Publishing Co.

Bromiley, P. *Corporate Capital Investment: A Behavioral Approach*. Cambridge, Eng.: Cambridge University Press, 1986.

Clarkson, G. P. E. (1962). *Portfolio Selection: A Simulation of Trust Investment*. Englewood Cliffs, NJ: Prentice-Hall.

Cyert, R. M. & March, J. G. (1963). *A Behavioral Theory of the Firm*. Englewood Cliffs, NJ: Prentice-Hall.

Dearborn, D. C. & Simon, H. A. (1958). Selective perception. *Sociometry*, 21, 140–144.

Eliasson, G. (1984). Micro heterogeneity of firms and the stability of industrial growth. *Journal of Economic Behaviour and Organization*, 5, 249–274.

Hogarth, R. M. (1980). *Judgment and Choice: The Psychology of Decision*. New York: Wiley.

Hong, J. T. & Plott, C. R. (1982). Rate filing policies for inland water transportation: an experimental approach. *Bell Journal of Economics*, 13, 1–19.

Ijiri, Y. & Simon, H. A. (1977). *Skew Distributions and the Sizes of Business Firms*. Amsterdam: North-Holland.

Kahneman, D., Slovic, P. & Tversky, A. (Eds.). (1982). *Judgment Under Uncertainty: Heuristics and Biases*. Cambridge: Cambridge University Press.

Katona, G. (1975). *Psychological Economics*. New York: Elsevier Publishing Co.

Kornai, J. (1971). *Anti-Equilibrium*. Amsterdam: North-Holland.

Kunreuther, H. et al. (1978). *Disaster Insurance Protection: Public Policy Lessons*. New York: Wiley.

Leibenstein, H. (1976). *Beyond Economic Man*. Cambridge, Mass.: Harvard University Press.

Lucas, R. E., Jr. (1978). On the size distribution of business firms. *Bell Journal of Economics*, 9, 508–523.

Marris, R. (1964). *The Economic Theory of 'Managerial' Capitalism*. New York: Macmillan.

Nelson, R. R. & Winter, S. G. (1982). *An Evolutionary Theory of Economic Change*. Cambridge, Mass.: Harvard University Press.

Roberts, D. R. (1959). *Executive Compensation*. Glencoe, Ill.: The Free Press.

Savage, L. J. (1954). *The Foundations of Statistics*. New York: Wiley.

Simon, H. A. (1951). A formal theory of the employment relationship. *Econometrica* 19, 293–305. Reprinted as ch. 5.2 in Simon (1982).

Simon, H. A. (1955). A behavioral model of rational choice. *Quarterly Journal of Economics*, 69, 99–118. Reprinted as ch. 7.2 in Simon (1982).

Simon, H. A. (1957). The compensation of executives. *Sociometry*, 20, 32–35. Reprinted as ch. 5.6 in Simon (1982)

Simon, H. A. (1979). On parsimonious explanations of production relations. *Scandinavian Journal of Economics*, 81, 459–474. Reprinted as ch. 4.4 in Simon (1982).

Simon, H. A. (1982). *Models of Bounded Rationality*. 2 vols, Cambridge, Mass.: MIT Press.

Simon, H. A. (1983). *Reason in Human Affairs*. Stanford: Stanford University Press.

Smith, V. L. (1976). Experimental economics: induced value theory. *American Economic Review*, 66, 274–279.

Soelberg, P. (1966). *A Study of Decision Making: Job Choice*. Cambridge, Mass.: Alfred P. Sloan School of Management, MIT.

Williamson, O. E. (1975). *Markets and Hierarchies*. New York: Free Press.

Winter, S. G. (1984). Schumpeterian competition in alternative technological regimes. *Journal of Economic Behavior and Organization*, 5, 287–320.

IV.3 Bounded Rationality

The term 'bounded rationality' is used to designate rational choice that takes into account the cognitive limitations of the decision maker—limitations of both knowledge and computational capacity. Bounded rationality is a central theme in the behavioral approach to economics, which is deeply concerned with the ways in which the actual decision-making process influences the decisions that are reached.

The theory of subjective utility (SEU theory) underlying neo-classical economics postulates that choices are made: (1) among a given, fixed set of alternatives; (2) with (subjectively) known probability distributions of outcomes for each; and (3) in such a way as to maximize the expected value of a given utility function (Savage, 1954). These are convenient assumptions, providing the basis for a very rich and elegant body of theory, but they are assumptions that may not fit empirically the situations of economic choice in which we are interested.

Theories of bounded rationality can be generated by relaxing one or more of the assumptions of SEU theory. Instead of assuming a fixed set of alternatives among which the decision maker chooses, we may postulate a process for generating alternatives. Instead of assuming known probability distributions of outcomes, we may introduce estimating procedures for them, or we may look for strategies for dealing with uncertainty that do not assume knowledge of probabilities. Instead of assuming the maximization of a utility function, we may postulate a satisficing strategy. The particular deviations from the SEU assumptions of global maximization introduced by behaviorally oriented economists are derived from what is known, empirically, about human thought and choice processes, and especially what is known about the limits of human cognitive capacity for discovering alternatives, computing their consequences under certainty or uncertainty, and making comparisons among them.

Generation of alternatives Modern cognitive psychology has studied in considerable depth not only the processes that human subjects use to choose among given alternatives, but also the processes (problem-solving processes) they use to find a possible course of action (i.e., actions that will solve a problem) (Newell and Simon, 1972). If we look at the time allocations of economic actors, say business executives, we find that perhaps the largest fraction of decision-making time is spent in searching for possible courses of action and evaluating them (i.e., estimating their consequences). Much less time and effort is spent in making final choices, once the alternatives have been generated and their consequences examined. The lengthy and crucial processes of generating alternatives, which include all the processes that we ordinarily designate by the word 'design', are left out of the SEU account of economic choice.

Study of the processes for generating alternatives quickly reveals that under most circumstances it is not reasonable to talk about finding 'all the alternatives'. The generation of alternatives is a lengthy and costly process, and one where, in real-world situations, even minimal completeness can seldom be guaranteed. Theories of optimal search can cast some light on such processes, but, because of limits on complexity, human alternative-generating behavior observed in the laboratory is usually best described as heuristic search aimed at finding satisfactory alternatives, or alternatives that represent an improvement over those previously available (Hogarth, 1980).

Evaluation of consequences Cognitive limits, in this case lack of knowledge and limits of ability to forecast the future, also play a central role in the evaluation of alternatives. These cognitive difficulties are seen clearly in decisions that are taken on a national scale: whether to go ahead with the construction of a supersonic transport; the measures to be taken to deal with acid rain; Federal Reserve policies on interest rates; and, of course, the supremely fateful decisions of war and peace.

The cognitive limits are not simply limits on specific information. They are almost always also limits on the adequacy of the scientific theories that can be used to predict the relevant phenomena. For example available theories of atmospheric chemistry and meteorology leave very wide bands of uncertainty in estimating the environmental or health consequences of given quantities and distributions of air pollutants. Similarly, the accuracy of predictions of the economy by computer models is severely limited by lack of knowledge about fundamental economic mechanisms represented in the models' equations.

Criteria of choice The assumption of a utility function postulates a consistency of human choice that is not always evidenced in reality. The assumption of maximization may also place a heavy (often unbearable) computational burden on the decision maker. A theory of bounded rationality seeks to identify, in theory and in actual behavior, procedures for choosing that are computationally simpler, and that can account for observed inconsistencies in human choice patterns.

Substantive and procedural rationality Theories of bounded rationality, then, are theories of decision making and choice that assume that the decision maker wishes to attain goals, and uses his or her mind as well as possible to that end; but theories that take into account in describing the decision process the actual capacities of the human mind.

The standard SEU theory is presumably not intended as an account of the process that human beings use to make a decision. Rather, it is an apparatus for predicting choice, assuming it to be an objectively optimal response to the situation presented. Its claim is that people choose as if they were maximizing subjective expected utility. And a strong *a priori* case can be made for the SEU theory when the decision making takes place in situations so transparent that the optimum can be reasonably approximated by an ordinary human mind.

Theories of bounded rationality are more ambitious in trying to capture the actual process of decision as well as the substance of the final decision itself. A veridical theory of this kind can only be erected on the basis of empirical knowledge of the capabilities and limitations of the human mind; that is to say, on the basis of psychological research.

The distinction between substantive theories of rationality (like the SEU theory) and behavioral theories is closely analogous to a distinction that has been made in linguistics between theories of linguistic competence and theories of linguistic performance. A theory of competence would characterize the grammar of a language in terms of a system of rules without claiming that persons who speak the language grammatically do so by applying these rules. Performance theories seek to capture the actual processes of speech production and understanding.

The question of the desirability and usefulness of a procedural theory of decision involves at least two separate issues. First, which kind of theory, substantive or procedural, can better predict and explain what decisions are actually reached. Does SEU theory predict, to the desired degree of accuracy, the market decisions of consumers and businessmen, or does such prediction require us to take into account the cognitive limits of the economic actors?

Second, are we interested only in the decisions that are reached, or is the human decision-making process itself one of the objects of our scientific curiosity? In the latter case, a substantive theory of decision cannot meet our needs; only a veridical theory of a procedural kind can satisfy our curiosity.

Bounded rationality in neoclassical economics It should not be supposed that mainstream economic theory has been completely oblivious to human cognitive limits. In fact, some of the most important disputes in macroeconomic theory can be traced to disagreements as to just where the bounds of human rationality are located. For example, one of the two basic mechanisms that accounts for underemployment and business cycles in Keynesian theory is the money illusion suffered by the labor force—a clear case of bounded rationality. In Lucas's rational expectationist theory of the cycle, the corresponding cognitive limitation is the inability of businessmen to discriminate between movements of industry prices and movements of the general price level—another variant of the money illusion. Thus the fundamental differences between these theories do not derive from different inferences drawn from the assumptions of rationality, but from different views as to where and when these assumptions cease to hold—that is, upon differences in their theories of bounded rationality.

What distinguishes contemporary theories of bounded rationality from these ad hoc and casual departures from the SEU model is that the former insist that the model of human rationality must be derived from detailed and systematic empirical study of human decision-making behavior in laboratory and real-world situation.

Bibliography

Cyert, R. M. & March, J. G. (1963). *A Behavioral Theory of the Firm*. Englewood Cliffs, NJ: Prentice-Hall; 2nd edn, 1975.

Hogarth, R. M. (1980). *Judgment and Choice: The Psychology of Decision*. New York: Wiley.

Nelson, R. R. & Winter, S. G. (1982). *An Evolutionary Theory of Economic Change*. Cambridge, Mass.: Harvard University Press.

Newell, A. & Simon, H. A. (1972). *Human Problem Solving*. Englewood Cliffs, NJ: Prentice-Hall.

Savage, L. J. (1954). *The Foundations of Statistics*. New York: Wiley.

Simon, H. A. (1982). *Models of Bounded Rationality*. 2 vols, Cambridge, Mass.: MIT Press (especially Sections VII and VIII).

Williamson, O. (1975). *Markets and Hierarchies*. New York: Free Press.

IV.4 Satisficing

A decision maker who chooses the best available alternative according to some criterion is said to optimize; one who chooses an alternative that meets or exceeds specified criteria, but that is not guaranteed to be either unique or in any sense the best, is said to satisfice. The term 'satisfice', which appears in the *Oxford English Dictionary* as a Northumbrian synonym for 'satisfy', was borrowed for this new use by H. A. Simon (1956) in 'Rational Choice and the Structure of the Environment'.

Optimization and its Problems

In the literature of economics and statistical decision theory, rationality has usually been defined in such a way as to imply some form of optimization, for example, maximization of utility subject to budget constraints. In simple situations, like the illustrative examples used in economics textbooks, computing a maximum may be a simple process, requiring, perhaps, nothing more onerous than taking a first derivative and setting it equal to zero. Even in much more complex situations, involving thousands of linear equalities and inequalities but also a linear criterion function, the powerful methods of linear programming often permit optimal choices to be found with tolerable amounts of computing effort.

In many (most?) real-world situations, however, genuine optima (maxima or minima) are simply not computable within feasible limits of effort (see Bounded Rationality). This is especially true when decisions must be made without benefit of computer, but it is frequently true even when powerful computing facilities are available. The complexity of the world is not limited to thousands or even tens of thousands of variables and constraints, nor does it always preserve the linearities and convexities that facilitate computation.

The Satisficing Alternative

Faced with a choice situation where it is impossible to optimize, or where the computational cost of doing so seems burdensome, the decision maker may look for a satisfactory, rather than an optimal, alternative. Frequently, a course of action satisfying a number of constraints, even a sizeable number, is far easier to discover than a course of action maximizing some function.

The example has been given of searching for a needle in a haystack. Given a probability density distribution of needles of varying degrees of sharpness throughout the haystack, searching for the sharpest needle may require effort proportional to the size of the haystack. The task of searching for a needle sharp enough to sew with requires an effort that depends only on the density of needles of the requisite sharpness, and not at all on the size of the stack. The attractiveness of the satisficing criterion derives from this independence of search cost from the size and complexity of the choice situation.

In a formal sense, a process of satisficing could always be converted into a process of optimizing by taking into account the cost of search, and only searching up to the point where the expected gain derivable from another minute of search is just equal to the opportunity cost of that minute (Simon, 1955; Stigler, 1961). However, this conversion imposes a new, possible heavy, informational and computational burden upon the chooser: the burden of estimating the expected marginal return of search and the opportunity cost. Solving these estimation problems may be as difficult as making the original choice, or even more difficult. An alternative is to search until a satisfactory alternative is found.

Conversely, most of the so-called optimization models of operations research and management science can more profitably be viewed as satisficing models. In the application of OR optimization techniques, some highly simplified approximation to a real-world situation is reduced to a formal model (e.g. a linear programming or integer programming model), and an optimum is then calculated for this approximation with respect to a similarly approximate criterion function. The resulting 'optimal' decision will often provide a satisfactory decision for the real-world situation, but without guarantee that it will be better than a decision arrived at by some alternative satisficing technique.

How may the satisficer set the levels of the criteria that define 'satisfactory'? Psychology proposes the mechanism of aspiration levels: if it turns out to be very easy to find alternatives that meet the criteria, the standards are gradually raised; if search continues for a long while without finding satisfactory alternatives, the standards are gradually lowered. Thus, by a kind of feedback mechanism, or 'tâtonnement', the decision maker converges toward a set of criteria that are attainable, but not without effort. The difference between the aspiration level mechanism and the optimization procedure is that the former calls for much simpler computations than the latter. It is somewhat analogous to the difference between adaptive and rational expectations, respectively, in the theory of choice under uncertainty.

Incommensurability of Goals and Outcomes

Satisficing can also provide another kind of computational advantage over optimizing. Human decision makers often find it very difficult to make trade-offs among aspects or dimensions of value that seem to them incommensurable. Of course, it is the function of the utility function to insure commensurability in all cases, but we may not know how to characterize it. Three classes of situations into which incommensurability is especially likely to intrude are: (1) cases of uncertainty, where, for each alternative, a bad outcome under one contingency must be balanced against a good outcome under another, (2) cases of multiperson choice, where one person's gain is another's loss; and (3) cases where each choice involves gain along one dimension of value and loss along another very different one.

It has been observed empirically that in circumstances of these kinds, and especially when each outcome entails unpleasant as well as pleasant consequences, decision makers do not proceed promptly to a choice, but instead seek to avoid the necessity for comparison. One common reaction, for example, is to refuse to choose among the given set of alternatives, and instead, to initiate a search for a new alternative that: in case (1), will ensure at least a minimally satisfactory outcome under all contingencies; in case (2), will ensure all participants a satisfactory outcome; and in case (3), will ensure an outcome that is at least minimally satisfactory along all dimensions. The acceptance of such alternatives comes within our definition of satisficing (Hogarth, 1980).

Consequences for Economic Theory

It is easier to reconcile a satisficing than an optimizing theory of economic decision making with what is known empirically of actual choice behaviour and of the computational limits of the human mind. On the other hand, a great deal is given up by the substitution of the former for the latter—given up in terms of the strength and variety of theorems that can be derived from the postulate of rationality in the two cases. To make predictions about behaviour on the basis of a satisficing theory requires much more empirical data about, for example, aspiration levels and their adaptivity, than does prediction on the basis of the optimizing theory. The magnitude of the difference becomes less, however, when we recognize that the optimizing theory says nothing about the shape or content of the utility function. It simply postulates a consistency of behaviour over time that may not be found if the decision maker is satisficing instead of optimizing.

In the last analysis, a choice between the two kinds of postulates will have to be made in terms of their relative effectiveness and accuracy in predicting and explaining economic behavior, at both micro and macro levels. There is still little consensus in the economics profession as to the circumstances under which one postulate or the other will be the more advantageous.

Bibliography

Hogarth, R. M. (1980). *Judgment and Choice: The Psychology of Decision*. New York: Wiley.

Radner, R. (1975). Satisficing. *Journal of Mathematical Economics* 2, 253–62.

Simon, H. A. (1955). A behavioral model of rational choice. *Quarterly Journal of Economics*, 69, 99–118. Reprinted in Simon (1982), ch. 7.2.

Simon, H. A. (1956). Rational choice and the structure of the environment. *Psychological Review* 63, 129–38. Reprinted in Simon (1982), ch. 7.3

Simon, H. A. (1982). *Models of Bounded Rationality*. Cambridge, Mass.: MIT Press.

Stigler, G. J. (1961). The economics of information. *Journal of Political Economy* 69, 213–25.

Winter, S. G. (1971). Satisficing, selection and the innovating remnant. *Quarterly Journal of Economics* 85, 237–61.

IV.5 Behavioral Research: Theory and Public Policy

Since the announced title of my remarks provides much too broad a canvas to be painted on in a reasonable time, I shall have to select just a couple of small areas as a sample of interesting issues relating to the topic as a whole. Obviously, in talking in Ann Arbor about behavioral research, I am bringing coals to Newcastle—for I can't think of any other place where that topic has been so carefully discussed.

In particular, for more than 30 years, George Katona has been making fundamental contributions—both theoretical and empirical—to the psychological foundations of economic behavior. It was many years before the economics profession was ready to acknowledge the relevance of psychological variables to economic phenomena, and even today the work does not receive the attention in macroeconomics that it deserves—and that it requires if we are to make progress in our understanding of economic phenomena at the societal level. The lag in acceptance may be due to the stubborness of economists; I prefer to attribute it to the originality of George's approach, which required a real restructuring of thought—a genuine paradigm shift—before it could begin to be assimilated. To any economists who are suffering malaise as a consequence of the current difficulties of business cycle theory with inflation, I recommended Chapter 12 of *Psychological Analysis of Economic Behavior*, a book published in 1951 but as relevant today as when it came from George Katona's pen.

Under these circumstances, the only rational grounds for my journey here must be the hope that the coals I am bearing may ignite the local fuel and cause an intense light to be thrown on the subject. So I will look forward with great anticipation to the discussion that is to follow my remarks.

Taxonomies

There are a number of ways in which the different kinds of possible behavioral research can be classified. I want to mention two of these that will be relevant to my subsequent discussion. Research can be classified by the methodologies it employs; and it can be classified by the goals at which it is aimed.

Methodologies The social and behavioral sciences are often distinguished by the particular phenomena they study. Psychologists study individual human behavior; economists, behavior in markets and the behaviors of production and consumption; political scientists, political institutions and processes; anthropologists, primitive societies; and sociologists, social phenomena not elsewhere classified. As with most taxonomies, the separations are not clean. Social psychology sits in uneasy suspension between psychology and sociology; some anthropologists regard modern industrialized societies as fair targets for their research weapons; the more sanguine among economists seek to discover economic man lurking in all manner of human behavior, whether "economic" in a narrower sense or not. Nevertheless, each discipline does locate its center of gravity in some domain of human behavior.

As one takes interdisciplinary journeys among the social sciences, one begins to notice the great varieties of methodologies that are available for the study of human behavior. Human behavior can be studied in the laboratory, using standard experimental techniques. It can sometimes be studied by setting up experimental designs in the field (the experiments on the negative income tax are a recent case in point). It can be studied by techniques of observation and interviewing in actual work settings (e.g., George Katona's [1957] studies of the banking practices of business firms, or our Carnegie-Mellon University studies of business decision making [Cyert and March, 1963]). It can be studied with the aid of formal opinion polling instruments—survey research (Katona, 1960, 1979a).

One begins to notice also, on these interdisciplinary journeys, that the several disciplines employ these methodologies quite selectively. In his doctoral training, a psychologist learns to design experiments, to carry them out, and to analyze the data with the help of such standard statistical tools as Chi-square and the T test. He may also learn to design instruments for measuring intelligence or specific abilities. Unless he is a social psychologist, he is unlikely to receive any special training in the conduct of field studies. An economist, on the other hand, learns to compute regressions on data obtained from published sources and to design statistical methods for testing and estimating the parameters of theoretical models; he does not learn how to design or run an experiment. Similarly, each of the other varieties of social scientist acquires, in his doctoral training, a small kit of sharp tools—and is left largely in ignorance of the tools of the other disciplines. If I were designing a short questionnaire to identify the discipline to which each of my respondents belonged, I think I could construct as discriminating an instrument by posing questions of methodology as by posing questions of substance.

This methodological specialization among the social sciences is an expensive luxury; for it means that most social scientists, in attacking the problems with which they are concerned, are not equipped to use the whole armamentarium of instruments that might be relevant. There are usually quite distinct methodological problems associated with each kind of technique, as well as distinct problems of applying the findings to questions of public policy. An obvious example of the former is the problem of inferring causal, or structural, relations from non-experimental data. In the laboratory, there is no ambiguity in the determination of the dependent by the independent variables. With non-experimental data, causal inferences depend upon identifying assumptions derived from prior knowledge.

An example of an application problem is the problem of extrapolating laboratory findings to the conditions of the "real world." Do the rewards and punishments, for example, that we can provide in laboratory settings have the same effects on behavior as the material and social sanctions associated with behavior in real-life settings? Approaching a research question with a composite body of data obtained from both laboratory and field can provide powerful leverage for attacking issues of these kinds; but the possibilities of employing such joint methods are likely to occur only to someone who has had exposure to both.

In general, economics has not been merely neglectful of, but sometimes even positively hostile to, using self-reports of economic actors about their expectations and intentions as data. This aversion to the direct observation of behavior in favor of postulating the behavior in order to derive predictions about macroscopic phenomena has been erected, by Milton Friedman's celebrated methodological essay, into a principle that makes a positive virtue of the unrealism of the behavioral postulates.

Exactly the opposite kind of tunnel vision afflicts psychology. Here at least since the early years of social psychology, aggregative data has played an insignificant role in the testing of theories. In Katona's recent paper calling for the development of macropsychology (Katona, 1979b), as in his long-term advocacy of an empirically based microeconomics (Katona, 1940, 1951, 1975), he has been a consistent advocate of a richer data-gathering methodology for both disciplines.

Goals A somewhat different approach to the taxonomy of behavioral research is to distinguish studies that are aimed at discovering and testing invariant laws of human individual or social behavior from studies that estimate parameters we need for fitting theoretical models incorporating known (or "believed") laws to particular situations where we wish to make predictions. This is the difference between research on the theory of the weather and research aimed at predicting tomorrow's weather in Ann Arbor. Or, to use a social science example, it is the difference between taking a poll of voting preferences as a step toward building a theory of voting behavior and taking such a poll in order to predict the outcome of the next Presidential election.

Of course, a study aimed at testing scientific laws may *use* prediction as a source of potentially disconfirming data. In that sense, there is no conflict between the two kinds of studies. Nevertheless, after a scientific theory has been established to our satisfaction, we continue to need empirical studies in order to apply that theory to specific, concrete policy questions. Even if we had an adequate theory of the business cycle (which I suppose only a few economists would claim we have today), we would still need observations of consumer and business expectations in order to make the predictions required for evaluating alternative cycle-damping policy measures.

Some Important Issues

On the basis of either or both of the taxonomies I have proposed, a plethora of significant issues can be defined with respect to the conduct of behavioral research and its application. I have already alluded to several of these issues: the selection of appropriate research techniques for addressing different problems, and the avoidance of disciplinary parochialism in that selection; extracting the implications of microphenomena for macroprocesses, and vice versa; and taking proper account of research goals—distinguishing between the testing of theory and its application. In the remainder of my remarks, I should like to introduce and discuss three somewhat more specific issues that seem to me to be of considerable importance. The first of these has to do with the use of human verbal reports as data. The second is concerned with the process of human decision making and the role of expectations in that process. The third is concerned with the use of public opinion polls and attitude surveys in guiding policy formation in a democratic society.

Human Verbal Behavior as Data

There is still a great deal of skepticism, in both the psychology and the economics communities, about the evidential value of the verbal responses of human subjects to task situations. In the case of the economist, there are probably several different reasons for this skepticism. First, as has already been suggested, microinquiry—obtaining data from individual economic actors—is a methodology that is foreign to most economists, and they have received no particular training that would make them knowledgeable about how to do it. If some of the data they use—census reports, for example—derive ultimately from individual responses, the user is not faced with the task of obtaining and editing the raw data or of determining how it should be aggregated. Beyond these technical problems, there is a common belief, not peculiar to economists, that people are not to be trusted to report their own expectations and attitudes, much less the motives for their actions. The chief lesson that has been learned from Freud, and learned rather indiscriminately, is that people are largely unaware of the roots of their own behavior, are driven by all sorts of unconscious motives, and, when asked about their motives, will supply plausible but inaccurate rationalizations.

The "introspection" controversy In the case of psychologists, the concern and skepticism about verbal reports goes all the way back to the great debate about "introspection" at the turn of the century. Nowadays, the term "introspection" is often used to refer to almost any kind of verbal report. Of course, introspection as carried out by Titchener and his fellow structuralists means something very special. It meant providing an exhaustive verbal description of a brief sensory stimulus in terms of a restricted vocabulary of "perceptual primitives." The method failed because reports could not be replicated from one laboratory to another and because there was no independent route for testing their veridicality.

This introspection was quite different from the kinds of verbal reports we elicit from subjects in thinking-aloud experiments on problem solving or in responses to questions about attitudes and intentions in public opinion polls. But these distinctions have been blurred in much professional discussion of these issues, and behavioral data have been tarred, indiscriminately and unjustifiably, with the brush of "introspection."

Information-processing interpretation of verbal reports Recently, my colleague Anders Ericsson and I have been reviewing the experimental literature on verbal reports (Ericsson and Simon, 1978a, 1978b). On the basis of the empirical findings we have examined, we believe that it is possible to state quite definite principles about the relation between subjects' verbalizations and their past or future behavior. These principles are consistent, in turn, with contemporary information processing theories of perception and of the working of short-term and long-term memories.

The central principle that emerges from our investigations is that information must, if it is to be reported verbally, be held in a verbal encoding in short-term memory (STM). In performing most tasks that require thought and attention, information (the inputs and outputs to the basic thought processes) flows continuously through short-term memory and, if it is encoded verbally, can be reported orally without imposing a significant additional burden on the processing system. Hence, subjects can provide rather full and veridical reports of the successive contents of STM while they are performing many kinds of problem-solving or other thinking tasks.

In tasks employing complex "pictorial" stimuli, however, verbal reports may be much less complete, because of the difficulty of recoding the STM information into words. Under these circumstances, the attempt to report may also interfere with performance of the assigned task. In either case, thinking-aloud reports are likely to be a less satisfactory source of data in tasks requiring recoding of the information in STM into a verbal code than in tasks where the stimuli are already encoded verbally, or in an encoding that is readily translated into verbal form.

Simple recognition processes do not readily lend themselves to verbal reporting. This is predicted by most information-processing models, since recognizing a stimulus *results* in a symbol being placed in STM, but there is no evidence that the process itself *uses* STM en route to the final recognition. Thus, subjects can report what they have recognized but cannot usually report what stimulus features or other cues they used to achieve the recognition.

In the case of retrospective reports, where the verbal data are obtained either immediately after performance of a task or some time later, interpretation is more complex. Some estimate must be made, on the basis of what is known about short-term and long-term memory, about the kinds of task information that could be expected to have been stored in memory during performance of the task. The verbal reports must come from these memories, from the subject's inference processes that are stimulated by the probe, or from some combination of these. The significance of the report and its proper interpretation depends on how complete the memories can be and how much inference has intervened in producing the report. These can be difficult questions to answer, but this does not mean that verbal reports are useless as data. It simply means that such reports, like all data produced by the reading of instruments, must be interpreted in the light of our knowledge of how the recording instruments operate. The same can be said of data obtained with the instruments of the physicist's, the chemist's, or the biologist's laboratory.

If, for example, we wish to obtain retrospective verbal reports that are drawn as completely as possible from long-term memory, and with a minimum of inference and reconstruction, then we must probe for specific events and not ask the subject to theorize about his behavior or even to generalize from a multiplicity of instances. Thus, instead of asking, "How do you make investment decisions?" we ask, "What was the last investment decision involving more than $X in which you participated? Please describe the history of that decision process." There is much evidence that memory can be tapped much more reliably by the latter than by the former procedure. The so-called "critical incident" technique of personnel assessment is based on this idea of discovering specific information from long-term memory, rather than by asking the respondent to provide generalizations about his own behavior.

Even in probing about specific past events, it must not be assumed that subjects can report all aspects of the processes they used in reaching decisions. Only those things can be recalled that were placed in memory at the time they occurred. Thus, a question like, "Why did you make that investment?" may evoke the subject's inferences, speculations, or rationalizations rather than his memories—not because he wishes to lie, but because the memories are simply not there. On the other hand, subjects may be able to report satisfactorily whether they were or were not aware of certain information at the time they reached a decision. The general principle here is that, when probing memories to obtain evidence about process, it is important not to incorporate in the probes assumptions about the nature of the processes that may not be valid.

The principles for eliciting and interpreting veridical memories have not, to my knowledge, been codified. Much could probably be learned by examining the rules the common law has developed for the interpretation of the testimony of witnesses and the rules applied by historians to the interpretation of both written and oral reports of past events.

These are samples of the ways in which our knowledge of human information processing can be used to improve our methods for obtaining behavioral data from verbal reports. Clearly, blanket statements about the "reliability" or "unreliability" of verbal reports are meaningless. With sophisticated techniques for eliciting them, verbalizations can be a rich source of microdata for testing theories of human choice.

Aggregation of microdata When we wish to use verbal reports for purposes that go beyond the theory-testing goals of the laboratory of individual psychology, new problems arise, and especially the problem of aggregation. How do we go from behavioral reports of individual subjects to aggregates that are relevant for testing macroeconomic theories or for estimating macroeconomic parameters? That is a legitimate question to raise, but it can usually be answered in a reasonable fashion for those kinds of research where procedures are available for sampling the relevant population. That condition is met by most survey research.

Suppose, however, our interest lies in the process that business firms use in reaching investment decisions. In every macroeconomic model, we find an equation representing that process. Of course, the phrase "the process" is already prejudicial, for it presumes that all firms make their investment decisions in the same way. The first result of any direct empirical inquiry will undoubtedly be to show that different firms have quite different methods for deciding upon their investments. Advocates of the "principle of unrealism" will not be dismayed by this finding, but for others it poses an aggregation problem. I think the right methodological attitude toward it is to acknowledge that where Nature has introduced individual differences, no amount of methodological magic will produce invariants. In the face of such variation, we can only hope that using appropriate averages will not introduce unacceptable inaccuracy in our results, or we must be prepared to use distributions instead of aggregates in our macromodels. That is a great inconvenience, but in empirical science we are not always allowed to choose the precise characteristics of the world we would like to study.

Moreover, as George Katona (1975, 1979b) has shown us, individual data may contain important information that is lost when averages are taken. He has pointed out that change of response from a first to a second interview may be caused either by the acquisition of new information or by uncertainty about the answer. But when the former is the cause, we would expect to find that most changes were in the same direction; when uncertainty is the cause, we would expect different respondents to be shifting their views in different directions. A measure of average change in view would not provide any information about the level of uncertainty. Yet, as Katona has observed, uncertainty itself may be one of the determinants of behavior.

Incidentally, panel studies of the sort just described illustrate also the vastly greater information that is contained in time series where changes in individual responses can be identified from one period to the next, as compared with time series that report only net shifts in responses.

While I will have more in a moment to say about the study of decision-making processes, the above remarks provide a global survey of some of the methodological questions that must be faced if verbal reports are to be used as data. These are methodological problems, not unclimbable barriers against the use of such data. Verbal reports have a central role to play in empirical inquiry in all of the social and behavioral sciences, and especially in individual psychology and in economics—a much enlarged role over the one they have played in the recent past.

Expectations and Decisions

A great many behavioral studies—perhaps most of them—are concerned with ascertaining people's expectations, their intentions, or their preferences. Others, a smaller number, are concerned with discovering the processes whereby expectations, intentions, and preferences are formed.

Price expectations and wages In models of rational behavior, preferences and information are the inputs on the basis of which actions are chosen. But information may lead to the formation of expectations about relevant future events so that these expectations become intervening variables in choice.

By way of example, let us consider the equation for the prediction of wages or of change in the wage level that is to be found in most contemporary macroeconomic models. A typical form for this equation is:

$$w_t = f(U_{t-1}, P_{et}) \qquad (1)$$

where w_t is the change in wages, U_{t-1} is the level of unemployment in the previous time period, and p_{et} is a variable representing expectations of the change in the price level. (Just *whose* expectations we are talking about will be considered in a moment.)

In the macromodel, the expectation variable that appears as an independent variable in Equation 1 may, in turn, be treated as an exogenous variable, or it may be treated as endogenous, appearing as the dependent variable in another equation of the system.[1] When the expected change in prices is viewed as endogenous, any one of a large number of different equations may be used to predict it, each representing a different hypothesis about the mechanisms of expectation formation. The classical "cobweb" equation simply assumed that the relevant actors would expect the next period's prices to be the same as current prices. A more sophisticated cobweb made the expected *change* in prices depend on the last period's price change. From this, it was an obvious generalization to introduce a distributed function of lagged prices for several periods. Soon the idea was introduced that a person forming expectations might learn from his mistakes, hence, that the error in predicting price changes in one or more past periods should appear as an independent variable in the expectations equations ("adaptive" expectations).

Particularly popular at the present time is the so-called "rational expectations" hypothesis, whereby, in the words of the author of that hypothesis (Muth, 1961)," ... expectations of firms (or, more generally, the subjective probability distribution of outcomes) tend to be distributed, for the same information set, about the prediction of the theory (or the "objective" probability distributions of outcomes)."

To the best of my knowledge, all of these equations have been conceived in the shelter of armchairs; none of them are based on direct empirical evidence about the processes that economic actors actually use to form their expectations about future events. The cobweb and adaptive expectations equations are pragmatic, in the sense of incorporating "plausible" assumptions about how an adaptive organism might use past experience to anticipate the future. The rational expectations procedure purports to be optimal in a certain sense, but rigorous proofs of its optimality are derivable only for a quadratic utility function. But optimal or not, it has never been checked directly against evidence of expectation-forming processes.

In the absence of direct behavioral evidence, the choice among alternative equations for the formation of expectations depends on econometric tests of how well the different equations predict macroeconomic time series. In the light of the many identifying assumptions that have to be made in order to carry out such tests, and the many open methodological issues relating to tests of goodness of fit, these indirect procedures can hardly be regarded as satisfactory. In sum, we have few solid reasons for preferring one of the equations for estimating expectations over the others.

Under these circumstances, it might appear obvious that we should take the other course and treat expectations as exogenous. We can then estimate them by quizzing the relevant economic actors directly. In fact, this is not obvious at all. First, we have to ask who the relevant actors are. Are they the workers, or the employers, or the bargaining agents on both sides of the table, or some combination of these? Moreover, the wage equation, as usually written, takes into account either the employers' expectations (a variable in the demand function) or the workers' expectations (a variable in the supply function), but not both. This will not be too serious if the society holds some common set of expectations, which may often be the case. Then the wage equation simply predicts how these common expectations, taken together with other features of the economic situation, affect the outcome of the wage bargaining process.

Even then we are not out of the woods. For now, if we ascertain by direct questioning what those expectations are, there is still a problem of determining the right form for the equation in which they are to be substituted—recognizing that this is an equation that represents a bargaining process (or rather, a whole host of bargaining processes in various industries and firms), and not a demand curve or a supply curve in a competitive market.

This particular problem would not have gone away had we followed the other route, treating expectations as endogenous and estimating them from some function of lagged variables. For such estimates still have to be plugged into the wage equation. Of course, if we estimate the parameters of the two equations simultaneously, we may hope that the errors of specification in each will somehow cancel out and that we will have enough parameters in the whole system to fit the data reasonably well. But if that is our justification for our procedure, then we can no longer regard our equations as structural, and we are faced with all of the limitations of reduced-form estimation—that is to say, any substantial change in structure in the real world will invalidate our predictions.

This is not merely a hypothetical difficulty. There is no reason to believe, for example, that the same equation will describe the formation of price expectations in both the 1960s and the 1970s. When structure changes, a considerable period of time must elapse under the new structure before the econometric data will be available that are needed to estimate expectations as endogenous variables. There need be no such lag in determining what the new structure is if decision makers can be asked directly not merely what their expectations of the moment are, but also what general model of the world they are using in forming those expectations.[2] I will say a little more in a moment about the prospects of getting veridical answers to such questions, but this approach at least suggests the possibility that a combination of direct behavioral data with econometric estimates may be more satisfactory than either alone. As a matter of fact, econometricians already use this approach informally, except that they depend on their own intuitions as the behavioral data for selecting the estimating model, a procedure that can hardly be recommended as good science.

Direct evidence on decision processes This brings us back to the question of whether respondents *can* describe their decision processes to us. The earlier discussion of methods of eliciting verbal reports suggests at least part of the answer. It will generally be futile to ask, "How much did X influence you?" There is no evidence that people can report reliably or consistently the weights that they attach to different factors entering into their decisions, that they are at all aware of these weights, or even that anything describable as a "weight" enters into the decision process. On the other hand, it may be quite useful to ask, "Just when did you learn of fact X, and from what source?" Although memory will not always be reliable on such matters, they are at least in principle accessible to recall and reportable.

Hence, if we are to use verbal reports to gain an understanding of decision processes, we should aim at reconstructing successive steps of the processes and the information available at each step. The denser our observations of the process, the more likely we are to discover the underlying mechanisms of information gathering, inference, and evaluation

(Newell and Simon, 1972). Verbal protocols with a density of a statement every three to five seconds have been obtained for a considerable range of problem-solving and decision-making tasks and have proved to be highly informative in reconstructing and simulating by computer the cognitive processes involved. Protocols taken concurrently with the decision process are generally more complete than those obtained retrospectively; but neither sort should be ruled out as valuable sources of data. Thus, behavioral methods need not be limited to ascertaining the respondent's "state" at a given moment—his beliefs, expectations, attitudes, and intentions. They can also be used to study the processes that form and transform his state, including his decision processes.

Let me offer a couple of conjectures about some things we are likely to discover when we pursue this kind of direct inquiry into the processes for forming expectations. If we were to ask, "What information do you have about how prices are likely to behave next year?" a frequent answer might be, "Everyone says they are going to go up at least ten percent." Another answer we might hear is, "If peace continues in the Middle East, prices may begin to stabilize." The first kind of reply illustrates the circularity (within a social system) of the process of forming expectations; the second illustrates the dependence of expectations about economic quantities upon political and other events outside the economic system. There is every reason to suppose that both these kinds of considerations play an important role in the formation of expectations and that both greatly complicate the prediction problem. The dependence of expectations on the expectations of others threatens the process with dynamic instability and makes it hard to trace the exogenous, or non-circular, sources of information that determine equilibrium. The likelihood that expectations will be strongly affected by political or meteorological events that are themselves hard to predict shortens severely the horizon of reliable prediction.

In spite of these limitations, an empirically based understanding of the processes by which expectations are formed, combined with opinion data on current expectations, holds promise of giving more reliable inputs to short-run prediction models than does the alternative econometric approach. It should promise us also an earlier awareness of change in structure of the estimating process than would be obtained from regressions using lagged data generated by the previous structure.

Polls and Policies

There is sometimes worry, in opinion or preference polling, that publication of the poll results will itself change opinions or behaviors. Such worries were often expressed in the early days of election polls, but the weight of evidence was that the concerns were unfounded, at least in the case of Presidential elections. We should not make an easy extrapolation to other elections, or perhaps even to Presidential elections when there are more than two candidates. Of course, whether it would be a good or bad thing that polls should have such effects, if in fact they did have them, is yet another question.

Polls and democratic theory There is another, even more important, question of the relation of opinion polls to public policies. It concerns the use of polls as an instrument of "direct democracy"—of going directly from the ascertainment of preferences and the counting of heads to the choice of public policies. I have even heard a distinguished physicist suggest that all homes should be provided with polling devices so that the electorate could, at the press of a button, instruct its representatives instantly about its views on any or all questions.

This kind of advocacy of a naive direct democracy—which seems quite widespread at the present time—needs serious review in the light of political theory, and the political theory itself needs badly to be informed by empirical research. The Founding Fathers, practical and experienced politicians that they were, did not think of the constitution of a body politic as a delicate instrument for titrating the acid of conservatism against the alkali of liberalism (or is it the other way around?). They regarded it as a very blunt instrument mainly aimed at preventing excessive accumulations of power anywhere in the system.

Any use of polling techniques as part of the political process must avoid the notion that democratic politics is an exercise in arithmetic. Our political institutions, as they now operate, do not give equal weight to all opinions and preferences, but tend to pay particular attention to those that are held passionately. The ability of minorities in this country to prevent the enactment of gun control measures or of liberal abortion laws are examples of this weighting of numbers by intensity of passion. I happen to regret the result in these particular two instances, but I see the mechanism that produces it an important means of protection against the tyranny of majorities. The response to a polling question may be too effortless a political act to serve as a real measure of "public opinion."

I do not wish to appear to be arguing against the utility of public opinion polls. Rather, I should like to argue that both the design of polls and application of their findings need to take place within a framework of political theory. On what kinds of topics can we expect the general public to have firmly held views? At what levels of abstraction or specificity should preferences be elicited? What part of the process of inferring policies from goals should be a public responsibility, and what part should rest with legislatures and the bureaucracy?

Of course, this set of issues is part of an even broader set that are concerned with the respective roles of voting, markets, bargaining, and other ways of registering preferences in the total social decision process (Dahl and Lindblom, 1953). It would be a useful exercise, for example, to explore the consequences of using opinion polls versus cost-benefit analysis versus other processes for determining the levels of protection we want against various environmental hazards. Whether it is useful to use a public opinion poll in this or any other public decision process depends on whether we are posing questions that our respondents can be expected to answer in a rational and informed manner.

Public attention In obtaining behavioral data and in interpreting it, we need to be concerned also with the relation between opinion formation and the focus of attention. As we have known at least since *The Voter's Choice* (Lazarsfeld, Berelson, and Gaudet, 1944) was published, expressions of preference or intention with respect to an issue that has not been long in the public eye may have little predictive value for preferences after attention has been focused for some time on that issue. We have come to understand that evocation of attitudes lying dormant in long-term memory may account for much more opinion change than any processes that can appropriately be described as "persuasion." Political processes tend to change views by reminding more than they do by convincing or persuading. Hence, polling data can only be interpreted intelligently in the light of information about the state of public attention when the data were gathered.

The importance of the attention variable is further underlined by the fact that attention is scarce—that only a very small number of issues can be in the focus of public attention at any one time. Thoughtfulness can be expected of respondents only with regard to matters they have had time to think about; and this means that, at any given time, they are prepared to be thoughtful about only a few things. A plausible answer to many opinion poll questions (I don't know how often this answer is given to pollsters) would be, "Come back and ask me after I have had a chance to think about the matter."

The process of opinion formation As I urged in the case of expectations, the most valuable information we might gain about opinions through behavioral study is an understanding of the processes that form them. Two points here are particularly important. First, opinions are held not only on the basis of evidence, but also on the basis of advice (i.e., because they are opinions held by legitimate and credible "experts."). Second, people may hold, on some topic, firmly rooted opinions on ends but not on the means for attaining them, or vice versa; discovering the right level in the means-ends hierarchy to pose the question may be crucial to the meaningfulness of the answer.

One facet of what I earlier called "naive direct democracy" is the principle that people not only have considered views on all important matters of public policy, but that these views are arrived at by weighing evidence. It is thought to be discreditable (especially in intellectual circles) to admit to voting for a candidate because of his party affiliation. Direct study of the process of opinion formation would reveal that many of our opinions are held because they were recommended to us by competent authority. Now this is by no means an irrational basis for belief. Generally, for example, it is better to ask an engineer whether the roof of our house is strong enough to withstand a heavy snowfall than to figure it out for ourselves; or to ask our attorney about our legal rights than to deduce them from our knowledge of the law.

By the same token, if the Democratic party has in the past generally pursued policies that have seemed consistent with my desires and interests, it may be quite rational for me to support Salt II, say, because it is supported by the Democratic administration, and more rational to support it for that reason than because I have examined the issues in detail and understand the technical arguments.

Perhaps in taking a political party as my example of a trustworthy opinion source, I have not made as strong a case as I could for my general point. In the current American culture, political parties are not generally in high repute. But the validity of the general point does not hang on this particular example. The point is that social processes for legitimating information and instilling confidence in it are central to the process of opinion formation. Hence, behavioral data on who trusts whom with respect to what, and who turns to what sources for information and policy recommendations, are crucial to developing and testing a theory of democratic institutions.

Let me turn now to the second point I raised at the beginning of this section: the importance of probing opinions at the right level of the means-ends chain. A central difficulty in the dialogue between an architect and his client (or between a city planner and the local population) is to find out what the client "wants." In part, this is a matter of attention: the architect is aware of many dimensions of design that have not occured to his client and wouldn't normally occur to him until he had actual experience of the future house. How do we know whether we like strawberries if we have never eaten strawberries? Only a thin line separates the architect's or planner's interpreting his client's tastes, educating those tastes, or creating them.

If we regard either of the latter two forms of social influence as legitimate (educating tastes or creating new ones), then behavioral data on present opinions or desires will have a correspondingly restricted value for purposes of planning. The main commodity that the planner may be offering us is the opportunity to enjoy new experiences, part of whose value may lie in our inability to anticipate them. Unless we recognize that tastes appear as both dependent and independent variables in the mechanisms of social processes, there is danger that we may build an assumption of fixed, pre-established tastes and goals into our democratic theory and into our practices for using opinion polls.[3]

Having urged all of these cautions in the use of polling data in the political scene, I should not ignore the other side of the coin. We need to learn much more than we now know about the political process—about how public opinions are formed, how tenaciously they are held, what changes them, how they are related to acceptance of the outcomes of political decisions. Perhaps the most important contribution that studies of public opinion can make to democratic processes lies in using them to study those processes themselves, rather than in making extensive use of polls as an instrument of direct democracy.

Conclusion

I am sure that my small sample of issues will bring to mind others of equal significance. But any of those I have mentioned could well occupy us for the afternoon and more. Much of the experience and empirical data we will need for dealing intelligently with questions like these must come from the work at The University of Michigan's Institute for Social Research, and a great deal of that, in particular, from the work of George Katona, whom we are gathered here to honor today, and who has himself had many perceptive and important things to say on these topics.

Notes

This research was supported by Research Grant MH-07722 from the National Institute of Mental Health.

1. An excellent brief survey of alternative treatments of wage determination in macro-models, with references to the literature, will be found in Turnovsky (1977), Chapter 5.

2. For a discussion of changes in the structure of expectations in recent decades, see Katona (1979b, pp. 123–4) and Katona and Strumpel (1978).

3. James March (1978) has commented insightfully on the processes of social choice in the absence of a fixed utility function.

References

Cyert, Richard M., and March J. G. *Behavioral Theory of the Firm*. New York: Prentice-Hall, 1963.

Dahl, Robert A., and Lindblom, Charles E. *Politics, Economics, and Welfare*. New York: Harper and Brothers, 1953.

Ericsson, K. Anders, and Simon, Herbert A. "Retrospective Verbal Reports as Data." Department of Psychology, Carnegie-Mellon University, C.I.P. Working Paper #338, 1978(a).

———, and Simon, Herbert A. "Thinking-aloud Protocols as Data." Department of Psychology, Carnegie-Mellon University, C.I.P. Working Paper #397, 1978(b).

Katona, George. *Organizing and Memorizing*. New York: Columbia University Press, 1940.

———. *Psychological Analysis of Economic Behavior*. New York: McGraw-Hill, 1951.

———. *Business Looks at Banks*. Ann Arbor: The University of Michigan Press, 1957.

———. *The Powerful Consumer*. New York: McGraw-Hill, 1960.

———. *Psychological Economics*. New York: Elsevier, 1975.

———. "Behavioral Economics." *Challenge*, September-October, 1978, pp. 14–18.

———. "Consumer Expectations as a Guide to the Economy." *Public Opinion*, January-February, 1979(a), pp. 15–19.

———. "Toward a Macropsychology." *American Psychologist* 34, 1979(b), pp. 118–126.

———, and Strumpel, Burkhard. *A New Economic Era*. New York: Elsevier, 1978.

Lazarsfeld, Paul; Berelson, B.; and Gaudet, H. *The People's Choice*, New York: Duell, Sloan and Pearce, 1944.

March, James. "Bounded Rationality, Ambiguity, and the Engineering of Choice." *The Bell Journal of Economics*, 9, 1978, pp. 587–608.

Muth, J. F. "Rational Expectations and the Theory of Price Movements." *Econometrica*, 129, 1961, pp. 315–35.

Newell, Allen, and Simon, Herbert A. *Human Problem Solving*. Englewood Cliffs, New Jersey: Prentice-Hall, 1972.

Turnovsky, S. J. *Macroeconomic Analysis and Stabilization Policies*. Cambridge: Cambridge University Press, 1977.

IV.6 Methodological Foundations of Economics

In order to talk about the methodological foundations of a subject, we must characterize that subject. Designing an appropriate set of methodologies for economics requires careful attention to some of the salient characteristic of economic phenomena. The most important seem to me to be these:

1. Economics has both a descriptive (positive) and a normative aspect: it describes how people behave in their economic decisions and actions, and it prescribes rational behavior.

2. Economics is a "science of the artificial," for it deals with systems that seek to adapt to their environments in order to reach goals, including survival goals. They may be subject to natural selection.

3. If we place no limits on the adaptive capacity of a system, then its behavior can be predicted completely from (1) its goals, and (2) the shape of the environment to which it is adapting.

4. The properties of the system itself influence behavior only to the extent that they limit the perfection of its adaptation to the environment. There may be limits both on its ability to compute what is the rational behavior and its ability to carry out the behavior computed.

5. It is convenient to draw the boundary of the system so that all limits on ability to carry out actions are outside the skin, while all limits on ability to calculate correct actions are inside the skin. Then only the latter limits (which define "bounded rationality") need be viewed as causes for departure from rationality.

Traditionally, economics (both positive and normative) has been viewed as the study of rational behavior. But this is only half of the story. The other half of economics is the study of the limits on human computational ability, and how these limits influence intendedly rational behavior. That half has been neglected in mainstream economic theory, with great detriment to the ability of economics to describe or prescribe correctly for human economic affairs. Notice that I am not talking about emotion, unreason, irrationality. I am talking about the limits imposed on rational calculation by the disparity between the complexity of the world and the finiteness of human computational capabilities, with or without computers.

To omit from economic theory a consideration of human computational power is like omitting gravitational forces from astrophysical theory. In a weightless world, or one with gravity shields, things would be quite different from the way they are in the actual world. A theory for the former would have little predictive value in the latter.

Nor is it sufficient to construct a theory of perfect rationality, and then to annex to it some modifications to take account of search behavior or response to uncertainty. As we shall see, introducing a neoclassical theory of search, like Stigler's (1961), simply compounds the computational problems; while handling uncertainty with rational expectations is a way of pretending that the problems aren't there. Economic theory needs to incorporate computational considerations from the very beginning, not as an add-on or amendment to a theory of omniscient rationality.

The criticism of neoclassical theory for ignoring the boundedness of human rationality is not new. I myself have been making the criticism for forty years (Simon, 1947), and many others have both preceded and followed me in voicing similar objections. It is fair to ask, and economists have often asked, what we have to offer instead. Hence, I will begin this essay with a description of the alternative theory. Then we can compare the two theories with respect both to their power and to their veridicality.

Foundations of a Theory of Rational Computation

Central to neoclassical economic theory is the notion of choice among a fixed set of alternatives by the criterion provided by a fixed utility function. The theory does not explain the origins of the alternatives, nor the content of the utility function, nor how items are placed on the agenda for decision, nor by what computational means the economic actor connects alternatives with their consequences, measured in terms of utility. Yet these four unexplained dimensions of choice are crucial to understanding economic behavior in the real world and to predicting the consequences of proposed economic actions.

The concept of bounded rationality provides a starting point for economic theory that deals with the areas of neglect without negating those findings of classical theory that have a good basis in empirical evidence. While neoclassical theory derives from a very small but powerful set of empirical assumptions about behavior (the assumptions of maximization of subjective expected utility), theories deriving from bounded rationality require more extensive empirical assumptions, hence call for wider observation of actual human decision-making behavior.

The Search for Alternatives

Most actual human choice begins with the recognition of the need for a decision, then proceeds to discover one or more alternatives that would meet this need. For a very wide range of human decision-making activities, the greatest part of the decision maker's time and effort is devoted to generating or identifying alternatives. Some examples will make this clear.

Some commodities are standard, or nearly so (sugar, wheat), but most commodities exist in numerous varieties that can be distinguished by purchasers, and their differences provide an important basis (along with price and other variables) for choice among them. Automobiles will serve us as an example. The automobile manufacturer does not make a decision to produce "cars," but to produce specific models of cars. These models, in turn, are not selected from a pattern book, they are designed. The design of product is a crucial part of the decision making in an automobile company, one might almost say, the most crucial. It certainly absorbs a significant part of the total cost of manufacture, and an even larger part of the decision-making costs that the company incurs in its operations.

In modem industrial economies, the decision-making costs of finding products are usually, but not always, borne by producers. (Buyers of new buildings participate in the design process, at least to a modest extent, but this is an exceptional domain.) The search for alternatives may take place in response to a specific customer order (request for a product that will meet certain specifications), or it may anticipate customers wants and produce "shelf goods" for market. In many industries (e.g., clothing, electric motors), both patterns exist side by side.

Not only the automobile industry, but many others, live under conditions where the life of a product is short, and where the continual discovery and introduction of new products is a key criterion of survival as well as profit. The pharmaceutical industry and the computer industry provide clear cases where manufacturing plays almost a secondary role to design. In the latter two cases, but less so in the case of the auto industry, an ongoing stream of scientific research, much of it outside the industry itself, provides the new knowledge from which the opportunities for continual product invention derive.

Today, we have a considerable body of theory, produced by research in cognitive science, that tells us how new alternatives, new designs, are discovered. Knowledge of the discovery process is available to economics as a starting point for filling this important gap in neoclassical theory. The cognitive theory shows that new alternatives are discovered by heuristic search through problem spaces. What does this mean?

The simplest kind of search involves two kinds of processes: generators and test. Generators make use of known, existing, components and combine these components into novel complex structures. Tests applied to the complex structures determine whether they meet the requirements of the object that is being sought. A classical experiment in Gestalt psychology illustrates the process. The subject is given a candle, a box of thumbtacks, and some matches; and is asked to mount the candle on the wall so as to provide light. One good solution is to empty the box of its thumbtacks, use a match to melt wax to fix the candle to the bottom of the box, and mount the box on the wall by means of thumbtacks pinned through its side. A clear (if primitive) example of product design.

For most real-world problems, the number of components and the number of ways of combining them are so large that undirected trial-and-error search "through all the possibilities" will not work. The possibilities cannot be exhausted, and most of them will be worthless. Hence, if it is to be effective and economical, the search must be directed by knowledge, so that likely directions of solutions are explored at an early stage. In human problem solving, search is usually directed by rules of thumb, called heuristics, that are based on prior knowledge of the structure of the domain. Hence the phrase "heuristic search."

Studies of human problem solving in a wide range of task domains, from puzzles and games like chess to professional activities like medical diagnosis and architectural design, have shown the processes of heuristic search to be ubiquitous and powerfully effective (Simon, 1981). Recent research on these lines has demonstrated that these processes can even account for scientific discovery as one form of creation of new alternatives (Langley, Simon, Bradshaw, and Żytkow, 1987; Kulkarni and Simon, 1988).

One important component of heuristic search procedures is the *stop rule*. If alternatives are being generated sequentially, as they are by these procedures, there must be some way of deciding when the search should be halted and a decision made. Seldom is there a guarantee that one of the alternatives already generated is the optimal one, and that a better one could not be found if search were continued. In the absence of such a guarantee, some standard must be set of what would constitute a "satisfactory" item, and search can be halted when an alternative is found that meets this standard (Simon, 1955). The psychological evidence shows that the standards of satisfaction take the form of *aspiration levels.* On the basis of past experience, the problem solver forms a judgment of the quality of solution he or she can expect to attain with a reasonable investment of effort. This judgment defines the level of aspiration and determines when search will stop. Aspirations tend to rise as it proves easy to find improved new alternatives and to fall if the search becomes unproductive.

Of course, if the relevant costs and yields of search were known, the stop rule could be determined as the solution of a problem of optimization (Stigler, 1961). But costs and yields can usually be estimated only grossly, at best. Hence, a theory to explain search must postulate some kind of a feedback mechanism to adjust aspiration levels, without the possibility of estimating the optimal values of the feedback parameters. The process of finding altematives by heuristic search with the use of a stop rule based upon adjustable aspirations is usually called *satisficing* (Simon, 1956a).

The Utility Function or Satisfaction Criterion

In solving problems by heuristic search, a criterion is needed for deciding when a satisfactory alternative has been found. This criterion can have much weaker properties than are required by neoclassical economics for a utility function. In particular, the criterion can be multifaceted, without a need for comparability across facets. For example, the criterion for a new automobile design may require that it be manufacturable at less than a specified cost, that its gasoline consumption be less than a specified amount per mile, that its exhaust gases meet legal standards for emissions, that it incorporate safety belts, that it have a "streamlined" appearance and chrome hubcaps, and so on. The list can be as long as we please, and there is no need to specify how much of one of these requirements would be traded off for a given improvement in another. All have to be satisfied in a satisfactory design.

Likewise, the theory does not postulate a utility function for consumers, but instead, a set of satisficing levels. If alternatives cannot be found that satisfice, then aspiration levels will drop until an alternative is found. This process has been observed, for example, in empirical studies of how students choose their first jobs (Soelberg, 1967). Only empirical evidence can determine which dimensions of the standard of satisfaction will be most malleable, and which most resistant to change. Like the theory of utility maximization, the satisficing theory does not completely determine, a priori, the content of the utility or satisfaction function, but the satisficing theory says a good deal more about that function than does utility theory.

Selecting Occasions for Decision

Neoclassical economic theory has nothing to say about how items are placed on the agenda for decision. In a theory of bounded rationality, the agenda-determining mechanisms are derived from psychological research on the phenomena of attention. In any system that can deal with only a limited number of problems at one time, there must be a mechanism to determine which problems will receive attention. This mechanism must assure that two kinds of needs are attended to sufficiently often for survival: (1) real-time needs, which can be thought of as representing threats (or opportunities) presented by the environment; and (2) periodic needs for the replenishment of resources on which there is a continuing drain (Simon, 1956a).

Biological orgainsms meet their real-time needs with the aid of sensory mechanisms that can detect external threats or opportunities, and can interrupt ongoing activities to put the new item on the agenda. The interrupter can be dealt with at least in sufficient depth to determine whether it really needs priority. Organisms meet their periodic needs with the aid of internal sensory mechanisms (drives like hunger and thirst) that monitor inventories and interrupt ongoing activities when the inventories fall too low.

The attention-directing mechanism in economic agents need not be built in biologically, but can include all sorts of learned behaviors. For example, business organizations can create specific units whose task it is to "plan," that is, to scan the environment and determine when particular matters require attention.

Thus, the functions that are attributed by neoclassical theory to the utility function are divided, in theories of bounded rationality, between the satisficing stop rules, in the forms of levels of aspiration that determine when search for alternatives should halt, and the mechanisms of attention direction that place new items on the agenda for decision.

I have commented here on some of the things that are known, through empirical research, about these mechanisms; but we clearly will have to investigate them much more extensively before we have an adequate empirical basis for a full economic theory of agenda fixing and search for alternatives.

Computation

In neoclassical theory, behavior is shaped by the environment, and takes on whatever shape the environment demands for utility maximization. In the theory of bounded rationality, behavior is shaped by interaction between the environment and the computational capabilities of the actor who is trying to adapt to that environment. If an account is to be given of behavior, then neither environment nor computation can be ignored.

Operations research provides an interesting domain for studying this interaction between environmental demands and computational capabilities. In its conceptual origins, operations research may be regarded as an offshoot of neoclassical economics—in particular, as an effort to apply the concepts of economics to actual, practical decision-making situations.

Operations research deals with the undefined utility function of economics by postulating, in any given situation, an objective function (often supplemented by a set of constraints that a solution must satisfy). The objective function is usually something like profit, which is to be maximized, or cost, which is to be minimized. Before the standard operations research tools can be applied, the range of possible alternative actions must be specified, and a production function must be provided that connects the actions with their outcomes in terms of the objective function. In all of these respects, operations research operates within the usual framework of neoclassical economics.

But the tool is only useful if actual (numerical) answers can be obtained from it. Hence, in the actual development and application of operations research, if not in its conceptualization from a theoretical standpoint, computational considerations play a central role.

First of all, observe that most of the research in OR is directed at improving the computational efficiency of OR tools. The cost and feasibility of computation is recognized as the main limit on the range of applicability of these tools. Hence, anything that can be done to make computation more efficient extends that range. Unlike economics, with its exclusive attention to the environment of decision, OR pays equal or more attention to the computational costs of the decision process and to its computational efficiency. Linear programming dominates dynamic programming in OR applications because LP has powerful computational algorithms of quite general applicability, while dynamic programming problems of any considerable size can only be solved for very special cases (e.g., the case of a quadratic cost function without side constraints (Simon, 1956b)).

The computations LP calls for can actually be carried out (at least when large computers are available), and hence specific decisions can be reached with its help. The simplex method and other algorithms allow the optimum solution to be found for problems that have very large numbers of variables. Hence, our awareness of the availability of linear programming and similar OR tools may give us the illusion that we can make optimal decisions in exactly the way called for by neoclassical theory.

But notice that the "optimum" can be found only after the problem has been formulated in a way that meets the definition of a linear programming problem. The objective function must be linear in the activities, and the constraints must take the form of linear inequalities. Few, if any, real-world problems meet these requirement literally. The first step toward an application of LP is to make the tool applicable by shaping the problem to fit it. Thus, the "optima" that LP provides are, at best, satisfactory solutions of the real-world problem. If we could embed LP in a system for finding approximate LP formulations for real problems, we would have a powerful device for satisficing.

LP has another interesting characteristic that brings it into close relation with theories of bounded rationality. The linear inequalities in an LP model can represent not only environmental constraints, but components of utility as well. In the famous Stigler optimal diet problem (Stigler, 1945), solutions were evaluated by a cost minimization criterion. The dietary requirements—vitamins, minerals, calories—were represented by linear inequalities. Thus, the utility function was represented by these inequalities, while the objective function represented a budget constraint. What was really being sought was a satisficing solution to the diet problem—the diet was to contain "adequate" amounts of vitamins, minerals, and calories, and among diets that satisficed on these dimensions, the cheapest was to be chosen.

When we recognize that computational feasibility is one of the necessary conditions a decision procedure must satisfy, and when we recognize also that replacing the goal of optimizing with the goal of satisficing is a powerful means for reducing computational demands, the way lies open to supplementing the usual repertory of OR tools with the methods of heuristic search, drawn from artificial intelligence, hence indirectly from research on human decision making. Today, we are making increasing use of so-called expert systems in practical decision making. Almost all of these new systems are based on the idea of heuristic search, hence are closely allied to the decision making methods known to be used by human beings.

Describing and Predicting Economic Phenomena

In comparing the computational (and behavioral) theory of economic behavior with neoclassical theory, we can ask several kinds of questions. We can ask which is the better normative theory—which provides the better advice to economic actors. And we can ask which is the better descriptive theory—which provides the more veridical picture of economic phenomena in the real world.

The answer to the first question, on the normative value of the theories, has already been answered in the section, above, on computation. A theory can be only of limited normative value if the computations it prescribes cannot be carried out. The development of operations research, and the more recent supplementation of OR techniques with the methods of artificial intelligence show us how computational requirements more and more take the center of the stage, and how these requirements shape the normative tools more and more in the direction of a theory of bounded rationality.

The Empirical Evidence

What about empirical, descriptive accuracy? Here the disparity between the theories is quickly revealed. In other essays I have shown that the main claims neoclassical theory has made for its validation "in the large" simply do not withstand close examination (Simon, 1979). The good fits to data provided by the Cobb–Douglas function, and the equality between the labor coefficient of that function and labor's share of total income have been shown to be statistical artifacts. The cost curves of business firms are not commonly U-shaped, as the theory requires, nor does the theory predict nearly as well as an alternative behavioral theory the size distribution of business firms. The distribution of executive salaries is better predicted by a behavioral theory than by neoclassical theory.

A major claim for the adequacy of neoclassical theory is that the mechanisms of supply and demand do seem to "work." When prices are freed from constraint, many markets (but certainly not all of them) keep fairly close to equilibrium, or return to it reasonably quickly. Unfortunately, this does not hold too well for the aggregate labor market or the market for capital goods, in both of which persistent underemployment is a familiar phenomenon.

When prices are regulated, usually by placing ceilings on them, shortages and black markets develop quite predictably; and minimum price agreements (as in the case of OPEC) prove difficult to protect against temptations to increase supplies.

The evidence, then, that markets tends to equilibrate is quite strong (especially if we overlook the few important exceptions, or hide them in terminological innovations like the phrase "natural unemployment"). But this evidence is not really evidence for the neoclassical theory. As Becker and others have shown, markets would tend to equilibrate, due to budget constraints and for other reasons, even if no one was seeking to maximize expected utility or profit. Moreover, it is quite consistent with a behavioral theory, taking into account computational limitations, that demand curves would generally have negative slopes and supply slopes positive slopes. Satisficing behavior is sufficient to account for this.

But what about the vast body of econometric work over the past half century? Does that not provide us with ample evidence for validating neoclassical theory? Unfortunately, it does not. First, we must rule out all econometric studies that use just-identified models. If the model that is fitted to data is not overidentified, it cannot be refuted by the data, hence cannot be tested by them. At most, we can determine, with such a model, what fraction of the variance in the data is accounted for. But that tells us nothing unless we compare the model with its potential competitors to see which explains the data best. Neoclassical models have seldom been compared explicitly with models of bounded rationality.

The evidence obtained from the relatively few studies that have used over-identified models is scarcely more helpful, Econometric data are so noisy, and the a priori restrictions that must be placed on models to identify them are so numerous, that the tests of hypotheses are seldom conclusive. Moreover, optimizing assumptions are usually represented in such gross, approximative form that they are virtually indistinguishable from satisficing assumptions. This difficulty is well illustrated by Jorgenson's endeavors to validate neoclassical investment theory using highly simplified models of firm behavior (Jorgenson and Siebert, 1968). At best, these tests show that firms are interested in making profits—not at all that they maximize them.

Theories Built on Unrealistic Assumptions

What is startlingly absent from the empirical literature of classical economics is evidence of optimization based on the direct observation of the behavior of economic actors. Milton Friedman (1953), of course, in his celebrated essay on methodology in economics, has sought to make a virtue of this deficiency. He argues that a theory cannot be judged by the realism of its assumptions, but only by its efficacy in making predictions.

Above, I have already indicated one of the difficulties with this argument as it is applied to economics. Neoclassical theory does not have, in fact, a notable record of correct predictions. In the one area, supply and demand equilibrium, where it has the best claims for success, it has never been compared with alternative theories that might make the same predictions—or better ones. It has been notably weak, even when supported by powerful modern computing resources, in predicting economic time series of any kinds. And even if we put some credence in "lead variables," the basis for postulating them is almost wholly empirical and does not derive from neoclassical theory. So neoclassical theory cannot be given high marks for its predictive power.

The second flaw in Friedman's argument is his claim that unrealism in the assumptions of a theory is a good thing, or that it is even acceptable. Among the inferences that can be drawn from any theory, hence among its predictions, is the truth of its assumptions. A theory can be falsified by falsifying its axioms as readily as it can be falsified by falsifying any of the theorems that can be derived from the axioms. There is no support in any system of logic with which I am familiar, or in any schools of philosophy of science, for Friedman's principle of unrealism.

Friedman was probably led into his error by a confusion between unrealism and approximation. It is true that we would like our theories to be as parsimonious as possible, and that under certain circumstances, we may be willing to trade off a little accuracy for a significant gain in parsimony. But as a neoclassical economist would (or should) say: it's all a question of the marginal gain from parsimony versus the marginal loss from inaccuracy.

Friedman takes as an example Galileo's neglecting air resistance in stating the law of falling bodies. Unfortunately, that is a misreading of history. Galileo did state the law in the simplified form, but he and his successors, when testing it, paid careful attention to its limiting conditions. Newton, or example, when testing the law with pendulums of different weights, embedded the weights in cork balls of the same size so that air resistance would be the same.

To put the matter more graphically, air resistance can be ignored when studying the fall of bodies in a near-vacuum, but not when designing parachutes. And in no case does a theory of approximation support the principle of unrealism, that it doesn't matter if the premises of a theory are false. Unrealism is no virtue, and unless careful attention is given to the goodness of approximation that is required, it can be fatal.

Another defense sometimes given to the principle of unrealism, as applied to economics, is that the axioms of neoclassical theory cannot be tested directly because the behaviors they describe (e.g., utility maximization) cannot be observed. The fallacy of this argument is that they *have* been observed (e.g., by Kahnemann and Tversky, 1973) and the observations have not agreed with the neoclassical assumptions.

Of greater significance, there is now a large body of experience of observing the decision making processes both of consumers and of business firms. (For an example of the latter, see, e.g., Bromiley, 1986.) A great deal, although not all, of the computation that is involved in making business decisions takes place "publicly," that is, in the writing of documents, or in discussion in meetings. Both documents and discussions are observable and analyzable, and under many circumstances business firms will permit them to be observed. Comparable observations of consumer decision making have, of course, been made for many years by market researchers. Techniques for carrying out such decision making studies are described in the literature, and could be (though they seldom are) taught to graduate students in economics.

Most recently, there has been a burgeoning of experimental work in economics (Vernon Smith, 1982; Charles Plott, 1982), which has also revealed an important role for computation and bounded rationality in making decisions in the environments of simulated markets. For example, phenomena remarkably like the 1987 crash in the New York stock market have been observed in rather simple laboratory settings, where optimal behavior could probably have been computed by the participants in the experiments, but wasn't.

There is no excuse today, on methodological principles or practical ones, for ignoring the evidence of actual economic behavior at all levels, micro, intermediate, and macro, and even less excuse for refusing to gather that evidence. It is not just a matter of finding evidence that will help decide between neoclassical theory and the theory of bounded rationality. The evidence is already more than ample for preferring the latter theory. But to strengthen the capabilities of the bounded rationality theories for making predictions about a wide range of economic phenomena, we need to learn much more than we now know about the details of human decision making behavior.

Power in Prediction

This raises the question of the respective predictive capabilities of different theories. The neoclassical theory gets great predictive power (even though its predictions are often wrong) from its parsimonious assumptions that human beings are maximizers of subjective expected utility. Accepting that axiom relieves us of the need to do any more empirical research on the foundations of human behavior—or so it is claimed. Certainly it must be admitted that applying a behavioral theory to concrete situations requires a great deal of empirical research.

But let us look more closely at the predictions of neoclassical theory, and how we apply them to real-world situations. Perhaps the appearance of predictive power is at least partly illusory. For in applying any theory to concrete circumstances (and this is true of theories in physics, too), initial conditions and boundary conditions must be specified, and these initial and boundary conditions can generally only be determined on an empirical basis.

In earlier essays, I have shown this to be the case for business cycle theories. Keynes cannot be distinguished from Lucas on the basis of first assumptions or modes of reasoning. On almost all of the pages of the

General Theory, Keynes (1936) use the assumptions and arguments of neoclassical economic thought: in particular that economic actors are utility maximizers. The same can be said of Lucas (1981) in his essays on the business cycle. But it has often been shown that, within these same assumptions, with competitive markets, the only equilibrium the system can reach and maintain is a full employment equilibrium. How does Keynes produce a business cycle in his system, and how does Lucas?

The recipe is the same in both cases. Take the rational-man hypothesis, but add just one speck of irrationality to it. Let labor suffer from just a bit of money illusion, so that it cannot distinguish changes in money wages from changes in the real wage. Or instead, attribute the money illusion to business: the businessman cannot distinguish a change of prices in his industry from a change in the general price level. Either speck of irrationality is adequate to produce a business cycle.

Of course, it matters where you insert the speck into the system. Different specks may have different implications for government policy. But the important point for our present purposes is that the business cycle in these theories does not come from the assumption of rationality, but rather from the assumption that rationality is, at least in some important respect or respects, bounded. Human computational limits do matter, and postulating them is essential to explaining the phenomena.

If the nature of the specks does matter, then it is important to determine the facts of the matter. Does labor suffer from money illusion; does management; or do both? These are empirical questions, to be answered by facts gathered through observation and experiment. Hence neoclassical theory, when we look at its applications more closely, is just as dependent upon empirical data as is the theory of bounded rationality—indeed, it explains such phenomena as business cycles only when it allows itself to be infected with elements of bounded rationality.

Within the framework of bounded rationality, a business cycle theory would not look wholly different from the theories we have now. But in its derivation, it would start with observed facts instead of detouring through, and then abandoning, the assumption of omniscient rationality.

Among the facts it would look at are some that are generally ignored by the individualism of neoclassical theory. For example, expectations rather obviously play a central role in such events as stock market booms and busts. Expectations are beliefs about the future. Those beliefs are formed, in a modern society, in an environment where each person is in constant communication with many other people. Surely, a realistic theory of belief formation, adequate to explain these phenomena, will have to take into account the processes of social communication, and the ways in which each of us is influenced by what we hear from others. These are empirical questions, which cannot be settled by reasoning from the model of omniscient rationality. They certainly cannot be settled within the context of "rational expectations."

Natural Selection in Economics

One other common defense of neoclassical theory must be mentioned. It is sometimes claimed that it doesn't matter if economic agents maximize. For only those who behave as *if* they maximized will survive the pressures of competition (Hirshleifer, 1977). As I have explained elsewhere, this argument rests on a misreading of Darwinian theory. In evolutionary theory, the survivors are those who are fitter than those who do not survive. The theory does not claim that there will be optimizers among the competitors, for there is nothing in the mechanisms of the theory to produce an approach to global optimization (as distinguished from local optimization) even in the long run.

Once we introduce the generation of new alternatives into our economic theories, as we must, we see that competition can cause the extinction of relatively inefficient businesses, but cannot prevent even very inefficient ones from surviving if they do not have competitors abler than themselves. Nothing in the evolutionary mechanism guarantees the existence of these abler competitors, hence nothing enforces profit maximization as against satisficing with aspiration values based on competitive standards.

The Aggregation Problem

Our current knowledge of human decision making is based largely upon research with individuals, supplemented by a rather small number of case studies of organizational decision making. In economics, our main interest (except for consumer economics and labor economics) is in decisions made by organizations, and the effects of decisions upon the operation of markets and the economy as a whole. Hence, while we have a rather extensive theory, and a well substantiated one, of human problem solving and decision making, it is not always clear how to derive from it inferences about organizations, markets and the economy.

When we look at the matter more closely, we see that we are not much worse off than neoclassical theory, except in those rare instances where we can be sure that all of the conditions for perfectly competitive markets are met. And even in these cases, the neoclassical theory leaves dynamics pretty well untouched—solutions are known only for static equilibrium.

In neoclassical theory, the typical route from individual behavior to aggregates is to assume a "representative individual" or "representative firm," and use this ideal entity for aggregation. We can do the same in a behavioral theory, with the added advantage of having some empirical basis for characterizing the units to be aggregated, instead of postulating their properties a priori.

We can, of course, go further. In the case of consumer behavior, we can sample the relevant population and arrive at aggregates by taking properly weighted sums or averaged of individual behaviors. In the case of business firms, sampling in any literal sense is seldom feasible, at least when behavior is to be observed at first hand and not simply inferred from formal reports or answers to questionnaires. But by intensive studies of even a few business firms, we can learn a good deal about the range of behaviors, and from that we can determine how robust our aggregation procedures are likely to be. Whatever the limits of such inferences, they are bound to be a great deal more accurate than a priori presuppositions, untainted by empirical observation, about how business firms behave.

Conclusion

My conclusion is a simple one. We have today a theory of economic behavior, that is, the theory of bounded rationality, that is far more veridical than the neoclassical theory. Applying either theory to answering specific economic questions requires empirical research to determine the initial and boundary conditions of the situation. It is so in every science, physical, biological, and social. Cultivation of empirical research at every level, including direct observation of the behavior of economic actors, is the only path that will enlarge economics as a science and enhance its powers of prediction and explanation.

Economics has developed very sophisticated econometric methods for handling aggregate data that, unfortunately, are usually extremely noisy. Corresponding effort directed at strengthening methods of observation at the micro level and at discovering how to aggregate micro data deserve high priority on the agenda of economic research. To give them that priority we will havc to provide new kinds of training for economics graduate students, and we will have to change the reward system of our discipline to assign higher credits to painstaking empirical work, and perhaps lower ones to mathematical virtuosity that detaches itself from the real word.

References

Bromiley, Philip (1986) *Corporate Capital Investment: A Behavioral Approach*, Cambridge University Press.

Friedman, Milton (1953) *Essays in Positive Economics*, Chicago: University of Chicago Press.

Hirshleifer, J. (1977) Economics from a biological viewpoint, *Journal of Law and Economics*, 20:1–52.

Jorgenson, D. W., and C. D. Siebert (1968) A comparison of alternative theories of corporate investment behavior, *American Economics Review*, 58:681–712.

Kahneman, D., and A. Tversky (1973) On the psychology of prediction, *Psychological Review*, 80:237–251.

Keynes, J. M. (1936) *The General Theory of Employment, Interest, and Money*, London: Macmillan.

Kulkarni, D., and H. A. Simon (1988) The processes of scientific discovery: The strategy of experimentation, *Cognitive Science*, 12:139–175.

Langley, P., H. A. Simon, G. L. Bradshaw, and J. M. Zytkow (1987) *Scientific Discovery: Computational explorations of the creative process*, Cambridge, MA: MIT Press.

Lucas, R. E. Jr. (1981) *Studies in Business Cycle Theory*, Cambridge, MA: MIT Press.

Plott, C. R. (1982) Industrial organization theory and experimental economics, *Journal of Economic Literature*, 20:1485–1527.

Simon, H. A. (1947) *Administrative Behavior*, New York: Macmillan.

Simon, H. A. (1955) A behavioral model of rational choice, *Quarterly Journal of Economics*, 69:99–118.

Simon, H. A. (1956a) Rational choice and the structure of the environment, *Psychological Review*, 63:129–138.

Simon, H. A. (1956b) Dynamic programming under uncertainty with a quadratic criterion function, *Econometrica*, 24:74–81.

Simon, H. A. (1979) On parsimonious explanations of production relations, *The Scandinavian Journal of Economics*, 81:459–474.

Simon, H. A. (1981) *The Sciences of the Artificial*, Cambridge, MA: MIT Press.

Smith, V. L. (1982) Macroeconomic systems as an experimental science, *American Economic Review* 72:923–955.

Soelberg, P. (1967) *A Study of Decision-Making Choice*, Unpublished Ph.D. dissertation, Carnegie-Mellon University.

Stigler, G. J. (1945) The cost of subsistence, *Journal of Farm Economics*, 2:303–314.

Stigler, G. J. (1961) The economics of information, *Journal of Political Economy*, 69:213–225.

IV.7 Preface to *La Théorie Moderne de l'Enterprise: L'Approche Institutionnelle*

Professor Gabrie and Jacquier have provided us with a highly instructive and insightful exposition and analysis of one of the principal developing trends in contemporary economic theory: the so-called "New Institutional Economics." Their book reviews the history of the new theory, the central theses put forth by some of its principal proponents, and also some of the problems it faces. Here is an alternative to the neoclassical economic theory which has reigned supreme through almost the whole of the Twentieth Century; the challenge to it from an earlier generation of institutional economists—Veblen, Commons and Mitchell, and to some extent Schumpeter—having long since largely withered and disappeared. Now there are new challenges, but it is important to understand what they are challenging.

Even the Keynesian "revolution," which seemed at first to counter neoclassical doctrine at the macro-economic level, was gradually reinterpreted by most economic theorists as a mild adjustment of neo-classical thought. They viewed it as straying from the fold only so far as to introduce short-run, transient departures from the classical assumptions of perfect rationality (e.g., "money illusion," "animal spirits"). Philosophers of science since Lakatos have argued that every theory has a central core that is defended by its adherents as inviolate, but that this core is almost always surrounded by a host of auxiliary hypotheses which tell us how the theory is to be applied to particular situations and circumstances. Keynesian theory gradually became, at best, such a set of auxiliary hypotheses. (It is not all clear that Keynes himself would have had it any other way, for the *General Theory* is replete with neoclassical reasoning.)

Now we see the rise of new challenges to neoclassicism. Among them, the New Institutional Economics has perhaps attained the greatest degree of attention and even acceptance from the profession. But as the reader of this book will learn, it is still an open question as to whether the new doctrine will be viewed, either by its proponents or by the rest of the economics profession, as displacing neoclassical theory. It is an open question how far it will be absorbed into that theory, as Keynesian theory has been, not changing the core but simply amending and adding to the auxiliary hypotheses that surround this core. Again, as Professors Gabrie and Jacquier point out, it is doubtful that the new-institutionalist writers themselves have any different intention, any deeply revolutionary goal of overthrowing the neoclassical core.

What are the central issues under discussion? Most specifically, there is the question of the adequacy of the neoclassical theory of the business firm. That theory is truly skeletal. As Professors Gabrie and Jacquier observe, the neoclassical business firm is little more than a production function and a cost curve that translate the costs of the factors of production into the costs (and hence the supply curves) of products. Institutional economists observe that in actual fact firms are much more than this: they are organizations, some of enormous size, that accomplish their work through the efforts of managers and other employees who have to be motivated to accept and retain their employment and to spend their working days furthering the objectives of the firm (its efficiency and profitability).

As the chapters of this volume show, the new institutional economics has focused on these questions—the terms of employment and the motivations for working toward the firm's goals—as the component of neoclassical theory most requiring amendment and amplification. The basic postulates of economic rationality are retained, and the amendment consists in introducing certain costs (transaction costs) and constraints on motivation (e.g., opportunism) and arguing that the economic system deals with them by means of actual or implied contracts and measures for enforcing them. The market flavor of all economic affairs is conserved by treating all relations among human agents as contractual relations governed by the laws of utility maximization, supply and demand. Even employment, which is strikingly different from the usual market relation of buyer and seller, is explained as a peculiar form of contract in which employers purchase authority over their employees. (As you will discover in Chapter III, I am one of those responsible for this point of view, in my essentially neoclassical interpretation of the employment relation.)

Little attention is given, in the new institutional theory of the firm, to organizational loyalty or identification: the possibility (indeed, the certainty) that membership in a work organization will engender loyalties to its goals and, perhaps even more important, will cause managers and other employees to envision the world in a company-centric fashion, much influenced by the highly selective environment of information in which they spend most of their waking hours. Instead, the theory assumes that people are mostly motivated by the prospect of personal economic gain (a much narrower concept than "utility gain," and a quite different one from "company gain"), and will respect their contractual obligations only to the degree that these can be enforced.

A second set of issues that the new institutional economics must address derive from neoclassical theory's core assumptions of perfect rationality and utility maximization. As Professors Gabrie and Jacquier show, these core assumptions are not generally questioned by the new institutional economics, unless we expand that term to include researchers who identify themselves by the rather different labels of "behavioral theory of the firm" and "evolutionary theory of the firm," people like Richard Cyert and James March, and Sidney Winter and Richard Nelson, respectively. Obviously I would align myself with these latter groups, in spite of my (and their) sometime use of the neoclassical apparatus to treat specific questions for which we regard it as appropriate and empirically defensible. In contrast to the advocates of the behavioral theory of the firm, who challenge the core assumptions of neoclassical theory, the new institutional economists with whom this book is mostly concerned do not offer such a challenge. The behavioral theorists find that the hypothesis of utility maximization does not conform to reality, and substitute for it a concept of bounded or limited rationality that takes into account the limits of human knowledge and of the abilities of decision makers to invent alternatives of choice and to compute consequences of proposed actions.

This brings me to the third class of issues, in many ways the most important. In our "neoclassical century" the search for solid empirical data to describe and explain economic behavior within the firm and to explain decision making in general has lagged far behind the elaboration of theory. Building theories and mathematical models of them has largely been an armchair exercise, and empirical economics has largely meant econometrics at a relatively high level of aggregation, aimed not so much at testing theory (which requires over-identified models) as at estimating parameters (which employs just-identified models). Milton Friedman and others have even tried to convert the paucity of data for testing the assumptions of economic theory into a virtue, claiming that the usefulness of a theory should be judged solely by its ability to predict aggregate outcomes, not by the correctness of the mechanisms it postulates for producing these outcomes. This view is not held by scientists in any other domain known to me. I do not want to debate the issue here (in a preface!) but simply call readers' attentions to the widespread acceptance in economics of this curious viewpoint.

When researchers have sought actually to observe the operation of basic economic processes, they have usually found that the assumptions of the neoclassical core theory are contradicted by their observations. Examples of such contradictions permeate the impressive empirical research on the consistency (or inconsistency) of human choice by Kahneman and Tversky and many others. As to business organization, works like *The Behavioral Theory of the Firm*, Chester Barnard's *The Functions of the Executive* and my own *Administrative Behavior* present a very different empirical picture of what goes on in business firms than the picture proposed by neoclassical theory, or even the picture drawn by the new institutional theories.

One of the progressive features of science, as distinguished, say, from theology, is that in the long run (sometimes a rather long run), disagreements about theory are settled empirically: it is gradually determined which theory best fits the facts. The important issues raised in this book about the differences between the new institutional economics and neoclassical economics, and about the partial dependence of the former on the latter, call for careful attention. But the issues are fundamentally empirical issues, and are only going to be settled when we learn what the facts are. To find the facts, we need new methods of empirical inquiry in economics to supplement, and in many cases to replace, the rather aggregative econometric methods that have dominated empirical economics. Reaching an understanding of the actual decision-making processes that determine the behavior of business firms and other economic actors calls for fact-gathering methods that have much higher resolutions and finer "grain sizes" than are typical in empirical economics today.

Fortunately, some of the needed methodologies are already at hand and have even been tested to a considerable extent. I refer especially to (1) two kinds of experimental methods: the choice experiments of Allais, Tversky, Kahneman and many others, and more recently, the experimental markets studied by Vernon Smith, Charles Plott and a growing number of other researchers; and (2) field studies that observe the actual decision processes within business firms, gather and analyze the verbal protocols and written records of the decision makers and use computer simulation programs to model them. Not only have these techniques gathered a mass of data in the past thirty years which provide extensive support for the new behavioral theories of limited rationality, but they have provided steadily improved methods for carrying out empirical work on decision-making processes. Regrettably, there has been a considerable lag in bringing these modern empirical methods into the standard curriculum for training economics graduate students. In the United States at least, business schools have been leading the way toward such training, but progress is still slow and doctoral degrees in economics are still awarded to numerous young scientists who have been taught no systematic ways of establishing facts beyond standard regression analysis.

As will be apparent from these remarks, my own view of the future of the theory of the firm, and economic theory generally, is more radical than are most of the views reviewed and analyzed in this book. I believe that the new institutional economics still gives too much credence to a highly rational utility-maximizing or profit-maximizing picture of economic actors. But I think there is great value in presenting the new institutional economics in a way that brings it into an understandable relation with neoclassical thought. This may be one important strategy for guiding economists, relatively few of whom are ready for a more radical rejection of neoclassical theory, in the direction of the Promised Land. The danger, of course (exemplified by the fate of Keynes), is that we may simply pour the new wine into old bottles, leading to a perception that nothing has changed. But if we pursue our empirical inquiries with vigor, the facts we discover will enable us, aided by books like this one, to explore and evaluate the intellectual underpinnings of alternative economic theories. I am grateful to the authors for lending their strength to the enterprise.

The stakes in the struggle to create an economic theory capable of explaining how economic institutions actually operate are not small. As Professors Gabrie and Jacquier emphasize, we are now engaged in a worldwide re-examination of the foundations of our economic institutions and their relation to our societies. This is not just an intellectual exercise; indeed, its main manifestations are not the writings of economists, but the real-world experiments, on the largest scale, that are now going on both in the nations that were until quite recently committed to Marxist doctrine and in those whose capitalist institutions have been buffeted by the winds of world trade and by international reallocations of people and resources on an unprecedented scale.

Central to this re-examination is an understanding of how business firms operate, of the effects upon their operations of different structures of ownership and control, of the relations between economic institutions and governmental and legal structures and above all, the respective roles of markets and organizations in the operation of the economy. All of these issues are addressed by the new institutional economics and the other heresies, revisionist or revolutionary, that Professors Gabrie and Jacquier examine in this valuable book.

IV.8 On the Behavioral and Rational Foundations of Economic Dynamics

1 Introduction

The study of the movement of economic systems through time has focused on two phenomena of particular interest and importance: the business cycle and long-run changes in technology and productivity. One of the impressive features of Joseph Schumpeter's economic theories is his unification of these two phenomena, accounting for business cycles as the byproducts of discontinuous advances in technology. The task I have set myself in this paper, however, is not to argue for this, or any other, particular theory of the business cycle or of economic development. Instead, I wish to look at the logical foundations of such theories, and particularly the assumption they make about the behavior of the human actors in the economic system.

If I may be permitted a personal remark, I observe that I am one of a very small number of pre-Keynesians present at this meeting.[1] By a pre-Keynesian I mean someone whose habits of thought about economics were already formed, or at least partially formed, before the publication of the *General Theory* in 1936. By that year I had already studied Ely's textbook, taken Henry Simons' course in price theory, and attended Henry Schultz's courses in econometrics. Of course, you cannot draw any strong conclusions about my economic views from those facts. Milton Friedman and Paul Samuelson are also pre-Keynesians, trained at the very same University of Chicago that I attended.

The significance of having a pre-Keynesian past is that it subjects one to occasional attacks of *deja vu*. Rational expectations theory, though innovative enough, does not come as a complete novelty to anyone who has reflected on Frank Knight's *Risk, Uncertainty, and Profit*. Reviewing the current explanations for the business cycle that are offered to us by monetarists, rational expectationists and supply siders, we may even convince ourselves that there is a genuine fifty-year cycle—not a business cycle but a cycle of business cycle theories.

Given the current disarray of macroeconomics, and the bewildering multiplicity of theories purporting to derive macroeconomic phenomena from microeconomic assumptions, it may be less useful to offer new ideas than to ask how we can winnow out the many and conflicting ideas we already have. In this paper, I will discuss the logical structure of some quite conventional ideas about how an economy like ours *might* operate. My main concern will be with the question of how we can subject these ideas to empirical test and use them effectively in the formulation of social policy.

Finally, I am among the economic majority who regard the heresies of Keynes as small (albeit important) heresies. Just as Luther accepted the Bible while rejecting the Pope, so Keynes' modes of reasoning in the *General Theory* are only locally heretical. His general form of argumentation is the one that is standard in economics: what might be called 'what would I do if I were a rational man' argumentation. So my remarks will cover Keynes as well as the classics.

2 Foundations of Classical and Neoclassical Theory

The economic theories that we call classical and neoclassical are based ostensibly on two tautologies and a postulate of rationality. The two tautologies are Say's Law (perhaps better referred to as the national income identity when intended as a tautology) and the monetary identity (alias the classical Quantity Theory of Money). The first of these says that, at any level of production, the income generated just covers the costs incurred. The second says that money changes hands at just the rate needed to cover total transactions.[2]

These laws can be thought of as describing a system in neutral equilibrium. A system governed by the national income identity can remain at full employment, or at a zero level of production. A system governed by the monetary identity can have stable prices or inflation, a high velocity of money or a low one. There is nothing in either law to produce a change in any of its variables—except, of course, in response to a change in one or more of the others. Nor is there anything inherent in the equations that forces the variables to remain constant.

We must be careful about thinking that, in labeling a law a tautology, we thereby make it innocuous. In fact, the tautological character of a law can only be determined in a context of the theory and observables in which it is embedded. Newton's Second Law, $F = ma$, is often referred to as a tautology—and so it is in a situation where only mass and acceleration can be observed. Then it is simply a definition of force. However, if independent operations exist for measuring the force applied to a body, then $F = ma$ is an empirical law, for it asserts that the measured force must equal the product of the independently measured mass and acceleration. (See 'The axioms of Newtonian mechanics', ch. 6.1 in my *Models of Discovery*; and 'The axiomatization of physical theories', ch. 6.5 of the same volume.)[3]

In much the same way, economic arguments can be, and frequently are, derived from Say's Law or the monetary equation by postulating something (often, *ceteris paribus*) about certain of the variables in the law and then deducing a relation among the others. Thus, we have the familiar argument that an increase in the quantity of money raises the price level (the velocity of money and the level of real product held constant). Say's Law lends itself to parallel arguments about an increased level of output 'creating' new demand by generating income.

Whenever we encounter such an argument, 'based on' Say's Law or the monetary equation, we must keep clearly in mind that the argument is really 'based on' the ceteris paribus or other auxiliary assumptions that are being made. We should not be seduced into accepting the argument because of its tautological appearance without careful consideration of the empirical bases for these auxiliary assumptions. Such assumptions commonly have the effect of transforming tautologies into conditions of equilibrium.

The third component of classical theories, the postulate of rationality, can take many forms. Its job is to get markets cleared by providing an opportunity for profit or increased utility whenever supply and demand do not balance, and to make sure that resources are used up to the proper margins. For a wide range of assumptions, rationality implies that, in equilibrium, people will have no motivation to modify their behaviors, and resources will be fully employed. The equilibrium need not, of course, be static. Instead, variables, exogenous or endogenous, like innovation, capital accumulation and population increases may produce a constantly changing steady state, but always with full employment of resources.

What is notably absent from these classical foundations is any specification of the mechanisms that restore equilibrium when it is disturbed. In fact, the only endogenous variable that is at all productive of dynamics in classical theory is the volume of capital, which is determined by the equilibrium requirements, and which in turn moves the system to new equilibria. In this respect it is much easier to derive a theory of economic development from the classical postulates than a theory of the business cycle. (Whether the theory thus derived is correct is a different question.)

I need to qualify the assertion that classical theory provides no specification of the mechanisms that restore equilibrium. The theory does assert that if the demand for a commodity is, for instance, below the supply at the market price, then suppliers will reduce the price and/or restrict the supply. What the theory does not provide, without additional postulates, is information about the relative magnitudes of the two adjustments or the rates at which they will occur.

The incomplete specification of the adaptive mechanisms leads to a problem and an opportunity. The problem is that it is precisely these mechanisms that determine the possibility and structure of cyclical movements about the equilibrium. The opportunity is to extend the postulate of rationality to specify a rational mode and rate of adjustment. Economic search theory and the theory of rational expectations are examples of responses to this challenge.

3 The 'Stylized Facts' of Dynamics

In his admirable little book, *Growth Theory*, Robert Solow reproduces the six 'stylized facts' that, according to Kaldor, characterize the process of economic growth in advanced economies:

1. Real output per man (or per man-hour) grows at a more or less constant rate over fairly long periods of time.

2. The stock of real capital grows at a more or less constant rate exceeding the rate of growth of labour input.

3. Moreover, the rates of growth of real output and the stock of capital goods tend to be about the same, so that the ratio of capital to output shows no systematic trend.

4. The rate of profit on capital has a horizontal trend.

5. The rate of growth of output per man can vary quite a lot from one country to another.

6. Economies with a high share of profits in income tend to have a high ratio of investment to output.[4]

There is a rather high level of agreement among economists, although not complete agreement, that these 'facts' do reasonably describe what has gone on in the economic growth of the advanced countries. A growth theory may be regarded as a plausible first approximation if it can predict (or retrodict) them; otherwise it is implausible. There is no guarantee that more than one theory will not pass the test, in which case new facts must be adduced that can discriminate among the competing theories, or some other criterion must be introduced that can select the 'correct' one.

Robert E. Lucas (1977) has provided a similar list of 'stylized facts' to describe what happens during business cycles. If his list will not command universal assent, it does not differ in important particulars from the lists that have been drawn up by others (e.g., by Mitchell in the essay whose title I have alluded to). Whatever the quarrels may be among business cycle theorists, they are not mainly quarrels about these facts.

> Technically, movements about trend in gross national product in any country can be well described by a stochastically disturbed difference equation of very low order. These movements do not exhibit uniformity of either period or amplitude, which is to say, they do not resemble the deterministic wave motions which sometimes arise in the natural sciences. Those regularities which are observed are in the *co-movements* among different aggregative time series.
>
> The principal among these are the following. (i) Output movements across broadly defined sectors move together. (In Mitchell's terminology, they exhibit high *conformity*, in modern time series language, they have high *coherence*.) (ii) Production of producer and consumer durables exhibits much greater amplitude than does the production of nondurables. (iii) Production and prices of agricultural goods and natural resources have lower than average conformity. (iv) Business profits show high conformity and much greater amplitude than other series. (v) Prices generally are procyclical. (vi) Short-term interest rates are procyclical; long-term rates slightly so. (vii) Monetary aggregates and velocity measures are procyclical.[5]

A business cycle theory may be regarded as a plausible first approximation if it can predict (or retrodict) these facts; otherwise it is implausible. Again, we may have to introduce additional considerations if we find ourself faced with several theories capable of explaining these facts.

A growth theory or a business cycle theory cannot be regarded as veridical, then, merely because it reproduces the appropriate collection of stylized facts. The empirical claims contained in these lists are so general that many theories, many different sets of structural equations, might fit them. But different structural equations will lead to different policy recommendations, and whenever structure changes, to different predictions. Why not test theories by comparing them with the aggregate empirical data instead of the derived stylized facts? The general answer is that any theory that will reproduce the stylized facts can very likely be fitted to the aggregate data with an R^2 value well over 0.9. [Nelson and Winter (1982, pp. 218–230) provide an example and a discussion of the problem in the context of growth models. Adelman and Adelman (1959) constructed a classical illustration of how a Keynesian macromodel can fit the stylized facts describing the statistical structure of business cycles.] It seems also that the details of the empirical data that go beyond the stylized facts in situations like these are also well below the noise level, and contain little information that can be used for model identification or prediction. As Leontief and Orcutt, among others, have pointed out, the idea of validating economic theories with aggregative data is a will-o'-the-wisp that has led econometrics down the garden path of ever more sophisticated statistical methodologies. The ponderousness of contemporary econometric techniques simply crushes the fragile data to which they are applied.

In the physical sciences, when errors of measurement and other noise are found to be of the same order of magnitude as the phenomena under study, the response is not to try to squeeze more information out of the data by statistical means; it is instead to find techniques for observing the phenomena at a higher level of resolution. The corresponding strategy for economics is obvious: to secure new kinds of data at the micro level, data that will provide direct evidence about the behavior of economic agents and the ways in which they go about making their decisions. [Support for this thesis comes from surprising directions. See Lucas (1980, pp. 288–289.)] a major purpose of this paper is to show how and why such empirical data are essential for the future development of economics.

4 The Formal Mechanisms for Dynamics

The mathematics of differential and difference equations delimits for us the range of mechanisms that are available for representing the dynamics of economic systems. The two most likely candidates are systems of linear equations subject to random shocks, and non-linear systems (with or without shocks) possessing limit cycles.

Linear systems call for exogenous shocks to drive them (e.g. sunspots, oil shocks). The systems themselves need to be stable, so that they will tend to return to equilibrium whenever displaced. The coefficients of all of the adjustment mechanisms are free parameters. They can, of course, be estimated from the empirical time series data themselves, but only with the loss of large numbers of degrees of freedom.

Non-linear systems have the attractive feature that they may behave in cyclical fashion, traversing so-called 'limit cycles', even in the absence of exogenous shocks. To explain real data with them, not only their parameters but also the forms of their functions must be estimated—or postulated. Again, these estimates may be made from available time series data at the cost of some degrees of freedom.

In the past forty years, an enormous number of dynamic models of these kinds, small, medium and large, have been fitted to empirical data. As we are all aware, these model-fitting exercises have not led to much consensus as to what is the right theory. A chief problem is that the parameter values turn out usually not to be very robust. As rational expectationists are fond of pointing out, coefficients estimated from past data often fail badly as predictors of the future. (Rational expectationists are especially pleased with this non-robustness of the coefficients of non-equilibrium theories because their theory leads them to expect it. The robustness of their own coefficients has not yet been tested extensively.)

5 The Behavioral Sources of Long-term Dynamics

We have now set the formal terms of our inquiry. We wish to know what kinds of assumptions will allow us to build dynamic models that possess the characteristics defined by the 'stylized facts' we have listed. But we will also be closely concerned with the bases, logical or empirical, for these assumptions. First, we will discuss models of long-term growth, and then turn to models of the business cycle.

I have already indicated in very general terms some ways in which dynamic movement is produced in long-term growth models and in models of the business cycle. For long-term growth in classical theory, three variables are important: one of these (technical innovation) produces a continuing shift in the production function. The other two, population and capital, produce a continuing growth in the factors of production. In most models, the shift in the production function and population are exogenous, while the capital formation is endogenous. A thoroughgoing pursuit of the goals of classical theory would try to define the processes of innovation and population growth as well as capital formation in economic terms—that is, to turn all of them into endogenous variables.

In a formal way, it is perfectly feasible to produce a theory of technical innovation based on the postulate of rationality. Since innovation is presumably produced by the investment of human and capital resources, we introduce a new production function for innovation, and equate the value of the marginal product of innovation with its cost. From a formal standpoint, we have simply replaced the task of estimating an exogenous variable, the rate of innovation, with the task of estimating the parameters of a function, the production function for innovation. The only obvious gain from the replacement is that we can now rest comfortably in the knowledge that everything is proceeding rationally. Human rationality is now only bounded by the characteristics of the external environment: the quality of the ore that is mined by the innovation production process. Of course, if we examine the metaphor too closely we see that 'quality' of the 'ore' is a euphemism for 'effectiveness of the thought processes of the human beings who are doing the innovating.' We have not removed the constraint from the human brain, just relocated it, so to speak, from one hemisphere to the other.

Something similar can be said about endogenizing the process of population growth. All we need here is something like the marginal utility of a child, and a reasonable respect for the technology of contraception. But Gary Becker and others have already built such a theory for us. By gently manipulating the part of the utility function that contains children, almost any kind of population growth function can be matched. Of course it might take considerable imagination to devise a function that would provide a rational explanation for fluctuations in the American birth rate over the past fifty years. Perhaps we would need, after all, some occasional alteration in the utility function, some changes in taste, to accommodate the data.

The conclusion that I draw is that to build an interesting and useful theory of long-term economic growth, even for developed countries, we have to go behind the principle of rationality. First, with respect to the production function we need an empirically based theory of innovation—a Schumpeterian component.[6] I say 'Schumpeterian' because the theory has to explain not merely that most inventors and 'risk capitalists' are motivated by the prospect of gain, but also has to specify just what the circumstances are under which those prospects will seem rosy and the circumstances under which they will seem bleak. Surely, a successful theory will have a large historical component—the prospects of gain from investment in genetic engineering are not independent of recollections of gain (one's own or others') from investments in electronics. A phenomenon that depends critically upon the strengths of beliefs in extremely uncertain events, as well as upon acquisition of esoteric and rapidly changing knowledge about new technological developments, must be influenced by psychological mechanisms that go far beyond the principle of rationality.

Second, the rationality principle will also do little to explain rates of population growth unless complemented by a historical and psychosociological theory of the determinants of the 'utility' of children. If we object that such historicizing, psychologizing and sociologizing are not the business of economics, then we must conclude that the objector thinks that long-term growth theory is not the business of economics.

6 The Business Cycle: Shocks

There is no difficulty in specifying various sources of unpredicted shocks as a means for causing departures of an economy from equilibrium. The weather is a perennial source of such shocks for economies that have an important agricultural component. The Oil Shocks provided spectacular examples of another sort, while wars, revolutions, and even elections supply a continuing sequence of disequilibrating events.

If we were to carry the logic of neoclassical economics to its limit, we would want to predict even these events (omitting the weather) as endogenous products of rational cogitation. However, a more limited goal, and the one usually accepted by economic theory, is to introduce them as unpredictable, hence unexpected, events. Then, in rational expectations theory, they need only be reacted to, not foretold.

Shocks, defined in this way, can make a valuable contribution to the testing of economic theories. For if they are genuinely unpredicted, they can be used after the fact to identify economic models and improve our estimates of their parameters. If there has been any systematic discussion in the economic literature of methods of exploiting this information, it has escaped my attention.

In business cycle theory we are concerned with the ways in which economic agents respond when they are faced with departures from equilibrium, or with expectations of such departures. Rather than discuss the matter in general terms, I think it more useful first to take up some examples: the inventory cycle, responses to price changes, and 'permanent' (or is it 'natural'?) unemployment.

7 Inventory Cycles

A businessman may receive signals from the economic system indicating that he is currently supplying more of his product than can be sold in the market at the current price. The usual signals are that inventories of finished product are increasing in stores or warehouses, or if the product is made to order, that new orders are arriving more slowly than products are being shipped. He may respond to these signals in a variety of ways—even ignoring them at his peril. He may reduce prices; he may reduce the production rate. If he reduces the production rate, he may reduce his labor force, put them on shorter hours, or simply divert some of them to maintenance work of some kind. In addition to price and product adjustments, he may increase (or decrease) his advertising, reorganize his sales efforts and sales organization, modify his product, or promise shorter delivery times. The actions he might take are limited only by his ability to imagine possible decision variables, and the range of values that each might take.

Moreover, there are many signals besides increasing inventories that might trigger the actions. The excess supply may be predicted prior to the actual accumulation of inventories or the depletion of orders and the prediction, in turn, may be based on many kinds of information, ranging from astrology, through the pages of the *Wall Street Journal*, to the latest turn of the Wharton model.

A business cycle theory must, somehow, capture or sum up these reactions—not for any single businessman, but for the aggregate of enterprises. This is usually done by introducing aggregate equations that are copies, writ large, of what is imagined to be the response process at the micro level. Of course the copy is not supposed to reproduce all the detail and variety of the individual functions, but only their gross, most important, features.

Now since management scientists and operations analysts have been rummaging about in business firms for many years, and since production scheduling has been one of their favorite concerns, we have a great deal of information—although it is rather unsystematic information not easily summarized in statistical distributions—about how inventories and production rates are actually controlled. I would like to make some generalizations, based on this knowledge, that I think could be verified by systematic sampling. First, production responses are more common than price responses, at least in the early stages of inventory buildup. This is probably not unrelated to the fact that prices are usually constructed by marking up costs. Second, in most business firms the response strategies are not formalized; responses are made 'judgmentally' by executives without definite rules to guide them. Third, the decisions about rates of production are often made by different persons, using different procedures, than the decisions about prices. These are 'stylized facts' at the micro level, accepted by most persons who have spent much time in business firms.

To avoid dropping into 'anything-can-happen' mode, let me describe an actual formal decision rule that has been devised to govern the production-level decision, and which has had at least some modest application to real factory situations: the so-called 'linear decision rule' devised by Holt, Modigliani, Muth and Simon (1960) (two Keynesians, a rational expectationist and a behavioralist!). Simply stated, the rule determines the desired level of production for the next scheduling period as a function of current inventories and expected values of sales for future periods. The level selected by the rule maximizes the present value of the expected profit stream for the given sales estimates, production function and cost of holding inventories. (A generalized form of the rule also makes decisions about the level of the labor force.) The price of the product, and the possibility of changing the price, are entirely ignored in the decision; the problem is to produce at minimum cost the stream of product that will be required to meet the predicted future sales.

Now I do not wish to claim that the linear decision rule solves the right optimization problem. But in my many conversations about the rule with practicing managers, I have never heard it criticized for its omission of price considerations, or as being over-simple. From this, I am tempted to conclude that the other rules used in industry are probably no more complex, and moreover, that there is probably a considerable variety of them, using different signaling information and different decision variables. Different decision rules and different forecasting procedures imply different dynamic behavior of the firm, and of the economy when the behavior of many firms is aggregated. Moreover, the rules and forecasts that firms use are subject to learning and fashion. That would be no great matter if the changes in them were random and independent, but they almost certainly are not.

It would not require an unconscionable amount of research effort to obtain, by investigations carried out in individual firms, a fairly good picture of the strategies actually used by firms to modulate their production levels. Such a picture would certainly provide a more satisfactory basis for an aggregate production decision rule than a complete reliance on aggregate time series for selecting relevant variables and estimating parameters. It could also provide some information about the circumstances that might cause firms to change their response strategies, and hence some basis for anticipating structural changes in the aggregative model.

In investigating and describing the production decision rules used by business firms, one aspect of particular interest would be the use or nonuse of forecasts of future sales, and the procedures for arriving at those forecasts. A decision rule that simply reacts to current inventory levels is a feedback system that is guaranteed to generate temporally damped cycles, but to amplify them each step backward in the production chain—from ultimate customers to producers of capital goods. Hence, if we found that such passive, reactive feedback systems were common (as I strongly suspect may be the case), we would have one source of explanation for Lucas' first and second stylized facts.

Introduction of sales forecasts into the decision rules could change the dynamics of a system drastically. If sales estimates were based on the extrapolation of recent history, they would not make a fundamental difference to the dynamic behavior of production rates. However, if expectations were formed in other ways (e.g., in whatever ways it is supposed that 'rational' expectations are formed), the sales forecasts could be either strongly stabilizing or strongly destabilizing. Possibilities for destabilization would be especially great if many firms drew upon the same sources of information for their forecasts.

Since these conclusions follow from well-known general properties of feedback and feedforward control systems, I will not try to justify them in detail here. I simply wish to point out that we cannot be satisfied that a theory explains the observed facts of the business cycle without knowing a good deal about the precise forecasting methods that it assumes. That brings me to the topic of rational expectations. But instead of discussing it in the context of inventory cycles, I would like to consider how businessmen respond to changes in the price level, and the relation of these responses to all types of business cycles.

8 Responses to Price Level Changes

An attractive feature of theories that incorporate rational expectations is that they purport to give a general explanation of how businessmen estimate future sales and prices, and hence to foreclose the need for any empirical inquiry into forecasting. We can ask, even of these theories, what information they use to estimate the structural parameters that determine equilibrium, but I wish, instead, to finesse that question and explore in another direction.

If expectations are formed rationally, in the most clear-eyed sense of that phrase, then the corresponding economic systems tend to steer very rapidly toward equilibrium and it becomes very difficult to understand how they can experience consequential cycles of any kind. It is interesting to see how Lucas deals with this difficulty. In brief, he handles it by assuming that forecasters are rational, but not *very* rational. He starts with the proposition that 'one would like a theory which accounts for the observed movements in *quantities* (employment, consumption, investment) as an optimizing response to observed movements in *prices*'.[7] But 'optimizing response' does not rule out delusions or illusions. For the critical assumption in Lucas' model, the assumption that creates the cycle, is that there is 'confusion on the part of agents between relative and general price movements'.[8] The unmoved mover is not the assumption of rationality, but an auxiliary assumption (unmotivated by empirical data) of a very particular failure of rationality—a failure of the businessman to interpret correctly the price information that is known to him.[9]

It appears that rational expectations theory, thus emended to account for the business cycle, does not at all relieve us of the burden of empirical inquiry at the microeconomic level. Instead, it instructs us loudly and clearly that to obtain a validated theory of the cycle, we must know not only what price signals the businessman receives and responds to, but also what misapprehensions he suffers under while he is interpreting these signals. Without such empirical inquiry, we are faced with the most casual of empiricisms. Removing this difficulty would seem to call for a rapid convergence of the research program of rational expectations to the program of behavioralism.

The problem to which I have just called attention—the critical role of 'irrationalities' in Lucas' business cycle theory—is not peculiar to that theory, or to rational expectationist theories, for that matter. Departures from rationality are endemic in classical and neoclassical economic theories. In earlier days, they were often described as 'stickinesses'. In partial equilibrium analysis, they take the form of ceteris paribus assumptions. In contemporary dynamic simultaneous-equation models, they most often show up as response rate parameters that determine which of the mechanisms in a system operate rapidly and which operate slowly. Whatever their form, conclusions about dynamic behavior and short-term equilibrium are extremely sensitive to them.

Since this last point is as important as it is obvious, I would like to perseverate upon it for a moment. In our research on near-decomposability, Albert Ando and I gave a formal rationale for partial equilibrium analysis, and for separating the short-term from the long-term dynamics of any system. The idea is that if a system can be 'nearly decomposed' into discrete subsystems by ignoring small coefficients, then the short-term dynamics of each subsystem can be determined by examining it independently of the others. This very strong conclusion, conversely, demonstrates the criticality of the choice of 'small' coefficients for the inferences one draws about a system's dynamic behavior.

The formal analysis of near-decomposability teaches us that rationality assumptions by themselves cannot provide macroeconomics with a satisfactory microeconomics. In addition, there remains at the very least the empirical task of determining which of the parameters is small enough to be ignored in partial equilibrium or (what is the same thing) short-term analysis. And a behavioralist would argue that the best way to do that is to look at behavior in the small—at the level of the individual firm.

Rational expectations theory moves the locus of parameter estimation, but does not eliminate the task. Moreover, as the particular example of Lucas' business cycle theory shows, it usually requires also its own complement of 'stickinesses' to make it fit the facts. The particular stickiness that Lucas proposes for his theory is a form of the money illusion. Let me try to put that illusion (as well as others) in a little broader psychological perspective.

The rationality assumptions of classical theory require implicitly that the economic actor attend to all of the important variables about which he has to make decisions or that can inform him in his decisions. Whether that is easy or hard to do—or even possible—depends on how many relevant variables there are in the world. In any realistic description of the environment of a human decision maker, the variables and information to which he might attend (and to which he must attend to satisfy the strict requirements of rationality) are innumerable. The hypothesis of bounded rationality claims that human beings handle this difficulty by attending to only a small part of the complexity about them. They make a highly simplified model of the world, and they make their decisions in terms of that model and the subset of variables that enter into it.

Now this approach may work very well (and may even give a good approximation to Olympian rationality) if the number of very important variables is small at any given time, *and* if this list of important variables does not change from time to time without the change being noticed. The decision maker of bounded rationality has both the problem of dealing with a simplified model of the decision situation *and* of noticing when he needs to change his model. Attentional mechanisms are critical to the quality of his rationality.

If the price level is not changing significantly, then one does not suffer from the money illusion if one fails to discriminate between real and money prices. One good way to simplify the world model in a world of stable prices is to ignore the distinction. That is almost certainly what most of us did in our economic decisions twenty years ago. At some point in time, however, we became aware that prices were no longer stable, and we began to take the price level into consideration; we began to index our commitments. The discrepancies between real and monetary quantities became so large that our attention was drawn to them as important enough—among the myriad of things we could consider—for our consideration.

Here we have a major discontinuity in the economic process, a major structural shift taking place from one set of mechanisms to another. The dynamics of the economic system depends on the timing of this shift, which of course will not be made by all persons simultaneously. To handle this discontinuity, and others like it, in our theories, we have to choose among three alternatives. The first is to treat attentional shift as an exogenous random shock. Then we simply give up the attempt to explain or predict it. The second is to apply the familiar marginal arguments: We allocate just as much effort to scanning the horizon for newly important variables as is justified by the marginal value (in terms of improved decision making) of the scanning. This second alternative is vacuous, providing us with no clue as to how these marginal costs and benefits are to be estimated. The third alternative is to study human attention and shifts of attention empirically in order to develop a theory of individual and social determinants of focus of attention. This important task of empirical inquiry has not yet been addressed by the economics profession.

9 The Debate on Unemployment

As a final example of how auxiliary assumptions or irrationality, or rather, bounded rationality, complement assumptions of perfect rationality in economic theories, both classical and Keynesian, I should like to turn to the much discussed topic of unemployment. The literature on this topic is so enormous that I don't really need to make any new arguments, but can simply point to those that have been made and repeated many times. Let me start with the notion, currently popular in some circles, of 'natural level of unemployment'.[10]

The most familiar of Keynes' local heresies was to introduce high viscosity into the adjustment of the wage level in order to permit the economic system to reside for considerable periods of time in a condition of below-equilibrium employment. The radical (should I call it 'ultraclassical'?) alternative to the Keynesian heresy is to insist that labor supply and demand are always in equilibrium, no matter what the official statistics of unemployment say. The level of unemployment is natural—all of those wanting empolyment at the current wage rate are employed.

The debate about natural levels of employment and unemployment can turn into a very refined philosophical discussion of the meaning of the phrase 'wanting employment'. Though I haven't seen it done, it might even be transformed into a classical discussion of free will versus determinism. But I think the debate misses the real issue, which has been pointed out by Thurow among others: Observed rates of unemployment fluctuate greatly from year to year. A theory that dismisses these fluctuations as irrelevant throws away an important aspect of the dynamics of the economic system. Why do these fluctuations occur, and what impact, in turn, do they have upon the other variables of the system?

A curious feature of the debate, nearly as true of the Keynesians as of their opponents, is that almost no one (Thurow is again a recent and notable exception) seems to question that there *is* a labor market in which workers offer their services at one or another price and/or employers simultaneously offer employment at one or another wage.

Thurow asks a very refreshing and revealing question: What *in fact* happens if an unemployed person presents himself to a business firm and offers to work (in a job for which he is qualified) at a wage below that being paid to the current occupant of a position? Here again, I would prefer to seek our answer by systematic empirical inquiry than by the methods of casual empiricism. Since I am not familiar with any inquiry into the question, I will hazard a casual answer. The offer would be refused, probably politely. If the jobseeker persisted, on the grounds that he was simply behaving as his economics textbook said he should, he would soon be referred for psychiatric examination.

For whatever good or bad reasons, employers during periods of high unemployment do not usually dismiss their current labor force and hire another at a lower wage. Sometimes, in extremity, they threaten to close down if their employees will not accept wage cuts. But I am reciting (stylized) facts that are familiar to all of us, no matter how indirect our information about labor markets.

Economic theory has been satisfied to substitute a hypothetical 'labor market'—whether the sticky one of Keynes or the perfectly adjusting one of the classical theory—for an actual study of the decisional and behavioral processes that lead to employees being dismissed and to job offers being made and being accepted or rejected. In the hypothetical labor market, the actors are, in some definable sense, 'rational'. But the assumption of their rationality does not provide answers to the important economic questions about the market. The actual level of employment predicted by such theories derives not from the rationality assumption, but from the particular limits that are supposed to operate on that rationality—whether they be stickiness of wages (Keynes) or unexplained shifts in the balance of preference for work and leisure (natural rate of unemployment).

One does not have to be a Marxist to notice an assymetry between the roles of employee and employer in the real labor market. Before there can be an offer or acceptance of employment, there must be a *job* to be filled. And jobs exist in the minds of employers. Employers decide, from time to time, that they want a work force of a certain size and composition. To be sure, these decisions are not made in a vacuum; they are made in the anticipation of profit, and in the light of a host of expectations about prices of output, costs of production and the quality of labor that could be hired at various wage rates. However they are made, there is a genuine decisional process going on here, involving all kinds of guesses, hopes and fears about the future, whose dynamics is central to the dynamics of the whole economic system. Since armchair conjecturing about what this process *must* be has only led to disagreement and confusion in the economics profession, it is probably not too soon to begin investigating empirically what the process actually is.

The picture I have just painted of the labor market is thoroughly Schumpeterian. Schumpeter focused mainly on those empolyers who were innovatively introducing new products, but the problem is not very different for employers in general. Employers must envision and 'create' jobs, before labor markets can operate. And if the number of jobs created is less than the number of workers available at the going wage, the difference between these numbers will show up in the official statistics as unemployment. It is less a matter of explaining how there can be a departure from equilibrium than it is of explaining how a system so constructed manges to keep close to equilibrium (as it does) much of the time.

Again, I must stop short of stating the answer to the question I raise. For my basic point is that, to find the answer, we must study the decision process in much greater depth and with far greater thoroughness than it has ever been studied.

10 Studying the Bounds on Rationality

A few main themes recur repeatedly in the previous sections. I should now like to sum up the findings of those sections in a new set of 'stylized facts'—this time, facts about the status and prospects of economic theory.

1. There is broad agreement, at the level of aggregate statistics, on the principal facts of economic growth in the developed countries, and the facts of business cycles, unemployment and inflation.

2. It is not likely that important new facts can be obtained by applying sophisticated statistical techniques to aggregate time series. The residual fluctuations in the data are mostly below the level of random noise.

3. The picture revealed by the agreed-upon facts about growth and cycles does not have high enough resolution to choose between major alternative economic theories. But different theories, all consistent with the aggregate data, lead to different policy prescriptions and to different predictions whenever structure changes.

4. The stylized facts of economic growth and business cycles cannot be derived from the rationality postulates of classical and neoclassical theory without introducing essential qualifications of those postulates. These qualifications take the form of assumptions of bounded rationality (e.g., the money illusion), or assumptions of exogenous shocks (e.g., unmotivated shifts in work-leisure preferences). Both neoclassical and Keynesian writings are mottled with such auxiliary assumptions, and their conclusions would not follow if the assumptions were removed. In fact, with removal of the auxiliary assumptions, which have mainly to do with the ways in which expectations are formed about uncertain future events, the neoclassical and Keynesian theories would become indistinguishable.

5. The auxiliary assumptions one finds in neoclassical and Keynesian analyses have no secure empirical base. They generally derive from the most casual of casual empiricisms. They are not adequately supported by aggregate data for the reasons already given. They are not adequately supported by micro-level data (data derived from actual studies of the decision-making processes of consumers and in business firms), because such data have not been gathered systematically for most of the phenomena under study.

A rather obvious conclusion follows from these facts: that the continuing progress of the economic theory of change and cycles requires massive empirical work at the level of the economic agents who make decisions—for example, the consumer and the firm. The dynamics of the economic system depends critically on just how economic agents go about making their decisions, and no way has been found for discovering how they do this that avoids direct inquiry into and observation of the processes.

This thesis, sometimes called Behavioralism, has been opposed on a number of grounds. First, it has been opposed as an abandonment of the principle of rationality. I have tried to show here that the principle of rationality has already been abandoned, and abandoned in fundamental ways, by classicists, neoclassicists, Keynesians, and rational expectationists alike. No new abandonment is proposed; just a major effort to discover which modes of abandonment are empirically defensible.

A second objection (e.g., Blaug) is that Behavioralism has not yet produced a complete theory that can compete with the classical one. It is not a theory, but a set of hopes and promises of a future theory. Blaug argues that you cannot beat something with nothing; there is no reason to abandon the neoclassical theory until a new theory is in place. This is a Catch 22 argument: behavioralism can't be developed without being pursued empirically; but there is no reason for pursuing it since it does not offer, here and now, an alternative to classical theory.

Behavioralism does not hold forward the hope of a theory that can be arrived at in an armchair. The new theory can only be built through extensive empirical research—on the scale, let us say, of the empirical research of the last century or two in field biology or geology. Moreover, the required research is of a kind that is novel to most economists. It does not rest on statistical data derived from secondary sources, but calls for direct observation of human behavior in the market and in the firm. The reason for undertaking that research is that the classical program has failed: it patches the rationality principle with ad hoc assumptions of bounded rationality, but it has no way to choose among alternative patches without obtaining new data. And macroeconomic studies are not a viable source for such data.

Empirical research on human decision making at the microeconomic level need not be, and should not be, a blind accumulation of facts. Priorities among the areas of decision to be investigated can be determined by the needs of macroeconomics. But there is an even more powerful source of heuristics for guiding the research. During the past twenty five years there has been developed in cognitive psychology a theory of the information processes that account for human problem solving and decision making for a wide variety of tasks.[11] The theory has by now reached the point where it has a good deal to say about complex, professional level human cognitive activities, like making medical decisions, using financial statements to identify and analyze corporate problems, or making investment decisions. In parallel with the theory, a methodology has been developed for using verbal thinking-aloud protocols and other verbal responses as empirical data for testing hypotheses about information processes, and a powerful technology for modeling the processes as computer programs and simulating their behavior. The substantive and methodological content of this work in cognitive psychology provide a theoretical framework for empirical work in microeconomics that was not available a decade or two ago. Lack of theoretical or methodological guidelines is no longer a credible reason for delaying the construction of an empirically based microeconomics.

11 Requirements for a Schumpeterian Dynamics

Let me end on a more substantive note, deriving from the earlier discussion of the labor market. In the language of classical economics there is little room for a fundamental asymmetry between the two parties to a bargain. There is no room for a concept like 'initiative'. In a Walrasian tâtonnement it is irrelevant who makes the first bid. Similarly, there is no distinction in classical economics between action and inaction. Each time period, the actors must choose some value of each decision value, and there is no special value called 'inaction'. An investment level of zero is not qualitatively different in the theory from a level of 100.

In the everyday world, matters are quite different. We do distinguish certain states as states of inaction. In a baseball game, 0-0 is a possible score, but there is a difference between a tie game and a day on which no game was played. Inaction is the state that prevails when no positive action is being undertaken, and it is qualitatively different from action. Action has to be motivated. The actor must attend to some stimulus, external or internal, that leads him to consider action relevant to it. In the absence of motivation, inaction prevails.

Applying these ideas to economic affairs, we arrive at a picture of them that looks very different from Walrasian equilibrium. In the Walrasian picture, there is at all times a fixed set of markets, each with its supply function and demand function and a price fluctuating around the equilibrium value. Markets are neither created nor destroyed. In an economy where actions must be positively motivated (let me call it a Schumpeterian economy), commodities are produced only after someone is motivated to consider producing them. Investments are made only when someone is motivated to pay attention to a potential investment opportunity and decides to invest. Job slots are created only when employers attend to the need for more workers and decide to try to employ them.

In a Schumpeterian world, human attention is a central endogenous variable, whose determination is a key to the direction and level of activity of the economic system, both in the long run and in the short. Attention, in turn, is a function of the information and communication flows in the society. There are habits of attention, a potent source of inertia and stability. There are also trends and fads in attention—societies as well as individuals may be said to have changing foci of attention.

There is a good deal of room for traditional economic variables in such a world. Economic actors may attend to prices, and they may become aware of, and be motivated to anticipate, the possibilities for price changes. One might even say that a Schumpeterian model is simply a next step in the same direction as that in which economic theories have been moving for forty years. During that time we shifted from an almost exclusive preoccupation with statics to a full concern with dynamics. We introduced expectations into the dynamic model, first describing those expectations as adaptations to the memory of the recent past. Then we (or the rational expectationists among us) took the leap of making expectations depend on an understanding of the economic system itself.

A very natural next step for economics is to maintain expectations in the strategic position they have come to occupy, but to build an empirically validated theory of how attention is in fact directed within a social system, and how expectations are, in fact, formed. Taking that next step requires that empirical work in economics take a new direction, the direction of micro-level investigation proposed by Behavioralism.

Notes

1. The original text of this footnote has been deleted as it only referred to the conference which is now subject of this book.

2. These brief statements are intended to identify the tautologies, not to characterize them with any precision.

3. Simon (1977).

4. Solow (1970, pp. 2–3).

5. Lucas (1977).

6. Nelson and Winter (1982).

7. Lucas (1977, p. 14).

8. Lucas (1977, p. 22).

9. Of course, in neoclassical theory these failures are not treated as irrationalities, but as rational responses to imperfect information. Whatever they are called, they will be understood only if they are subjected to empirical study at the microlevel. They cannot be deduced as consequences of the rationality assumption.

10. If awards were made for outrageous audaciousness in the coining of terms, certainly the author of 'natural level of unemployment' would deserve one, as would Jack Muth, the author of 'rational expectations'. The virtue of such terms is that they win the argument instantly by taking the breath away from would-be disputants, whose very skepticism now accuses them of 'unnaturalness' or 'irrationality', as the case may be.

11. See, for example, Newell and Simon (1972).

References

Adelman, I. and F. L. Adelman, 1959, The dynamic properties of the Klein-Goldberger Model, Econometrica 27, 596–625.

Becker, G. S., 1981, A treatise on the family (Harvard University Press, Cambridge, MA).

Blaug, M., 1980, The methodology of economics (Cambridge University Press, Cambridge).

Hicks, J. R., 1950, The trade cycle (The Clarendon Press, Oxford).

Holt, C. C., F. Modigliani, J. F. Muth and H. A. Simon, 1960, Planning production, inventories and work force (Prentice-Hall, Englewood Cliffs, NJ).

Keynes, J. M., 1936, The general theory of employment, interest and money (Macmillan, London).

Leontief, W., 1971, Theoretical assumptions and nonobserved facts, American Economic Review 61, 1–7.

Lucas, R. E., Jr., 1977, Understanding business cycles, in: K. Brunner and A. Meltzer, eds., Stabilization of the domestic and international economy (North-Holland, Amsterdam).

Lucas, R. E., Jr., 1980, Methods and problems in business cycle theory, in: Studies in business-cycle theory (The MIT Press, Cambridge, MA).

Muth, J. F., 1961, Rational expectations and the theory of price movements, Econometrica 29, 315–335.

Nelson, R. R. and S. G. Winter, 1982, An evolutionary theory of economic change (Harvard University Press, Cambridge, MA).

Newell, A. and H. A. Simon, 1972, Human problem solving (Prentice-Hall, Englewood Cliffs, NJ).

Samuelson, P. A., 1947, Foundations of economic analysis (Harvard University Press, Cambridge, MA).

Schumpeter, J. A., 1934, The theory of economic development (Harvard University Press, Cambridge, MA).

Simon, H. A., 1977, Models of discovery (D. Reidel, Dordrecht).

Simon, H. A. and A. Ando, 1961, Aggregation of variables in dynamic systems, Econometrica 29, 111–138.

Solow, R. M., 1970, Growth theory (Oxford University Press, Oxford).

Thurow, L. C., 1983, Dangerous currents: The state of economics (Random House, New York).

Turnovsky, S. J., 1977, Macroeconomic analysis and stabilization policies (Cambridge University Press, Cambridge).

IV.9 Rationality in Psychology and Economics

The task I shall undertake here is to compare and contrast the concepts of rationality that are prevalent in psychology and economics, respectively. Economics has almost uniformly treated human behavior as rational. Psychology, on the other hand, has always been concerned with both the irrational and the rational aspects of behavior. In this paper, irrationality will be mentioned only obliquely; my concern is with rationality. Economics sometimes uses the term "irrationality" rather broadly (e.g., Becker 1962) and the term "rationality" correspondingly narrowly, so as to exclude from the domain of the rational many phenomena that psychology would include in it. For my purposes of comparison, I will have to use the broader conception of psychology.

One point should be set immediately outside dispute. Everyone agrees that people have reasons for what they do. They have motivations, and they use reason (well or badly) to respond to these motivations and reach their goals. Even much, or most, of the behavior that is called abnormal involves the exercise of thought and reason. Freud was most insistent that there is method in madness, that neuroses and psychoses were patients' solutions—not very satisfactory solutions in the long run—for the problems that troubled them.

I emphasize this point of agreement at the outset—that people have reasons for what they do—because it appears that economics sometimes feels called on to defend the thesis that human beings are rational. Psychology has no quarrel at all with this thesis. If there are differences in viewpoint, they must lie in conceptions of what constitutes rationality, not in the fact or rationality itself.

The judgment that certain behavior is "rational" or "reasonable" can be reached only by viewing the behavior in the context of a set of premises or "givens." These givens include the situation in which the behavior takes place, the goals it is aimed at realizing, and the computational means available for determining how the goals can be attained. In the course of this conference, many participants referred to the context of behavior as its "frame," a label that I will also use from time to time. Notice that the frame must be comprehensive enough to encompass goals, the definition of the situation, and computational resources.

In its treatment of rationality, neoclassical economics differs from the other social sciences in three main respects: (a) in its silence about the content of goals and values; (b) in its postulating global consistency of behavior; and (c) in its postulating "one world"—that behavior is objectively rational in relation to its total environment, including both present and future environment as the actor moves through time.

In contrast, the other social sciences, in their treatment of rationality, (a) seek to determine empirically the nature and origins of values and their changes with time and experience; (b) seek to determine the processes, individual and social, whereby selected aspects of reality are noticed and postulated as the "givens" (factual bases) for reasoning about action; (c) seek to determine the computational strategies that are used in reasoning, so that very limited information-processing capabilities can cope with complex realities; and (d) seek to describe and explain the ways in which nonrational processes (e.g., motivations, emotions, and sensory stimuli) influence the focus of attention and the definition of the situation that set the factual givens for the rational processes.

These important differences in the conceptualization of rationality rest on an even more fundamental distinction: in economics, rationality is viewed in terms of the choices it produces; in the other social sciences, it is viewed in terms of the processes it employs (Simon 1976/1982). The rationality of economics is substantive rationality, while the rationality of psychology is procedural rationality.

Substantive and Procedural Rationality

If we accept values as given and consistent, if we postulate an objective description of the world as it really is, and if we assume that the decision maker's computational powers are unlimited, then two important consequences follow. First, we do not need to distinguish between the real world and the decision maker's perception of it: he or she perceives the world as it really is. Second, we can predict the choices that will be made by a rational decision maker entirely from our knowledge of the real world and without a knowledge of the decision maker's perceptions or modes of calculation. (We do, of course, have to know his or her utility function.)

If, on the other hand, we accept the proposition that both the knowledge and the computational power of the decision maker are severely limited, then we must distinguish between the real world and the actor's perception of it and reasoning about it. That is to say, we must construct a theory (and test it empirically) of the processes of decision. Our theory must include not only the reasoning processes but also the processes that generate the actor's subjective representation of the decision problem, his or her frame (Simon 1978/1982).

The rational person of neoclassical economics always reaches the decision that is objectively, or substantively, best in terms of the given utility function. The rational person of cognitive psychology goes about making his or her decisions in a way that is procedurally reasonable in the light of the available knowledge and means of computation.

Embracing a substantive theory of rationality has had significant consequences for neoclassical economics and especially for its methodology. Until very recently, neoclassical economics has developed no strong empirical methodology for investigating the processes whereby values are formed, for the content of the utility function lies outside its self-defined scope. It has developed no special methodology for investigating how particular aspects of reality, rather than other aspects, come to the decision maker's attention, or for investigating how a representation of the choice situation is formed, or for investigating how reasoning processes are applied to draw out the consequences of such representations.

All these investigations call for empirical inquiry at the micro level—detailed study of decision makers engaged in the task of choice (Simon 1979*b*/1982, 1982). They are not questions that are easily answered by even the most sophisticated econometric analysis of aggregate data. To understand the processes that the economic actor employs in making decisions calls for observing these processes directly while they are going on, either in real world situations or in the laboratory, and/or interrogating the decision maker about beliefs, expectations, and methods of calculation and reasoning.

Securing access in order to observe decision processes in business firms or government organizations is difficult but often quite feasible—there are already a substantial number of successful studies of this kind in the literature. To extrapolate and generalize the findings requires attention to problems of sampling and aggregation; but these problems are surely easier to solve than the problem of going from the micro level of hypothetical "representative firms" or "typical consumers" to the level of markets.

Laboratory experiments on decision processes raise questions of their generalizability to real world situations. Studies that depend on interrogation of one kind or another raise questions of the veridicality of responses. There is no dearth of methodological issues but no reason to suppose that these issues are any more intractable than those encountered in standard econometric practice. But since experimental economics is well represented at this conference, I will say no more about the methodological issues it faces. They are best discussed in the context of concrete examples, a number of which will be provided here.

To move from substantive to procedural rationality requires a major extension of the empirical foundations of economics. It is not enough to add theoretical postulates about the shape of the utility function, or about the way in which actors form expectations about the future, or about their attention or inattention to particular environmental variables. These are assumptions about matters of fact, and the whole ethos of science requires such assumptions to be supported by publicly repeatable observations that are obtained and analyzed objectively.

In the following sections of this paper, I should like to illustrate, with concrete examples, the difficulties that contemporary neoclassical economics faces on a number of fronts owing to the insufficiency of its empirical foundations. These examples will also suggest the directions in which empirical work needs to go. My topics will include the shape and dimensions of the utility function, the role of attentional processes, the formation of expectations, and the sources of the empirical parameters and models that characterize cost and supply functions.

In all these examples we will see that the conclusions that are reached by neoclassical reasoning depend very much on the "auxiliary" factual assumptions that have to be made to define the situation and very little on the assumptions of substantive rationality—in particular, the utility-maximization assumptions. Indeed, in many cases, provided that the factual assumptions are retained, the conclusions reached within the utility-maximization framework could be reached as readily from much weaker assumptions of "reasonableness" in behavior (Becker 1962). Almost all the action, all the ability to reach nontrivial conclusions, comes from the factual assumptions and very little from the assumptions of optimization. Hence it becomes critically important to submit the factual assumptions to careful empirical test.

Empirical Basis for the Utility Function

Contemporary neoclassical economics provides no theoretical basis for specifying the shape and content of the utility function, and this gap is very inadequately filled by empirical research using econometric techniques. The gap is important because many conclusions that have been drawn in the literature about the way in which the economy operates depend on assumptions about consumers' utility functions.

To illustrate this claim, I will take two examples from the work of one of my discussants, Gary Becker, at the risk, of course, of introducing circularity by discussing a discussant. Both examples are drawn from Becker's well-known *A Treatise on the Family* (1981).

The Opportunities of Children

My account of the first example is not original but follows an enlightening analysis that has been carried out recently by Arthur Goldberger (in press) of Becker's (1981, chs. 6, 7) theory of the opportunities of children and intergenerational mobility. On page 116 of his book, Becker follows a mathematical demonstration with the interpretation: "If parents correctly anticipate their children's luck and endowment, an increase in either would not add an equal amount to the income of children." This interpretation is later (pp. 125–26) used to question whether public compensatory education programs will achieve their goal since parents whose children participate in these programs simply reallocate elsewhere resources they would otherwise have invested in these children.

I will return in a moment to the empirical evidence for the conclusion and its application. First, however, I would like to report Goldberger's analysis of the underlying argument that leads up to it.

Goldberger shows that Becker's conclusion follows from specific assumptions that parents' utility grows positively with parent's consumption and child's income and that the child's income is an additive function of parents' investment and child's luck. If the latter function is multiplicative instead of additive, the conclusion does not follow. Moreover, the whole derivation employs a homothetic utility function. No empirical support is provided for these assumptions.

But Milton Friedman (1953) would tell us that we should concentrate our efforts on testing the conclusions, not the assumptions, and this is what Becker does. Three pieces of evidence are cited, one relating to compensatory education and two to other public "compensatory" programs. On education, Becker quotes Arthur Jensen's "famous and controversial essay" (the characterization is Becker's) to the effect that "compensatory education has been tried and it apparently has failed" (p. 125). The essay quoted is, indeed, controversial; others have subsequently reached quite different evaluations of Headstart and other compensatory education programs. Moreover, Jensen himself attributes their failure—if there was one—to causes very different from the utility functions of parents. To choose among Jensen's explanation, Becker's, and the thousand others that could be dreamed up, it would surely be important to find out directly whether families whose children participated in such programs diverted their money, nurturance, or attention away from those children. That would provide a relatively direct test of the nature of their preferences (although very far from a test either that they possessed consistent utility functions or that they were maximizing anything).

Becker's other two pieces of evidence are more to the point. It does appear that public health programs cause people to devote less of their private budgets to health matters (the programs are presumably intended to do this) and that food supplements to pregnant women are to some extent diverted by reallocation of private budgets. To that extent we can conclude that some substitutions of the sort that utility theory predicts do actually take place. But of course as Becker has pointed out elsewhere (Becker 1962), price elasticity of demand is not a very strong test of utility maximization.

What one sees in this example are matters of substantial practical as well as theoretical importance disposed of on the basis of unsupported theoretical assumptions and scanty evidence about the conclusions. Economics is too important, intellectually as well as practically, to be treated with this kind of casual empiricism.

What one also sees in this example is that the conclusions depend primarily not on the assumption of optimization but on the (untested) auxiliary assumption that the interaction of luck and endowment is additive rather than multiplicative. Utility maximization is neither a necessary nor a sufficient condition for compensatory behavior.

Finally, in this example one begins to understand the real decision making when one undertakes (as in the public health and food supplement research) to gather direct evidence about behavior through field studies or field experiments.

Labor Force Participation of Women

Let me now turn to a second example from Becker's (1981) book. On pages 245–56 he gives us his interpretation of the evolution of the

American family since World War II. The salient fact around which the analysis revolves is that there has been a steady rise in the labor force participation of married women, including those with small children. At the outset (p. 245), Becker tells us that he believes "that the major cause of these changes is the growth in the earning power of women as the American economy developed." This credo is then buttressed by the empirical observation that the weekly earnings of employed women grew substantially during this period. This, he observes, implies an increase in the opportunity cost of staying in the home and also raises the relative cost of children, thereby reducing the demand for children.

However, the question is never raised as to (a) whether the increase in real earnings of women was more rapid than the increase in real earnings of men during this same period or (b) whether the increase in women's weekly earnings might not have been in some measure due to an increase in average hours worked—itself a form rather than a consequence of greater labor force participation.

Moreover, Becker places the whole weight of explanation on an unexplained shift in the demand curve for women's labor. No account is given of why this event should have taken place at this particular moment in American history or whether it was a sudden shock or a continuing development. Nor is any evidence provided (except the circular evidence that women moved into the labor force) that the event in fact took place. In particular, the possibility is not explored that a shift in the utility function of women caused a shift in the supply of women in the labor market in the face of a highly elastic demand curve and generally rising productivity in the economy.

So in this example as in the previous one, the action comes, not from the assumption of utility maximization, but from factual assumptions about the shifting or stability of particular supply and demand curves. The true explanation will be obtained not by raising the sophistication of the economic reasoning but only by painstaking examination of occupations in manufacturing and service industries and an even more difficult empirical examination of changes in women's attitudes about where they prefer to work. Utility maximization is neither a necessary nor a sufficient condition for the conclusion that was reached. The action comes from the empirical assumptions, including assumptions about how people view their world.

Attention and Representation

In a substantive theory of rationality there is no place for a variable like focus of attention. But in a procedural theory, it may be very important to know under what circumstances certain aspects of reality will be heeded and others ignored. I wish now to present two examples of situations in which focus of attention is a major determinant of behavior. The first rests on very strong empirical evidence; the second is more speculative, but I will try to make it plausible.

The Purchase of Flood Insurance

Kunreuther et al. (1978) have studied decisions of property owners whether to purchase insurance against flood damage. Neoclassical theory would predict that an owner would buy insurance if the expected reimbursable damage from floods was greater than the premium. The actual data are in egregious conflict with this claim. Instead it appears that insurance is purchased mainly by persons who have experienced damaging floods or who are acquainted with persons who have had such experiences, more or less independently of the cost/benefit ratio of the purchaser.

If we wish to understand the insurance-buying behavior, then we must determine, as Kunreuther and his colleagues did, the circumstances that attract the attention of a property owner to this decision alternative. Utility maximization is neither a necessary nor a sufficient condition for deducing who will buy insurance. The process of deciding—in this case, the process that puts the item on the decision agenda—is the important thing.

Voting Behavior

Voting behavior provides a more complex example of the role of attention in behavior. Both before and since Marx, it has been widely believed that voters respond, at least to an important extent, to their economic interests. Let us assume that is so. A substantial number of empirical studies have shown correlations between economic conditions and votes in American elections (Simon 1985). But such studies use a great variety of independent variables as measures of voters' perceptions of the economic consequences of their choices. (See, e.g., Hibbs 1982; and Weatherford 1983.) Some investigators have tried to measure the economic well-being of voters at the time of the election as compared with their well-being at some previous time. Others have measured the state of the economy—the level of the GNP, say, or of employment. Which of these (or what other measure) is the true measure of economic advantage? Quite different predictions can be made if different measures are chosen.

Consider the situation of a voter at the time of the 1984 presidential election who wished to maximize his or her economic well-being. Which of the following facts about the economy should influence the vote? (1) Real incomes of a majority have increased over the past 4 years but at less than the historical rate of a couple of decades earlier. (2) Dispersion of incomes has increased. (3) The rate of inflation has declined dramatically. (4) The rate of interest remains high compared with the historical past. (5) The national debt and deficit have increased dramatically. (6) The balance of trade has "worsened" dramatically. (7) Farm foreclosures have increased substantially. (8) Unemployment has decreased recently but is higher than it was 4 years previously. If we throw noneconomic considerations into the voter's utility function, we may add such facts as, the armament situation has changed in complex ways, et cetera, et cetera, moving into race tensions and equity to minorities, energy, the environment, creationism, abortion, and what not.

To predict how a voter, even a voter motivated solely by concern for his or her economic well-being, will vote requires much more than assuming utility maximization. A voter who attends to the rate of inflation may behave quite differently from a voter who attends to the federal deficit. Moreover, in order to predict where a voter's attention will focus, we may need to know his or her economic beliefs. A monetarist may consider different facts to be salient than the facts to which a Keynesian will attend. In any model of voting behavior that has any prospect of predicting behavior, almost all the action will lie in these auxiliary assumptions about attention and belief that define the decision maker's frame.

Expectations

Neoclassical theory, either with or without the assumption of rational expectations, cannot explain the phenomenon of the business cycle. In previous papers (e.g., Simon 1984) I have shown that auxiliary assumptions, which in this case amount to departures from objective rationality, must be annexed to the neoclassical model before a business cycle can be made to appear. I will repeat the argument here very briefly.

If we examine Keynes's reasoning in *The General Theory of Employment, Interest and Money* (1936), we see that, at most points, it fits perfectly the neoclassical mold of substantive rationality. Auxiliary assumptions (it does not matter whether we view them as "irrationalities" or simply as expectations) are introduced, however, at points that are critical to the explanation of the business cycle. One of these auxiliary assumptions is the postulate that labor suffers from the money illusion—that unions cannot distinguish between changes in real and money wages, respectively. The addition of this postulate is sufficient to produce underemployment stagnation in the Keynesian theory.

Remarkably enough, when we move from Keynes to the other end of the spectrum of economic theories—for example, to Lucas's (1981) rational expectations models—the same picture presents itself. The business cycle in these models derives, not from the assumptions of rationality, but from the appearance of money illusion in an erstwhile Eden. Only, in Lucas's theory, the illusion is suffered by businessmen, who cannot distinguish between general price movements and price changes in their industry, instead of by workers.

The action in business-cycle theories appears to reside not in the rationality assumptions but in auxiliary assumptions about the processes that people use to form expectations about future events. A theory of procedural rationality would have to employ empirical research to investigate these expectation-forming processes. Again, the assumption of utility or profit maximization provides neither a necessary nor a sufficient condition for the existence of business cycles.

We already have experience in using direct methods to learn how people form expectations about the future. Direct inquiries into people's expectations about business conditions, pioneered by George Katona (1951) at the University of Michigan, have for many years supplied inputs to econometric models of the economy. Studies have been made of planning methods and investment decision processes of business firms (for examples, see Eliasson 1976; and Bromiley 1986) that give us considerable information about what the forecasting firms do and whether and how forecasting enters into the process of choosing investments. This kind of information, which could easily be multiplied, provides us with powerful means for testing the rational expectations theory or other theories about how expectations are formed. There is no need to fall back on casual empiricism or on dubious indirect inferences from econometric data.

Other Empirical Parameters

My two final examples of the role of facts in economic reasoning are a little different from the previous ones. There are important cases in which not only are assumptions of substantive rationality insufficient to account for the observed phenomena but also parsimonious alternative explanations can be provided with only a minimal reference to rationality. The two examples I will discuss are the distribution of business firm sizes and the magnitudes of executive salaries.

Distribution of Business Firm Sizes

There is no unequivocal neoclassical theory of the distribution of business firm sizes. The traditional theory of the determinants of firm size was expounded by Jacob Viner (1932) and, by some kind of intellectual Gresham's Law, has survived to this day in elementary economics textbooks and books on intermediate price theory. It postulates a family of U-shaped short-run cost curves; a U-shaped long-run cost curve that is the envelope of the short-run curves; and a firm whose size corresponds to the scale of minimum cost on the long-run curve.

There are innumerable difficulties with this account. The most serious is that empirical studies very often show cost curves to be J shaped, without a recognizable minimum, rather than U shaped. With a J-shaped curve, that is, decreasing costs at all sizes, there is no upper bound on firm size. Nearly as serious is that the theory says nothing about parameter values of the cost curves, hence nothing about what sizes of firms will actually be observed. In particular, no conclusions can be drawn about the distribution of firm sizes.

If the theory is interpreted to mean that all firms in an industry have identical cost curves (which, in the absence of rents, should be the case), then, in equilibrium, all firms will be the same size. But this prediction is contradicted by the facts as squarely as any prediction could be. The actual distributions are highly skewed, with many small firms and a few that are very large.

If, on the contrary, each firm has its own cost curve, bearing no relation to the curves of the others, then the theory predicts too little: any size distribution whatsoever can be accommodated. But the fact is that the actual distributions are quite regular and similar, approximating the Pareto distribution in the upper tail. The traditional theory is therefore a total failure in predicting actual firm size distributions and should be banished from the textbooks.

But here we face the difficulty that nature abhors a vacuum, that a bad theory is preferred to none. However, in this case, a wholly satisfactory alternative is available. It rests on plausible (although not well-tested) premises, and these premises are even consistent with possible behaviors of reasonable men and women. The key premise (Ijiri and Simon 1977) is that the expected rate of growth of a firm during any period is proportionate to the size it had attained at the beginning of that period—the so-called Gibrat assumption. With this assumption and a little attention to boundary conditions, the Pareto distribution can be deduced as the steady-state equilibrium of the system.

Such tests as have been made of the Gibrat assumption have had generally positive results. But even if we were satisfied that the assumption is empirically valid, we might wish to probe deeper. In a world in which people have reasons for their actions, why would such a relation hold? This is not the place for a full discussion of the matter, and I limit myself to two comments. First, if average rate of return on capital is independent of size of firm (as seems to be true to a first approximation), it is rather easy to think of reasons why access to internal or external capital for expansion should be, on average, roughly commensurate with present size. Second, we really do not need to do this kind of armchair guessing. We can undertake to study business firms to determine how growth comes about. What we should not do is to cling to a theory that predicts very little and that little incorrectly.

Distribution of Executive Salaries

My second example of a failure of classical theory that can be remedied within a framework of procedural rationality is the prediction of the distribution of the salaries of top executives.

Neoclassical theory would, of course, explain the salaries of executives in terms of individual abilities for managerial work. Moreover, a very able executive would presumably have greater productivity when engaged in large affairs, as in managing a large business firm. Hence the combined forces of supply and demand would produce a strong correlation of executive ability with firm size. Rees (1973, p. 201), in his textbook exposition of the theory, puts it this way: "The person who alone among hundreds of competing junior executives in a large corporation eventually rises to the presidency must surely have special qualities that account for this rise, although they differ from the qualities that make a successful scientist or a successful salesperson. In any event, a business that is not a monopoly would soon run at a loss if it selected executives without any regard to those kinds of ability relevant in managing a business well."

The claim is moderate and plausible. It does not require any assumption of maximization, only the assumption that those who select executives will behave reasonably, by taking ability into account. It leaves open the question of the processes of selection: how ability is judged and how accurately it can be estimated. It also leaves open the question of whether the characteristics that allow a person to compete successfully for advancement are closely correlated with the characteristics that make for effective management. But we will ignore the Peter Principle and other postulates that have been put forward challenging the close relation between managerial ability and selectability.

Difficulty arises, however, when we try to move from these premises to an account of the observed salary distribution function. A number of studies (e.g., Roberts 1959) have shown that the average compensation of top executives increases with the cube root of the size of the firm. I have been told, though I have not seen the data, that this relation continues to hold when executive bonuses and fringe benefits are included in salary. How shall we explain this very regular and persistent distribution?

Neoclassical theory, without strong auxiliary assumptions, is helpless. As Lucas (1978) has pointed out, what are needed are an assumption about the marginal product of managerial work as a function of firm size and managerial ability and an assumption about the distribution of managerial ability measured in the same units as in the previously mentioned function. Since there are no empirical data either on the marginal productivity of managers (except the salary data themselves) or on the distribution of ability, it is easy to manufacture functions that will produce the desired distribution of salaries. However, it should be noted that certain "obvious" choices of function will not work—for example, the

Gibrat assumption that the marginal productivity of a manager is proportional to the size of the firm. If a function is found that fits the data, it is, of course, not refutable and hence profoundly uninteresting as a theoretical premise.

As an alternative route to an explanation of the observed salary distribution (Simon 1979*a*/1982), we can introduce two factual assumptions that can be verified (and for one of which we already have sufficient empirical data). The first assumption is that business organizations have a pyramidal form and that the number of subordinates reporting directly to an executive does not vary much from one organization to another or from one organizational level to another—that the span of control is relatively constant. This is a well-known fact about business organizations. The second assumption is that, by some generally accepted norm of "fairness," the ratio of the salary of an executive to the salaries of his or her immediate subordinates is a constant over organizations and over levels.

With these two assumptions, it follows immediately that the log of the salary of the top executive will vary linearly with the log of company size; and with reasonable assumptions, fitting observed facts, about the sizes of the two parameters of the theory (the span of control and the "fair" ratio of salaries), the coefficient in this linear relation can be predicted to be in the neighborhood of .3—very close to the observed value.

Of course, we will be more confident that this is the correct explanation when we have more direct evidence that the postulated norm of fairness really exists in peoples' minds. My only claim at the moment is that here we have an explanation that takes process into account, that does not rely on any assumption of utility or profit maximization, and that does describe a realizable decision process that is not dependent on quantities that are unobservable by the actors and by economists studying the phenomena. Of course this explanation does make the correct prediction—quantitatively as well as qualitatively.

Neoclassical economists have raised several objections to the explanation I have just outlined. Rees (1973, p. 201) argues that the theory "is too special, since it applies only to hierarchical organizations." He points out that the salary distributions of such professionals as architects and attorneys, who typically work in small organizations, also are highly skewed. Of course, there is no reason to suppose that salaries in all occupations are fixed in the same way. A procedural theory of rationality would predict that the method of salary determination would depend on what kinds of information were available for assessing worth.

Position in hierarchy provides such information in large organizations. In the case of architectural and legal firms, direct measures are generally available of the magnitude of the revenues associated with an associate's work and the magnitude of the contracts he or she is able to attract. Moreover, the sizes of jobs have a highly skewed distribution for a variety of reasons that we could explore empirically. Hence the fact that the salaries of professionals other than executives of business firms are skewed hardly seems a reason for rejecting the theory of executive compensation I have proposed.

Recently, new information has been gained about bonuses and other nonsalary awards that make up an increasing part of executive compensation. This information shows that bonuses vary strongly with profits and other statistics that might be taken as measures of the effectiveness of executive performance. But such evidence merely shows that companies try to motivate their executives to make profits (often, alas, with excessive attention to short-run profits, as has been pointed out in the literature). It does not show that the incentives bear any close relation to the marginal worth of the executives or even that the fluctuations in profits are the result of the incentive compensation.

The evidence that incentives are offered to executives to increase profits is just what a procedural theory would predict. It would predict also that the rewards would be related to available statistics of company performance, even in the absence of reliable information about the exact relation between performance and managerial behavior. It would make no assumption that profits are maximized since the observable evidence provides no basis for that assumption. It would assume only that executives (and corporate boards) believe that executives can influence profits through their behavior and that a bonus plan would thereby motivate them to try harder.

A procedural theory would assume that people have reasons for what they do when they set executive salaries and that these reasons take account of the highly imperfect and incomplete information available to them. However, it would be essential, in order to predict behavior more precisely, to have good empirical information both about the kinds of information to which the decision makers have ready access and about their beliefs and opinions on the mechanisms of the world on which their decisions operate. The most likely sources of such information are direct studies of the behaviors, values, beliefs, and opinions of the actors.

Summing Up

Between supporters of substantive and procedural theories of rationality there are fundamental differences about what constitutes a principled, parsimonious, scientific theory. We may put the matter in Bayesian terms. Neoclassical economists attach a very large prior probability (.9944?) to the proposition that people have consistent utility functions and in fact maximize utilities in an objective sense. As my examples show, they are prepared to make whatever auxiliary empirical assumptions are necessary in order to preserve the utility-maximization postulate, even when the empirical assumptions are unverified. When verification is demanded, they tend to look for evidence that the theory makes correct predictions and resist advice that they should look instead directly at the decision mechanisms and processes.

Given the magnitude of the Bayesian prior that expresses confidence in the theory and the weakness of the kinds of indirect evidence that are allowed for testing it, neoclassical economics becomes, as has been observed more than once, essentially tautological and irrefutable. Because of its preoccupation with utility maximization, it fails to observe that most of its "action"—the force of its predictions—derives from the, usually untested, auxiliary assumptions that describe the environment in which decisions are made. The examples show that the important conclusions it draws can usually also be drawn, with the aid of the auxiliary assumptions, from the postulate that people are procedurally; rational and without assuming that they maximize utility.

It is too easy, within the neoclassical methodological framework, to save the theory from unpleasant evidence by modifying the auxiliary assumptions and providing a new framework within which the actor "must have been operating." Hence neoclassical theory, as usually applied, is an exceedingly weak theory, as shown by the difficulty of finding sets of facts, actual or hypothetical, that cannot be rationalized and made consistent with it.

Behavioral theories of rationality attach a high prior probability (.9944?) to the assumption that economic actors use the same basic processes in making their decisions as have been observed in other human cognitive activities and that these processes are indeed observable. In situations that are complex and in which information is very incomplete (i.e., virtually all real world situations), the behavioral theories deny that there is any magic for producing behavior even approximating an objective maximization of profits or utilities. They therefore seek to determine what the actual frame of the decision is, how that frame arises from the decision situation, and how, within that frame, reason operates.

In this kind of complexity, there is no single sovereign principle for deductive prediction. The emerging laws of procedural rationality have much more the complexity of molecular biology than the simplicity of classical mechanics. As a consequence, they call for a very high ratio of empirical investigation to theory building. They require painstaking factual study of the decision-making process itself.

What is to be done? What prescription for economic research derives from my analysis?

First, I would recommend that we stop debating whether a theory of substantive rationality and the assumptions of utility maximization provide a sufficient base for explaining and predicting economic behavior. The evidence is overwhelming that they do not.

We already have in psychology a substantial body of empirically tested theory about the processes people actually use to make boundedly rational, or "reasonable," decisions. This body of theory asserts that the processes are sensitive to the complexity of decision-making contexts and to learning processes as well.

The application of this procedural theory of rationality to economics requires extensive empirical research, much of it at micro-micro levels, to determine specifically how process is molded to context in actual economic environments and the consequences of this interaction for the economic outcomes of these processes. Economics without psychological and sociological research to determine the givens of the decision-making situation, the focus of attention, the problem representation, and the processes used to identify alternatives, estimate consequences, and choose among possibilities—such economics is a one-bladed scissors. Let us replace it with an instrument capable of cutting through our ignorance about rational human behavior.

Note

In writing out my remarks for publication, I have had the benefit, of course, of hearing the observations of my discussants at the Chicago meeting. I shall take the liberty of commenting, from time to time, on their remarks, but I shall try to indicate when I do so, in order to avoid a confusing anachronism.

Reference

Becker, G. S. 1962. Irrational behavior and economic theory. *Journal of Political Economy* 70:1–13.

Becker, G. S. 1981. *A Treatise on the Family*. Cambridge, Mass.: Harvard University Press.

Bromiley, P. 1986. Corporate planning and capital investment. *Journal of Economic Behavior and Organization* 7:147–70.

Eliasson, G. 1976. *Business Economic Planning*. New York: Wiley.

Friedman, M. 1953. *Essays in Positive Economics*. Chicago: University of Chicago Press.

Goldberger, A. S. In press. *Modeling the Economic Family*. Ann Arbor: University of Michigan Press.

Hibbs, D. A., Jr. 1982. Economic outcomes and political support for British governments among occupational classes. *American Political Science Review* 76:259–79.

Ijiri, Y., and Simon, H. A. 1977. *Skew Distributions and the Sizes of Business Firms*. Amsterdam: North-Holland.

Katona, G. 1951. *Psychological Analysis of Economic Behavior*. New York: McGraw-Hill.

Keynes, J. M. 1936. *The General Theory of Employment, Interest and Money*. London: Macmillan.

Kunreuther, H., with Ginsberg, R.; Miller, L.; Sagi, P.; Slovic, P.; Borkan, B.; and Katz, N. 1978. *Disaster Insurance Protection: Public Policy Lessons*. New York: Wiley.

Lucas, R. E., Jr. 1978. On the size distribution of business firms. *Bell Journal of Economics* 9:508–23.

Lucas, R. E., Jr. 1981. *Studies in Business Cycle Theory*. Cambridge, Mass.: MIT Press.

Rees, A. 1973. *The Economics of Work and Pay*. New York: Harper & Row.

Roberts, D. R. 1959. *Executive Compensation*. Glencoe, Ill.: Free Press.

Simon, H. A. 1976. From substantive to procedural rationality. In S. J. Latsis (ed.), *Method and Appraisal in Economics*. Cambridge: Cambridge University Press. Reprinted in *Models of Bounded Rationality*. 2 vols. Cambridge, Mass.: MIT Press, 1982.

Simon, H. A. 1978. Rationality as process and product of thought. *American Economic Review: Proceedings* 68:1–16. Reprinted in *Models of Bounded Rationality*. 2 vols. Cambridge, Mass.: MIT Press, 1982.

Simon, H. A. 1979*a*. On parsimonious explanations of production relations. *Scandinavian Journal of Economics* 81:459–74. Reprinted in *Models of Bounded Rationality*. 2 vols. Cambridge, Mass.: MIT Press, 1982.

Simon, H. A. 1979*b*. Rational decision making in business organizations. *American Economic Review* 69:493–513. Reprinted in *Models of Bounded Rationality*. 2 vols. Cambridge, Mass.: MIT Press, 1982.

Simon, H. A. 1982. *Models of Bounded Rationality*. 2 vols. Cambridge, Mass.: MIT Press.

Simon, H. A. 1984. On the behavioral and rational foundations of economic dynamics. *Journal of Economic Behavior and Organization* 5:35–55.

Simon, H. A. 1985. Human nature in politics: The dialogue of psychology with political science. *American Political Science Review* 79:293–304.

Viner, J. 1932. Cost curves and supply curves. *Zeitschrift für Nationalökonomie* 3:23–46.

Weatherford, M. S. 1983. Economic voting and the "symbolic politics" argument. *American Political Science Review* 77:158–74.

IV.10 The Failure of Armchair Economics

Q. This month you and a group of co-authors are bringing out a new book, *Scientific Discovery*. You call it a report on scientific work in progress. To what is your research ultimately leading?

A. We arc aiming to provide a comprehensive theory of the processes that scientists use to make scientific discoveries. We developed a rough taxonomy of discovery processes—there are many that scientists actually use—and we designed computer programs that simulate human thought processes as scientists work toward discoveries. In this project we have come to grips with some of the central issues in the philosophy and history of science. We are trying to find out what drives the development of new science. Is theory the driving force, or do data lead and theories follow?

Q. Do you have any answers yet?

A. The evidence from the simulations with our computer programs certainly puts new light on these issues, but we don't think we have reached definitive answers to all the questions. We started out with the "paradigm" of contemporary, information-processing psychology, or cognitive science. The currently accepted theory in this field suggests that the processes of scientific discovery may be described as special cases of problem-solving processes. Scientists carry on a variety of activities in the discovery process—gathering data, describing, explaining and theory-testing—but our new book reports on just one subset of them; namely, how to induce descriptive and explanatory theories from the data. But even before you can begin the induction of a scientific law from data, you have to begin with a new phenomenon.

Q. What for example?

A. Discoveries such as the X-ray, the effect of penicillin on bacteria, the synchrony between the pulsation of the heart and arteries, the Brownian movement—these are among the most important discoveries in science. Or maybe the story of discovery begins with the invention of a new instrument—Seeboek's battery, Ampere's ammeter that was used by Ohm in formulating Ohm's law, or Fahrenheit's thermometer. Whatever the initial discovery, it leads to new data. From it we get new theories and the verification of theory. Our concern is not whether discovery is data-driven or theory-driven. What we try to do in our research is to

This interview was conducted on September 17, 1986 in Pittsburgh by Richard D. Bartel, Editor of *Challenge*.

understand how scientists carry out these processes. We use artificial intelligence—our computer programs—to replicate the scientific process. We take examples of major discoveries in the history of science, start out with their raw, content-free data and replicate the scientific process that led to new laws: Johann Kepler's laws of planetary motion from the early 17th century, Ohm's law of electrical resistance in circuits, to cite just two.

Q. My mind is already jumping quickly from natural science to economics. What does this hold out for future progress in the social sciences, particularly economics?

A. We demonstrate how a lot of successful science was done—by looking at the world, getting puzzled by it, getting data, and then developing and testing a theory. That direction of movement is not impossible in economics, of course. As a matter of fact, the small amount of empirical work I have done in economics was mostly of this kind—my study of firm size distribution, for instance. But there is a lot of resistance among economists to going out and looking at the world until you have a theory about it. Economists tend to start with some global theoretical assumptions as if they were handed down from the mountain by Moses, and then they reason from them. If the world doesn't fit the assumptions, or you have a hard time with the regression results, so much the worse for the world. Economists don't start at the other end of the discovery process with some new phenomenon out there, which they ought to explain, and then first try to find some descriptive explanations and then identify a mechanism that would produce this. Of course, I exaggerate a bit, but in economics there is a distancing of theory from data that is unlike any other fields that I know in the natural or social sciences.

Q. Not only is economics clearly different from the natural sciences, you also argue that economics differs from other social sciences, especially in the way economists treat the concept of rationality.

A. I see the contrast particularly between economics and psychology. Economists are quick to defend the belief that humans are rational. But you can only determine whether certain behavior is rational if you study that behavior in the context of certain premises or assumptions about the environment in which the behavior takes place, or in the light of the goals that the individual is looking to achieve, and also the means for computing or calculating how the goals can be achieved. But neoclassical economics departs from other social sciences in three ways. It says nothing about the contents of goals and values that are assumed. It assumes uniformly consistent behavior as if there were one world, whether we are talking about the present or the future, or even as the individual moves through time, and it assumes that behavior is objectively rational.

Q. How do other social sciences treat rationality?

A. Other social sciences are more concerned about studying the individual and social processes in which individuals decide and act on their decisions. They study empirically the origins of values and how and why values change as individuals move through time and gain new experience. Economic theorists assume givens, as if they were facts, whereas in other social sciences, the investigator tries to determine empirically the substance of those givens. Other social sciences also try to determine the calculating strategies that individuals use in the reasoning process that leads to decisions and actions; people have limited information and limited computational abilities with which to function in a complex real world. In psychology, at least, researchers also have to describe and explain how nonrational processes—human emotions, sensory stimuli—shape the individual's focus of attention, which in turn fixes those aspects of the decision-making process that economists typically assume as givens. In short, economists see rationality in terms of the choices that people make. Other social scientists view rationality in terms of the processes. I call the rationality of economics *substantive rationality* and the rationality of psychology *procedural rationality.*

Q. I don't see where this is driving. It's too abstract for me.

A. Let me put it in terms of economic theory. In the theory of consumer choice, economists start off with an assumed utility function for an individual. These utility functions are simply assumed—all the values and preferences influencing choice are given and fixed. Economists then assume that individuals working in the economy have an objective description of the world in which the consumer has to function, and also that the decision-maker has unlimited computational powers. In this environment we don't have to distinguish between the real world and the decision-maker's perception of it. So the individual's choices can be made entirely from their knowledge of the real world.

In psychology, for example, we don't start with any knowledge about the decision-maker's perceptions or his means of calculation. In fact, we take them as being terribly limited. Then it is important to distinguish between the real world and the decision-maker's perception of it, and how he reasons about it. In psychology we have to use empirical data to construct a theory of the processes of decision. In economics, that's a given. As a result, neoclassical economics has created no strong methodology for studying empirically the process in which values are developed. Economists simply take the utility function and its underlying values to be defined and given.

Q. So there is a great difference in the way economists and psychologists view human behavior and theorize from it.

A. Yes, and in order to move from the economist's substantive rationality to the psychologist's procedural rationality requires a major extension in the empirical foundations of economics. Economists will have to observe decision-makers in the actual process of making decisions in the real world or in laboratory experiments, or study the actors' beliefs, their expectations and their methods of calculation and reasoning. This fundamental failure in the very basic methodology means that the conclusions reached in neoclassical economics rest largely on the auxiliary assumptions that economists make in defining any given situation. The conclusions rest very little on the economists' basic assumptions of substantive rationality; for example, the assumption that economic actors always maximize their utility. Conclusions from economic theory come mainly from the factual assumptions, rather than from the assumptions about maximizing utility or optimization more generally.

Q. Could you give me some examples?

A. I often use several examples from Gary Becker's work to illustrate my point. Becker follows Milton Friedman's advice that economists should focus on testing the conclusions of a theory, not testing the factual assumptions that underlie it. In his *Treatise on the Family*, Gary Becker looks at the steady rise in the labor force participation of married women since World War II. The major cause for this change, he believes, is the growth in the productivity of women as the American economy developed. He observes how the weekly earnings of employed women grew substantially and interprets this to mean an increase in the opportunity cost for women of staying at home. That also raises the relative cost of children, thereby reducing the demand for children. Becker never asks, though, whether the increase in real earnings of women was more rapid than the increase in real earnings of men. He could also have asked if the increase in women's weekly earnings might have resulted from an increase in average hours worked; that is a form rather than a consequence of greater labor force participation. But he explains it all in terms of an unexplained shift in the demand curve for women's labor. He doesn't say why this event should have taken place at this particular moment in American history. Was it an unexpected shock, or a continuing development? And even more basic, there could have been a shift in the utility function of women which led to a shift in the supply of women to the labor market in the face of a highly elastic demand curve and generally rising productivity in the economy.

Q. I can imagine another possible factor at work: accelerating inflation in the 1970s eroded the weekly earnings of husbands, motivating many women to enter the work force in order to maintain the real standard of living of the family.

A. There are many possibilities, but my point is that the action in this example comes not from the assumption that women maximize utility, but from the underlying factual assumptions about whether the particular supply and demand curves shifted or remained stable. If economists are to provide a true explanation of this phenomenon, they will not get it simply by increasing the level of sophistication of economic reasoning. That will come only from much more empirical study of changes in women's attitudes about their preferences to work at home or to work in the marketplace. That requires looking into the evidence on occupations in manufacturing and service industries. In this example, the assumption that women maximize utility in making their decisions is neither necessary nor sufficient to make the conclusions that Becker reaches. The action comes from the empirical assumptions, particularly about how people view the world in which they have to function.

Q. In contrasting the theory of rationality used in economics and psychology, you single out the procedural theory of rationality that is common among psychologists, but neglected by economists. In that context you talk about a variable you call "focus of attention." It is commonly used in psychology, and you feel economists should consider it when they study economic decision-making. How would you do that?

A. Economists should study how economic actors heed or ignore given features in the economic world in the same way that psychologists observe human behavior. I have an example from consumer decisions to purchase flood insurance that makes the theoretical point more concrete. Neoclassical economists have a neat theory that predicts that a homeowner would buy insurance if the expected reimbursible damage from floods is greater than the insurance premium. Yet, there are actual empirical data, gathered by Kunreuther and others, that are in egregious conflict with the economists' theory. The data indicate that people purchase insurance if they have experienced damaging floods or if they know others who have had such experiences. They make the decision quite independently of the cost/benefit ratio which they can calculate. So in this example, the economists need to know the factual circumstances that actually attract the attention of a property owner when he comes to make the decision to buy or not to buy insurance. Again, the economists' utility-maximization is neither a necessary nor a sufficient condition for deducing who will buy insurance.

Q. You have also written about voting behavior in this context.

A. Yes, but voting behavior offers a more complex example of the role of focusing attention in the decision process. People now widely believe that voters respond to a significant degree to their economic self-interests. Many empirical studies have shown correlations between economic conditions and how Americans vote. These studies use a broad range of independent variables as measures of voters' perceptions of how the economy is performing and how their voting choices affect their economic interests. Looking at the 1984 presidential election, people who wish to maximize their economic well-being could point to a variety of facts about economic performance when they decide to vote. They might refer to the real incomes of a majority of the population, changes in the income distribution, changes in the rate of inflation and prospects for the future, the rate of interest relative to historical experience. I could go on and on; at the moment—the growing national debt and the size of the federal deficits, the worsening balance of trade, farm foreclosures, and the problem of unemployment.

My point is that for economists to predict how a voter will vote, he has to know much more than assuming that each voter maximizes utility in his model. A senior citizen who lives on a fixed income and who worries about what is happening to the rate of inflation may behave quite differently from a young worker with a family who is mainly concerned about the threat of unemployment. In order to predict where a voter will focus his or her attention, we have to know their respective economic beliefs. If a model of voting behavior is to predict the outcome accurately, almost all of the voter action will come from these auxiliary assumptions about the focus of attention and underlying beliefs that define a voter's state of mind. Of course, in the economist's approach, that state of mind is subsumed in the voter's utility function.

Q. Does macroeconomic theory lack the same empirical and behavioral foundations that you see as a problem in microeconomic theory?

A. It's all much the same in both microeconomics and macroeconomics. Economists don't develop the same empirical approaches in theorizing as in other social sciences and in the natural sciences because we had, first of all, the great fortune—or maybe it was a misfortune—to have inherited a really neat theory. Anybody with the slightest mathematical bent can't help but view neoclassical, general equilibrium theory, with utility-maximization as a driving mechanism, as a very, very beautiful thing. So all economists start out with that. It's basic at every level of training and education, from the elementary textbook to the graduate school courses and seminars. We don't want to depart very far from such a powerful deductive theory. Economists are very reluctant to recognize and accept facts in the real world that seem to fly in the face of that beautiful theory, or undermine its basic assumptions.

Especially in macroeconomics, theory and methodology progressed along with a huge and growing body of aggregated numerical data. The supply of data on prices, the GNP accounts, money and financial statistics grew with the demand. With all these good things, economists created some powerful statistical tools. That's the preoccupation of most graduate students in economics these days—their training, their research, and the very criteria of their success. But it is also true that these aggregated data are horribly noisy. Economists have to make all sorts of alarming assumptions in order to get anything identified at all. This leaves tremendous room for creative analysis.

Q. Do you mean manipulation of the data?

A. Yes, manipulation in the sense that, by making appropriate identifying assumptions, it becomes—as we know by reading the literature every month—very easy to find true or false just about any theory that any good or bad economist puts forward. So we get these long wrangles about whether rational expectations theory, for instance, does or doesn't hold. These are not just debates in a vacuum about logical reasoning. They are fights about whose regression equations are right. By the very nature of prevailing methodology in economics, you have to make identifying assumptions in order to get the equations, and those identifying assumptions are made on the basis of very casual armchair feelings about how the world must be.

Q. I heard you describe those problems in the context of business-cycle theory at the 1985 meetings of the Eastern Economic Association in Pittsburgh.

A. Business-cycle theory illustrates my point exactly. You go back and read Keynes, the great revolutionary, and he reasoned just like our contemporary textbook economists. One wonders why Keynes doesn't come out where all the other neoclassical economists of his day came out—with a full employment equilibrium. Reading *The General Theory*, I note at one or two places Keynes allows people in his theoretical world to depart from the strict assumptions of rational utility-maximization. I'll just take one example: labor somehow doesn't quite see the difference between real wages and money wages; in the language of economists, labor suffers from money illusion. So they bargain for money wages instead of real wages; and unemployment results. But just about everybody else in Keynes's model behaves quite rationally, just the way Marshall leads us to expect.

Now look at the business cycle with Bob Lucas's eyes. He also starts out from a beautiful Marshallian position that should lead to a full-employment equilibrium. Except that in the Lucas model there is also a little grain of sand in the oyster: businessmen aren't terribly bright, or perhaps not quite informed. Businessmen can't quite distinguish a price change in their industry—that is, a change in relative prices—from a general movement of prices in the economy as a whole—a change in the price level. So they suffer from money illusion. Their behavior leads to investment fluctuations and the business cycle. So both Keynes and Lucas start off together with neoclassical theory. They march together 98 percent of the time. Except each throws a grain of sand of irrationality into the beautiful Marshallian oyster and we get quite different pearls.

Q. Again we have economic theory created in the armchair with no empirical evidence?

A. They don't talk about evidence at all. You read the pages where Lucas talks about why businessmen can't figure out what's happened to prices and it is just what he feels as he sits there smoking his cigarettes in his armchair. I don't know what Keynes smoked, but when you look at the pages where he talks about labor's money illusion, no evidence is cited. So the real differences in economics, as compared with psychology, is that almost everybody operates within the theoretical logic of utility-maximization in the neoclassical model. When economists want to explain particular phenomena in the real world, they have to introduce new assumptions. The distinctive change in the behavior of the economic actors comes from a change in the behavioral assumptions. No empirical evidence is given to support those changes. They emerge from the mind of the economic theorist sitting in his armchair.

The Swedish economist Assar Lindbeck recently did a survey of some 30 business-cycle theories. When I read it, I saw a pattern emerging as one theorist after another attempted to explain how unemployment developed. Each introduced into his model some particular behavioral departure from perfect economic rationality. I'm sure each departure led to a journal article on business cycles, and in response, other economists soon joined the debate. All of this theory and debate was over assumptions, but not one was bolstered by evidence from empirical observation. Economists treat behavior as if it were in fact the right behavior for the actual circumstances: that the world is out there, people see that world accurately, understand that world, and adapt perfectly to it. That is what I call "substantively rational behavior."

Q. Is that what distinguishes theory in economics from psychology?

A. The economist believes the good Lord looks down on earth and couldn't improve on it. But the psychologist says, here are people or other organisms living in a world where they have to find food, shelter, wages, or whatever. They have to solve that problem. So they go through certain processes which we call thinking, or problem-solving processes and they get solutions. They aren't always very good solution; they certainly aren't perfect solutions. The Lord could certainly improve on them.

No matter how hard they try, their thinking capacities are not anywhere near a match for the complexity of the situations they have to cope with. Economists talk about what it would be like if actors knew everything about a situation, while the psychologist looks at the processes an organism can use to deal with a complexity that's far beyond its capabilities. He sees procedural rationality in those processes; the economist sees substantive rationality in his model.

Q. Can utility theory be salvaged?

A. If so, economists will have to learn something from the psychologists. They will have to get evidence on what information people actually have, what calculations they actually make on that information, and how they go about making their decision. If they do, economists will find out that in complex, real-world situations, the principles underlying the theory of subjective expected utility and standard utility-maximization simply break down. From that theory you can deduce that there ought to be a certain internal consistency in the choices people make. If they prefer a to b, and b to c, then they should prefer a to c. Empirical evidence and experiments show how egregiously bad people are in satisfying these transitivity requirements.

I have a good example for that. Take a physician who tells a patient about a certain surgical procedure and evaluates the chances for a successful outcome: If the physician says there is an 80 percent chance of survival with this treatment, then a certain percentage will agree to undergo the procedure rather than face certain death without it. If the physician says there is a 20 percent chance that the patient will die, the evidence shows a much smaller percentage of people will take the treatment. It is very hard to reconcile that kind of inconsistent behavior with any form of utility maximization. You really have to add something new to the theory.

Q. Have economists put the wrong stress on optimization theory in consumer preference and resource allocation?

A. The stress is wrong and so is the methodology for testing their theories. Virtually no economics students get training in methods of observation that would lead the researcher to find out how the consumer actually makes choices, or to go inside a business firm to see how decisions are actually made there. Marketing people in business schools are learning something about that, but it's not part of the training of the Ph.D. economist. In business schools there is a surge of interest in decision-*making*, not in decision *theory*. As a matter of fact, in the Cathedral itself—the University of Chicago Business School—there is a very lively group working on decision-making.

Q. Wassily Leontief has also called for much more empirical content in economic theory (*Challenge* interview, March/April 1985). And in Alfred Eichner's recent book, *Why Economics is not yet a Science*, he makes similar criticisms of economic theory. He also sees no empirical foundations for the economists' utility functions, marginal productivity theory, and upward sloping supply curves, among other economics building blocks. But if you accept these criticisms, aren't you really dismissing the very foundation stones of microeconomics as it is taught today?

A. Tough. If it is wrong, why not throw it away? Yes, I am throwing it away. I think the textbooks are a scandal. I think to expose young impressionable minds to this scholastic exercise as though it said something about the real world, is a scandal. The most widely used textbooks use the old long-run and short-run cost curves to illustrate the theory of the firm. I find that inexcusable. I don't really expect economists to purge their texts of these invalid theoretical elements, certainly not soon. But I don't know of any other science that purports to be talking about real world phenomena, where statements are regularly made that are blatantly contrary to fact.

Q. What is your criticism of the textbook use of cost curves?

A. It goes back to the famous controversy over Jacob Viner's drawings of the short- and long-run cost curves of the firm and industry. That theory has survived for fifty years, as if Gresham's law were operating. Bad theory survives; it doesn't predict very much, and when it does, it predicts incorrectly. Viner drew a family of U-shaped short-run cost curves for a group of firms in an industry, and then traced a U-shaped long-run cost curve that is the envelope of the short-run curves.

Q. What was that model supposed to predict?

A. First of all, it postulated that in the long run the size of the firm would increase to a scale associated with the minimum cost on the long-run curve. It was supposed to predict something about the size distribution of firms in the industry. It doesn't do that and there are other problems.

Most serious is the fact that empirical studies show the firm's cost curves not to be U-shaped, but in fact to slope down to the right and then level off, without a clearly defined minimum point. Such a curve implies decreasing costs in all sizes, with no upper boundary on the size of the firm. In short, with this theory we end up knowing nothing at all about what sizes of firms we should expect in the real world. Many have thought that the theory means that all firms in an industry have identical cost curves, so that in equilibrium, all firms will be the same size. But again, this prediction does not square with empirical evidence. Actual distributions of firm size are highly skewed: there are many small firms and a few very large ones.

Q. If economics is successful in banishing the Viner model from the textbooks, what would you use in its place?

A. I can think of a completely satisfactory alternative for predicting the growth of firms and the distribution of firm size. It is based on the plausible premise that firms, on average, have an opportunity to grow that is about proportional to their existing size. Their access to markets, to the banks for money and credit, to information is likely to increase with size. In any case, the distribution of firm size and how their growth occurs can be easily studied to get empirical evidence. So far, some empirical tests of this premise generally support it. In any case, economists don't have to sit in their armchairs to think up new models.

Q. If you were to return to focus more on economics, what problems would you look into—the foundations for a theory of the firm?

A. Throughout my whole career I really have been interested in the decision-making process and, in particular, how human beings with very limited access to information, very limited research and computational capacities deal with the world they live in. Economics is only one of the disciplines in which you have to ask those questions, but it applies to all other aspects of life. If you trace out what I have been doing, you will see that I gradually backed away from studying organizations and big economic systems and focused more and more on studying individuals—how they make decisions and how they solve problems. The work on *Scientific Discovery* is a part of the research program that I have been engaged in for over 30 years now. Decision-making and problem-solving are a very core part of human activity. Having a realistic theory of what goes on, what the processes are that enable human beings to solve problems and to make decisions is bound to influence the way we look at all our social, economic, and political institutions.

Q. Would that lead you back to the theory of the firm, then?

A. Oh, I expect I would get back to the theory of the firm again and try to do it right this time. We badly need better ideas of how to put together the stuff we find out at the micro-micro level and aggregate it. For that, economists need much more data.

Q. Would that require a new role for government statistical agencies?

A. Not necessarily. It depends on who collects the data. Look at how the biologists do it. Most of the data would be collected in the private sector by individual investigators, just as individual biologists collect data on organisms in nature or from experiments. If the government plays a role, it would provide the megabucks. This costs money as does everything else.

Q. Is the biologist concerned with aggregating in a way that the economist would have to be concerned?

A. If the biologist is interested in the larger ecology, he surely is. In biology it is sometimes safe to assume that if you examine one organism in a species, you can generalize for them all. In the case of humans, we wouldn't be satisfied with extrapolating from one human being to the entire population, though economic theorists don't seem to hesitate to extrapolate from themselves to the population. But they shouldn't.

Q. But if you study one firm, can you generalize for 1,000?

A. The flip answer to that is you learn a heck of a lot more than if you studied no firms. But the serious answer is that if you studied about a dozen firms, you have a pretty good feeling of the range of behavior you are likely to encounter in firms, just as we find in our psychological experiments. Take a mechanical puzzle, like this one on my desk, and give it to ten people. You will get quite a range of individual behavior in trying to solve it. But you won't learn very much more from the next ten people you give it to. So the idea that we must have huge samples in order to know how a system works is not necessarily so. Human beings aren't that variable.

Q. Where does economics go from here?

A. Economists should stop worrying over a theory of substantive rationality and the assumptions about maximizing utility and profits. They should be looking directly at the decision mechanisms of people—to use Marshall's words—in the ordinary business of life. Because of their preoccupation with utility and profit-maximization, economists fail to see that most of the action derived from their theories—the real force of their predictive powers—comes from the auxiliary assumptions that define their environment. The evidence is overwhelming that this can't provide a sufficient base for explaining and predicting economic behavior. I can only conclude that the economics profession should allocate just a small fraction—say 5 percent—of our research resources to studying the actual behavior of human beings in the process of making decisions. If the profession did that, we'd be headed for a golden age in economics. Then we could begin to recover from the embarrassment of our current inability to deal with some of the central economic problems and policy issues of our day.

IV.11 Why Economists Disagree

It is common knowledge today that economists disagree; they disagree very much in public; they disagree about the causes of the present economic situation; they disagree about the policies that will improve that situation. We have all sorts of labels for difference schools of economics: we have Keynesians who have been around since the Great Depression; we have monetarists, Milton Friedman being the best known person who flies that banner; we have, more recently, supply-side economists who set up quite an establishment in Washington D.C.; we have another slightly more esoteric group called rational expectationists, who argue that people are not only rational in general, but that they are rational even about the way they form expectations about the future; and, of course, we have budget balancers; and I probably left out a few breeds along the way. They disagree about the policies that should be followed by the government with respect to the economy, and they often disagree as well about the forecasts that they make for the near future of the economy. And in the light of this apparent disarray, I think it's fair to ask whether economics really is, as some would claim, a science.

There are other sciences that also sometimes show a less than completely unanimous front. Meteorologists have been known to disagree about their forecasts, but I think most of us would concede that meteorology is a science. It's a science because it makes use of models of atmospheric processes that are consistent with the basic laws of physics. But even the possession of such basic laws does not necessarily make it possible for a group of scientists to predict the behaviour of a very complex system like the atmosphere or the economy; some would even say "a chaotic system like the atmosphere or the economy."

While the disagreements among economists are very well known and evident and public, it's perhaps less well known that there is, in fact, a very high level of agreement among economists. Economists, in fact, do subscribe, nearly to a man and woman, to a central core of theory and to a particular way of reasoning about economic and sometimes non-economic questions. I mean to include all to the groups to economists mentioned earlier: the Keynesians, the monetarists, the supply-siders, the rational expectationists, the budget balancers and any others that I left out.

As an example, suppose we put the following question to a random sample of citizens of Canada, (and I was told that the question has actually been put): "during a period of gasoline shortage, rationing tickets for gasoline are issued to the poor so that they can be sure to have enough gasoline to meet their transportation needs. The question is whether the recipients of those ration tickets should be allowed, if they wish, to sell the tickets to others who may want more gasoline than they can get and who are willing to pay for those tickets." When that question was actually put in a proper survey, to a random sample of laymen, somewhere between 80 and 85% said "no". This majority felt that those people who were given ration tickets because they need gasoline should not be allowed to sell the tickets and use the money for other purposes, even though they would feel better off after the sale, and even though the other people who voluntarily offer them money for the gasoline tickets would presumably feel better off after the sale as well.

I haven't taken that poll among economists, but I will say with complete certainty that virtually 100% of economists of all persuasions believe that the sale of ration tickets should be legal—that the poor who would rather have money than gasoline should be allowed to make that decision, and that other people in the society who wanted to pay whatever price was negotiated for that gasoline, and give their money for it, should be permitted to do so. Here's a case where not only do economists as a group of professionals have a very different view than that which is evidently current in the general population, but in spite of all their disagreements about public policy, they have nearly a unanimity of view on this question.

I would like to describe first the theory that virtually all brands of economists share, and then discuss their way of common reasoning. The theory is very simple: all people, or at least all economic decision units in society, such as business firms, consumers and members of the labour force, are utility maximizers. That is, in making our choices, we consult our utility function which tells us which bundles of goods and services we prefer to which other goods and services, and we make our choices subject to budget limitations. We make these choices in such a way that we get the most preferred bundle of goods and services that our money will buy, including such credit as we can raise. Now, that hypothesis by itself has some implied premises buried in it. The first is that each of us carries around in us a consistent, comprehensive utility function, although we may not be aware of it and there are no conscious calculations involved in its use. It is assumed that we are able to order, in terms of preference, any bundles of goods and services that may be provided to us.

No matter how plausible you find this assumption with respect to your own behaviour, or how consistent you view your own behaviour over a period of time, this is a very basic hypothesis that enters into all economic reasoning. And that, of course, includes choices among uncertain things. Many, if not most, of the choices that we make in our lives involve expectations about the future. Even for such things as buying a car or house, our decision will involve not only our present situation, but also our guesses as to whether next year we will be able to afford maintaining a house, whether we will need a car, whether we will be living in the same place, what the state of the economy will be, and so on. All of these decisions involve expectations about the future and also a lot of guesses about the present: information about the alternatives, and consequences of our actions.

The economic premise is that even in the midst of all this complexity, of all these things we would have to balance and juggle, we can make choices that will maximize what is called our "subjective expected utility". "Subjective", because we have to make probability estimates about events, "expected", meaning the average value under these probability estimates, and "utility" as already described. If we are to believe the economic theory, this is the underlying process involved, not necessarily conscious or deliberate. Somehow we act as if we were doing all of those things.

That assumption leads also to a way to reasoning in which an economist, faced with a policy problem, will apply the utility maximization assumption to every decision process and will recommend policies that produce a "Pareto optimum" in a world of equilibrium. A world of equilibrium means one in which everything has settled down, markets balance, supply equals demand, and people's expectations reflect the world as it really is. Economists, by and large, in their policy recommendations are talking about a world of equilibrium. Most of the more refined and powerful economic theories we have today, especially mathematical theories of economics, are theories about equilibrium and usually about competitive equilibrium; that is, a world in which most firms are operating in competitive industries and these industries have reached some kind of a balance.

A "Pareto optimal policy" is one whose outcome is such that you could not improve the lot of any one person without damage to the lot of at least one other person. That does not define a unique state of affairs, but a whole set of possible states that are optimal in the sense that you could not give further benefits to any one person without taking benefits away from someone else. This doesn't say who's going to get lots of benefits or who's going to get few benefits. It's a very restricted claim. When a economists says that income taxes are a good thing or a bad thing, or says anything about taxes, it is usually on the premise that the recommendation being made will bring us closer to a Pareto optimum, the desirable state of affairs where resources are used in the most efficient way.

In terms of the example of gasoline ration tickets, if we could bring about a trade so that I want to give away my gasoline for money, and you want to give away your money for gasoline, then obviously, from our own standpoints, we are both better off after the trade than before. If we are utility maximizers, both of us have increased our utility by that trade. And if both of us can thus increase our utility, then clearly the situation before the trade was not a Pareto optimum. We just improved two people's lots without harming anybody else. And that is the reason why I feel so confident that virtually every economist would agree that the legality of that trade was a good thing. In fact, you will find that in the economic theory presented in *Das Capital* basically the same point of view is taken—that people are utility maximizers. If Marx has quarrels with the present economic system, you could describe them as complaints that businessmen are too effective as utility maximizers for the good of other people. But the reasoning in *Das Capital* is, by and large, and with the exception of a couple of premises here and there, reasoning with which other economists feel quite comfortable. The same thing is true of Keynes' *General Theory*. On almost every page of that book, he uses standard economic reasoning about utility maximizers. I will explain a little later why Keynes comes to different conclusions about business cycles than some other people do.

The allegiance of economists to this core theory of subjective expected utility maximization, and to the way of reasoning that follows from that theory, is hardly less unanimous than the allegiance of physicists to Newton's Three Laws of Motion as revised by relativity. How then in the midst of this agreement on doctrine can economists still disagree? There are two basic reasons. The first is that in order to apply this grand theory to most real world problems, at least problems a little more complicated then the rationing ticket example, it has to be augmented by additional assumptions. Before you can apply the theory, you have to know some facts about the world in which the theory is going to be applied. These may be assumptions about what information people really have. Even when people are subjectively trying to maximizc their utility, they may reach different conclusions if they think the world is one way rather than another. You have to make assumptions about the facts that people have or the information that they are acting on; how, in fact, they are going to deal with uncertainty; how they make up their minds; or what probability they're going to assign to an event. One very large area of disagreement among economists today is about these auxiliary assumptions. Let me give you some examples.

I will start with business cycle theory. Keynes' analysis, which seemed to many people very radical when he published his *General Theory* in 1938, is really a classical economic theory of equilibrium, except for several small deviations from orthodoxy of which I will just mention one. Keynes assumes that everybody is acting perfectly rationally except that labour is kind of stupid. (That's a little surprising because we think of Keynes as a liberal economist.) He thought that labour and labour unions didn't distinguish very clearly in their minds between money wages and real wages. Now all of us having been through a few inflationary years have been taught that there is a difference between money wages and real wages; that before you take your pay cheque home with great pride to your husband or wife with the raise you got last month, you had better look at the price index to see whether the raise was more or less than the increase in prices. We all learned those lessons during the years of inflation. But what Keynes assumed was that labour and labour unions bargained for money wages and that they really didn't understand the difference between these and real wages. If you look at the explanation of underemployment equilibrium or stagnation in Keynes, it really comes basically out of that assumption. We have a perfectly classical economic theory with one little deviation from the assumption of perfect rationality which is capable of changing, very drastically, the behaviour of that system. The classical theory, in contrast, had no room in it for unemployment; everything is balanced, and supply equals demand; if there's unemployment, wages go down to the point where employers are motivated to hire all the unemployed and you return to equilibrium. By making one change in assumptions as did Keynes, you can have a theory with genuine unemployment and therefore fit the facts of the 1930's.

Now let's take an economist from the other end of the spectrum. One economist who is regarded as one of the conservatives, Bob Lucas, adheres to "the rational expectations" doctrine. The doctrine means that people are not only rational in a maximizing way, but also that when they form expectations about the future, they have in mind a model of how the economic system really operates, and they make the decisions which would be reasonable decisions if everybody has such a model in their mind and behaves rationally. The idea is that we have expectations that are rational, in the sense that they would be the expectations that would be very reasonable for people to have, if everybody had them (that would settle the economic system down to equilibrium). How can Lucas possibly get a business cycle into his economic model? He does it just the way that Keynes does. He assumes that everyone behaves this way except that sometimes businessmen are stupid. (And again it's a rather interesting fact that the conservative economist gets his business cycle by attributing the irrationality to businessmen rather than to labour). If you assume that businessmen, when they see a price change taking place, can't tell whether it's a price change in their industry or a change in the general price level of the economy, then you can get a business cycle in the theory. You can see from this that the auxiliary assumptions are extremely powerful in pulling the results of the model around no matter what assumptions you basically make about rationality.

Let me take an example of quite a different kind. The American economist Gary Becker has been very active in trying to explain a vast range of phenomena on grounds of rational behaviour. He deals with phenomena that previously we had thought were in the domain of sociology or some other science than economics. Becker wrote an interesting book called a *Treatise on the Family* in which he tries to explain many phenomena of family life: for example, how many children we have, and why there has been an increase over recent years in the employment of women in the labour market. Why is this taking place? On the one hand, you could suppose that the demand for the services of women had increased. That chases your inquiry a little farther, and you would have to ask why it has increased. Another possibility would be that women feel differently about life that they used to or, in economists' terms, their utility functions have shifted. They now get more utility out of earnings from work than from working around the house. This would cause, of course, a shift in the supply of women in the labour force. The question of why we have more women in the labour market turns out to hinge not just on the rationality assumptions. Assuming that women are making a rational choice as to whether they are going to be employed or stay in the household, or whether they're going to do something else, isn't going to settle the question of how many women are in the labour market until you know some auxiliary facts: has there been, for some reason or another, a change in the demand for women workers, or has there been a shift in their utility function. All of the power in the theory that enables you to make predictions doesn't come from the rationality assumption at all—but comes from the assumptions you make about these auxiliary facts. Becker, for reasons I don't particularly understand, opted for an increase in the demand for the services of women. If I had to guess, I would say that there had been a shift in their utility functions, but neither of us happens to have any facts about the matter.

Auxiliary assumptions, as my examples show, are empirical. It's an empirical question whether labour is confused about the difference between money wages and real wages. It's an empirical question whether businessmen do or do not discriminate accurately between changes in price levels in their industry relative to changes in the overall price level. It's an empirical question whether, for one reason or another, there has been a shift in the demand curve for women employees in the last years.

Since these are empirical questions, we might ask why economists don't take the next step and test these hypotheses, go out and see what the world is like. You can talk to union people, and ask them what they understand about the economy. There are all sorts of skills for asking people about their beliefs, attitudes, hopes, and a lot of other things. You can ask businessmen how they go about making their decisions. You can ask what they think is going to happen in the next three months. By and large, the economics profession has been very leery about going out and posing these kinds of questions. Not the whole profession, however. There have been a few voices in the wilderness. George Katona, at the University Michigan, for many years was pushing the idea of increasing our understanding of how people make decisions by direct enquiries of those people. But most economists have found that empirical work of that kind is rather arduous and messy and that it's more fun to play with theory. There is today a very strong tradition of *a priorism* in economics, or what might be called deductionism. There is a very strong tradition of accepting the utility maximization hypothesis and then seeing, often with the aid of very powerful and elegant mathematical tools, what kind of conclusions you can draw from those premises, preferably by mathematical means. And there are even some economists who think that the theory is analytic and not refutable. I find it a rather curious point of view that a theory which purports to be about the real world should, somehow or other, follow from unrefutable premises and therefore not be subject to empirical test.

I should not say that economists are totally uninterested in empirical work, because at the same time that the field has become highly mathematized, it also has developed extremely sophisticated statistical techniques. Economists spend a lot of time taking data and fitting regression lines to those data, testing them statistically in every which way. But largely, almost exclusively, these data have been produced by others, usually by public sources. They are general economic data on the price level, on the kinds of things we gather in the census of manufacturing and the like. While economists have applied very sophisticated econometric techniques to these data, the data themselves are almost all highly aggregated and concerned with society as a whole or very large segments thereof. They are not detailed data about how individuals or individual business firms are behaving.

Increasingly, we have come to realize that these data are very noisy indeed. They give us a very rough and approximate picture of the economic system and, in particular, of what changes are taking place in that system from time to time. No matter how sophisticated the analytical techniques, if you start out with bad data, you're not going to squeeze very much information out of them. In other sciences, statistical techniques are also utilized, but usually to determine the precision of measurements. When measurements turn out to be insufficiently precise for the theories that are being tested, scientists go back to the drawing board to invent better instruments to get better information and better measurements.

Since World War II, economics has largely taken the other path of thinking that if you make your analytical tools sufficiently sophisticated and powerful, you can squeeze meaning out of extremely rough statistical data. That's a little like looking at things from the wrong end of the telescope—seeing how small you can make them in order to see how sharp your vision is. It's a challenging intellectual game and many people are caught up in it; but it may not be the way to advance our empirical knowledge of the economic world.

Why do economists behave so perversely if my description is correct? First, like all scientists and perhaps all professionals and most people, economists do what they know how to do. It's not a bad rule, by and large, to do the things you know how to do. Economists are very well trained today not only in the economic theory I have been talking about, but also in econometric methods for examining data. What economists are not trained to do today in most graduate schools is to gather data at the micro-level, at the level of individual consumers or individual business firms. They are not trained in their doctoral work to conduct opinion and attitude studies; they are not trained to observe actual decision-making processes in business organizations. Some such observations have been made, but they have largely been made by people in fields like organization theory and in other parts of the business school; not in the economics department. I think a change in this situation will require a very serious revolution within economics departments and within the profession. It will require a change in methodological viewpoints and a change in the whole Ph.D. program. I was glad to see that in a recent issue of The *Journal of Business Administration*, Professor A. M. Moore (1984/85), who recently retired from the Economics department at U.B.C., expressed very much the same opinion.

But there's still one further reason why economists disagree. Some people, largely outside of economics, have begun to do empirical research which bears on the question of how people actually do make decisions; on the question of whether we really do carry around in our heads something equivalent to a utility function; and whether if we do carry it around, we do in fact maximize. It turns out that the beliefs on which economists agree are simply false; they do not fit the facts. At Carnegie-Mellon University in the 1950's we began to make rather extensive studies of decision making in business organizations. We watched the processes that firms used to decide what investments they were going to make in new products, or new factories, new facilities, new machinery and so forth. We made empirical studies within business firms about how they actually used the accounting information that was developed in their books. What inferences did they draw from it; how did they draw those inferences?

Out of that research came a good many publications; one that's especially well known is *The Behavioural Theory of the Firm* by my colleagues

Dick Cyert and Jim March. They were able to show from this kind of empirical work that the decision-making process in business firms was very different from the model that is presented in standard economic theory. Business firms, for example, when they were making reasonable levels of profits, often coasted along until difficulties arose, and their most intense search for new possibilities, cost cutting, and new products often took place when profits were falling off, or were falling below their expectations.

A term like "reasonable profits" does not exist in present day economic theory. It's a term well known to businessmen who form expectations of what they should be able to accomplish, and whose search for new alternatives and possibilities is very much influenced by whether what they are accomplishing does or does not meet those expectations. That is a kind of behaviour that is very different from knowing that you have a mountain to climb and always finding yourself on the top, which is the maximization theory. Today there are, in several places, economists who are actually conducting experiments to see whether groups of business school students placed in a trading situation will, in fact, trade according to classical economic theory. Vernon Smith, at the University of Arizona, and Charlie Plott at Cal Tech, have developed a whole field of experimental economics, where they put people, usually motivated by money, in laboratory situations where you can make predictions using standard economic theory. In the earlier experiments of this sort, they often confirmed that a group of bargaining students would soon reach an equilibrium between supply and demand at the price that theory would have predicted. When they began to complicate the experiments a little bit to make them look like real world situations, important deviations between actual behaviour and that predicted by the classical theory immediately began to appear. Economists are now beginning to pay attention to the findings of people like Vernon Smith and Charlie Plott.

A third body of empirical research relevant to the heartland of economic theory has been carried out primarily by psychologists. This research bears on the ability of people to choose in terms of a consistent utility function, especially under conditions of uncertainty where probabilities and risks are attached. Perhaps the most famous team of these psychologists are Amos Tversky and Danny Kahneman at Stanford. They present people with various kinds of risky gambles; for example, would you prefer to do this with a 40% chance of winning, or do that with a 80% chance of winning? By manipulating the possible bargains a little bit, you can confront people with alternatives that allow you, after they have made their choices, to test their consistency. You can test whether rational people who are maximizing subjective expected utility could have made these choices.

In experiment after experiment, we find large inconsistencies in behaviour. Is it surprising that confronted with a variety of uncertainties and probabilities, we sometimes and under certain circumstances, opt for highly risky things; and other times and other circumstances, we opt for highly conservative things; that there are lots of people in the world today who both buy lottery tickets and carry insurance at the same time? So we have a large and growing body of evidence today that people do not have consistent utility functions; that they do not reason correctly and consistently about probabilities and risks; that they use all sorts of rules of thumb to simplify choice; and that they satisfice—that is, they look for good enough outcomes rather than optimizing. So we don't have just a suspicion that people are not profit maximizers or utility maximizers. We have a large body of evidence today and the beginnings of some notions of what it is people in fact do when they are confronted with uncertainty and complexity; when they can't carry out either explicitly or implicitly the kinds of calculations that would be required for the consistent behaviour that is predicted by economics. I think the next steps in the story are to secure a wider knowledge about these new theories among economists and bring them into the mainstream of economics.

If the situation that I have described is even 80% correct, maybe even if it's 40% correct, then we have a real problem in our society. Economics is important to society and to the effective operation of our institutions. It's the means by which we satisfy our material and some of our immaterial wants and needs; and if we are to have wise public policies in society, we need to have a deeper and better understanding of how the economy actually operates. I have already suggested what my remedy would be for the present situation. Most of that remedy is going to have to be implemented by the economics profession itself. Maybe a little bit of encouragement from outside and a little bit of nudging will help. First of all, the auxiliary assumptions of economics, which are factual assumptions, as well as the central theoretical assumptions of classical economics, will have to undergo rather massive revision on the basis of empirical evidence. And we have only the beginnings of the evidence that we need in order to do that job.

A field like biology, which now has very powerful theories underlying much of molecular biology, genetics, and biochemistry, long before it got to that stage, had paid its dues in terms of doing the empirical work that had to come first. The task has never been done in economics of providing a detailed description of actual economic behaviour that has to underlie any kind of satisfactory theory. Secondly, to build that kind of empirical body of evidence, economists are going to have to receive new kinds of research training; they are going to have to borrow and learn from psychology and organization theory, which have at least some, or perhaps most, of the techniques that would be needed. The situation isn't completely bleak. Increasing numbers of mainline economists are beginning to perceive and accept the need for these reforms, but there is far from a consensus within the profession about these issues.

As a matter of fact, that is an understatement. While the views I'm presenting represent a minority position in economics, I'm not alone. Economists as distinguished as Ken Arrow, Wassily Leontief, and others have made similar complaints. It's going to take these reforms to make economics really useable and to allow it to play the policy role to which it aspires. The desire of economics to play that role and the desire of all of us to have good advice from economists are in themselves major sources of pressure toward the sort of reform which I have described. The reform will not be rapid, it also will not turn economics from a difficult to an easy science. There is no reason to suppose that an economics that correctly describes and theorizes about the world is going to be any easier for laymen to understand than bio-chemistry, which actually describes what goes on in chemical reactions. It's not going to become an easy science, but reform will gradually remove what I regard as the present scandal in economics. This is not just the public scandal of disarray, not just the public scandal of showing in public that you can't get together, that there's no unity in the family. It's the private scandal, known best to economists themselves, about a science that, during a period I hope is nearly over, almost renounced the practice of looking at the empirical evidence that is supposed to provide, and necessarily must provide, its foundations.

Questions and Answers

Question Is it possible to re-educate economists in the directions you suggest?

Answer If the mainstream of the profession becomes increasingly persuaded that it needs to move in the directions I've suggested, then a lot of re-education will take place. There are many professions whose knowledge has changed very rapidly during the lifetime of participants and practitioners in the profession. Medical knowledge changes every year and we expect the profession to develop institutions that re-train and update physicians. The same kinds of procedures would allow economists to move with their profession as it changes, although I don't see that change happening overnight. I perhaps didn't emphasize enough that there are some good things about economic training. One is that economists are very good in reasoning from premises and doing it pretty rigorously and logically. The thing that is needed are the right premises to reason from. Maybe people who can reason very accurately from dubious premises will do quite well when they have better facts to reason from. I think we can have some optimism about that.

Question During the 1970's there were some attempts to test, in the field especially, hypotheses about the effects of an negative income tax. This was a very important proposal in the United States as a basis for welfare reform. There were some very interesting experiments carried out on this proposal. In light of the fact that the experiments were quite expensive and only tested a narrow range of circumstances, can we really expect to establish the facts on which economic reasoning can rest, or should we be rather humble in our expectations of how much of a science we can build of economic behaviour?

Answer The budget for the experiments on the negative income tax was probably less than ten million dollars. The NASA budget has been somewhere in the neighbourhood of three billion dollars. The decimal point is in a different place! One of the troubles with the social sciences is that, except for the periodic census which historically was started for other reasons, we've had our decimal point in the wrong place when it comes to undertaking empirical work in the field. We should be spending hundreds of millions of dollars a year understanding our economy. We can spend this amount yearly understanding quarks, but I think that economic processes and human beings making decisions are almost as interesting. The modesty we have, and the modesty we shouldn't have, is the modesty in thinking small about the kind of empirical inquiry we ought to be making. If we made it on the NASA scale, I think we would find that our facts would be firm enough to arrive at more sensible policies then we have today. The negative income tax enquiry should have been the beginning of something extremely important but the resulting tax proposals were left to die. We still have the same welfare system basically that we had 15 or 20 years ago.

Question How much of a paradigm shift would be implied by carrying on the kind of empirical research that you suggested. Are we going to have a complete revolution in economic theory, or just a little revolution?

Answer I really shouldn't predict that because I've been arguing that what we most need are not new prescriptions or new theories but evidence about how the world really works. We would have to find out how big the revolution is after we begin to gather that evidence. The evidence we have already shows that the decision-making processes of firms, for example, are rather drastically different from the notions of a profit maximization environment where we really know supply and demand curves. In view of discrepancies that have already appeared in the facts we find, I would suppose that present theory would not remain unscathed.

Question Since most of the existing theory is based on equilibrium, and a large part of our problem is to predict what's going to happen in the future, what are our possibilities and prospects of really developing a science that will have some power of prediction?

Answer This hinges, in turn, on your views as to how patterned and rule-like human behaviour is. I think I see a fair amount of regularity in human behaviour. All of us in our own lives and interactions with other people make many predictions about how others are going to respond. The local transportation company makes many such predictions, otherwise they wouldn't know how many buses to have out tomorrow morning. So this is a relative matter. Any increase in the quality of our predictions about behaviour certainly will increase our ability to respond in intelligent ways and to adopt intelligent public policies. It is not as though we were not acting now; we have to act; inaction is action. The question is how far can we move in improving it.

We are going to reach a point where we realize that the economic decision making of people is not itself history-free. After people have been experiencing inflation for 5 years, they probably do take account of the difference between real and nominal prices. That type of information would play an important role in our predictions. In contrast, after people have not been experiencing much inflation for 5 years, they would probably ignore differences between real and nominal changes in prices. As we make advances in economic theory and understand more about human decision-making, we'll find that human beings, since they can't be aware of everything at once, are doing their decision-making in terms of a few crucial factors in situations, and these factors are themselves history-dependent. That does not condemn the science to futility, it just makes it a little more complicated and sophisticated.

Question Would some of the differences among economists be based on their different philosophies and ideals of political life?

Answer The closer you come to policy prescription, the more that differences in basic values and goals can enter into those prescriptions. What I find striking is that when I listen to debates among economists, especially the internal debates on the policy side, they hinge around which policies will produce Pareto optimality. They are debates about the efficiency of the operation of the economic system. Now maybe if those debates were settled, economists would get on to some more fundamental debates about values. For example, attitudes about economic measures that redistribute income, and which are certainly highly value tinged are, among economists, often debated in considerable measure in terms of the effects of the redistribution of income on incentives; namely, on the efficiency of the system. So, to that extent, these issues become technical and the more philosophic issues tend to get muted within the profession.

Question What are the basic problems in the U.S. economy today?

Answer We need to know a great deal empirically that we don't know in order to answer questions concerning the current plight of the U.S. economy. I can recite some of the usual wisdom—the United States dollar has been overpriced in world markets and this is why we have had terrible trade balance problems; we have a very large debt burden which is worrisome because of high interest rates and because the debt is not internal, etc. But I think we need to learn a great deal more about how people actually react to uncertainties about the future, especially to know what the implications of those facts are. During the 1950's and 60's we thought we knew fairly well, using primarily Keynesian techniques, how to fine tune an economy. And then with the beginnings of what was later called stagflation, we discovered we didn't know how to fine tune with respect to employment at the same time we kept stable price levels. The fact that something which seemed to be all in hand, something we thought we understood very well in the profession, became unhinged has been a major force in bringing about a change in attitude, perhaps a loss of morale, in the profession. This fact is beginning to make more and more members of the profession willing to rethink some of the fundamental economic issues. I don't have answers for those questions. I could join any one of the groups I mentioned at the beginning and give you their answer, but I don't think we are going to have answers we can believe until we do the hard job of gathering the facts.

Question What importance would you attach to providing economists with a sense of historical perspective?

Answer It is highly possible and probable that as we understand better the economic system and the fact that human beings when trying to be rational or reasonable are still able to look only at a very selected part of the whole world, we are going to realize the importance of attentional variables. What are people attending to today? Are we worrying about energy, environment or inflation? And what are we ignoring? These kinds of issues are going to play a larger role in economic theory. This theory is going to have to include, which it never did, a theory of attention; of what people are attending to. That is going to make economics much more a historical science; that is, a science in which behaviour has to be understood in relation to the events that preceded it, as well as the immediate economic situation that people find themselves in. The time dimension has to be brought into economics, not merely in the current form of regressions on time series, but as a real understanding that there can be qualitative shifts in the variables that people take into account in making their decisions.

Question You have described economists as working from assumptions which are accepted as being true and proceeding to make deductions very rigorously on that basis. You are now suggesting that economists be asked to examine the assumptions to be able to decide on some empirical basis whether those assumptions are true, false, somewhat true, or somewhat false. Is it going to be possible for economics to survive that kind of shift in terms of this sort of reasoning that is supposed to come forth from economics?

Answer I've argued that economists reason quite rigorously from given premises, but that the premises now need re-examination and may have to be replaced. I think many of them will. The question is whether economics is going to survive that. If by economics we mean the study of and understanding of economic institutions and decision-making processes in those institutions, I don't think we are going to give up that kind of study. Whether the same people will be studying it in all cases is another question.

Professions do change. I used earlier the example of biology. There's been a major revolution in biology in my lifetime. Partly that was brought about because a lot people who were already biologists moved in the direction of understanding and making use of some of the new developments in the areas of molecular biology, biochemistry, genetics and so on. Also there has been a great inflow of people from chemistry, and younger people who are trained in new ways of looking at things. The cadre of people who call themselves biologists today are very different with respect to their knowledge and skills than the people who called themselves biologists 50 years ago. If economics moves in the direction which I devoutly hope it will, I expect that much the same thing is going to happen. I would expect an ingestion of people from fields like psychology who can bring in some of the empirical techniques that are needed and help economics hone those techniques and apply them to its own purposes. These people will not only bring in techniques, but also the body of knowledge we have been acquiring in cognitive psychology about how people behave. Contributions will also come from people in business schools who have done field research in business organizations. So, some will survive and there will be lots of newcomers.

Question Present economic theory, in a certain sense, has no pathway from one Pareto optimum to another. It can have lots of efficient solutions with different allocations of goods to different groups of people, and there is nothing in the current theory that tells you which of these is to be preferred to the others.

Answer One should not expect that anything that's going to happen to economics is going to solve problems of distribution in a society, because these problems are not simply technical issues of how that society can operate its economic institutions efficiently. They are questions of fairness—as to who should get how much of the rewards of that system. Economists are extremely clear in understanding that distinction. Economics as a science can only tell you what's efficient; it cannot tell what constitutes a fair distribution of wealth or income. Sometimes the technical question and the question of fairness can intermingle when actions are undertaken that particular people, groups, or society think unfair. For example, some economists think that the present income tax causes a departure from the efficient allocation of resources. So, in economic debates, you often hear economists opposing resource distribution measures on grounds of inefficiency of resource use. The two are connected in that sense. But economics by itself, or any science, really has nothing to say, as a matter of justice, about how egalitarian or inegalitarian a society ought to be.

Question Would the changes you have been suggesting take care of the political biases that one seems to encounter in the economic positions of economists and others?

Answer We have to realize that in the management of a society, there are not just questions of building institutions that will make that society efficient in meeting human needs and wants. That is the main business of the economic mechanism; but there are also questions of justice between people, and relative welfare. And those are not technical questions; they are moral questions and they are going to be with us just as strongly as ever. Of course, you describe them as political questions, as a large part of politics is concerned with the question of who gets what in the society. I would be a little worried about a society that didn't leave those questions to politics; it would be a very different society then the one that any of us know.

Question Since economists are well trained in the use of computers, have they created models to build in satisficing and cooperation in a multi-value system. That's ideal for computers and you originally suggested this in 1947. If they do make these models, the only thing I'd worry about is that economists might inadvertently bias the results with their own values.

Answer There has been a good deal of modelling in economics by people like Larry Klein, for example, who has devoted his whole career to trying to improve macro-economic models that will make relatively short-run predictions, of a year or couple of years, for economies. There are other speculative models of the sort that Jay Forrester built for the Club of Rome a few years ago in which he tried to model what would happen over a longer period of years with respect to resource exhaustion and related problems. There has been a good deal of modelling done but, of course, those models are only as good as the assumptions you put into them. Each equation you put in a computer model is a description of the behaviour of some module in the economic system. If you don't have your facts right, the models are going to predict wrong. It is probably true today that Larry Klein's model of the American economy does better than chance. That's small praise, but it is praise. If we say that of the weatherman, that is also praise.

Question Are these models satisficing models?

Answer In models of the sort that Larry Klein builds, or any kind of a national model of an economy at such an aggregated level, there are gross equations which are supposed to describe behaviour which would be the consequence of utility maximization; but utility maximization is not in there explicitly. Therefore, it's not completely impossible that these models could be describing satisficing rather than maximizing behaviour. But certainly insofar as theoretical assumptions work their way into these models, they tend to be the mainstream assumptions of maximization.

Question Would you like to comment on the usefulness of the long-wave theories as a power of prediction, given that they have a basis in historical empirical evidence?

Answer The long-wave theorists are people who have looked at really long-term data, sometimes 150 years or a little less, and believe that they have detected in those data long-term economic fluctuations such as the "Kondratief" cycle and others of that kind. This is a little like sun-spot theory in that we know that there are periodicities in a lot of celestial events, some of them very long. The evidence is very difficult to interpret because it is extremely hard to discriminate between a dynamic system that is bubbling along and undergoing various kinds of random shocks, and a dynamic system that is undergoing periodic cycles. Under very many circumstances, random shocks do cumulate over periods and produce waves that look as though there were cycles underlying them.

Furthermore, there can be various kinds of cycles. There can be cycles that are paced by some kind of periodic event and recur, like the cycles of weather through the year. If they ever get out of phase, the sun gets the cycle back into kilter again. It's a rigorous 12 month cycle that changes from year to year, but we have no difficulty detecting this cycle in the weather. Another kind of cycle is not synchronous in that sense, and does not necessarily stay in phase. It might average 20 or 21 years, or some of the cycles might be longer or shorter. These are very hard to distinguish from random fluctuations of a dynamic system. There are still other possibilities. If you have a system whose equations have non-linearities, then there may be built into the system so-called "limit cycles" which may, in simple cases, have definite periods. I don't think anyone has shown from the few available series of long-term data which of these alternatives is the correct one. One reason for not completely dismissing the concern with the longer cycles is that some people have theorized that economic stagnation and bursts of economic activity are associated with them. Schumpeter, for example, thought that the economy tended to get into stagnation and then a new burst of innovation would shove it off and that, in fact, this process might be correlated with these kinds of cycles. So I don't want to dismiss them completely, but I think we are going to learn more about the shorter run operation of the economic system before we fully understand its long term behaviour.

Acknowledgement

This Chapter is based on an address to The Vancouver Institute on February 8, 1986.

Reference

Moore, A. Milton, (1984/85) "Could Business Schools Succeed Where Economists Have Failed?", *Journal of Business Administration*, Vol. 15, Nos. 1&2, pp. 87–109.

IV.12 The State of Economic Science

The title of this volume of essays is "The State of Economic Science," but I should not like to limit myself to just describing where economics is now: I would like also to say something, however conjectural, about the future. Since, in contrast to Larry Klein, forecasting is not my professional metier, perhaps I can avoid some of the dangers of amateurism by putting more emphasis on the prescriptive than on the predictive; by taking high moral ground and telling economics what it should be doing that it is not now doing.

Consensus and Dissention Among Economists

With this agenda, my emphasis will be on methodological issues: on what kinds of research economists should be doing and what tools they will need for doing it. But my methodological prescriptions need to derive from a view of the substance of economics and its problems, and should rest on an assessment of where economic science stands today. Let me begin with that.

Public Disagreement Among Economists

I must first explain why economists are seen by the general public to be constantly disagreeing with one another. Of course that is not wholly true with respect to my distinguished colleagues in this volume. I have observed that Ken Arrow, Larry Klein, Jim Tobin, and Bob Solow often agree even on public policy issues—they may more often disagree with Jim Buchanan. But if Milton Friedman, or George Stigler, or Ted Schultz—to mention just a few equally notable luminaries—had happened to be present in this year's sample, the disagreement/agreement ratio would have increased quite sharply. And we could perhaps liven up the discussion even further by adding Bob Lucas or Sam Bowles. I have not even begun to exhaust the spectrum of policy views we can find within the economics profession.

Although you may have seen relatively little disagreement among the authors in this volume, the public is not mistaken in its perception that economists disagree frequently and vociferously. The fact of the matter is that, no matter what our views on matters of public policy, we can almost certainly find a relatively prominent economist to defend them; and this democratic indiscipline of the profession is well known to all readers of the daily press. We have Keynesian economics, monetarism, supply-side economics, rational expectations, and budget balancing, not to mention free trade, protection for infant industries, and proponents of the income tax, the single tax, the sales tax, and almost no taxes at all.

When national economic problems are under discussion, economists disagree as to whether to give priority to inflation, the public debt, employment, taxes, the trade balance, or the rate of interest. Clearly, these priorities have much to say about what policies economists will advocate. During the late seventies, there was a massive shift in primary concern from employment to inflation, but the shift was not unanimous and left the profession in as much disarray as before—or more. Likewise, it is easy to start a lively argument about whether taxes should be raised in order to stem the rise in the national debt, or whether the burden of the national debt on the federal budget should be relieved by lowering interest rates.

And finally, economists disagree about their forecasts for the economy over the coming months or years. We can almost always find optimists, pessimists, and flat-planers, although their relative numbers vary from time to time. Nor do these proportions much correlate with what the economy actually does. Economic forecasting is in low repute, often also among economists, who can even provide theoretical reasons why it should be impossible to predict the course of the business cycle or the stock market. The last recession saw a high casualty rate among economic forecasting units attached to business firms—at a time of budget crunch, they were seen as dispensable.

With this cacophony of economic voices, it is not surprising that the status of economics as a science is sometimes challenged by a bemused public. Isn't science supposed to provide accurate predictions about its phenomena? Is economics therefore not a science? We had best reserve our judgment a bit until I get on with my story. We are aware that meteorologists also disagree widely in their forecasts, but we would not doubt that meteorology is a science. For meteorologists have built a model of the atmospheric processes that is consistent with the basic, well-supported, laws of physics. Possessing such a model does not guarantee an ability to predict the future of the weather with any great accuracy.

In recent years, there has even been a very exciting development in the field of mathematics that suggests that certain complex systems (systems of nonlinear equations) may behave in a way that makes them inherently unpredictable. Such systems are called "chaotic," and their central characteristic is that a tiny displacement of their initial conditions sometimes causes them to go off on completely divergent paths. We don't know whether the atmosphere is actually a chaotic system, but if it is, the wingbeats of a butterfly in Singapore may cause a tornado in Chicago.

We also don't know whether the economy is a chaotic system. There are some statistical tests that can be applied to time series—the money supply, or stock prices, or other economic series—to distinguish between simple randomness and the kind of chaos and unpredictability I am describing here. Some attempts have been made recently by economists to test whether various economic time series are chaotic, but the results so far are inconclusive. (The September 1987 issue of the *Journal of Economic Behavior and Organization*, Volume 8, Number 3, which is devoted to the subject of chaos in dynamic economic systems, will provide the reader with a good introduction to the topic.) I mention chaos to indicate that we should be wary of using prediction as a test of science, and especially of whether economics is a science, for an understanding of mechanisms does not guarantee predictability.

Private Agreement among Economists

If it is well known that economists disagree, it is less well known to the general public, although perhaps not among economists, that there is a very high level of *agreement* among them. I will try to explain the apparent paradox and show why this is so. In spite of the disagreements I have enumerated, economists subscribe, nearly to a man and woman, to a common central core of theory, and above all, to a way of reasoning about economic questions. Before I state what the common core is, let me give an example of the kind of agreement that this communality produces.

Suppose that during a period of gasoline shortage, the government issues ration tickets to the poor to guarantee them an adequate supply of gasoline at a moderate price. Should the law be written so that the poor may sell their ration tickets to others if they would prefer the money to the gasoline, or should such exchanges be prohibited by law?

When this question was presented to a national sample of lay persons, about 80 percent replied that the exchange should be prohibited—that the poor should be able to use the tickets only to purchase gasoline.

When the same question was presented to a national sample of economists, virtually all responded that the exchange should be allowed.[1]

The reason economists are able to agree on this conclusion is that they apply to the problem a common set of assumptions and inference procedures. All (or nearly all) economists assume that every person is a utility maximizer: (1) possesses a consistent, comprehensive utility function that orders all the possible alternatives of choice, and (2) selects among alternatives so as to maximize subjective expected utility. "Subjective expected" means that the decisionmaker assigns (subjectively) probabilities to all possible outcomes of each available alternative, and averages the utilities of these outcomes, using the subjective probabilities as weights. Economists (nearly all economists) claim that people do behave so as to maximize utility, and that they *ought* to behave in this way, which they regard as uniquely rational.

Now in the rationing case, if the potential seller and buyer both agree on a price for the tickets, this must mean—using the standard economic reasoning—that each one thinks that his or her utility will be increased by the exchange. Hence, they will make the exchange if they are permitted to, and they should be permitted to because then everyone will be better off. When certain other conditions are also satisfied, the exchange is said to produce a *Pareto optimum*, a situation that could not be altered in any way to produce an increase in utility for *both* participants. Economists also refer to solutions of decision problems that are Pareto optimal as producing an *efficient allocation of resources*.

My account of the core of standard economic theory is, of course, something of an oversimplification. Many of the conclusions, particularly the normative ones, depend on the economic system being in a stable state of competitive equilibrium, and only under these conditions can a Pareto optimum guarantee an efficient allocation of resources. My simplified version, however, gives a clear enough picture of the nature of contemporary economic reasoning that is subscribed to by almost every school of thought.

Even Marx, in *Das Kapital* subscribes to this theory and this way of reasoning. So does Keynes; for the *General Theory* uses, on every page, standard economic reasoning. So do the rational expectationists, like Lucas and Sargent, and the monetarists, like Friedman. So do my predecessors in this volume. The allegiance of economists of all sects and descriptions to subjective expected utility maximization is hardly less unanimous than the allegiance of physicists to Newton's Three Laws of Motion in their relativised form.

Disagreement from Consensus

Now I appear to have hooked myself on a serious dilemma. If economists agree in the way I have just outlined, how can they disagree in the ways I described earlier? They can disagree because, in order to apply the standard core theory to real-world problems, that theory has to be augmented by additional assumptions, especially assumptions about what information people have, and how they deal with uncertainty and with their own limited capacities for computation. Economists disagree about these auxiliary assumptions; and as a result of the disagreement, reach very different conclusions even though applying identical modes of reasoning. That is not surprising: conclusions depend on premises. Using identical laws of logic, we will reach quite different conclusions about the visibility of swans in dim light from the premise "All swans are white" than from "All swans are black."

Let me provide an example of the sources of disagreement in economics from a central topic of macroeconomics: business cycle theory. The theory of static equilibrium under perfect competition developed by Arrow, Debreu, and others proves that, under equilibrium conditions, all resources will be fully employed: labor, capital, and so on. However, most (not all) economists concede that the real world is plagued by a fluctuating level of employment of both labor and production facilities, with periods, from time to time, of substantial unemployment. How can we, within the framework of the accepted theory and method of reasoning, reconcile general equilibrium theory with the fact of unemployment and underemployment of resources. We can do it by making one small change in the assumptions of rationality—by introducing one small grain of irrationality or nonrationality into behavior, and allowing that grain to grow into the pearl of unemployment of resources.

Keynes uses several mechanisms to produce this result; I will refer to just one of them. Starting with a standard classical model, he assumes that labor is not always quite rational, specifically, that in bargaining for wages, labor sometimes confuses the money wage, in current prices, with the real wage, adjusted for price changes. Labor is just a little stupid, and this stupidity draws the system away from full-employment equilibrium into a situation in which unemployment can appear and persist.

Lucas, a rational expectationist usually regarded as standing at the opposite end of the policy spectrum from Keynes, also admits that there is sometimes unemployment in the real world. He too starts out with a model of perfect rationality, which of course leads to full-employment equilibrium. He also introduces a grain of sand to displace that equilibrium and produce unemployment. His grain of sand consists in assuming that businessmen are not always quite rational, specifically, that they sometimes stupidly mistake a shift in the general price level for a change in relative prices in their own industry. This mistake (from lack of knowledge or ignorance in calculation) draws the system away from full-employment equilibrium into a state where there is unemployment.

So both Keynes and Lucas depart from the assumptions of perfect rationality in order to account for a fact of the real world, the fact of periodic unemployment. Both introduce a grain of irrationality in the form of a confusion between monetary and real prices—what economists usually call "money illusion." In the case of Keynes, the liberal, the money illusion is suffered by labor; in the case of Lucas, the conservative, it is suffered by businessmen. Presumably we know our friends better than we know strangers! Not only do they introduce irrationality in different ways, but they draw different conclusions, as a consequence, as to what policies should be followed to deal with the resulting unemployment.

In understanding the disagreement between Lucas and Keynes, it is important to remember where it comes from. It does not come from the central theory of rational economic behavior, on which they both agree, but from the auxiliary assumptions—the grains of sand—on which they disagree. That might lead us to ask where these auxiliary assumptions come from. They are empirical assumptions, assumptions about how particular groups of human beings behave in the real world, about what they know and don't know and how they use that knowledge or are affected by that ignorance. But you will search the pages of Keynes and Lucas vainly if you want to know the evidence from which these crucial premises are drawn. They are presented simply as "obvious" facts, as something "everyone knows." A dangerous procedure for a science that purports to give an account of the real world!

It is not only in business cycle theory that the auxiliary assumptions do all the work of deriving the conclusions. Here is an example drawn from microeconomics. In recent years, we have seen a kind of economic imperialism in which microeconomists seek to demonstrate that they can use the standard theory to explain not only strictly economic phenomena but the phenomena of politics, the family, and indeed of all of our social institutions as well. A vigorous and well-known leader of this intellectual imperialism is Gary Becker, of the University of Chicago; and James Buchanan also belongs to this schools of thought, especially as it applies to political institutions.

Let us see how Becker, in his book on the family, deals with the observed fact that the employment of women has increased rapidly in recent years. Becker explains that this is due to the fact that the demand curve for women employees has shifted upward during this same time—more women will be employed at any wage, and hence wages will rise as more women attracted from the home to the labor market. Becker cites no particular evidence for the shift in the demand curve, and indeed, it is not clear that during the period he is concerned with, the wages of women increased much more than the wages of men.

Moreover, there are alternative explanations we could consider. Perhaps the utility function of women has shifted, for example, as a consequence of consciousness raising, so that they prefer outside work to homework more than they did before. Or perhaps the productivity of homework has increased with the availability of household appliances, while the demand for it is relatively inelastic. All of these shifts would cause an increase in the number of women employed outside the home, and we are far from exhausting the list of possible explanations.

Again we see that the conclusion (which matches an observed fact) is not a consequence of the theory of rationality. The real work is done by the auxiliary assumptions, and without additional empirical evidence (which Becker does not bother to provide), we do not know which of the possible auxiliary assumptions is actually satisfied, and hence is causing the phenomenon. Without taking seriously the task of verifying the auxiliary assumptions empirically, we can find an "explanation" for any fact; our theory becomes tautological and vacuous. As Poincaré once remarked about another theory: "An explanation was necessary, and was forthcoming; they always are; hypotheses are what we lack the least."

In economics, hypotheses are certainly what we lack the least. Auxiliary hypotheses, frequently manufactured in the armchair, are in good supply. What is lacking is empirical evidence to test them. Why don't economists devote themselves more vigorously to testing their auxiliary hypotheses? I can only conjecture (the question is one that should also be settled by facts, historical and sociological facts about the economics profession).

First, there is a tradition of a priorism and deductivism in economics, which goes back at least to Adam Smith (although Smith was not reluctant to take facts where he could find them). It is more fun, and easier, to play with theory, especially mathematical theory, than to grub for facts. As long as the tradition persists in the profession, editors will accept analyses based on postulated facts or facts tested by casual empiricism.

Second, a few philosophers of economics, for example Boland, think that the standard theory is true by definition, and not empirically refutable. Friedman holds a related position, arguing that economic theory can only be tested by assessing the empirical correctness of its "predictions," and not by testing the correctness of its "assumptions." I have not the time here to argue the fallacies in these positions, which have been pointed out by numerous economists on other occasions. I mention these erroneous beliefs simply to account for the relative indifference of economists to empirical evidence.

Third, economists of course do carry out a very considerable amount of empirical work to test their theories, but they employ only a narrow range of methodologies in doing so. As a result, they spend much of their time viewing the world through the wrong end of a telescope, with correspondingly foggy results. By "the wrong end of a telescope" I mean that economists usually test their theories with the help of rather aggregated data about the economy which have mainly been gathered for practical purposes unconnected with economic theory and whose concepts and units bear only a faint resemblance to the concepts to which they are matched in the theory.

Robert Eisner has described these difficulties eloquently in his recent presidential address to the American Economic Association, which appears as the lead article in the March 1989 *American Economic Review*, 79:1–14. His summary (p. 11) displays the seriousness of his concerns:

> I have ... noted some pitfalls in using current and past variables in analyses that depend critically upon expectations of the future. I have warned of confusion in employing narrowly defined measures of income and product in evaluating flows and trends in comprehensive earnings and output. I have argued that particularly large dangers abound in basing policy on conventional measures of private and public saving, investment and capital. I have suggested that usual estimates of

some of the critical behavioral relations of macroeconomics may be suspect because of a failure to match theoretical constructs with appropriate empirical counterparts.

Very generally, I conclude, it is important in economics—as elsewhere—to know what we are talking about.

A very sophisticated body of econometric theory and methodology has been created since World War II to deal with the problem of carrying out economic analyses with data that are too aggregated, measure the wrong concepts, are too infrequently collected, and are exceedingly noisy. The experience of the past 50 years has shown that these sophisticated econometric tools do not compensate for the poor quality of the data to which they are applied.

Other kinds of data can of course be obtained; data that tell us something about the expectations, preferences, and choices of economic actors at micro levels. Opinion and attribute studies can be conducted (and of course have been). Actual decisionmaking processes can be observed in business organizations (and of course have been). But polling data and "case studies" of individual behavior are mistrusted in orthodox economic methodology. The use of these kinds of data to discover the realities of economic life and to provide an empirical basis for the auxiliary assumptions we need will require a revolution in methodological beliefs in economics, and a revolution in the training of economists, who are not now trained to use these techniques.

Validity of the Standard Theory

If casual empiricism and the neglect of available sources of empirical evidence are a major scandal in contemporary economics, equally scandalous is the retention of beliefs, central to the standard theory, that are empirically false. For when investigators have begun to examine, in field and laboratory, the central assumptions of the standard theory—not just the auxiliary assumptions this time, but the very core of the theory—it has turned out that these assumptions do not fit the facts.

For example, research in the 1950s, reported in *The Behavioral Theory of the Firm* and elsewhere, shows that business firms are not the simple profit-maximizing entities that the standard theory assumes them to be. They sometimes settle for "satisfactory" profits. They operate with slack that is only reduced under the pressure of hard times. They suffer from internal power struggles. They simply do not behave as required to meet the conditions of competitive equilibrium with efficient use of resources.

Second, an increasing number of studies of experimental markets, operated under the controlled conditions of the laboratory, have shown that it is easy to construct market situations where behavior will depart widely from the predictions of the standard theory. Vernon Smith, Charles Plott, and others have shown that behavior tends to settle toward the predicted market equilibrium in simple markets, but that it is not at all difficult to produce booms and busts even under conditions where participants could easily compute the correct, rational behavior that would produce stability and equilibrium.

Third, a long series of studies by Allais, Kahneman, Tversky, and others have shown serious departures from utility-maximizing rationality when choices are made under conditions of uncertainty. Respondents, for example, opt much less frequently for a surgical operation where there is a 20 percent chance of dying than for an otherwise identically described operation where there is an 80 percent chance of living.

The sum and substance of these findings is that people just do not maximize utility. They do not have consistent utility functions (Allais). They do not reason correctly and consistently about probabilities and risks (Kahneman and Tversky). They use rules of thumb (heuristics) to simplify choice (Cyert and March). They look for satisfactory courses of action, they satisfice, instead of optimizing (Simon).

Nature is supposed to abhor vacuums, and the demonstration that a theory is empirically false, as the standard theory of economic choice most certainly is, appears to leave a large vacuum. Is there anything to fill it? Indeed there is. Over the past 30 years, cognitive psychology has developed a large body of empirically tested theory of decisionmaking and problemsolving. So far, economists have mostly ignored it.

The theory of decisionmaking to be found in psychology today substitutes satisficing for optimizing. It gives central position to the limits of human ability to deal with real-world complexity, and to the methods of radical approximation that are used to remove this mismatch of adaptive power to problem difficulty. Enlarging the scope of economic decision theory, it does not assume that the alternatives of choice are given *a priori*, but shows how they can be generated by selective (heuristic) search in problem spaces. It is beginning to investigate the processes that focus human attention on certain problems so that others are ignored, and the processes of representing or framing problems in terms of their most important dimensions, omitting those that are less important.

The research that has produced the new theory has also produced new methodologies that are relevant for economic research. Methods have been devised to use computers to simulate complex human thought processes and thereby to model problemsolving and decisionmaking situations of real-world complexity. The theory and practice of taking thinking-aloud protocols from human subjects while they are thinking and solving problems has been developed and explored.

Of course these developments do not mean that the problems of economics have been solved and that economists need merely to replace their standard theory with the new theory and apparatus. Certainly few of the economic implications of the new theory have been worked out. But a vacuum does not exist, and would not exist if the standard theory, or its invalid components, were simply abandoned. There is a firm foundation on which economic research can proceed.

What Is to Be Done?

I have described what I believe to be the serious problems facing economics and a path toward their solution. Both the auxiliary assumptions and the central postulates of classical economics must be revised on the basis of sound empirical evidence. To get the proper evidence, economists must receive new kinds of research training, much of it borrowed from cognitive psychology and organization theory. Doctoral candidates must learn how to obtain data about beliefs, attitudes, and expectations. They must learn how to study decisionmaking processes inside and outside business organizations. They must learn how to analyze and interpret the verbal reports of human subjects in both laboratory and field situations. They must learn how to conduct laboratory experiments.

Increasing numbers of mainline economists are beginning to perceive and accept the need for these reforms. I have already mentioned some of them, and I could add many names to the list. But there is a long way to go.

The inability of economics today to play the policy role to which it aspires is a major source of pressure toward reform. The hubris of the 1950s, when many economists thought we knew how to fine tune the economy, has disappeared in the face of stagflation and the ideological struggles between Keynesians and rational expectationists. Nevertheless, the reform will not be rapid.

As it progresses, however, the alteration of economics toward a responsible empiricism will gradually remove the present scandals in economic science: not just the public scandal of disarray in the policy arena, but the private scandal, known best to economists themselves, of a science that nearly renounced the practice of looking hard at the empirical evidence that was supposed to provide its foundations.

The late Tjalling Koopmans, a distinguished econometrician and a Nobel Laureate in economics, warned, in a celebrated book review, against "measurement without theory." The remarks of Robert Eisner, quoted earlier, echo the same concern. The concern for economics that I have emphasized in my remarks is the complement of that one—theory without measurement. What distinguishes science from every other form of human intellectual activity is that it disciplines speculation with facts. Theory and data are the two blades of the scissors. But the metaphor is not quite right, for the blades are not symmetric. When theories and facts are in conflict, the theories must yield. Economics has strayed from that simple principle, and it must return to it.

Note

1. I have only a newspaper reference to the original survey, which was conducted in Canada. I have repeated the finding by polling several audiences at my talks; but I must confess that when I tried to replicate the result during my talk in Kalamazoo, a majority of the noneconomists present voted like economists. Perhaps most of my audience had been taking economics courses from a very persuasive faculty.

IV.13 Effect of Mode of Data Presentation on Reasoning about Economic Markets

(Hermina J. Tabachneck and Herbert A. Simon)

Introduction

People are faced with having to process a diversity of percepts, i.e., verbal, visual, etc., including text, diagrams, graphs, and mathematical representations. What types of mental representations and processes do people use to deal with these? We know much about verbal processes, but non-verbal mental processes have been more difficult to trace. Little has been done either on complex visual problem solving or on the interaction between verbal and visual representations in problem solving. Non-verbal mental processes become more accessible to study if (1) one assumes computational reality of modality-specific representations; (2) one assumes that environment-initiated representations and memory-based representations use the same medium and processes; and (3) one has evidence that a subject is working with a particular representation. If these three criteria are satisfied, then concurrent verbal protocols can be used to trace complex problem solving in a domain using a multiplicity of representations.

To study both visual and verbal processes and their interactions in the context of learning difficult concepts we presented different formats of the same data to subjects in a between-subject design. We guarded against contamination from previous experience and gave all subjects the same domain information. To obtain information on subjects' problem solving processes and computations, we recorded subjects' interactions with the environment-initiated representations in detail. We also modeled the subjects' behavior, but our computer models are not described in this paper.

Using this methodology in the domain of economics we found many differences in behavior between subjects using different data formats. The findings strongly confirmed the hypothesis that subjects' verbalizations would reflect, and thereby reveal, their internal representations of the information.

Processing Different Representations

Diagrams, somewhat veridical drawings of objects that preserve spatial relations, were first used by engineers to keep track of their designs in the 15th century; later, they began to appear in printed works. Drawings provided a logical medium for exchanging ideas in a Europe of many languages and low literacy. Graphical displays, which are a form of quantitative data representation more abstract than diagrams, did not make their appearance until the late 18th century. Current textbooks use a mixture of representations including text, photographs, diagrams, graphs, and many types of mathematics. and geometry.

How do people interact with different representations? What types of mental representations and processes do they use? We know much about verbal mental processes, especially through verbal protocol analysis (cf. Ericsson & Simon, 1980), but much less about non-verbal mental processes. Most of the research on visual representations after the Gestalt era has investigated the beginning and ending states of some elementary process (e.g., Kosslyn, 1980; Shepard & Cooper, 1982), but little has been done on complex problem solving.

Before we discuss why, we should distinguish between the external display (the information provided to the subject), the environment-initiated internal display (the information after it is filtered through the senses) and the memory-based internal display (combinations of information filtered through the senses and information retrieved from memory). A human can only work with the latter two since the external display is never "seen" until it has been filtered through the entire perceptual/cognitive process. Moreover, once the external display has become an internal display, it consists of both more and less than the original external display. More, because the memory interacts nearly immediately with the environment-initiated information, supplying it with semantic knowledge. The percept now has a meaning, the viewer's meaning, to be precise. Less, because only a subset of the percept's information ends up in the internal display.

Recognition of the external stimuli we perceive is fast and partly subconscious. The interaction between memory-based representations and environment-initiated representations is very efficient; in fact, it is hard to think of a percept that would not immediately attain at least *some* semantic meaning from interaction with information stored in memory. It is parsimonious to assume that these two sources of information use the same medium and the same processes when we are actively perceiving the world. There appears to be no empirical or other reason to assume that we use different media and processes for handling information about stimuli we are viewing than we use for the same information as we image it in memory.

This is not a universally held viewpoint, especially historically. Before the early seventies, visual mental processes were often considered to be epiphenomenal: imagery was viewed as a result of cognitive processes and not a cause. Evidence that images could cause processes resulted in discarding this view (Shepard & Metzler, 1971; Kosslyn, 1980).

Currently, the main question is whether there are computations and processes that are specific to the type of representation involved (i.e., imagery, verbal, etc.), or whether the same general cognitive computations and processes manipulate the information in all representation types. The strongest form of the latter view is held by Pylyshyn (1981). He argues that imagery is a simulation of physical or perceptual events, carried out by general thought processes. A number of researchers, including Shepard (1981), Shepard & Cooper (1982), Kosslyn (1980), and Farah (1984), argue for specificity of only a part of the process. These researchers believe, as we do, that imagery uses representations and processes that are also used in visual perception, with the exception of very early processes in the retina and perhaps early in the visual cortex. Farah reported neurological evidence showing a physiological link between visual perception and visual imaging. Shepard's experiments and model and Kosslyn's seminal work are well known; Kosslyn's model contains many modules that are vision-specific (e.g., zoom, pan, rotate, scan). Larkin and Simon (1987) demonstrated computational advantages of having different processes operating on different representations.

Thus, there is acceptance that visual processes are not epiphenomenal, and a growing body of evidence that many of them are unique to imagery. It has been recognized that research on mental visual processes is needed. The problem is that processes more complex than elementary operations are difficult to trace. We do have an excellent methodology for researching complex verbal mental processes by the analysis of concurrent verbal protocols. Visual processes have been traced with eye-tracking equipment; this method was recently used to unravel the processes subjects use when taking the Raven Intelligence test, a task that has a very strong visual component (Carpenter et al., 1990). However, eye-movement equipment usually restricts the subject to looking at a computer screen (the head is immobilized), limiting the type of problems that can be researched with this tool.

Verbal protocols have not been considered to be usable for visual mental processes, since they require the visual representations to be translated into verbal form for speech. Pinker (1985) expressed a common view of the use of verbal protocols in imagery research while arguing that subjectivity, along with the homunculus and the epiphenomenon problems, should be considered non-issues:

"It is dangerous to take people's introspective reports about the contents or properties of their images as evidence in characterizing imagery, because such reports can be unreliable and subject to bias, because the referents of people's descriptions of imagery are unclear, and because interesting cognitive processes are likely to take place beneath the level of conscious accessibility. Again, a non-issue: all parties agree that much of image processing, whatever it is, is inaccessible to consciousness, that experimental data and computational and neurological feasibility are the proper source of constraints on imagery theories, and that introspective reports are psychological phenomena to be accounted for, not accurate descriptions of underlying mechanisms." (p. 38)

We agree with the general unreliability of *introspective* reports. However, *concurrent* reports, when properly elicited, are *not* introspective, but provide a partial record of the contents of verbal working memory. They have repeatedly been shown to be both reliable and valid for elucidating mental processes (see Ericsson and Simon, 1980, for an in-depth discussion on verbal protocols and their analysis).

While there is ample evidence that the referents of people's descriptions of imagery are often unclear, one must distinguish here between elementary visual operations and more complex visual mental processes. Just as in the case of elementary verbal operations, many elementary imagery operations may be beneath the level of conscious accessibility; Pinker's constraints on imagery theories (as well as verbal theories) for this level are consistent with the evidence.

But complex visual mental processes such as those used in problem solving are difficult to trace not because they are "beneath the level of conscious accessibility," but because of the problem of translating them from visual to verbal form. A concurrent verbal protocol of a visual mental process generally consists mainly of references to the representation that are difficult correctly to interpret if we cannot be sure of the nature of the subject's visual representation.

This is especially true if the visual representation has been induced by verbal means, for a verbal description can generally be interpreted visually in many different ways. "The ball is on the box" says nothing about the attributes of the ball, the box, the position of the box, or where exactly the ball is on the box.

Objectives of the Research

While there are quite probably processes that are unique to visual representations just as there are for verbal representations (see also Paivio, 1971; Just & Carpenter, 1985), there also appear to be processes that are the same for both. Little research has been done on either complex problem solving using visual information or on how visual and verbal representations interact in such problem solving; we need a reliable and small-grain method to trace such processes. If we can ensure the content of subjects' visual mental representations, we can interpret the pointers to the visual representations within their concurrent verbal protocols and obtain a sufficient trace to identify the problem-solving processes.

We have argued that mental processes and computations are the same for environment-initiated representations as for memory-based representations. This means that when subjects are set to work on an external display, the processes inferred from their protocols will be nearly the same as the processes they would use if they were working on a memory-based representation.

But before we can interpret the evidence about the representation that can be found in a verbal protocol, we must ensure that the subjects work with visual representations that are close enough to the external ones to make mapping possible. In order to deal with these problems we made the following decisions:

1. Use novices in the selected domain—in this paper, the field of economics. Use subjects of differing abilities since individual differences will contribute to the variety of processes that can be detected. ("Naive" economic theories can of course not be avoided, just as naive physics theories cannot be avoided in testing children.)

2. Use tracing methods that yield a lot of detail. Verbal protocol analysis is a proven method that is uesable in imagery research if the referents to imagery representations can be mapped.

3. Run the experiment on a computer, thereby making it possible to constrain and record access to different types of information (the different quantitative data formats, the qualitative introduction, the questions). Obtain accurate timing data for key processes through the computer.

4. Elicit different types of reasoning to detect whether a particular type of reasoning would be easier in one representation than another. Give the subjects both qualitative questions (presence or absence of change and direction of change in the market) and quantitative questions (exactly how much change), as well as explanatory questions (why did the system change?).

5. Use three equivalent quantitative data formats, which are different computationally but not informationally, between subjects, and one qualitative format within subjects. The qualitative format (here, verbal) should contain as few imagery-inducing words as possible. Using different formats exposes their relative weaknesses and strengths and enables validation of the method.

6. Use computer programs to simulate the processes and computations obtained from the verbal protocols and time analyses to ensure sufficiency of the simulations; use these models to predict future behavior. Model the differences in the processes observed in the different quantitative data formats; assume the lowest level of understanding needed to account for the reasoning.

We chose a task from the domain of economics. The task began with reading verbal explanations of demand, supply and equilibrium in a competitive market, and how economic forces can influence demand or supply and thus displace the equilibrium. Twelve subjects were then given quantitative data sets either in a graphical, tabular, or algebraic format (4 subjects each), and asked to calculate the equilibrium price before and after such economic forces had acted. (see Appendix 1 for the data screens used for the third set of questions).

Several of our findings from the empirical data are summarized below:

• Statistically significant differences were found in time and accuracy data between the data formats. Subjects using the graphical data had more answers correct in the quantitative questions than those using the tabular format; users of the algebraic format were worst (90% vs. 47% vs. 34% correct; $F(2,9) = 5.87$, $p < .05$). The differences in quality of responses to the qualitative and explanatory questions were in the same direction, but not statistically significant. Subjects using the tabular format were consistently fastest in answering the questions, followed by graphical and algebraic format users (except in the qualitative questions, where algebraic users were just a bit faster than the graphical users—mainly because they did not consult the data as often); none of these differences reached statistical significance, however. Subjects in the graphical data format spent more time than the others examining the data while answering qualitative questions (27 vs. 11 vs. 14 sec. for graphical, tabular, and algebraic formats; $F(2,0) = 4.40$; $p < .05$), but the pattern was different for quantitative questions, where the algebraic subjects spent more time with the data (not statistically significant).

Many other differences in the processes were not reflected in differences between the groups in either time or accuracy.

• None of the subjects showed any sign of having translated the given quantitative data format into another one. Only one subject showed awareness of the existence of a data format other than the one given; this resulted in an intrusion, but not a translation. It actually netted the subject a wrong answer.

• The language used by subjects in the different groups was very different. Typical answers to the question "What is the current equilibrium price?" included:

Graphical data format: "being that demand and supply—are dependent on each other I would think that the equilibrium would occur where those two lines meet ... the price per knife—uh, let's go to where they intersect. So, at 7.5 ... whatever unit the price per knife is—dollars."

Tabular data format: "let's see—at 7 dollars, it's 60,000 and over here it's reversed, so it would be—7.50."

Algebraic data format: "price = 2 + quantity; price = 13–quantity; quantity means 10,000 knives; (solves equation) Q = 5.5, that is 5 dollars and 50 cents."

• Errors made in the calculations and in the reasoning were different in each data format. Two examples of the many instances: (1) 3 of 4 subjects in the algebraic format calculated Q (quantity) rather than P (price), as illustrated by the *algebraic data format* example above. No subjects in the other data formats did this. (2) 3 out of 4 users of the tabular format did not interpolate; interpolation to obtain the correct answer was also required in the graphical format. In the latter format interpolation was not a problem. Interpolation was irrelevant in the algebraic format.

• Much of the language used by subjects would be completely uninterpretable without knowledge of which data format a subject had been given. However, the referents and reasoning processes were nearly perfectly mappable within each data format; moreover, the language and the type of reasoning used by a subject in one data format could not be mapped onto another data format. Hence the findings strongly confirmed the hypothesis that subjects' verbalizations would reflect, and thereby reveal, their internal representations of the information.

• The differences in the processes used in the different data formats affected more than just calculations. For instance, while answering qualitative questions, subjects used the data to different extents; the graphical subjects using the data the most, followed by the tabular and algebraic subjects.

• Interestingly, the subjects' verbal qualitative reasoning was not qualitatively different in the various data formats when they were reasoning without direct reference to using data, although *how often* they engaged in such reasoning was affected by the data format: algebraic and tabular subjects, instead of underpinning their qualitative answers with evidence from the data, often reasoned qualitatively.

• We were able to document individual differences as well. Two examples: (1) The subject who did worst on the graphical data format looked much like an algebraic format user in her use of the data, and declared that she hated interpreting graphs and always had a hard time with them. (2) Another subject, in the algebraic format, was weak in calculations involving simultaneous equations and solved them by a method of successive approximations, while the others did so by substitution.

• Computer models simulating the behavior of a "good" and "not-so-good" subject in all three data formats were written; the data from the concurrent verbal protocols combined with the data recorded by the computer were sufficient to specify the models almost precisely.

In conclusion, our method successfully and reliably traced complex visual and verbal mental processes in problem solving in a real learning situation. We traced the subjects' performance in both visually- and verbally-based data formats. The method consisted of analyzing concurrent verbal protocols, combined with accuracy and timing data, in a situation where the experimenter could ensure (to a practical degree) that the subject was indeed working with a particular known representation. We believe that the complex visual mental processes we found are valid both for the environmentally-initiated representations that we used, and for memory-based representations. This methodology holds much promise for elucidating complex mental imagery processes and the interaction of imagery processes with verbal and other processes in different types of reasoning.

Appendix

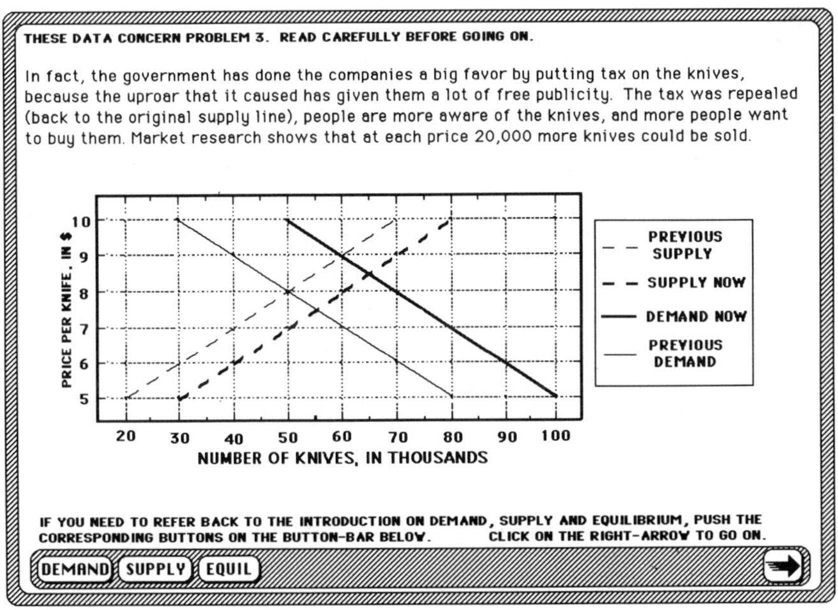

Figure A.1
The graphical data screen for the third set of questions

THESE DATA CONCERN PROBLEM 3. READ CAREFULLY BEFORE GOING ON.
In fact, the government has done the companies a big favor by putting tax on the knives, because the uproar that it caused has given them a lot of free publicity. The tax was repealed (back to the original supply schedule), people are more aware of the knives, and more people want to buy them. Market research shows that at each price 20,000 more knives could be sold.

This is the **old demand** schedule:

at this price:	this many would be bought:
$ 5.	80,000
$ 6.-	70,000
$ 7.-	60,000
$ 8.-	50,000
$ 9.-	40,000
$10.-	30,000

This is the **old supply** schedule:

at this price:	this many would be supplied:
$ 5.-	20,000
$ 6.-	30,000
$ 7.-	40,000
$ 8.-	50,000
$ 9.-	60,000
$10.-	70,000

This is the **new demand** schedule:

at this price:	this many would be bought:
$ 5.-	100,000
$ 6.-	90,000
$ 7.-	80,000
$ 8.-	70,000
$ 9.-	60,000
$10.-	50,000

This is the **new supply** schedule:

at this price:	this many would be supplied:
$ 5.-	30,000
$ 6.-	40,000
$ 7.-	50,000
$ 8.-	60,000
$ 9.-	70,000
$10.-	80,000

IF YOU NEED TO REFER BACK TO THE INTRODUCTION ON DEMAND, SUPPLY AND EQUILIBRIUM, CLICK THE CORRESPONDING BUTTONS. **CLICK ON THE RIGHT-ARROW TO GO TO PROBLEM 3.**

DEMAND SUPPLY EQUIL

Figure A.2
The tabular data screen for the third set of questions

THESE DATA CONCERN PROBLEM 3. READ CAREFULLY BEFORE GOING ON.

In fact, the government has done the companies a big favor by putting tax on the knives, because the uproar that it caused has given them a lot of free publicity. The tax was repealed (back to the original supply equation), people are more aware of the knives, and more people want to buy them. Market research shows that at each price 20,000 more knives could be sold.
These equations are valid for $4 < P < 11$

The **old supply** for knives conformed to this equation:

$$P = 3 + Q$$

The **old demand** for knives conformed to this equation:

$$P = 13 - Q$$

The **new supply** for knives conforms to this equation:

$$P = 2 + Q$$

where P = price per knife, in dollars
Q = units of knives supplied
(1 unit = 10,000 knives)

The **new demand** for knives conforms to this equation:

$$P = 15 - Q$$

where P = price per knife, in dollars
Q = units of knives bought
(1 unit = 10,000 knives)

IF YOU NEED TO REFER BACK TO THE INTRODUCTION ON DEMAND, SUPPLY AND EQUILIBRIUM, CLICK THE CORRESPONDING BUTTONS ON THE BUTTON-BAR BELOW. **CLICK ON THE RIGHT-ARROW TO GO ON.**

DEMAND SUPPLY EQUIL

Figure A.3
The algebraic data screen for the third set of questions

References

Carpenter, P. A., Just, M. A., & Shell, P. (1990). What one intelligence test measures: A theoretical account of the processing in the Raven Progressive Matrices test. *Psychological Review*, 97(3), 404–431.

Ericsson, K. A., & Simon, H. A. (1984). *Protocol analysis: Verbal reports as data*. Cambridge, MA: The MIT Press.

Farah, M. J. (1984). The neurological basis of mental imagery: A componential analysis. *Cognition*, 18, 248–272.

Just, M. A., & Carpenter, P. A. (1985). Cognitive coordinate systems: Accounts of mental rotation and individual differences in spatial abilities. *Psychological Review*, 92(2), 137–172.

Kosslyn, S. M. (1980). *Image and mind.* Cambridge, MA: Harvard University Press.

Larkin, J. H., & Simon, H. A. (1987). Why a diagram is (sometimes) worth ten thousand words. *Cognitive Science*, 11, 65–99.

Paivio, A. (1971). *Imagery and verbal processes*. New York, NY: Holt.

Pinker, S. (1985). Visual cognition: An introduction. In S. Pinker (Ed.), *Visual cognition*. Cambridge, MA: The MIT Press.

Pylyshyn, Z. W. (1981). The imagery debate: analogue media versus tacit knowledge. *Journal of Behavioral and Brain Sciences*, 3, 382–389.

Shepard, R. N. (1981). Psychophysical complementarity. In M. Kubovy & J. Pomerantz (Eds.), *Perceptual organization*. Hillsdale, NJ: Erlbaum.

Shepard, R. N., & Cooper, L. A. (1982). *Mental images and their transformations*. Cambridge, MA: The MIT Press.

Shepard, R. N., & Metzler, J. (1971). Mental rotation of three-dimensional objects. *Science*, 171, 701–703.

Index

Abstraction techniques, 89–93. *See also* Aggregation; Equilibration
Adelman, F. L., 348
Adelman, I., 348
Advertising activities, electronic, 157
Aggregate variables, 34
Aggregation
as abstraction technique, 89–93
causal ordering and, 85–93
in mixed structure, 89–93
of dynamic structures, 74–93
causal ordering and, 85–93
completely decomposable systems, 76
nearly decomposable systems, 75–79
variables, 79–85
large-scale systems, simulating by, 105–113
nearly decomposable systems and, 5, 107–109
sensitivity analysis versus prediction and, 111–113
simplification of, need for, 109–111
unknown system mechanisms and, 105–106
of manufactured and agricultural products, 143–144
methodologies for economics and, 333–334
of microdata, 306–307, 334–335
of mixed structures, 89–93
modeling and, 45, 124–126
of non-linear systems, 96
of variables, 79–85
conditions for, 84–85
numerical example of, 81–84
procedure for, 80–81
Aggregative time series, 347
Agreement among economists, 401–402
Agricultural employment, 140, 143
Agricultural products, 143
AI. *See* Artificial intelligence (AI)
Air conditioning invention, 164
Alienation of workers and management, 183–195
automation and, 189–194
computers and, 189–194
executive work and, 184–188, 195
Golden Age myths and, 183, 188–189, 195
human condition and, 195
Industrial Revolution and, 188–189, 195
in preindustrialized society, 188–189
technology and, 183–184
Allais, M., 340, 430
Alternatives, generation of, 291–292
Altruism, 205–216
bounded rationality and, 205, 244–246, 257–259
definitions of, 241–243
docility and, 205, 209–214, 229–230, 244–246
in everyday life, 242
in evolutionary theory, 241–242
fitness and, 206–207
glory and, 246
group identification and, 253, 262–263
implications of, for economics and politics, 214–216
intelligence and, 259–260
loyalty and, 201–204
modeling, 208–209
alternative models, comparison with, 213–214
natural selection and, 205–206, 228–229
neo-Darwinist framework of, 205, 207–208, 241–244, 257
in politics, 251–252
implications of, 214–216
power and, 246
reciprocal, 205, 247
role of, in society, 247
selection of, 206, 285
selfishness and, 206–207, 216, 228, 253, 260–261
social learning and, 209–213
social meanings of, 260–261
in utility function, 285
wealth and, 246
AM program, 180
Ampere's Law, 64
Ando, Albert, 5, 26, 46–47, 75, 78, 91, 356
Andronov, A. A., 116
Arrow, Kenneth, 412, 421, 425
Artificial intelligence (AI)
causal knowledge and, 43
cognitive science and, 166–167, 181–182
expert systems and, 152–153, 166–167, 178–179
future of, 179–180
Information Management Systems and, 148
language and, 166–167, 179–180
learning and, 180
originality and, 180
robotics and, 166, 180
scientific process and, 388
Artle, R., 131, 137–138, 140–141, 143
Aspiration levels, 296–297, 323, 324–325
Asymmetry and causal ordering, 10, 14, 18, 21–22, 48

Attention, public, 313–314
Attentional process, 357, 374–375, 392–393
Authority, organizational, 223–226
Automation
alienation of workers and management and, 189–194
dehumanizing effects of, 190
employment shifts and, 193–194
future of, 195
human interaction and, 156
job satisfaction and, 193–194
productivity and, 194
Automobile invention, 164

BACON program, 168, 180
Barnard, Chester, 340
Baumol, W. J., 283
Bayesians, 4, 382
Becker, Gary S., 242, 284, 350, 371–373, 390–391, 406, 427
Behavior. *See also specific types*
of dynamic structures, 29–30
modeling, 46, 303–307, 325
of organizations, 199
rational, 233, 307–310, 355, 383, 406
Behavioral economics, 277–289
case studies, 288
choice processes and, 286–287, 292
classical economic theory and, 275–276
computer modeling, 289
concept of, 275–276
conventional behavior and, 279–280
decision-making processes and, 285–286
experiments, 289
individual utility and, 284–285
interest in, 276
modeling, 289
neoclassical economic theory versus, 277–278, 327, 334
New Institutional Economics and, 281–282
research
directions of, 278–279
methods of, 287–288
utility function of organization and, 282–284
Behavioral research, 299–316
decision-making processes and, 307–311
human verbal behavior as data and, 303–307
inconsistencies in behavior and, 411
polls and policies and, 312–315
taxonomies, 299–302
goals of, 299, 301–302
methodologies of, 299–301
Behavioralism, 361–362, 364
Berle, Adolf, 222
Berlyne, Daniel, 186
Biology, 399, 412, 417
Black, Joseph, 168
Black's Law of temperature equilibrium, 180
Blaug, M., 362
Blauner, Robert, 191–193
Block-diagonal form, 31–32
Block-triangular matrix, 30
Bok, Derek, 169
Boredom in workplace, 185–187
Bounded rationality, 291–298
alternatives and, generation of, 291–292
altruism and, 205, 244–246, 257–259
behavior in, 325
choice and
criteria of, 292
processes, 286–287
concept of, 291
consequences and, evaluation of, 292
decision-making processes and, 324, 357
docility and, 202–203, 244–246, 252–253, 258–259
economic dynamics and, 360–363
economics and, 269
neoclassical economic theory and, 294, 334
procedural theory of rationality and, 271, 293
subjective utility theory and, 291, 293
substantive theory of rationality and, 271, 293
Bouwman, Marinus, 179
Bowles, Sam, 421
Boyd, R., 208, 213
Brown, J. S., 45–46
Buchanan, Jim, 421
Bulletin boards, electronic, 157–158
Business-cycle theory
disagreement of economists about, 405–406
economic dynamics and, 343, 351–352
expectations theory and, 375–376
inventory cycle and, 352
Keynes and, 286, 394–395
Lucas and, 394–395
neoclassical economic theory and, 275, 375–376
rational expectations theory and, 355–356
shocks in, 351–352
stylized facts and, 347

CADUCEUS system, 152–153, 179
Canonical form of equations, 19, 58–59, 62, 66

CAOS, 93–96
Capitalist economies, 238
Carbonell, Jaime, 126–127
Carnegie, Andrew, 184–185, 246
Causal dependency relations, 43–44, 67
Causal ordering, 3–5, 9–97
abstraction hierarchy and, 89–93
account of (1953), 13
aggregation and, 85–93
asymmetry and, 10, 14, 18, 21–22, 48
bathtub example, 53–56, 60–62, 67–68
comparative statics and, 25–26
concept of, 13–14, 47
defining, 15–18
derivation of, 19, 29
in dynamic structures, 26–31, 58–65
aggregation of, 85–93
bathtub example, 60–62
behavior of, 29–30
equilibrating, 69–70
examples of, 26–28
exogenizing, 63, 69, 72–73
exogenous variables in, 62–65
long-term, 31–35, 78
in Maxwell's equations, 63–65
mixed approximation to, 35–39
mixed structures and, 65–74
nearly decomposable systems, 75–79
self-contained, 28–29, 58–60
short-term, 31–35, 78
static structure, matrix for, 29–31
in equilibrium structures, 48–57
example of, 50–52
long-term, 33, 78
minimal complete subsets with multiple variables, 11, 15, 17–18, 29–30, 48–49, 53
qualitative equations, 56–57
self-contained, 48–50, 57
short-term, 32, 78
examples of, 13–14
extended, 19–20
formalization of, 11, 14
identifiability of, 11–12, 22–23
linear systems and, empirical evidence for, 23–25
in Maxwell equations, 63–66
in mixed structures, 65–74
aggregation of, 89–93
applications of, 97
definitions from, 35, 38–39
dynamic structures and, 69–74
self-contained, 38–39, 66–67
model aggregation and, 45
notations, 9, 38
possible worlds and, 20, 22–23
research on, 4–5
semantic meaning of, 20, 22–23
in static structures, 19, 29–31, 44, 93
system of equations and, 9–11, 24–25
theory of, 3–5, 44–45, 47
of variables, 24
CAusal Ordering System (CAOS), 93–96
Causal relations, 5, 10, 16–18, 93. *See also* Causal ordering
Cavalli-Sforza, L. L., 208, 213
Centre Mondiale de Informatique et Ressource Humaine, 146
Chaikin, C. E., 116
Chaos theory, 115–117
Chaplin, Charlie, 190
Children's economic opportunities, 371–372
Choice processes, 286–287, 292
Choice, theory of, 269
Clarkson, Geoffrey, 179
Classical economic theory
behavioral economics and, 275–276
economic dynamics and, 344–346
foundations of, 344–346
growth in, long-term, 349–351
monetary identity and, 344
rationality and, 344–346
Say's Law and, 344–345
Clayre, Alasdair, 188–189
Club of Rome report (1972), 110–111, 118–119, 123, 419
Coal burning invention, 164
Cobb-Douglas function, 271, 327–328
Cobweb theory, 10
Cognitive science, 126, 166–167, 181–182
Commons, John R., 200, 275, 337
Communications, market versus internal, 236. *See also* Electronic communications
Comparative statics, 25–26, 138–140, 143–144
Completely decomposable systems, 76
Completely subsets of First order, 49
Computation
capability, 325–327
load of, acceptable, 6–7
rational, 230, 319–320
Computer-aided instruction, 166
Computers. *See also* Information technology
advertising activities with, 157
alienation of workers and management and, 189–194
behavior economics modeling, 289

Computers (cont.)
bulletin boards with, 157–158
capacity limits of, 147–150
computer-aided instruction, 166
design of, 147
criteria for, 160–161
in economics, 289
in educational system, 170–172
first use of, 189
"flaming" phenomenon with, 158–159
graphics, 166
human interaction and, 155, 190–191
implications of technology of, 146–147
learning about, 168–171, 180
mail systems, 169
Management Information Systems, 148, 176–177
medical diagnosis programs, 153, 167, 179
modeling, 289, 440
need to know and, 151–154
networking with, 149–152
potential of, 159–160, 162, 165–168
power and, 159, 162
problem solving programs, 167, 179
removing people from loop of, 154–155
satisficing models, 418–419
social interaction and, 157–159
sophistication of, growing, 6, 145–146
symbols processed by, 126
as testbeds for study of information storage alternatives, 153
thinking and, 182
workplace and, 155–157, 161
Conformity, 185, 213, 347
Consequences, evaluation of, 292
Constancy, 63, 69
Consumer preference, 321, 389–390, 396–397
Conventional behavior, 279–280
Cooper, L. A., 435
Coordination, organizational, 232–237
Copernicus, 182
Correlation, spurious, 12
Cost curves, 271–272, 328, 377, 397–398
Courtois, P. J., 109
Cowles Commission for Research in Economics, 3
Cyert, Richard M., 283, 339, 410

Darwin, Charles, 182. *See also* Evolutionary theory
David, P. A., 251
de Kleer, J., 45–46
Dearborn, D. C., 231
Debreu, G., 424
Decision-making processes
behavioral economics and, 285–286
behavioral research and, 307–310, 362
bounded rationality and, 324, 357
evidence about, direct, 310–311
expectations theory and, 307–311
human activity and, 398–399
interest in, 397
methodologies for economics and, 324–325
neoclassical economic theory and, 324, 369
observation of, 320, 330
rationality in psychology and economics and, 374–375, 389–390
flood insurance, 374, 392
voting behavior, 374–375, 392–393
stop rule in, 322–323
theory of, 362–363
uncertainty in, 285–286, 292, 307
Decomposable systems, 32, 75–79
Demand
elasticity of, 142–144
supply and, 328
Democratic theory, 312–313
Demography, 118
Demsetz, H., 222, 232
DENDRAL program, 180
Dependent variables, 9, 11, 18–19, 28
Derived structure of first order, 49
Device Modeling Environment (DME), 96–97
Devons, Ely, 234, 343
Directly causally dependent variables, 49
Disagreements of economists, 401–413, 424–428
agreements versus, 401–402
business-cycle theory, 405–406
Pareto optimum and, 403–404, 423
philosophies, 415
public, 401, 421–425
subjective expected utility and, 403–405
Discovery process, 322, 387–388
DME, 96–97
Docility
altruism and, 205, 209–214, 229–230, 244–246
bounded rationality and, 202–203, 244–246, 252–253, 258–259
cognitive component of, 244
fitness and, 202–203, 285
intelligence and, 260
motivational component of, 244
taxing, 205, 252–253, 258–259

Donne, John, 4
Duck, Stephen, 188–189
Dynamic equations
 equilibrating, 69–70
 exogenizing, 72–73
Dynamic structures
 aggregation of, 74–93
  causal ordering and, 85–93
  nearly decomposable systems, 75–79
  variables, 79–85
 causal ordering in. *See* Causal ordering in dynamic structures
 nonlinear, 116

Econometrics
 economics and, 3–4, 334–335
 identification problem of, 12
 motivation in organizations and, 253
 neoclassical economic theory and, 328–329
 theory of causal ordering and, 45
Economic dynamics, 343–364
 bounded rationality and, 360–363
 business-cycle theory and, 343, 351–352
 formal mechanisms for, 348–349
 inventory cycle and, 352–355
 long-term, 349–351, 356
 neoclassical economic theory and, 344–346
 price level changes and, 355–358
 Schumpeter and, 350, 363–364
 stylized facts of, 346–349, 361
 unemployment debate and, 358–360
Economic phenomena, 327–333
 evidence for, empirical, 327–329
 prediction, power in, 331–333
 theories built on unrealistic assumptions, 329–331
Economic theory. *See also specific types*
 armchair, 395
 assumptions in, 390–391, 417
 behavioralism and, 362
 characterizations of needed, 270–272
 consumer preferences and, 389–390
 empirical evidence for, 397
 human computational power, 319–320
 labor force and, 359
 markets in, 217
 motivation in, 264
 problem solving and, 417–418
 psychology theory versus, 395–396
 rational computation and, 319–320
 revolution in, 414
 satisficing and, 297–298
 traditional, 319
 validity of, 429–430
Economics. *See also* Behavioral economics; New Institutional Economics; Rationality in psychology and economics
 altruism and, implications of, 214–216
 assumptions of, shift in, 417, 431–432
 bounded rationality and, 269
 computers in, 289
 discovery process and, 388
 econometrics and, 3–4, 334–335
 empirical evidence in, 395
 experimental work in, 331
 future of, 398–400
 group identification and, 247–248
 historical perspective of, 416
 irrationality in, 367
 methodologies for, 319–335
  aggregation problem, 333–334
  alternatives, search for, 320–323
  behavioral, 287–288
  computational capabilities, 325–327
  decision-making processes, 324–325
  economic phenomena, 327–333
  natural selection, 333
  rational computations, 319–320
  satisficing criterion, 323–324
  utility function, 323–324
 of modern industrialized society, 237
 natural selection in, 333
 political biases and, 418
 a priorism in, 407
 profession's view of, 272–273
 public face of, 272
 reform in, 270–272, 412, 431–432
 research on reasoning in, 273
 revolution in, 409
 of rural-urban population balance, 137–144
  comparative statics and, 138–140, 143–144
  neutral technological change and, 138–140
  non-neutral technological change, 140–141
  price elasticities and, 140–143
 satisficing and, 269
 self-reports of actors and, 301
 social sciences versus, 388–389
 state of, 421–432
  consensus and dissent, 421, 425–429
  public disagreement among economists, 421–423
  reform, 430–431
  validity of standard theory, 429–431
 statistical practice in, 3–4
 voting behavior and, 375

Educational system, 170–172, 181, 371–372
Efficiency, organizational, 222–223, 232
Eisner, Robert, 428–429
Elasticity of demand, 142–144
Electronic communications
capacity limits of, 147–150
design of, 147
criteria for, 160–161
human interaction and, 155
implications of computer technology and, 146–147
need to know and, 151–154
networking with, 149–151
possibilities of, technical, 159–160, 162
power and, 159, 162
removing people from loop of, 154–155
sophistication of computers and, 6, 145–146
in workplace, 155–157, 161
Employees, organizational identifications of, 199, 230–231
Employment
agricultural, 140, 143
boredom with, 185–187
contract, 200, 223–224
free-riding and, 228
job satisfaction and, 185–186, 189–190, 192–194
pride in work and, 227–228
relations, 223–226
Endogenous expectations, 309
Endogenous variables, 10–11
Engineering analysis, 117
Entrepreneurial behavior, 184–185, 287
Equilibration
as abstraction technique, 89–93
exogenization versus, 73–74
of dynamic equations, 69–70
of markets, 328
Equilibrium structures, causal ordering in. *See* Causal ordering in equilibrium structures
Evolutionary theory
altruism in, 241–242
competition and, 250
fitness, 202–203, 206–207, 229, 250, 257, 259–261, 285, 333
natural selection, 205–206, 228–229, 250–251, 333
Executives
authority and, 223–226
motives of, 222–223
salaries of, 328, 378–382
work of, 184–188, 195
Exogenization
constancy and, 63, 69
dynamic equations, 72–73
equilibration versus, 73–74
of expectations, 309
Exogenous equation, 51
Exogenous expectations, 309
Exogenous variables, 10, 14, 16–17, 25, 51, 62–65, 72–73, 95, 349
Expectations
business-cycle theory and, 375–376
decision-making processes and, 307–311
endogenous, 309
exogenous, 309
neoclassical economic theory and, 375
rational, 233, 308–310, 343, 349, 355–356
rational behavior and, 233, 307–311, 355
rationality in psychology and economics and, 375–377
Expert systems, 152–153, 166–167, 178–179
Extended causality, 19–20

Faraday's Law, 63–65
Farah, M. J., 435
Feedback loop, 27, 44, 58
Feedback mechanism, 296–297
Feldman, M. W., 208, 213
Firm. *See also* Organizations
growth of, 378
size distribution of, 328, 377–378
theory of, 338–339, 398–399
Fisher, Franklin M., 26, 46–47
Fitness, 202–203, 206–207, 229, 250, 257, 259–261, 285, 333
"Flaming" phenomenon, 158–159
Forbus, K. D., 96
Ford, Henry, 184
Forrester, Jay, 419
Free-riding, 228
Friedman, Milton, 301, 329–330, 339, 343, 371, 390, 401, 421, 424, 428
Functional relations, 43

Gabrie, H., 337–339, 341–342
Galileo, 330
Generators process, 322
Gibrat assumption, 279–280, 378
Glory, desire for, 246
Glymour, Clark, 4
Goldberg, Walter, 145
Goldberger, Arthur, 371
Golden Age myths, 183, 188–189, 195
"The Goldwater Machine" program, 126–127

Goodwin, Richard M., 26
Government statistical agencies, 399
Granger causality, 4
Graphics, computer, 166
Gresham's Law, 377, 397
Group identification, 199, 247–248, 253, 262–263
Guilt, 210

Haggerty, Pat, 185
Halliday, D., 65
Handbook of Behavioral Economics, 275–276
Hawkins-Simon theorem, 235
Headstart program, 372
Hewlett, William, 185
Hierarchy, organizational, 151
Holt, C. C., 353
Hooke's Law, 60
Hoos, Ida, 190, 193
Humes, C., Jr., 131, 137–138

Identification
- cognitive, 284
- econometrics and, problem of, 12
- group, 199, 247–248, 253, 262–263
- mechanism of, 284
- organizational, 199, 201–204, 227–232, 247–249, 263
- questions about, empirical, 248
- social motivation for, 284

Ijiri, Y., 236–237
Immersion, education by, 164–165
Income tax, negative, 413–414
Incommensurability of goals and outcomes, 297
Independent variables, 19, 36
Individual utility, 284–285
Individualistic ethic, 184–185, 332
Industrial Revolution
- alienation of workers and management and, 188–189, 195
- First, 163–165
- Second, 165–168

Infection theory of learning, 170–171
Information
- abundance of, 131
- management of, 148, 175–178
- in memory, 434
- need to know and, 151–154
- plentiful, 173–174
- in print media, 174–175
- scarce, 173–174
- about stimuli being viewed, 434–435
- storage of, 153
- strategies
  - organizational, 175–178
  - personal, 174–175

Information society, 173
Information technology. *See also* Computers
- abundance of information and, 131
- changes in, 138–140
- prediction of effects of, 134–136
- workplace relations and, 131–132

Information-processing interpretation of verbal reports, 304–306
Information-rich society, 173–182
- artificial intelligence and
  - cognitive science and, 181–182
  - expert systems, 178–179
  - future of, 179–180
  - language, natural, 179–180
  - learning and, 180
  - originality and, 180
  - robotics and, 180
- information strategies in
  - organizational, 175–178
  - personal, 174–175
- knowledge in, gaining, 174–178
- plentiful versus scarce information and, 173–174

Innovation theory, 350–351
Insignificant root of subsystem, 34
Instructability. *See* Docility
Intelligence, 259–260, 435
Interest rates, 280, 292
Intergenerational mobility, 371
The Internet, 132
Intervention into system, 49–50
Introspection controversy, 303
Inventory cycle, 352–355
Investment theory, 329
Irrationality in economics, 367
ISAAC program, 179
Iwasaki, Yumi, 4, 96

Jacquier, J. L., 337–339, 341–342
Jensen, Arthur, 371–372
Job satisfaction, 185–186, 189–190, 192–194
Jorgenson, D. W., 329
J-shaped cost curve, 377

Kahneman, D., 120, 340, 410–411, 430
Kalagnanam, J. R., 96
Kaldor, N., 346
Katona, George, 275, 299–301, 306–307, 376, 407

Kepler's Third Law of planetary motion, 168, 180, 388
Keynes, J. M., 331–332, 344, 359, 394–395, 404–406, 424–426
Keynesian revolution, 337
Keynesian theory, 286, 294, 358, 376, 401
Klein, Larry, 419, 421
Knight, Frank, 343
Knowledge
 causal, 43
 compilation system, 97
 of discovery process, 322
 of economic world, 408
 expert, 178–179
 in information-rich society, 174–178
 need for, 151–154
 prior, 12
 technology and, 171–172
Kondratief cycle, 419–420
Koopmans, Tjalling C., 3–4, 432
Kosslyn, J. M., 435
Kuipers, B., 47
Kunreuther, H., 374, 392

Labor force
 economic theory and, 359
 money illusion and, 332
 women in, 372–373, 390–391, 406–407
Lambert, H., 97
Language, artificial and natural, 166–167, 179–180
Large-scale systems, simulating, 6–7, 105–128
 by aggregation, 105–113
  nearly decomposable systems and, 5, 107–109
  sensitivity analysis versus prediction and, 111–113
  simplification and, need for, 109–111
  unknown system mechanisms and, 105–106
 world-modeling problems and, 7
Learning
 altruism and social, 209–213
 artificial intelligence and, 180
 about computers, 168–171, 180
 by computers, 180
 immersion and, 164–165
 infection theory of, 170–171
Lehn, K., 222, 232
Leibenstein, H., 283
Leonardo, Anthony, 273
Leontief, Wassily, 348, 397, 412
Lincoln, Abraham, 173
Lindbeck, Assar, 395
Linear systems, 11–12, 19, 23–25, 115–116, 348, 353
Locality principle, 46
Long-term dynamic structures, 31–35
Long-term economic dynamics, 349–351, 356
Long-term equilibrium structures, 78
Long-wave theories, 419–420
Low, C. M., 96
Loyalty
 ethnic, 262
 group, 247–248, 253, 262–263
 organizational, 199, 201–204, 227–232, 247–249. *See also* Identification
LP computation, 326
Lucas, Robert E., Jr., 280, 294, 331–332, 347–348, 354–356, 376, 379, 394–395, 406, 421, 424–426
Lumsden, C., 208, 213

Macroeconomics, 269, 275, 301, 306–308, 343–344, 393–394
Macro-social processes and models, 111–112
Mail systems, electronic, 169
Management, business. *See also* Alienation of workers and management
 information strategy and, 175–178
 Management Information Systems and, 148, 176–177
 organizational identifications of, 199
 thinking and, 181
Management Information Systems (MIS), 148, 176–177
Manipulability
 of phenomenon, 21
 of variables, 49, 55
Manufactured products, 143
March, James G., 283, 339, 410
Mark Hopkins and a log theory, 170
Market economies, 237
Markets
 communications, 236
 in economic theory, 217
 equilibration of, 328
 neoclassical economic theory and, 234–235
 New Institutional Economics and, 218–219
 organizations and, 199–200, 217–221
 reasoning about, 433–441
  processing different representations, 433–437
  research objectives, 437–441

Marschak, Jascha, 3
Marshall, Alfred, 275, 400
Marx, Karl, 188, 262, 374, 404, 424
Mathematical relations, 43–44. *See also specific types*
Maxwell's equations, 63–66
Means, Gardiner, 222
Mechanisms, concept of, 47, 49. *See also specific types*
Mechanization. *See* Automation
Medical diagnosis computer programs, 153, 167, 179
Methodologies for economics, 319–335
 aggregation, 333–334
 alternatives, search for, 320–323
 behavioral, 287–288
 computational capabilities, 325–327
 decision-making processes, 324–325
 empirical, 327–333
 natural selection, 333
 rational computations, 319–320
 satisficing criterion, 323–324
 utility function, 323–324
Microcomputers, 166
Microdata, aggregation of, 306–307, 334–335
Microeconomics, 269, 334–335, 369, 393–394
Minicomputers, 166
Minimal complete subsets, 11, 15, 17–18, 29–30, 48–49, 53
Minimal self-contained subsets, 11, 17
MIS, 148, 176–177
Mitchell, Wesley, 337
Mixed structures, causal ordering in, 65–74
 aggregation of, 89–93
 applications of, 97
 bathtub example, 67–68
 definitions from, 35, 38–39
 dynamic structures and, 69–74
 self-contained, 38–39, 66–67
Mobility, intergenerational, 371
Model abstraction and causality, 43–103. *See also* Modeling
 aggregation of dynamic structures, 74–93
  causal ordering and, 85–93
  nearly decomposable systems, 75–79
  variables, 79–85
 applications of, 97
 dynamic model, 58–67
  of bathtub, 60–62
  exogenous variables in, 62–63
  in Maxwell's equations, 63–65
  self-contained, 58–60
 economic system, 105–106
 equilibrium model, 47–57
  of bathtub, 53–56
  example of, 50–52
  minimal complete subsets with multiple variables, 53
  qualitative equations, 56–57
  self-contained, 48–50, 57
 future directions of, 95–97
 knowledge of causal dependency relations and, 43–44
 mixed model, 65–74
  of bathtub, 67–68
  generating, 69–74
  self-contained, 65–67
 related work and, 45–47
 size distribution, 106
 theory of causal ordering and, 44–45
Modeling, 115–128. *See also* Model abstraction and causality; *specific models*
 aggregation and, 45, 124–126
 altruism, 208–209
  alternative models, comparison of, 213–214
 behavior, 46, 303–307, 325
 behavioral economics, 289
 business firm growth, 283
 chaos theory and, 115–117
 Club of Rome, 110–111, 118–119, 123, 419
 computer, 289, 440
 linear systems and, 115–116
 in mathematics, 116
 nonlinear systems and, 116
 in physics, 116
 prediction in, 117–122
 prescription in, 122–124
 principles, 115
 symbolic systems, 126–127
Modigliani, F., 353
Modules for reasoning, 93–96
Monetary identity, 344–345
Moore, A. M., 409
Morgenstern, O., 121
Motivation
 in economic theory, 264
 of executives, 222–223
 in organizations, 222–223, 248–250
  correct, natural selection of, 250–251
  econometrics and, 253
  rewards, 226–227
 in politics, 251–252
 social, 284
Mr. Chips theory, 170

Muth, J. F., 353
MYCIN system, 153, 179
Myers, J., 152–153

Naive direct democracy principle, 314
NASA budget, 413–414
Natural selection, 205–206, 228–229, 250–251, 333
Nayak, P. P., 50
Nearly decomposable matrix, 32–33, 76
Nearly decomposable systems, 5, 75–79, 107–109, 113, 356
Nelson, Richard R., 283, 287, 339
Neoclassical economic theory
 adequacy of, 328
 assumptions of, 277
 behavior in, 325
 behavioral economics versus, 277–278, 327, 334
 bounded rationality and, 294, 334
 business-cycle theory and, 275, 375–376
 computational problems and, 320
 decision-making processes and, 324, 369
 econometrics and, 328–329
 economic dynamics and, 344–346
 employment contract and, 223
 flood insurance decision and, 374
 foundations of, 344–346
 individualism and, 332
 markets and, 234–235
 monetary identity and, 344–345
 organizations and, 248
 Pareto distributions and, 221
 prediction and, 329, 331
 rationality and, 344–346
 salaries of executives and, 378–380
 Say's Law and, 344–345
 social sciences versus, 367–368
 utility function and, 382
 weaknesses of, 370, 382
Neo-Darwinist framework of altruism, 202–203, 205, 207–208, 241–244, 257
Networking, computer, 149–152
Neutral technological change, 138–140
New Institutional Economics
 behavior of organizations and, 199
 behavioral economics and, 281–282
 concept of, 281–282
 Gabrie and Jacquier's work on, 337–342
 identification with organizations and, 263
 interest in, 200
 markets and, 218–219
 opportunism and, 218
 organizations and, 248
 questions focused on by, 338
 theory of firm in, 338–339
 transaction costs and, 218
Newcomen, Thomas, 163, 166
Newell, A., 135
Newton, Sir Isaac, 330
Newton's Second and Third Laws, 27, 59–60, 344, 404, 425
Nishida, T., 96
Node capacity, computer, 147–148
No-function-in-structure principle, 46
Non-linear systems, 96, 116, 349
Non-neutral technological change, 140–141
Nonnumerical models, 126
Non-self-regulating variables, 71
Non-verbal processes, 433
Numerical aggregation module, 94

Ohm's Law, 180, 388
Operations research OR, 325
Opinion formation, 314–315
Opportunism, 218
Optimization, 295–297, 325–327, 329, 396–397
OR optimization techniques, 296, 325–327
Orcutt, G., 348
Organization Man, 184–185, 195
Organizational economies, 237
Organizational slack hypothesis, 283
Organizations, 217–238
 authority in, 223–226
 behavior of, 199
 coordination of, 232–237
 efficiency in, 222–223, 232
 employment relations in, 223–226
 goals of, 231–232, 248
 hierarchy and, 151
 identification with, 199, 201–204, 227–232, 247–249, 263
 information strategy for, 175–178
 markets and, 199–200, 217–221
 motivation in, 222–223, 248–250
  natural selection of, 250–251
  rewards, 226–227
 New Institutional Economics and, 248
 theory of, 238
 ubiquity of, 219–221
 utility function of, 282–284
Originality, artificial intelligence and, 180

Pareto distribution, 221, 279
Pareto optimum, 282, 403–404, 424
Path analysis, 3
Pearl, Judea, 4

Pepys, Samuel, 186
Phone communications, 149–150
Pictorial stimuli, 304
Piecewise Linear Reasoner, 96
Pinker, S., 436
Plott, Charles, 340, 410, 430
Poincare, Raymond, 427
Politics
 altruism in, 251–252
  implications of, 214–216
 democratic theory and, 312–313
 economics and, 418
 motivation in, 251–252
 opinion formation and, 314–315
 polls and, 312–313, 428
 public attention and, 313–314
 voting behavior and, 264, 314, 374–375, 392–393
Polls, 312–313, 429
Pople, H., 152–153
Population. *See* Rural-urban population balance, economics of
Possible worlds, 20, 22–23
Power, desire for, 246
Prediction
 of information technology's effects, 134–136
 long-wave theories and, 419–420
 in modeling, 117–122
 neoclassical economic theory and, 329, 331
 power of, 331–333, 414
 sensitivity analysis versus, 111–113
 World Dynamics models and, 112
Preindustrialized society, 188–189
Prepotency principle, 21–22
Prescription in modeling, 122–124
Price
 compensated change in, 142
 elasticities, 140–143
 expectations, 307–310
 level changes, 355–358
 regulation of, 328
 theory, 377
Pricing practices, 235
Pride in work, 227–228
Primary root of subsystem, 33
Print media, 174–175
Prior probability, 382–383
Problem solving, 324, 398–399, 417–418, 433
 computer programs, 167, 179
Procedural theory of rationality, 271, 293, 368–370, 376, 382–383, 389–392
Productivity, 137–140, 194
Profits, 283, 410
Protestant ethic, 184
Psychology, 395–396. *See also* Rationality in psychology and economics
Public attention, 313–314
Public choice, theory of, 264
Puccia, C. J., 28
Pylyshyn, Z. W., 435

QPT, 46, 96
Qualitative aggregation module, 94
Qualitative equations, 56–57
Qualitative prediction module, 94
Qualitative Process Theory (QPT), 46, 96
Quantity Theory of Money, 344–345

Rational behavior, 233, 307–310, 355, 383, 406
Rational computation, 230, 319–320
Rational expectations theory, 233, 308–310, 343, 349, 355–356
Rationality in psychology and economics, 367–383
 attentional process and, 374–375
 children's economic opportunities and, 371–372
 comparing and contrasting, 367–368
 decision-making processes and, 374–375, 389–390
  flood insurance, 374, 392
  voting behavior, 374–375, 392–393
 expectations theory and, 375–377
 other empirical parameters and, 377–382
  executive salaries distribution, 378–382
  size distribution, 377–378
 other social sciences versus, 367–368, 388–389
 substantive and procedural, 368–370, 374, 382–383, 389–392
 utility function, 370–371
 women in labor force and, 372–373
Rationality principle, 344–346, 350–351
Raven intelligence test, 435
Reasonable profits, 410
Reasoning about markets, 433–441
 processing different representations, 433–437
 research objectives, 437–441
Reciprocal altruism, 205, 247
Reduced form equations, 12, 24
Re-education of economists, 409, 413
Rees, A., 380
Reiersol, O., 4
Rescher, Nicholas, 13, 59
Resnick, R., 65
Resource allocation, 396–397
Rewards as motivations, 226–227

Reynolds Numbers, 116
Richerson, P. J., 208, 213
Risk capitalists, 350
Robotics, 166, 180
Roots of subsystems, 30, 33–34, 77, 79–80
Rousseau, Jean Jacques, 183
Rural-urban population balance, economics of, 137–144
 comparative statics and, 138–140, 143–144
 neutral technological change and, 138–140
 non-neutral technological change and, 140–141
 price elasticities and, 140–143
RWA program, 97

Sacks, E. P., 96
Salaries, 280, 328, 378–382. *See also* Wages
Samuelson, Paul, 343
Sargent, T., 424
Satisfaction criterion, 323–324
Satisficing, 295–298
 computer models, 418–419
 concept of, 295
 consequence of economic theory and, 297–298
 economics and, 269
 incommensurability of goals and outcomes and, 297
 optimization and, 295–297
Saving to income ratio, 280
Say's Law, 344–345
Scheines, Richard, 4
Schultz, Henry, 138
Schultz, Theodore, 421
Schumpeter, Joseph A., 200, 275, 287, 337, 343, 350, 360, 363–364
Schumpeterian economy, 363–364
Scientific process, 388
Self-contained subsets, 11, 17
Selfishness, 206–207, 216, 228, 249, 253, 260–261
Self-regulating variables, 70–72
Sensitivity analysis, 111–113
Service occupations, 194
SEU theory, 285, 291, 293, 403–405
Shame, 210
Shepard, R. N., 435
Shocks, business-cycle, 351–352
Shortliffe, E., 153
Short-term dynamic structures, 31–35
Short-term equilibrium structures, 78
Short-term memory (STM), 304
Significant root of subsystem, 34, 79
Simon, Herbert A., 13, 26, 44, 46–47, 59, 75, 78, 91, 137, 139, 231, 353, 435
Simon, Henry, 343
Size distribution, 328, 377–378, 388, 397–398
Slovic, P., 120
Smith, Adam, 428
Smith, Vernon, 340, 410
Social ethic, 184–185
Social interaction by electronic communications, 157–159
Social sciences. *See also* Rationality in psychology and economics
 economics versus, 367–368, 388–389
 goals of, 299, 301–302
 human verbal behavior as data in, 303–307
 methodologies of, 299–301
 rationality in, 367–368, 388–389
Socialist economies, 238
Solow, Robert, 421
Spirtes, Peter, 4
Stability analysis module, 94
Stark, Oded, 259
Static structures, 19, 29–31, 44, 93
Statistical practice, 3–4
Steady-state models, 6–7, 112
Steam engine invention, 163–164
Stendhal, 186
Stigler, George J., 320, 421
STM, 304
Stop rule, 322–323
Structural equations, 12, 24
Stylized facts, 346–349, 361
Subjective expected utility (SEU) theory, 285, 291, 293, 403–405
Subsets
 complete, minimal, 15, 17–18
 self-contained, minimal, 11, 17
Substantive theory of rationality, 271, 293, 368–370, 374, 382, 389–390
Supply and demand mechanisms, 328
Survey research, 288, 306
Symbolic models, 126–127
System of equation, 9–11, 24–25

Tabachneck, Hermi, 273
Technology, 163–172. *See also* Computers; Electronic communications; Information technology
 air conditioning invention and, 164
 alienation of workers and management and, 183–184
 automobile invention and, 164
 Blauner's studies of, 191–192
 dehumanizing effects of, 190
 educational system and, 170–172
 employment shifts and, 193–194

First Industrial Revolution and, 163–165
immersion in learning about, 168–169
infection theory of learning and, 170–171
knowledge and, 171–172
potential of computers and, 165–168
steam engine invention and, 163–164
Whisler's studies of, 193
workplace and, 183–184
Telephone system, 149–150
La Théorie Moderne de l'Enterprise, 337–342
Thinking, human, 181–182
Thurow, L. C., 358–359
Time precedence, 21
Tobin, Jim, 421
Transaction costs, 218
Tversky, Amos, 120, 340, 410–411, 430

Uncertainty in decision-making processes, 285–286, 292, 307
UNDERSTAND program, 179
Unemployment
in agriculture, 143
debate, 358–360
U.S. economy, problems in, 415–416
Unrealism, principle of, 306, 329–332
U-shaped price curve, 271, 328, 377, 396
Utility function, 277, 282–285, 320, 323–324, 370–371, 382
Utility gain, 338–339
Utility, individual, 284–285
Utility theory, 396
Utility-maximization framework, 277, 284–285, 325, 370–372, 382, 404, 407–408

Varaiya, P., 131, 137–138
Variables
aggregate, 34
aggregation of, 79–85
conditions for, 84–85
numerical example of, 81–84
procedure for, 80–81
root system, 79–80
causal dependency among, 43, 67
causal ordering of, 24
dependent, 9, 11, 18–19, 28
direct causal dependence, 28, 49
endogenous, 10–11
exogenous, 10, 14, 16–17, 25, 51, 62–65, 72–73, 95, 349
independent, 19, 36
manipulability of, 49, 55
minimal complete subsets with multiple, 53
non-self-regulating, 71
of order zero, 11
self-regulating, 70–72
Veblen, Thorstein, 275, 337
Vcrbal processes, 433–447
Verbal reports, 303–307
Viner, Jacob, 377, 397–398
Visual processes, 433–437
Von Hayek, F., 234
Von Neumann, J., 121, 145
Voting behavior, 264, 314, 374–375, 392–393

Wages, 307. *See also* Salaries
Watt, James, 163, 166
Wealth, desire for, 246
The Web, 132
Whisler, Thomas L., 193
Whyte, William H., 184–185
Williams, B. C., 45–46
Williamson, Oliver E., 200, 263, 281, 284
Wilson, E. O., 208, 213
Winter, Sidney G., 283, 287, 339
Women in labor force, 372–373, 390–391, 406–407
Workplace
alienation of workers and management in, 183–184
authority in, 223–226
automation and, 156
boredom at, 185–187
electronic communications in, 155–157, 161
employment relations in, 223–226
executives in, 184–188
free-riding and, 228
information technology on relations at, 131–132
job satisfaction and, 185–186, 189–190, 192–194
preindustrial, 188–189
pride in work and, 227–228
technology and, 183–184
World Dynamics models, 110–112
World-modeling problems, 7
Wright, Sewall, 3

X-efficiency concept, 283

YAKA program, 97